Before They Were the Bombers

Before They Were the Bombers

The New York Yankees' Early Years, 1903–1915

by JIM REISLER

McFarland & Company, Inc., Publishers

Jefferson, North Carolina, and London

To a couple of big swingers,
Tobie and Julia,
with love

Library of Congress Cataloguing-in-Publication Data

Jim Reisler, 1958–
   Before they were the Bombers : the New York Yankees' early years,
1903–1915 / by Jim Reisler.
      p.   cm.
   ISBN 0-7864-1226-7 (illustrated case binding : 50# alkaline paper)
   1. New York Yankees (Baseball team)— History.   I. Title: New York
Yankees' early years, 1903–1915.   II. Title.
   GV875.N4R45   2002
   796.357'64'097471 — dc21   2002001087

British Library cataloguing data are available

Cover photograph: Dave Fults (*National Baseball Hall of Fame Library,
Cooperstown, NY*)

Manufactured in the United States of America

McFarland & Company, Inc., Publishers
  Box 611, Jefferson, North Carolina 28640
    www.mcfarlandpub.com

Table of Contents

Acknowledgments

Putting this volume together was such a solitary endeavor that I sometimes lost track of the contributions of others. Eric Enders and Bill Burdick of the National Baseball Hall of Fame were always there with their help, as were several members of the Society for American Baseball Research, particularly the late Jack Kavanagh, a true mentor.

Friends like Jim Gardener, Ken Pearlman, Joe Sterling and Ken Levinson offered their ongoing support, even as I rambled on with long-ago tales of Jack Chesbro's streak and Hal Chase's shenanigans. And Don Phillips of the Mercy College Library in Dobbs Ferry, New York, made sure the microfilm machines were always working. A bag of Hilltop Park popcorn for all.

But the biggest thank you of all goes to my wife, Tobie, and daughter, Julia. Their understanding, patience and support of this time-consuming endeavor were worth more than they will ever know.

Introduction

Histories of the New York Yankees' storied first century generally skim the dubious early years, heading right to the familiar 1919 tale of Red Sox owner Harry Frazee. You probably know a little about it — how Frazee peddled a young slugger named Ruth to the team to bankroll a Broadway show (which trivia buffs and baseball fans who need another hobby can tell you was *No, No, Nanette*).

The show failed. Ruth didn't. He hit lots of home runs and the Yankees won both games and pennants. That started it; from there, those histories generally proceed to legendary stories of Lou Gehrig's iron will, Joe DiMaggio's grace, Mickey Mantle's knees and Whitey Ford's big-game grit. Along the way, the books will get into that old Yankee pin-striped arrogance and the old saying that rooting for them was kind of like rooting for U.S. Steel. There would be some down years — the Horace Clarke era of the mid-to-late 1960s for instance — but those periods would end.

The history books then generally proceed to the familiar story of the wacky Steinbrenner years, starting most likely with Reggie Jackson's three home runs on three swings to take the 1977 World Series. And they'll conclude with the current dynasty-in-the-making with stars like Derek Jeter and Bernie Williams. All in all, it's been an extraordinary ride for America's most celebrated, most successful sports franchise.

For the most part, those histories gloss over the beginnings of the franchise — 12 years when they were first the Highlanders, occasionally the Americans, sometimes the Invaders and finally the Yankees, but not really *the* Yankees, the big, bad boys from the big, bad city, a team that has won far more pennants than anyone — 26 to be exact, almost three times more than the next most prolific team, the St. Louis Cardinals, winners of nine. The only other professional team in any sport on this continent that comes close to Yankee dominance is hockey's Montreal Canadiens, with 24 titles.

So why ignore those first few years? There are three main reasons:

• The "Golden Age" of sportswriting had not yet arrived;

• Although the Highlanders were sometimes strong, they won no pennants and were, for the most part, pretty mediocre; and,

• Babe Ruth wasn't there yet.

No, they didn't have Ruth, who would arrive in 1920, when the team suddenly became successful and basically never stopped winning. The original, pre–Ruth Yankees were lousy, but they constitute an important part of the team's history.

Assembled in 1903 from the remnants of the old Baltimore Orioles, the Highlanders were part of the two-year-old American League. The brainchild of a dictatorial former sportswriter named Ban Johnson, the

A.L. had been hatched two years earlier as a new, more fan friendly and wholesome major league. Here was a direct challenge to the presumed vice of the more established National League, where gamblers ruled the roost, fights broke out on the field and in the stands, foul language flew and few women or children ventured near a ballpark.

Johnson was a visionary, a man who saw baseball as integral in the growing emergence of the new American leisure class. How ironic then that to secure a franchise in New York, he would turn to the Tammany Hall—connected talents of the flamboyant, flagrantly corrupt ex–New York City Police Chief "Big" Bill Devery, and his partner, pool hall king Frank Farrell. In the beginning, Big Bill and Farrell were friends and political allies, who figured running a baseball team would buy them both connections and respectability. In time, they argued so bitterly that they no longer spoke.

Having a successful team in New York wasn't just a nice idea. It was a major step in rivaling the more established National League in prestige and gate receipts. Johnson did everything he could to make it so—stocking the team by actually ordering other teams to transfer good players there; imagine anyone even trying that today! That went for the Orioles, which were essentially dismantled and rebuilt on Washington Heights as the Highlanders.

Too bad the celebrated sportswriters of the day—people like Damon Runyon, Grantland Rice and the great Ring Lardner—weren't yet around to cover it. Runyon and Rice both hit New York in 1911, and Lardner much later—all too late to report on characters like Big Bill Devery, Ban Johnson and "Happy" Jack Chesbro, along with other early Highlander happenings. Too bad nobody was around to romanticize the era for future generations; it would have been fun.

In time, Broadway, or more accurately, the life around Broadway became Runyon's

true beat. His forte was incorporating the characters he met along the way—the actors, race-track bookies, dancers, agents, promoters and wise-guys—into memorable short stories and plays.

Runyon's joint was Lindy's, the well-known restaurant he immortalized as Mindy's in many of his stories. It was there that many of his enticing bookies, ballplayers and hangers-on congregated, only to find themselves worked into a short story sometime later. Never a drinker, Runyon would occupy a seat at Lindy's for long hours, consuming quarts of coffee, as he hosted a steady stream of characters. Said one regular, after reading a Runyon piece: "It ain't hard to spot the guys in the stories."

Runyon's men were "guys." Women were "dolls" and money, "potatoes." Complimentary show tickets in those politically incorrect times were "Chinee"—his reference to the holes punched in the tickets that he thought resembled a Chinese coin. Even the names of his plays and short story collections were classics: *Guys and Dolls, Blue Plate Special* and *A Slight Case of Murder.* Nice, but that was all in the future in 1903. An integral part of Runyon's eventual voice: baseball, particularly the Giants of John McGraw and all the action around the Polo Grounds.

And while the papers did file baseball reports and had done so since 1895—when William Randolph Hearst, of all people, created the sports section for his *New York Journal*—the coverage was terse and pedestrian. For the most part, game coverage until writers like Rice and Runyon arrived was relegated to box scores and brief game summaries under the heading "Yesterday's Baseball."

At their start, the Highlanders were the most expensive major league team ever assembled. Big things were expected of a team led by established stars and future Hall of Famers like "Wee" Willie Keeler and Jack Chesbro. Their manager: Clark Griffith, another future Cooperstown inductee. Hey pal, this *was* New York, where money talks, okay? The team, however, had a little trouble getting started in 1903 and never got on track, finishing fourth.

The Highlanders came close in 1904, with Chesbro winning 41 games — yes, 41 games — and although they nearly won the American League pennant, they lost out on the season's final day. It was their finest moment; not until Ruth was on the scene would they win so many games again.

Big things were expected of the Highlanders in 1905. A new first baseman that year, a 23-year-old Californian named Hal Chase, added excitement with both his bat and his glove and quickly became the Highlanders' first homegrown star. He did so in other ways too, as arguably the most corrupt player in major league history. Chase, known as "Prince Hal," quickly became a fan favorite and a legend in the process — sure, he was the team's big gate-attraction, but he was a rogue, a gambler and a game thrower, so blatant in his sinister behavior that he couldn't be trusted. The taunt of the day late in his career, when everyone knew what he was up to: "Hey Hal, what are the odds today?" What was that again about fan friendly?

The Highlanders didn't do much in 1905, but came close the following year, when they again led the American League in late September before tailing off to finish three games behind Chicago. That was the last time for 14 years that they contended seriously for the title. The Highlanders finished dead last twice — once in 1908, when they lost a club-record 103 games, and again in 1912, suffering their most distant finish ever, 55 games behind A.L. champs Boston.

In 1913, the lowly, newly christened Yankees, too poor to renovate or rebuild the Hilltop, their outdated little ballpark in Washington Heights, became humble tenants of those lordly Giants at the Polo Grounds. Even the story of the name change

was more a matter of convenience. A patriotic nod to veterans? No. A way to honor the flag? Hardly. Jim Price, a sportswriter with *The New York Mirror*, figured the name "Yankees" was a better fit for a headline than "Highlanders," and the name stuck.

The team's misfortunes bankrupted Farrell and Devery. They stumbled on for a couple more years, changing managers with the wind to make things happen. Nothing worked, and the two fell into a bitter feud they'd take to their graves. Virtually bankrupt, they sold the team in January 1915 to two respectable businessmen: Jacob Ruppert, a brewer, and Tillinghast L'Hommedieu Huston, an engineer whose mother really did give him that name. Both were sportsmen of the smart set. Both were veterans who preferred to be addressed by their ranks — "Colonel" Ruppert and "Captain" Huston.

Ruppert and Huston decided to buy a baseball team because it sounded fun. They paid $450,000, but the basic math of the transaction was misleading. The extent to which Farrell and Devery transferred capital from other business activities into their baseball business isn't known, but on their deaths, Farrell left a net estate of $1,072, and Devery left debts of $1,023.

The sale turned the Yankees toward immediate respectability. Both men were businessmen with deep pockets and a fierce hatred of failure. In 1915, they purchased A's pitcher Bob Shawkey, who the very next year led the Yankees to 24 victories, giving them their first winning season in six years. In 1919, Shawkey, back from military service, won 20 and the Yankees climbed to third at 7½ games out, their closest finish in 13 years.

That winter, on the recommendation of Manager Miller Huggins, Ruppert paid a then-record $125,000, with a $300,000 loan, to the Red Sox for a slugger named Ruth. Things were never quite the same again. Glory days had begun.

Ruth sparked the Yankees to big things. In his first year with the team, 1920, he hit 54 home runs, obliterating the record of 29 he had set the year before. Shawkey and Carl Mays together won 46 games and the team was off on a roll that lead to A.L. pennants in '21 and '22 and the team's first World Series triumph in 1923, the same year the Yankees moved into the stadium that to this day bears the team's name.

But amidst all the success, something was lost. Virtually forgotten was the birth and the weird, wacky first decade of the New York Highlanders–turned–Yankees when baseball giants like Chesbro, Keeler, Chase and Ban Johnson roamed the land. Granted, they lost most of the time, but they did occasionally come close and by God, they made things interesting in a lovable, early Mets way.

So, as the Yankees celebrate their glorious first century and sail into the next, it's a good time to look back at their origins. The story of those early years is a story about a city, its politics, its personalities and a vanished time in American history. But most of all, it's a story of the interlopers, a team that for a time was actually known as the "Invaders." And it comes complete with dark splashes of Tammany Hall intrigue; the titanic, clashing egos of the baseball moguls; and the daffy, raffish behavior of the ballplayers, who make today's players look like choir boys by comparison. Phooey on all those accounts describing American life a century ago as more innocent. No way.

Yes, the Yankees have been America's greatest sports franchise hands down. But not so in the team's first decade. Even so, it was a pretty wild start.

1

Enter the Prince

"When I lose, I drink, and when I win, I celebrate."

— *Bo Belinsky*

Overcast, threatening skies greeted the early arrivals this Labor Day morning of Monday, September 2, 1912, to New York's Hilltop Park, on the upper reaches of Manhattan in New York City. Their quest wasn't so much to see the hometown Yankees, mired in a neck-and-neck race for last place with the St. Louis Browns, as it was the opportunity to see that season's kings of the American League, Boston's mighty Red Sox, and young, exciting players like Tris Speaker, Harry Hooper and pitcher "Smokey" Joe Wood.

None of that mattered to Yankee first baseman Hal Chase. The team's star, a big-time player of lightning quickness, a brash personality that seemed to fit New York and a nickname to match — "the Prince" — had other things on his mind as he took his cuts in the batting cage this gray morning.

Turning between pitches to Gabby Street, a Yankee utility catcher, Chase said, "Gabby, poker game, two tables going, down at McGraw's tonight, 8 o' clock."

"Pass me, Prince," said Street, whose annual salary at the time was $1,400. "The stakes are too high."

"That's okay," countered Chase, who made $10,000 a year, among the highest salaries in the league. "Come anyway.

There's plenty of good food and lovely dolls. You don't have to play. Gee, they even got that good beer you like so much, Gabby."

"McGraw's" was the popular pool hall operated by feisty New York Giant manager John McGraw at 1328 Broadway in the Marbridge Building on Herald Square. Well-paid and the toast of New York, McGraw surrounded himself with a steady stream of acquaintances from show biz, racetrack, gambling and wise guy circles. Many shared a penchant for action with money to burn.

Open since 1908, this was McGraw's second Manhattan pool hall venture in New York, and one he was financing with the aid of an average $300 monthly police "protection" supplement and a young partner named Willie Hoppe, a pool champ in the making. Nobody mentioned that McGraw, who in a few short years had transformed the Giants into the class of the National League and the toast of New York, had another partner in his pool hall named Arnold Rothstein.

Known to his many acquaintances as "AR," and more starkly to writer Damon Runyon as simply "the Bankroll," Rothstein had made a name for himself three years before as a slick man with a pool cue, when he'd taken on and beaten Jack Conroy of Philadelphia in a match for the ages that lasted 34 hours — that's right, 34 hours — before McGraw sent everyone home to get some sleep. Rothstein, described as a cigar salesman, was all of 30 and well on his way to making himself the biggest bookmaker in New York City. A cold man with little use for pleasantries, he once told an interviewer that "money talks … I learned that fast … the more money, the louder it talks." A few years later, AR would achieve lasting fame as the money man behind the 1919 World Series fix for which he never served a day in jail.

But never mind. McGraw's was *the* place to be in New York in the early days of the 20th century. It was a joint where anyone who was anyone went in the days when the lines between ballplayers, boxers, Broadway starlets, vaudeville performers, gamblers, wise guys and hangers-on tended to blur. So, Street went, expecting to see a star or two and maybe a bit of glitz. He wasn't disappointed.

"I walk in," Street said. "The first guy I walked into was George M. Cohan. He was a hell of a baseball fan. And guess what? He bet big money on baseball games. I go into the backroom. There are two big card games going on. Must have been 50 people there. Almost half of them were the most gorgeous women I had ever seen. They were all very tall. I later found out they were show girls from the Follies. Big as life. Sure enough, I hear this whistle. It's the Prince. Right in the middle of the action at the big game table. He motions me over and says real loud for everyone to hear, 'Stand behind me, Gabby, and watch a master at work.'"

For the record, the Red Sox, despite a steady rain during the first game, had taken two from the lowly Yankees that day in a pair of tight pitcher's duels before a packed Hilltop crowd estimated at 20,000. Sox pitcher Hugh Bedient outpitched Russell Ford to take the first game 2–1. In the sec-

ond game, Wood struck out eight Yankees for a 1–0 win — his 30th victory of the season and 14th in a row. Chase's contribution: one single in eight at-bats.

None of that mattered that night at McGraw's, where Chase, who may have been a "Prince" on the ballfield, was truly a king. "Now, this table drew most of the spectators because of the stakes and the players," Street says. In addition to Chase, there is Hooper of the Red Sox and Guy Zinn, the Yankee centerfielder.

By now, Chase is smoking a cigar and smiling. Street again: "He was always smiling…. He sure as hell loved life."

He sure did. Indeed, Hal Chase was more than the Highlanders' first great homegrown star, known far and wide and the most graceful first baseman of his generation — and a feared, line-drive batsman. He was a man of many faces, a complex, restless soul — popular with his teammates yet mistrusted; a gregarious, easy interview with a passion for the game, but known to consort with gamblers as much as his manager; and a man who was married with a young son, but with a fondness for showgirls and the action of the craps table.

In some ways, Chase had it too easy. So good, so young, he hit New York in the spring of 1905, hailed as the young Californian who could do wondrous things, and promptly lived up to expectations. The baseball writers couldn't contain themselves; even the crusty, old *New York Times*, whose sober analysis in those days made the *Titanic* sinking seem boring, got mushy when it came to Hal Chase: "His display in the field was the work of an artist," it gushed after his first New York area appearance, an exhibition game April 8, 1905, in Jersey City. "The opinion of old baseball 'fans' was that was undoubtedly the greatest 'find' seen on a baseball field in a long time."

As the years wore on, Chase proved his mettle, as the smitten writers droned on. By 1907, *Sporting Life* called Chase "perhaps the

Prince Hal Chase — wonderful, wacky, willful, erratic and never boring. (National Baseball Hall of Fame Library, Cooperstown, NY)

biggest drawing card in baseball." But even by then, cracks were appearing in the general good humor of the Highlander star: in 1908, he bolted the team for California. Back for 1909, he had a bitter falling out with his new manager George Stallings but somehow replaced him as manager.

Even his personal life was by then starting to unravel. Married in 1908, he and wife Anna had a son in 1910, but separated in 1912. In the papers that September as Chase held forth at McGraw's were headlines that detailed the messy divorce proceedings. Among them: "Hal Chase, Idol of Fans, Claims He Wasn't Idol Home," "Hal Chase is 'Put Out' in Game with Wife," and the irresistible "Hal Chase 'Fans Out' Before Pitcher Cupid." Such detailed coverage of private affairs was unusual in the newspapers of those post-Victorian days. Not so when it came to Chase; he was great copy.

Back at McGraw's it was time for action. They cut for deal and Chase wins. Straight cards are dealt, Zinn opens, the other two call and Chase raises. Zinn then reraises and around they go. Finally, somebody calls and cards are drawn. Chase asks Zinn how many and he says, "I'll play these, Prince." Hooper and other player do a fast fade and fold.

Street again: "Now, I'm looking over Hal's shoulder," he says. "He drew three cards. He had a pair of kings going in. I see his new cards. No help. The Prince is dead in the water. Zinn bets $100, and the Prince drags on his cigar and says, 'And $100.' This goes on a couple of more times. I think he's nuts. Zinn's not getting out as he had a pat hand going in. Finally, Guy calls the Prince. Hal fans his cards in front of Zinn and says, 'Four Kings, Zinny, can you beat 'em? For the record, he couldn't. A Full House was second best. But where did the other pair of Kings come from? I was standing right behind Prince Hal and he turned that pair of Kings into four of a kind right in front of my eyes. It's the damndest thing I've ever seen."

It may have been. The fact that Street, who eventually became the well-known manager of the "Gashouse Gang" St. Louis Cardinals teams of the 1930s, remembered the night so vividly in a 1950 interview from which these remarks are taken — that's right, 38 years later — speaks volumes.

More astonishing is the sharpness of the detail Street remembered. The pot was at $2,500, mostly from Chase and Zinn. "Hal winks at me, rakes in the pot and says, 'Isn't life beautiful, Gabby, me boy?' Cheat?

Later that night, I see Zinn talking to a pretty young thing at the bar. He's happy, smiling, and I'm thinking to myself, 'what an actor.' He calls me over and buys me a beer and tells me what a great guy Hal Chase is. He says the Prince calls him over and says, 'What's the matter, Zinny? Have you lost your best friend?'"

It was worse. Zinn had lost six months' pay. And with that, Chase dropped $1,000 in his pocket, with the words, "Hell, it's only money."

"Funny thing," recalled Street, "I never thought of it as cheating. More like beating the system. For some reason, Hal was showing off for me. He wanted to show he could palm a pair out of his sleeve in that tough company and not get caught. But, it's like he wanted somebody to know it. Know it! I can't forget it."

That was Chase. How fitting that this talented but wayward man was, of all people, the player who symbolized the wacky, weird ride of the early New York Yankees, a team with a long way to reach before reaching the pinnacle of its more celebrated days. And how fitting that perhaps the defining moment of that team took place, not even on its home field, but 130 blocks south in a Midtown pool hall on a cool night in September 1912.

So it went in the first nearly dozen years of the Highlanders-turned-Yankees — a time that ranged from the team's birth in 1903 until it was sold December 31, 1914, and got respectable. One of the new owners was Colonel Jacob Ruppert of the Upper East Side, a brewer and sportsman; while, the other, the improbably-named Captain Tillinghast L'Hommedieu Huston of Havana, was a soldier-turned-engineer. Both were millionaires and went about molding the Yanks into a franchise for the ages.

Those early Yanks could show some promise, as in 1903, when they finished fourth. Sometimes, they were even decent, as in 1904, when they came within a game of winning the American League pennant. Mostly though, they were mediocre on the field, colorful off and just plain lousy, as in the long, painful year of 1912 when they lost and lost again, but did so with their patented brand of zaniness that was par for the course.

Adding to the on-the-field ineptitude — "hoodoo," the writers called it — was a brand of corrupt ownership. This wasn't a case of meddlesome owners and odd decisions, as the team would endure much later under Steinbrenner. This was downright corrupt, a dozen years rife with political intrigue, backroom deals and good, old-fashioned brawling. It was a bumpy ride — but it sure was entertaining.

2

A Normal Start at Least

"Don't tell me about the world. Not today. It's springtime and they're knocking baseballs around fields where the grass is damp and green in the morning."
— Pete Hamill

On the surface, it was a normal start at least. On April 30, 1903, American League baseball came to New York. It was an unseasonably warm Thursday in which the temperature reached 85 degrees, the hottest anyone could remember for that time of the year on the East Coast. It had been a rush job from the get-go and it showed; just weeks before, newspaper reports described the grounds of the ballpark as a "wild waste of huge boulders and brushwood," causing many to wonder how the opening-day deadline would ever be made.

After all, it had only been six weeks since Frank Farrell and Bill Devery had paid $18,000 for the Baltimore American League franchise and moved it to New York as the Highlanders. Getting a toehold in New York, America's largest and most important city, and challenging the domination of the politically-influential, establishment Giants was considered crucial if the spanking new, more fan-friendly American League was to be a success.

The place they chose was Washington Heights in the northern reaches of Manhattan, between 165th and 168th streets, east of Broadway and overlooking the Hudson River. It doesn't seem that out of the way

today, but back then, it was a haul — from Midtown, a 55-minute ride on the 3rd Avenue El, which included changing cars at 125th Street to the Amsterdam Avenue line. Few New Yorkers at the time had ever ventured to those northern fringes, where years later, ballplayer-turned-evangelist Billy Sunday would preach the gospel under big tents and where, after that, Columbia Presbyterian Hospital would be built. Even fewer had realized the flurry of events unleashed by the American League's decision to locate in New York; the ballpark was on secretly-leased land belonging the New York Institute for the Blind.

More than $200,000 had been poured into the project — big bucks for the time — much of it spent blasting some 12,000 cubic yards of rock to create a suitable playing service. It took another $15,000 to hastily throw up the wooden grandstand. But the contractors had made it — barely — and the ballpark, Hilltop Park, was ready, thanks to an army of laborers and mechanics who had helped them over the last few weeks. The blasting had gone on both day and night, with horse carts hauling away the debris. Finally, the stone foundations were set, the curved grandstand up, the roof nearly

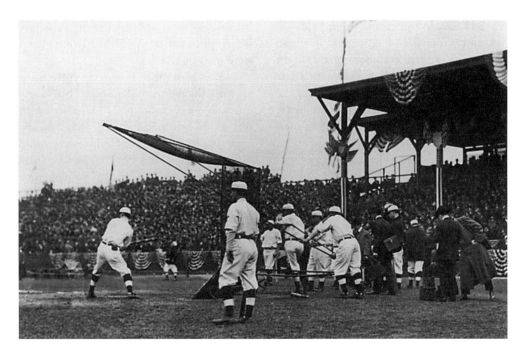

The bunting is out during batting practice of opening day at the Hilltop. (National Baseball Hall of Fame Library, Cooperstown, NY)

finished, and the infield sodded — smooth as glass and ready for baseball.

On one hand, it was a pretty location — fans (or "cranks" as they were called in those days) could enjoy the majestic river views, provided they turned their backs on the game. On the other hand, the Hilltop was a fairly utilitarian place — dominated by the single-decked grandstand that curved around home plate and extended a few feet beyond both the first- and the third-base lines. Open, single-decked bleachers then started from there and extended down the foul lines to the outfield — not until 1911 was a roof put over the stands down the left-field line.

The outfield was just a 15-to-20 foot high fence — except for a crude, roped-off hollow in right field, for which team officials developed an unusual ground rule: doubles would be awarded to those batters driving the ball past the ropes. In June, a fence would be put up, to be plastered four years later with advertising signs for products like

Bull Durham tobacco, Regal Shoes — "A Pair Free For Every Home Run" read the sign — and Morisco Cigarettes. Not until 1912, when the Highlanders built center field seats for their final year at the Hilltop, did the team have permanent seats in the outfield.

A decade or so later, after the Highlanders had become the Yankees and moved to the Polo Grounds, nobody could quite recall whether anyone ever hit a home run that cleared the fence at the Hilltop. That's because the park was an immense place built within to conform to the geography of the area. Not that it really mattered anyway how far the fences were in the deadball era, when baseball games were won — not with home runs, but mostly with good pitching, singles, stolen bases and "hittin 'em where they ain't," as a well-known Highlander, the diminutive hometown legend Willie Keeler, would say.

Wacking a home run at the wonderfully-lopsided Hilltop was a feat — left field was 365 feet down the line, right field 400 feet and center field a downright Ruthian distance of 542 feet from home plate. Right field? The big stone wall in right with a gate leading out to the street for fans leaving the ballpark was about 400 feet from the plate, angling sharply to 100 feet in the corner. That nobody thought to record the exact distance is one of those enduring mysteries of the game in the dead-ball era.

The Hilltop's spaciousness wasn't unusual for ballparks of the dead-ball era. By 1905, the top seating capacity of any park was only about 18,000. And although pennant contenders of the era often drew far greater crowds for big games on weekends, the penny-pinching owners typically had the overflow crowds sit and stand behind ropes around the outfield, down the foul lines, and even behind home plate. Lacking either the capital or the willingness to pay for increases in the seating, most owners preferred keeping outfield fences far away from the diamond, so they could continue to sell as many 25-cent standing-room tickets as possible. It helped: major league attendance rose from 3.5 million in 1902 to 4.5 million the following year and more than more than 5 million each of the next five years.

Some 16,243 cranks journeyed to northern Manhattan that first day for the Highlanders' first game ever, paying $1 for boxes, 75 cents for the grandstand and 50 cents for seats down the lines. A degree of pomp filled the air; fans were handed little American flags at the gate. Then, promptly at 3 p.m. with the fans waving their flags and cheering lustily, the baseball players, their pre-game practices completed, streamed out of the center field clubhouse and marched in toward the infield.

The teams formed in lines in the outfield, with the day's opponents, the Washington Senators, looking natty in their combination uniforms of white shirts and blue pants. And resplendent in their new white flannel uniforms and caps with black facing, topped off with natty maroon coasts were the Highlanders.

As part of the uniform, the New Yorkers wore the white on dark blue "NY" logo, but with the "N" and the "Y" separated with one on the left breast and the other on the right. For the record, the Highlanders would wear that design until 1905, Chase's first season, when the "N" and the "Y" were merged side by side into a monogram on the left breast.

(They'd go back to the old design for the following three years, before, in 1909, returning to what became the most recognizable insignia in sports — the interlocking "NY," a design that was actually created in 1877 by Louis Tiffany for the a medal given by the New York Police Department to Officer John McDowell, the first city policeman shot in the line of duty. The design was adopted by Devery.

Kicking off the opening day's parade to the strains of "The Washington Post March," a compliment to the day's opposing team, was Bayne's 69th Regiment Band. Across the diamond they marched to a medley of increasingly patriotic tunes including "Yankee Doodle Dandy." Pausing within a few feet of the grandstand, the players then removed their hats as Bayne's lit into "The Star-Spangled Banner," then considered a jaunty, patriotic tune and later adopted as the National Anthem.

With the fans waving their flags and cheering lustily — so loud that the echoes went clear across the Hudson to the Palisades and back again — the players broke ranks and went into their last-minute pre-game warm-ups. All in all, said a scribe, "the scene was both picturesque and inspiring."

There was one final bit of ceremony to do — the time-honored throwing out of the first ball. Chosen for that was one Ban Johnson, the American League President and the man most responsible for creating the Highlanders. A onetime Cincinnati sports editor, the blustery, dictatorial Johnson had used his sheer force of will in transforming the money-losing Western League into the American League two years before. And he had forced the rival National League to treat his upstarts as equals.

Johnson, seldom seen without his trademark pince nez glasses and double breasted suit and tie, accepted the honor with relish. He had realized how much maneuvering it had taken to get a team into New York. After all, it was Johnson who had cleverly figured that for all his talk about a more moral league, it made good business sense secure the good graces of New York City's insatiably-corrupt Tammany Hall Democratic machine. Indeed, it was Johnson who had leased the land for the ballpark, a move made possible the previous fall by donating $2,500 to Tammany's election fund.

So here he was looking supremely happy and seated next to G. Hector Clemes, a director of the Senators, and Highlander President Joseph W. Gordon, a well-connected coal baron and a former state assemblyman whose baseball roots in the city went clear back to the 1870s when he had been president of the late, great New York Metropolitans, and more recently, a Giants stockholder.

Gordon's role was apparent; he was a Tammany Hall ally and secured a critical link to the city's government. In turn, Gordon, who had recently lost his position as deputy superintendent of buildings, was looking forward to the pomp and stature afforded the owner of a major league team to help his coal business.

And it was Gordon, who despite the city's large Irish population, had provided the team with its most common nickname, after Gordon's Highlanders, a famous Scottish regiment, as well a reference to Hilltop Park being built on northern Manhattan's highest peak. There were other, more common names: Americans, followed by Hill

Dwellers, Porch Climbers, Burglars and Cliffmen and Invaders.

But Gordon was a figurehead. Seated side-by-side, down near the Highlanders' bench were the real power behind the team: That would be Farrell and Devery, the big two among the seven-person consortium that owned the Highlanders, and arguably the most corrupt pair of owners in major league history.

Both were Tammany Hall bigshots — Farrell, the New York pool room tycoon, reportedly worth $750,000; and Devery, known as Big Bill, the fabulously corrupt ex-chief of the New York Police Department and a man who boasted of never having read a book. Big Bill's most famous sermon? "When ye're caught with the goods, don't say nothin'" — a saying generally credited as the origin of the famed blue wall of silence. In Devery's book, the problem wasn't the crime; it was getting caught. Neither appeared under the masthead of official owners. But everyone knew and seemed to enjoy the open secret.

"Rumor has it that William H. Devery, ex–Chief of Police, is a stockholder in the New American League team," *The Sporting News* coyly reported May 9, 1903. When questioned on the subject, the big ex–Chief became quite suddenly evasive: "Me a backer!" he said. "I only wished I did own some stock in a base ball club. I'm a poor man, and don't own stock in anything. What would I do with a ball team? Me pitch with a stomach like this! Not on your life."

"Undoubtedly, he is a poor man," the newspaper countered, "but he has managed to purchase for cash about half a million dollars worth of property on Manhattan Island."

The irony is that for all Johnson's talk of a New York team in a fan-friendly league, making it happen had required the services of a couple of disreputable Tammany Hall types. But on this day, it didn't matter, for there was excitement in the air and lo and behold, a team that seemed to stack up well.

It was the peace agreement of January 10, 1903, that had made it possible for the American League to pick up the dormant Baltimore franchise and move it wholesale to New York. Amidst the cigar smoke and brass spittoons of the St. Nicholas Hotel in Cincinnati, the grim-looking magnates of both leagues ironed out an agreement designed to end two years of costly cross-league player raids and trigger an era of peaceful prosperity.

For starters, the magnates agreed to a rule limiting major league rosters to 16 after June 1. Then, the American League strove for consistency by adopting the foul-strike rule that had been used in the N.L. since 1901. Most importantly, they agreed to a policy of territorial rights in which the American League allowed the N.L. to retain its exclusivity in Pittsburgh, while accepting Johnson's plan to enter New York. Flying into action, Johnson promptly arranged for the transfer of the Orioles to Manhattan.

And yet the Highlander team that started the season in mid–April bore little resemblance to the sorry Baltimore franchise of 1902, a team that finished dead last, 34 games behind the A.L. champion Philadelphia A's. In all of six weeks, the Highlanders had assembled an attractive cast of bona fide veteran major league stars with a decidedly local flavor, chiefly the 5'4" Brooklyn homegrown Wee Willie Keeler, late of the borough's Bridegrooms — he of the 30½

inch bat, the majors' shortest; a .373 lifetime batting average, baseball's heftiest; and, the quote — "I hit 'em where they ain't" — among the game's best known.

And thanks to Johnson's mandate to raid other big league teams, in came talent from 11 other major league teams. From the Pirates came star pitchers Jack Chesbro, a 28-game winner the previous season and Jesse Tannehill, a 20-game winner. Along came Jimmy Williams from the dormant Baltimore Orioles and Germany Long from the Boston Braves.

And at the helm of what became the most expensive team in the majors — this was New York after all — was the old warhorse, 33-year-old Clark Griffith. The well-known player-manager of the Chicago White Sox, had joined the Highlanders after Johnson had prevailed on his friend, White Sox owner Charles Comiskey, to engineer the transfer. Bringing the crafty, sometimes crabby and always competitive Griffith in was Johnson's idea; Griffith was thought to be past his prime, which he would eventually prove to be wrong.

Keeler got the Highlanders started, with a single in the first and scoring the team's first ever run on Williams's double over the left field rope; the outfield fence wasn't yet built. They added another run in the second and two more in the fifth, which is all they needed with the stocky, spitballer Chesbro shutting down the Senators with two runs on seven hits. Most notable in their failure was Big Ed Delahanty, who would tragically lose his life later in the year, who didn't reach base in five at-bats. Final score: Highlanders 6 Washington 2.

3

Origins

"Don't bite the hand that's feeding you—there's more meat further up."
— *Bugs Baer*

It was more than a good start. For Ban Johnson, having a team in New York *and* building them a ballpark in Manhattan was a monumental coup over the elements, the terrain and, most critically, the political forces of Tammany Hall. He had outfoxed them all.

The game itself was not the real beginning. That had happened months before on a cold winter's evening at Johnson's suite in the Criterion Hotel in New York, as the American League magnate played host to some 20 American League executives.

"Gentleman," he said, raising his cocktail glass in a toast, "the American League!"

"The American League!" they answered in unison, polishing off their drinks.

And so it was in this atmosphere of unity, good cheer and spirits that the American League's New York franchise was born.

Johnson was an ambitious man whose goal was to create a new major league. The path he chose was to take the Western League, of which he had also been president, and make it major. By 1902, despite some heavy infighting along the way, Johnson had assembled teams in Baltimore, Philadelphia, Washington, D.C., Cleveland, Detroit, St. Louis and Chicago.

Just as critically, he had brought to-gether a powerful group of allies, ranging from Ben and Tom Shibe, the Philadelphia sporting good manufacturers, to Charles Somers, a Cleveland contractor. Along the way, he got onto his side a group of wily baseball men such as Comiskey, the Old Roman, Connie Mack and Griffith, all of whom worked hard to lure name National Leaguers in search of larger salaries.

But the one change Johnson felt was mandatory to secure the success of his new venture was a team in New York. His plan was to take the Baltimore Orioles, a once great team that had fallen on hard times and unsteady support, and plop them some-where in Manhattan.

Johnson would succeed and find suc-cess in New York—eventually. But it would sure take some doing.

Ban Johnson was a magnate who looked the part. Just shy of 40 years old, he was tall and hefty, which made him look a decade older. With trademark wire-rim glasses pinching his nose, he was a man whose loud, overbearing personality and limitless energy nonetheless inspired fol-lowers. The first thing biographers often say

Ban Johnson — inspirational, dictatorial and the force behind American League baseball in New York. (National Baseball Hall of Fame Library, Cooperstown, NY)

about Johnson is that he attended Marietta College and the University of Cincinnati law school. It's ironic, since Johnson graduated from neither; it was among the few failures of his life.

Law would have bored Johnson. He spent about 10 years on the staff of the *Cincinnati Commercial-Gazette*, becoming its sports editor. His position led to establishing friendships with baseball people like Charles Comiskey, then the player-manager of the Reds. In the 1890s, Johnson jumped into the sport fulltime — leading the Western League and holding it together, critics said, by will of his personality at a time when the sport was in turmoil.

Johnson inspired loyalty. He paid his umpires well. He disciplined players who misbehaved. And when the National League

dropped four franchises, he swung into action: First, he contacted Comiskey, who, since retiring as a player, had taken over and shifted the Western League's Sioux City team to St. Paul. On March 16, 1900, Johnson announced that he had persuaded Comiskey to move his team from St. Paul to Chicago's South Side, where he resurrected the moniker White Stockings, formerly used by the city's N.L. team. The name stuck, although the team wasn't able to use "Chicago" in its official name.

Then, he announced franchises in Kansas City, Minneapolis, Milwaukee, Indianapolis, Detroit, Cleveland and Buffalo. And he renamed his collection of teams, the American League — still a minor league in conformance with the National Agreement. But when the Nationals refused to grant the A.L. equal status, Johnson took the extra step again, announcing they'd no longer abide by the pact. Welcome to the majors, American League. Welcome to the baseball wars, National League.

Johnson's timing was solid. At the time, quite a few minor leaguers in concert with a number of well-known National Leaguers had formed a union, the Ball Players Protective Association. Among their demands: an increase in the salary ceiling from $2,400 to $3,000, which was quickly turned down by N.L. owners.

And with that, a number of disgruntled players began jumping to the Americans. There was Griffith, the star pitcher of the N.L.'s Chicago Cubs and a force behind the players union, who traveled crosstown to Comiskey's White Sox, encouraging several former teammates to jump as well. There was John McGraw, having nixed the idea of managing the Reds, who joined the A.L. Baltimore Orioles, where he had starred a few years before as a scrappy third baseman, manager and part-owner. And then there was the tall, taciturn Mack, manager of the old Western League's Milwaukee club and seemingly more suited to the priesthood than baseball. Johnson encouraged him to take over in Philadelphia.

Johnson closed in on kicking off the American League in 1901. With the new year, events unfolded quickly. On January 4, the Orioles incorporated, with McGraw at the helm. Eighteen days later, Mack, as manager and general manager of the Philadelphia Athletics, signed a 10-year lease on grounds at 29th and Columbia in Philadelphia to be called Columbia Park. The contract called for construction of single-deck stands to seat 7,500.

Then, on January 28, the American League formally organized. The Orioles, Athletics (or A's), and White Stockings joined the Boston Somersets, Washington Senators, Cleveland Blues, Detroit Tigers and Milwaukee Brewers. Three of the original clubs — Buffalo, Indianapolis and Minneapolis — were dropped, meaning that in its first year as a self-proclaimed major league, the Americans would take the N.L. head-on only in Chicago, Philadelphia and Boston.

Oh yes, A.L. President Johnson was named trustee for all teams' ballpark leases and majority stockholdings. And the player limit was established at 14 per team, with schedules set at 140 games.

Johnson, meanwhile, had other aces up his sleeve. Lake Erie millionaire Charles Somers, in addition to his role as majority stockholder of the Cleveland club, was another ally who loaned funds to keep various franchises afloat. And as the magnates organized, Griffith, Mack and McGraw spent the winter racking up railroad miles, crisscrossing the country in a cumulative effort to sign ballplayers. They did well, as 11 former National Leaguers signed on with the Americans.

The jumpers included some of the game's biggest stars. Pitcher Cy Young, already the winner of an astounding 286 games in 11 big league seasons — an average of 26 a year — went from St. Louis to Boston. Going crosstown in Philadelphia to

the A's from the Phillies was Napoleon Lajoie, a second baseman of extraordinary skills and in only five years, a cumulative batting average of .362. Also jumping to the A's were "Strawberry" Bill Bernhard and Charles "Chick" Fraser, two solid pitchers.

Raided particularly hard were Boston's N.L. Beaneaters, who lost Ted Lewis, Chick Stahl and Jimmy Collins, all of whom went with Young to the Somersets; and Hugh Duffy, a two-time batting champion, to Milwaukee. The Brooklyn Bridegrooms, N.L. champions of 1899 and 1900, lost outfielder Fielder Jones to Chicago and pitcher Joe McGinnity to McGraw's Orioles. Johnson even secured veteran N.L. umpires Jack Sheridan, Tim Hurst and Tom Connolly.

In most cases, a few hundred dollars more a season was all it took to bring over both players and umpires, many of them sore at their treatment by chintzy N.L. owners. Young, in signing for about $3,500 — the same as Lajoie — had some delicate parting words for St. Louis owner Frank Robison: "Your treatment of your players has been so inconsiderate," he said, "that no self-respecting man would want to work for you if he could do anything else in the world."

All in all, 1901 was a decent first season for the Americans. On April 24 in Chicago, the White Stockings kicked things off with a 8–2 win over Cleveland behind pitcher Roy Patterson, who would win 20 games and lead his team to the pennant. Five days later, Admiral George Dewey saw the Senators beat Baltimore in the AL opener in the nation's capital. On May 8, Cy Young got off on the right foot, pitching Boston to a 12–4 home opener win over the A's.

It was an entertaining season too. On May 23, Lajoie was intentionally walked with the bases loaded by Chicago. On September 3, the Orioles' McGinnity gave hints of his Hall of Fame career and a good nickname—"Iron Man"—by pitching two complete games against Milwaukee, winning 10–0 and losing 6–1.

Indeed, a spirited pennant race between the White Stockings and Boston—Chicago won by four games—kept the crowds coming and by season's end, more than 1.6 million had paid to see A.L. games, only about 236,000 less than National League teams. Dominating the league was Lajoie, a triple-crown winner with a whopping .426 batting average—86 percentage points over his nearest competitor, Baltimore's "Turkey" Mike Donlin, who batted a mere .340—along with 14 home runs and 125 RBIs. On the mound, Young would win 33 games with a 1.62 ERA. McGinnity won 26 and Griffith 24.

Despite the strong A.L. start, the Nationals didn't budge when it came to establishing labor peace. After all, they had problems of their own, mainly what to do with one Andrew Freedman, owner of the New York Giants.

If at times the questionable behavior of today's owners is enough to test the patience of even the most loyal baseball fans, their collective self-righteousness barely holds a candle to the fiery, cantankerous turn-of-the-century Freedman, who never met a man he didn't like suing.

A real estate operator who studied law at City College of New York, Freedman became a force in Tammany Hall, using his political ties to make numerous choice real estate and government bonding deals, including the bonding for construction of New York's subway. In 1895, he purchased controlling interest of the Giants for $48,000 from local Republican politicians and promptly drove this proud team from contenders to cellar dwellers.

The Sporting News called Freedman "vain, arrogant, ruthless—and cheap." That was kind: Another paper said that "whenever a man's work didn't suit him, it was off with his head." The irascible Freedman knew so little about baseball that he couldn't tell where the bases were, but ran the team like a Tammany fiefdom, feuding with players, managers, sportswriters, policemen, rival club owners and city officials.

When Giant pitcher William "Dad" Clarke, short of funds one winter, wrote Freedman and asked for an advance of $200 on his salary, Freedman sent him $100, with a note that read, "Since $20 is not enough to live on until the season opens, I am sending you $100." Managers were hired and fired for no conceivable cause, rowdyism on the field was encouraged, and both players and sportswriters were habitually bullied and barred from the ballpark.

During Freedman's "Reign of Terror," as his tenure was known, 13 managers passed in and out of the Polo Grounds' Giant dugout. Among them: Cap Anson and Buck Ewing, future Hall of Famers who didn't last because they couldn't stand Freedman's second guessing. Another manager, one Harvey L. Watkins, was hired in 1895 from P.T. Barnum's Circus, where he'd been business manager. He lasted 35 games.

Also in 1895, Freedman picked a fight with the finest pitcher of the day, Amos Rusie, who was fined $200 after a 23-win season, causing the so-called "Hoosier Thunderbolt" to sit out the following season in protest. When sportswriter Sam Crane wrote a series of stories critical of Freedman's management style, he was banned from the Polo Grounds.

Freedman's talent drain landed the Giants in the cellar. In the winter of 1901–2, he drove fellow National League to distraction with an offbeat power grab. Freedman's plan was to reorganize the N.L. into a kind of national trust, proposing that it issue common stock in its different franchises. The catch: New York would get 30 percent of the stock, far more than any other club.

The catch, part two: Freedman planned to take his stock plurality, combine it with the 12 percent to be awarded to his close friend, Cincinnati Owner John T. Brush, and dominate things.

Part of Freedman's power grab made sense: By seeking to establish this trust, he wanted to ground the sport in sound business principles, including tight control over wages and shifting franchises to the most profitable sites. But the other owners had heard enough and turned him down.

Then, in late 1902 Freedman sold the Giants because they didn't meet anticipated profits. John T. Brush bought most of Freedman's stock for $200,000 after selling the Cincinnati Reds. But even after the sale, Freedman continued to exert his influence by using his position as a director of the IRT to block the subway from subsidizing a new American League team in New York. In response, the A.L. needed to find investors with personal political clout in Tammany Hall capable of overcoming Freedman's opposition and breaking into the lucrative big city market.

The feuding only made Johnson work harder. With N.L. owners bickering, he and his allies strengthened the A.L.— moving Milwaukee, the league's weakest club, to St. Louis, where the new club raided the crosstown Cardinals for pitcher Jesse Burkett and shortstop Bobby Wallace. Elsewhere, the Washington Senators signed the great Philadelphia Phillies slugger Ed Delahanty, and the Boston Somersets landed another crosstown star, Beaneaters pitcher Bill Dinneen, winner of 35 games the last two years. In the A.L., Dinneen would win 20 or more games in each of next three seasons.

But even the American League couldn't survive the season without the obligatory dose of wackiness. Just after the season's start, injunctions were served in Pennsylvania's Supreme Court against Napoleon Lajoie, Bill Bernhard and Chick Fraser, pro-

hibiting them from playing for any Philadelphia team but the Phillies. It was the outcome of a suit brought by the Phillies a year earlier against the raiding A's and it could have meant a major problem, had it not been for Johnson's quick thinking.

Johnson's decision-making process was creative. He just reassigned the contracts to Cleveland, with Lajoie and Bernhard signing up and Fraser heading back to the Phillies. On May 23, Cleveland financier Charles Somers met with Lajoie, offering him an annual contract at $7,000 no matter what the legal outcome of his case.

Even so, Lajoie and Bernhard played it safe, enjoying the beach at Atlantic City and staying clear of Philadelphia during Blues visits there. With Lajoie batting .379 and Bernhard going 17–5, the Blues jumped to a fifth place finish, up from seventh. A year later, Cleveland fans voted to rename the clubs the Naps in honor of Lajoie.

The A's did just fine anyway, thanks largely a stroke of good fortune in the name of one George Edward "Rube" Waddell. "Rube" was a common name of the day given to players from the hinterlands, unused to life in the big city. Waddell, a native of Bradford, Pennsylvania, fit the bill in more ways than one.

In 1900, as a member of the Pittsburgh Pirates, Waddell won the N.L.'s earned run average title. But the 24-year-old's incurable drinking and carousing set the standard even in those days, causing the Pirates to release him the following year. But Mack liked what he saw and wrote Waddell at his home in Punxsatawney, Pennsylvania, asking him to sign. Waddell's response: a terse wire that read, "Come and get me."

So Mack went to Punxsatawney. Traveling with Waddell to the train station for the trip to Philadelphia, the pitcher insisted that Mack stop at virtually every store in town and pay off Waddell's substantial debts.

Reaching the station, the almost penniless Mack and Waddell were surrounded by a group of seven men. Now, here was a situation, thought Mack, in which bad things were about to happen. But just then, one of the men stepped forward and thanked Mack for taking Waddell away. At least that's the story Mack would relate years later.

Waddell made it Philadelphia in mid–June and went 24–7 for the remainder of the 1902 season, finishing behind only Cy Young in wins and joining another native Pennsylvanian, Eddie Plank, as an A's 20-game winner. That was "Gettysburg Eddie's" first 20-win season; when he was done, he had won 326 games in a 17-year career, good enough for inclusion in the Baseball of Hall of Fame.

Waddell would make to Cooperstown too: He'd win 193 games in a 13-year career, including four straight 20-win seasons with the A's. Along the way, he continued to confound Mack by periodically going AWOL from the club to wrestle alligators, join a minstrel show and chase fires. Eventually, Mack paid Waddell's $2,200 salary in one-dollar bills, thinking it might make the pitcher keep it longer.

Waddell stories are legion, many of them involving a vast consumption of alcohol and some kind of violence. It is said that a drunken Waddell once told his teammates he could fly. Stepping from the window of his hotel and flapping his arms, Waddell ended up, not flying, but in the hospital. Waking up the next day, he asked a teammate why he hadn't stopped him.

"I could have been killed," said the incredulous Waddell. "Why didn't you stop me?"

"What?" said the teammate. "And lose the hundred I had bet on you?"

In his handling of the Napoleon Lajoie controversy, Ban Johnson demonstrated his genius at trench warfare. But his troubles weren't finished. Enter one John J. McGraw.

How best to describe McGraw? To do it right, you'd need an encyclopedia. For starters, he stood all of 5'4", had a bulbous nose, fought all comers, held grudges for years and in time may have, next to Ty Cobb, been the most loathed figure in baseball history.

In time, McGraw would become one of the game's greatest managers and personalities. His genius was in taking and molding the prospect from coal country or the big city into a ballplayer of consummate skill and part of a team with, as one writer put it, "the look of eagles." Most of the players that McGraw influenced — like many players of the day — were the product of society's bottom rung; for them, the baseball life was preferable to one at the mill.

McGraw had earned his stripes as third baseman for the Baltimore Orioles of the 1890s, a team whose brand of rough, rowdy tactics was extreme even for the National League. If these were Orioles of the skillful Willie Keeler, they were also the team who raised umpire baiting to an art, slid into bases with spikes up high and cheated when they could. For them, winning came any way possible.

But when McGraw insisted on using the same rough tactics on A.L. umpires that he had in the National League, Johnson bristled. Fines and suspensions didn't help, particularly when McGraw became convinced that Johnson was trying to make an example of him. "If [Johnson] was planning to ditch me," McGraw recalled years later, "I ditched him first." That sealed it: The two became enemies for life.

In June 1902, McGraw, aided by Andrew Freedman, lashed back. The two launched a plan to bring McGraw to New York to manage the inept Giants. First, he negotiated with the Baltimore directors to release him from his contract in return for $6,500 in stock. In a complex series of maneuvers, he then transferred the stock and other holdings to Freedman — enough to ensure that the Giant owner had firm control of the Orioles as well.

On July 8, Freedman signed McGraw to a four-year contract to manage the N.L. Giants for a record annual salary of $11,000. Then, he went to work on the players, directing the releases of six of the 14 Baltimore players. Pitcher McGinnity, and three others — Dan McGann, Roger Bresnahan and Jack Cronin — joined the Giants. Two more Orioles — Joe Kelley and Cy Seymour — went to Cincinnati, where Kelley would manage as well. By doing so, Freedman helped both himself and his close friend, Brush, who owned the Reds, and was preparing to take over the Giants himself.

Just like that, one of Johnson's franchises had fallen into a hostile camp. But once again facing a major crisis, he rose to the challenge. The Baltimore raids had ravaged the Orioles, leaving the team with four players in uniform — that's right, four — for their July 17 game against St. Louis. Having hustled into Baltimore that morning, Johnson quickly invoked a league rule stipulating that unless a full team was placed on the field, the franchise would automatically be forfeited to the league.

So, on the morning of July 18, Johnson declared the Baltimore franchise vacant and took control of the team in the name of the American League. The call went out for players to fill the roster, and although some fairly borderline major league talents volunteered, it allowed the Orioles to finish the season — in last place, 34 games behind the pennant-winning A's. Thirty-nine men players toiled for the Orioles that season, among them, Baltimore mainstay Wilbert Robinson, he of eventual "Uncle Robby" fame, who caught 91 games in his final season, hit .293, but more significantly, replaced McGraw. It kicked off a long managing career that would land him in Cooperstown.

But none of that much mattered much

to Johnson. By then, he had pretty much decided that with or without McGraw, the Orioles were a franchise more trouble than they were worth. "The weakness of the club always was one of my worries," Johnson wrote later, as related in his 1982 biography, *The Czar of Baseball*, by Eugene Murdock. "I tried constantly to bolster it, for the league's sake and also for McGraw."

According to Murdock, Johnson had told McGraw some time early in 1902 that he had hoped to scrape up the Orioles and plop them in New York for 1903, installing him as the manager. But that plan went haywire when McGraw jumped to the Giants, and leaving Johnson still determined to find an A.L. team good enough for the bright lights of New York.

The McGraw situation only intensified the baseball raids. The only National League team considered truly off-limits in the previous two-year inter-league trench warfare had been the Pittsburgh Pirates. That was due to the Pirates' internal wars of their own, leaving what Johnson thought was the desire of Pittsburgh owner Barney Dreyfuss to bolt to the American League. These were no ordinary Pirates — they were the National League defending champs of '01 and a powerful team led by a young shortstop named Honus Wagner that would run away with the '02 race by a whopping 27½ games. How nice it would be, Johnson thought, to have a truly good team aboard.

But when Dreyfuss decided to stick to the N.L., the Pirates became open game. And so it was in truly dramatic fashion that Johnson slinked undercover into the Steel City one night in August to meet Pirates catcher Jack O'Connor and others at the Lincoln Hotel in an attempt to sign up players for the New York franchise. Dreyfuss and his secretary Harry Pulliam caught wind of the trip and stood guard in the hotel lobby, making the ballplayers use the freight elevator.

Johnson outwitted everyone again. All

in all, it was a big coup for the American Leaguers: by the time his work had finished, he had signed up not just O'Connor, but those twin 20-game winners, Jesse Tannehill and Jack Chesbro—along with Tommy Leach, Lefty Davis and Wid Conroy.

The great, late-night freight elevator raid cut deeply into the Pirate lineup but did not completely devastate it. Paced by Wagner, whom the Americans tried to get, Pittsburgh would take its third consecutive N.L. pennant in 1903, this time by a measly 6½ over the second place Giants. But it would sting enough that at the baseball peace agreement of 1903, National Leaguers would insist that in return for A.L. entry to New York, Johnson agree to steer clear of Pittsburgh.

On August 25, Johnson made it official, announcing his intention that the A.L. team set for the following season in New York be managed by Clark Griffith. And when, on December 9, Johnson announced he had bought the Washington Heights ballpark site, the N.L. took all of one day to make their move. The next day, December 10, it declared its readiness to make peace.

The National League magnates recognized that peace was essential to their survival. Attendance at N.L. games had declined more than 300,000 in 1902, a fact due in part to the farce of a pennant race, dominated by the Pirates and that laughable 27½ game advantage ahead of second place Brooklyn. Meanwhile, the upstart A.L. had swiped many of their best players, and managed to outdraw the N.L. by more than 500,000—all without a team in New York.

To fortify themselves, the N.L. owners elected 33-year-old Henry Clay "Harry" Pulliam as their new president. A graduate of the University of Virginia Law School,

Pulliam was a Louisville newspaper reporter and a Kentucky state legislator-turned-baseball executive, thanks to his friendship with Barney Dreyfuss when he was still running the Louisville Colonels. When the Colonels merged with the Pirates in 1898, the move credited with making them a powerhouse, Pulliam went along, working as team secretary.

Pulliam didn't seem like the man for the job. He liked poetry, nature and especially, flowers. A slight, generally unhealthy man, he also suffered from depression over business affairs and just may have been too gentle for steely nerves, iron-fisted negotiating abilities and resilience in dealing with the squabbling, egomaniacal team owners. "A lot of poltroons and dogs [who] eke out their existence through the receipts on the New York grounds," he once called them.

Even so, it came as a surprise, when, on the evening of July 28, 1909, Pulliam ended his life, shooting himself in his apartment at the New York Athletic Club with a revolver through his right temple. He died the next morning. The beginning of his end may have kicked off around 1907 or so, when, according to *The New York Times*, Pulliam's health "began to give way under the strain of the multitude of duties."

But all that was far off in December 1902 when Pulliam leapt into the fray, getting National League owners to agree to approach Johnson with a peace overture. The final straw had come after Frank Robison, the St. Louis owner, was won over to the cause by happenstance. Traveling to the N.L. meeting at the Victoria Hotel in New York, Robison had happened to share a train berth with Charles Somers, who was headed to New York for an American League meeting. Somers told Robison that the American Leaguers had in fact secured a playing site in Manhattan, leaving the impression that to carry on the fight was hopeless. In truth, no site had been found.

It took some doing, but led by Robison, the National League magnates decided it would be in their best interests to pursue peace. So over the strident opposition of Brush, Robison and Pulliam, along with Cincinnati's August "Garry" Herrmann and Chicago's Jim Hart, met with Johnson, Comiskey, Somers and Henry Killilea of the Boston Braves. Keyed by Herrmann's longtime friendship with Johnson and Comiskey, hostilities came to an end January 9, 1903.

For once, both sides won. Meeting in Cincinnati, league magnates agreed to mutually recognize each league's player contracts, reserve lists and existing operating territories. They agreed to play under a common set of rules, meaning that the A.L. adopted the N.L.'s foul-strike rule. In the rewarding of disputed contracts, the hottest competition came with the case of Reds outfielder Sam Crawford, signed by both Cincinnati and the Tigers. Crawford went to the Tigers, who signed him first.

On the surface, the peace agreement was a wash. But everyone knew that Johnson had gotten his way once again with his long-term goal of getting the Orioles to New York. "Brushism can never equal in diplomacy and wise management what is fondly termed 'Johnsonism,'" wrote H.G. Merrill in *The Sporting News.* "The American League has thus far made good on every proposition and its influence and example have been felt throughout the realm of professional baseball."

Not that New Yorkers would quite be seeing the pathetic old Orioles either, for Johnson, through his Pittsburgh raid and by securing Griffith, was steadily securing the services of quality major leaguers. And with that, a destructive baseball war was finally at an end, with a structure that would endure, more or less, for the next half-century.

4

Hell of a Town

"Baseball, gentlemen, baseball."

— *Sportswriter Jimmy Cannon, said to stop
a press box conversation on football*

For all the peace and harmony of the Cincinnati meetings, considerable minefields still awaited Ban Johnson in New York. And so began the next phase in the career of the strong-willed A.L. president — resumed warfare with his old New York adversaries, Brush and Andrew Freedman.

Just why Brush, the Giants' owner, so loathed Johnson may never be fully known. The discord had started a few years back, when Brush had owned the Indianapolis club of the Western League that Johnson ran, and it endured into the trials and tribulations of the dead ball era.

This much is certain: A gaunt man with a crooked nose and a perpetual frown on his face, John T. Brush did not resemble a New York baseball magnate. Anything but a bombastic type, Brush suffered from locomotor ataxia, a progressive disease of the nervous system, was thin to emaciation and walked with a cane. But leave it to this unusual baseball magnate to bring excitement and a dash of glamour — not to mention McGraw and Christy Mathewson — to his New York Giants and to the Polo Grounds, the ballpark he would build by Coogan's Bluff.

An Indianapolis clothing store owner,

Brush took to baseball as a means of promoting his sale of "ready made" suits for men and boys. He had already built a diamond and organized a semi-pro team when, in 1886, he learned that the St. Louis club of the National League was for sale. Brush promptly bought the team and moved them to Indianapolis.

In 1890, the league dropped Indianapolis and Brush sold some of his players to the New York Giants for cash and stock. In 1891, while holding on to his portion of the Giants, Brush bought the Cincinnati Reds. That arrangement continued for more than a decade until he sold the Reds in 1902 and spent $100,000 in taking over majority ownership of the Giants the following year.

As a transplanted New Yorker, Brush lived at the Lambs Club, the city's oldest theatrical club and the meeting place and temporary residence to a generation of entertainers and actors, among them W.C. Fields, John Barrymore, Al Jolson and Spencer Tracy.

Unlike Freedman, Brush poured money into the Giants and made them winners. He also brought a showman's touch to life at the Polo Grounds — bringing in brass bands at least once a series, leather cushions for women, along with thousands of card-board fans bearing an ad for his clothing company.

Brush vs. Johnson became a cat and mouse game. Through December of 1902, Brush beat Johnson to options on most of the available spots. When Brush failed, Freedman picked up the slack by threatening, with the help of Tammany tycoon Richard Croker, to have streets created through properties that Johnson eyed. As for the league peace of early 1903, "Lip service was all [Brush] gave," writes Yankee historian Frank Graham, "for he continued to combat Johnson and, through the Giants' secretary, Fred Knowles, to denounce the new league and scoff at its pretentions."

But Johnson needed more than a ballpark. Like Brush, what he really needed was an ally, someone plugged into the Tammany bureaucracy who could help him skirt the slings and arrows of the city politic, and helping nail down a ballpark. But there wasn't much time: How fortunate then that he was able to reach back into his vast repertoire of acquaintances, among them, New York sportswriter Joe Vila.

Johnson's friendship with Vila dated back to 1892, when they'd been young reporters covering the John L. Sullivan–Jim Corbett fight in New Orleans. As it turned out, Vila, who would eventually become sports editor of the *New York Sun*, knew a few people himself, notably big-time gambler Frank Farrell.

It was just the connection Johnson needed. Farrell and his partner, Big Bill Devery, along with Tammany boss Tim Sullivan — make that "Big" Tim — comprised a syndicate that handled protection services for gambling establishments. That was big business at the turn of the century in New York, as proven by *The New York Times*, responding in 1900 to the failure of the 1899 Mazet Committee to fully investigate the state of the city's gambling, provided a breakdown of the syndicate's income:

- 400 pool rooms at $300 per month each, totaling $120,000 per year;
- 500 crap games at $150 per month or $75,000 annually;
- 200 small gambling houses at $150 per month, or $30,000 per year;
- 20 large gambling houses at $1,000 per month, or $20,000 annually;
- 50 envelope games or pawnshop swindles at $50 per month, or $2,500 per year; and,
- policy operations at $125,000 per year.

The entire operation totaled nearly $3.1 million a year, an airtight scheme since between Sullivan and Devery their syndicate took in the supervision of the police, the state senate and the State Gambling Commission.

Heading the Mazet Commission was one William Travers Jerome, elected district attorney in 1901, who had taken on the noble mission of abolishing gambling. But standing in his way was Tammany Mayor Robert Van Wyck (1898–1901), who had other ideas, and let gambling houses run open all over town.

To open a gambling hall of any size, owners had to apply in person at their local precinct. The $300 initiation fee — paid directly to the captain — was returnable in the improbable event that the application was denied. In turn, the owners were assured all the cooperation they could hope for, to the point that in March 1900, it was reported that when a well-known establishment on 13th Street moved to the next block, attendants simply carried dismantled roulette wheels and green baize covered poker tables brazenly through the streets.

So it went in Tammany Hall just after the start of the 20th century. The organization's roots dated back 100 years or so, its rise attributable to the city's more exclusive clubs. In the early 19th century, the Society, as it was known then, supported Aaron Burr and Martin Van Buren, along with such progressive policies as universal male suffrage, and the abolition of imprisonment for debt and lien laws to protect craftsmen.

In time, the government became riddled by graft and corruption, which by the 1840s had reached epidemic proportions. Even so, Tammany leaders managed to steadily expand their base by granting aid to immigrants. They also opposed nativist and anti–Catholic movements of the era, securing loyalties that were maintained for decades.

John Kelley ran Tammany Hall from 1872 to 1886, making it a political machine. The first of 10 straight Irish-American leaders, he is said to have "found the society a horde and made it an army," as one observer put it. Kelley's system of organizational improvements appointed precinct captains to help families in their neighborhoods — finding them jobs in times of need and smoothing the way with the law when problems arose.

In return, Tammany Hall asked for votes. To help the process, its leaders occasionally resorted to the time-honored New York political traditions of stealing ballot boxes on election day and ensuring that dead people cast their votes. The machine controlled virtually all local nominations to elected office, ensuring them the last word in appointments made by successful candidates for municipal office.

It was a lucrative system. As part of the corruption, Tammany soldiers received considerable funds and kickbacks from contractors, builders and candidates hoping to conduct business in New York. Along the way, legal fees and brokerage commissions were directed to district leaders, who earned handsome profits from what was called "honest graft." Said one wealthy machine contributor: "I saw my opportunities and I took 'em."

At the top of turn-of-the-century Tammany Hall were Sullivan and Devery, who would eventually split and argue bitterly. A beefy man given to skimmers and bow ties, Big Tim emerged from the tough Irish tenement of Five Points and rose to a colorful career of politics and business, with each helping the other. With Tammany's backing, he rose rapidly from the state assembly (1886–1893) to state congress (1893–1902 & 1908–1912) and the U.S. Congress (1902–1906). He also managed to own a vaudeville circuit, which extended to a lucrative chain of more than 40 theaters, and lucrative investments in nickelodeons, Coney Island and at racetracks.

Sullivan ruled the districts of lower Manhattan for a quarter century, forging an effective style that mixed the traditional machine tactics with his considerable influence in business and organized crime. Ironically, his domination of city politics can be described by considering the enormous crowd that, of all things, attended his funeral. The eventual victim of tertiary syphilis, Big Tim was classified insane in 1913 and was killed that August when struck by a train in Eastchester. His funeral drew 75,000 mourners, among the largest in the city's history.

Big Bill Devery was another story. So fat he could barely squeeze his 250 pounds into his suit, the fleshy Devery was so flamboyantly crooked that it became his badge of honor. Working as a bartender on the Bowery, he bribed Tammany Hall to become a policeman in 1878. Promoted to sergeant in 1884 and captain in 1891, he became chief of police in 1898 and reportedly told his men during his inaugural address: "If there's any graftin' to be done, I'll do it. Leave it to me!"

"He was no more fit to be a chief of police than the fish man was to be director of the aquarium," muckraker Lincoln Steffens wrote of Devery, "but as a character, as a work of art, he was a masterpiece." Working

It's Opening Day at the Hilltop and Big Bill Devery, clearly living up to his descriptive nickname, is throwing out the first ball. (Brown Brothers)

the system made Big Bill rich. He became so wealthy that when the state legislature, overwhelmed in one of its periodic bursts of reform, voted to abolish his position and replace it with a commission system, Devery owned real estate worth $640,000.

Devery operated his network of police protection each night from a West Side street corner, where a stream of gambling bosses, criminals and pimps diligently delivered their envelopes stuffed with cash. When *The Mail and Express* reported a list of prices the police charged for such protection — including $50 a month for pool-hall gambling houses, $25 a month for rumrunners and $3,000 for illegal abortionists — a Devery associate suggested they hire a detective to find the leak. "A detective?" pondered Devery. "We need a plumber."

Rigging elections was a particular Tammany specialty. Shortly before a vote, Devery would send his aides to saloon keepers, promising protection should the ticket be elected. It all made for colorful copy in the newspapers, and although Devery was

frequently brought to task by Steffens and other reformers, none of that mattered very much. After all, Big Bill never fined a policeman for dereliction of duty, only for getting caught.

In Devery's baseball partner, 37-year-old Frank Farrell, the Highlanders had the backing of Manhattan's biggest pool room and bar owner. Together, Devery and Farrell were baseball's odd couple, a turn-of-the-century Oscar and Felix. For all of Big Bill's bluster and bombast, Farrell was everything his partner wasn't: reserved, charming, slightly natty in a Nathan Detroit kind of way and passionate, not about baseball, but horse racing. He and his wife, Anna, had no children, and lived well but quietly on West End Avenue on the Upper West Side.

The site of Farrell and Devery seated side-by-side in their private box at the Hilltop was a treat. Seated next to the obese former Chief, Farrell seemed even more slight than his 5'6" frame, 160-pound frame. The reason could have been the massive handlebar mustache he sported until around 1909, which gave him an eerie resemblance to the writer Stephen Crane. After shaving it off, Farrell looked just unassuming.

"Everybody knows him but few persons truly know him," a New York newspaper wrote of Farrell in 1908. Suffice it to say that Farrell was a Tammany Hall businessman who realized early that the best way to get ahead was to get along, mixing with all kinds and on all levels. "Act on the square toward everybody," he would say, "and make them do likewise by you."

Interviews with Farrell could be tough going. He was cordial, but he knew the advantages of seeming a little dull, unassuming and ever-so-slightly respectable. Farrell was also tight-lipped and hated to criticize in the overstated, blustery way of most other baseball moguls. But ask him about horse racing and Farrell would get downright misty-eyed.

"If there is one thing that I care for more than anything else, it is my horses," he once said. "There is no finer sport than racing. To see one of your horses dash home the winner in front of a big field of contestants makes your nerves jump and your blood tingle with joy. In that brief period of glory, you forget your many previous disappointments and the expense they have entailed."

The roots of this baseball odd couple's relationship dated to the days when Devery was captain of the West 13th Street police station and Farrell owned a saloon a half-block away on the corner of 13th Street and 6th Avenue. Farrell's business success tended to rise and fall with the city's political fortunes; for a time, he owned a luxurious casino designed by Stanford White, where the city's café society met.

But in the 1901 election campaign, when William Travers Jerome, the reform candidate for district attorney, accused Farrell of being a leader of the infamous New York gambling trust that included Devery, Sullivan, Police Commissioner Joseph Sexton and Mayor Van Wyck. Farrell lost his police protection as Tammany Hall suffered mightily at the polls.

So, he began to diversify, purchasing Empire Racetrack in Yonkers for $217,000 and waiting awhile before opening his next gambling establishment. This one, at 33 West 34th Street, opened in August 1902 and featured double iron front gates; a secret button that turned off the lights and closed the windows and doors; and a concealed iron door upstairs that led to the building next door. Even so, Jerome, by now the district attorney, raided it that December and closed it down. But the ever-resourceful Farrell was back at work three months later at another new place, 11 blocks north.

So, this was the crowd to whom Johnson turned in his driving ambition to place an American League franchise in New York. Within a few days of the Cincinnati meeting at which the peace pact was signed, Joe Vila brought Johnson and Farrell together.

Farrell got right to the point, offering to buy the Baltimore franchise within minutes. But Johnson hesitated, thinking, as he would recall later, that the New York gambler seemed a tad too eager. But when Farrell produced a certified check for $25,000, Johnson's doubts were erased.

"Take that as a guarantee of good faith, Mr. Johnson," Farrell said. "If I don't put this ball club across, keep it."

Johnson hadn't expected that. Prepared, if needed, to finance the club from the American League war chest to which the Shibes and Somers were the major contributors, he described the amount as "a pretty big forfeit."

Vila offered a knowing smile. "He bets that much on a race, Ban," he said.

Farrell explained his intention of bringing his friend Devery into the partnership.

Big Bill had retired only two years before and had money to burn, in part due to a lucrative real estate business. Besides, Farrell added, they had a good spot for a ballpark.

"Where?" Johnson asked.

"It runs from 165th Street to 168th Street on Broadway."

Johnson doubted a place so far north would work. "That's a long way uptown," he said.

"It won't seem so far uptown in a little while," said Farrell. "The neighborhood is growing; and the subway, which will start operating in the fall, will be extended up there sooner than most people believe."

He was spot on. Johnson, swayed by the ready cash and pleasantly stunned at how quickly everything had come together just like that, quickly inked the deal, agreeing to sell the Baltimore franchise to Farrell and Devery for $18,000. In return for their ready-made team, the late Baltimore Orioles, that even came with a name manager, Griffith, Farrell and Devery agreed to buy the property and build the park. But they needed to hurry; the season was all of six weeks away.

5

New Yawk, New Yawk

"In Boston, they ask, 'How much does he know?' In New York, they ask, 'How much is he worth?'"

— Mark Twain

For all their bluster, Farrell and Devery knew what they were talking about. For starters, the territory was familiar and their pipeline to Tammany Hall assured that the ballpark would be built, even against the formidable opposition of Brush and Friedman.

The fact that the Hilltop would have to be so far uptown may have scared off most mortals. But Farrell and Devery had another ace in their favor — the promise of New York City's subway system. Plans for the subway — the Interborough Rapid Transit or IRT — had been in the works for decades, and although it was generally expected to ease the congestion of a growing city to a point, very few expected that it would be such an overwhelming success.

The dream was that the IRT would hurl passengers from City Hall in the southern part of Manhattan clear up to 145th Street in Harlem in all of 15 minutes. But even as the phrase "15 minutes to Harlem" became a kind of mantra for the subway zealots throughout 1902 and 1903, others were doubtful. It all seemed a bit too good to be true.

After all, the idea for a New York subway had kicked around for more than 25 years. When, on February 26, 1870, Alfred Ely Beach demonstrated his creation of the pneumatic subway, he was gambling that intense press and public attention would be enough to make it work.

Beach had designed a single car, which fitted into the nine-foot-wide cylindrical tube. Propulsion was supplied by a giant fan that subway workers christened "The Western Tornado." Operated by a steam engine, the subway drew air through a valve that blew into the tunnel. So back and forth it went between Warren and Murray streets. Beach even topped off his couple of stations with frescoes, a fountain and a fish tank.

The single 22-seat subway car was a wonder of the age. Newspapers crowed, as Beach had hoped. "The waiting room is a large and elegantly furnished apartment, cheerful and attractive throughout," gushed *The New York Sun.* "Fashionable Reception Held in the Bowels of the Earth!" trumpeted *The Herald.* But public and press attention weren't enough, for Beach didn't bother to secure the support of the person whose endorsement he needed most — Boss William Marcy Tweed, the spiritual father of Tammany Hall.

So, plans for a subway in New York

stalled. Other cities opened their underground railways — London came first, in 1863, followed by Glasgow in 1886, Budapest in 1896 and Paris in 1900. In the U.S., underground rapid transit kicked off in 1901 when the Boston Elevated Railway opened for business.

It took the forceful will of financier August Belmont II, backed by reform Mayor Robert Van Wyck, to get the New York project started. Belmont had succeeded his father as head of his family's banking firm and managed to retain their close business relations with the wealthy Rothschild family. When Belmont became president of the Rapid Transit Subway Construction Company in 1900, the Rothschild money poured in, assuring the project's success.

On March 24, 1900, 12,000 laborers — most of them Italian, Irish and Polish — began tunneling their way through the streets of New York. A year later, with the subway under construction, horses were taken off streetcars, which converted to electricity. It was a stopgap measure, for the trolley cars proved so dangerous that Brooklynites started calling themselves, "Trolley Dodgers." So did the borough's baseball team, eventually called the Dodgers.

Those subway workers made a mess but they made it. On October 27, 1904, the city's new mayor, George B. McClellan, Jr., son of the former Union General, followed by Belmont and more than 200 mustached Wall Street bankers, walked into the gleaming, new City Hall station, got on the train and pulled its silver throttle. Off went the city's first subway — heading north under Broadway, then to Grand Central Terminal, west to Times Square and north again to 145th Street. At a top speed of 45 miles an hour, the subway traveled the 9.1 miles in its advertised time — 26 minutes.

All in all, it was quite a day. Its opening, according to subway historian Stan Fischler, author of *Uptown Downtown: A Trip Through Time of New York's Subway,*

was "a day rarely … equaled in the city's long history of major celebrations."

"Only Armistice Day, V-E Day, V-J Day and the return of Charles Lindbergh after his solo flight across the Atlantic produced as enthusiastic an explosion of public joy," wrote Fischler. In building the subway line, some 3,508,000 cubic yards of earth had been excavated.

It had been a long haul and it was a huge success. Suddenly, Harlem and other Uptown areas really weren't so far away. And getting to Hilltop Park, overlooking the Hudson River, would be a quick trip after all.

The IRT was more than a way of moving people uptown, downtown and all around. It helped bring a disparate population closer together, and it opened up tracts of land in the Bronx and Queens and other areas once thought too far away for homes. Most of all, it helped the city's emerging middle class, struggling to get ahead, find their piece of the American dream.

New York was then, as it is now, gargantuan. Then, as now, it was the big town, the city of lights and a place, as the novelist Caleb Carr puts it, where "whatever happens, happens in the rest of the country 10 years later."

So it goes that as the country's most important city, New York is and has always been the destination of the world's most ambitious people. As the *Times* once wrote: "It was the ultimate harbor, the ultimate trading post, the ultimate real estate deal, and most important, a crucible of democracy and capitalism like no other."

New York was also the most crowded, the dirtiest and the noisiest city in the country. Many there had yet to find that American dream in the early part of the 20th century; then, as now, it was diverse in the extreme, a place with more Irish than in

Dublin, more Italians than in Naples, and more Jews than in Jerusalem. Yet its blend of what the *Times* called "frontier democracy and greed acted as a growth hormone of frightening power." It still does.

Indeed, you won't find cherished tales of a city founded on heroism and principle that its citizens get misty-eyed talking about. This wasn't Philadelphia or New England, where the Puritans and Quakers talked of religious freedom, tolerance and the chance to worship without persecution. This was New York, pal, with all its grubby, loud glory.

Blame it on the Dutch. They founded the city, and as writer and preservationist Brendan Gill once observed, "didn't give a damn about anything except making money." Legend has it that Peter Minuit paid the Narragansett Indians $24 in beads and trinkets for Manhattan Island. The lesson? The art of the deal, as Donald Trump would say, lives on.

From the start, capitalism took center stage in New York, affecting every transaction and everything else done there for that matter. It took the Dutch 17 years to build a church there. Even Manhattan's street grid, adopted in 1811, appears to have been laid out with efficiency and commerce in mind.

Financial events multiplied in New York through the 19th century. Alexander Hamilton solidified a deal that secured the city as the country's money center. By the 1830s, New York created a financial district on Wall Street in what is thought by historians to be the first time that a district was created for the single purpose of commerce. A few years later came the Erie Canal, upstate, which streamlined the movement of goods from the Great Plains to the rest of the world.

In time, the language of New York came to revolve around bulls and bears. Fortunes were made and lost, as the winners built stately mansions and handsome town houses. On the other extreme was an appalling poverty in which poor Irish and poor blacks lived in areas like the seamy Five Points in lower Manhattan near today's Foley Square, with its gang fights, violence as a way of life, unpaved roads, open sewers and foul-smelling air.

Such was the state of New York just after the turn of the century when the Highlanders moved to the Hilltop. Even then, it was a sprawling place of extraordinary diversity, a city of horse-drawn milk wagons, opulent mansions, bustling shipping docks, men who wore hats and streets where gaping holes for subways and skyscrapers were common.

For most, wages were low, with city employees putting in 10-hour days and many having to work even longer. To work from 5 a.m. to 9 p.m. was the norm and 12-year-old children could be paid if they attended school 80 days a year.

Yes, life was arguably harder in turn-of-the-century New York than it is today. More than 1.5 million New Yorkers lived in slums just after the start of the 20th century, many of them in the section of lower Manhattan, like that of Five Points, bounded by the East River, East 14th Street, 3rd Avenue, the Bowery and Catherine Street that was probably the world's most densely populated area.

For many, conditions were grim. The mortality rate for children was more than five times higher than it is today and life expectancy at birth was far lower. Hospital conditions was poor. It wasn't until 1910 that the city's water was chlorinated, and the milk wasn't pasteurized until 1912.

Like today, New York was the city that was constantly reinventing itself. Then, as always, it was in a flurry of transition. In an age where 60 percent of Americans lived in small towns or on farms, the city, which itself had more than 2,000 farms, was in the midst of a building boom. Buildings and land on Manhattan were valued at $3.6

billion, compared to $1 billion back in 1865. Meanwhile, the city's 40,000 manufacturing accounted for 60 percent of the manufacturing of the entire state.

Large-scale population shifts were at work as well. Of the city's inhabitants, 37 percent were foreign-born. Between 1880 and 1919, more than 23 million persons emigrated to the U.S., and of those, 17 million entered through New York City. The two largest groups were Russian Jews and Italians, who, unlike most immigrants of previous years, who moved to farms or small towns, a large number remained in New York, where opportunities for jobs were plentiful.

After all, New York was the nation's largest port, which provided a lot of jobs along the waterfront. It was the largest center of light manufacturing. It was the center of finance, trade, the garment industry, construction and manual labor. And although immigrant workers were frequently exploited, most were compelled by work to remain in the city.

Immigrants of the time generally settled in working class, ethnic neighborhoods, like "Little Italy," which took form in the area of Mulberry Street on the Lower East Side; a Jewish area closer to Hester Street; the German section of Yorkville on the Upper East Side; and, African Americans near West 53rd Street. The rhythms of the neighborhoods changed with the new arrivals, who created homes, shops, ethnic and religious festivals, theaters and coffee houses, all in the flavor of their former homes.

Then, as now, New York was intent on being consistently hip. Blue was the choice color of suits for well-dressed businessmen, who preferred their shoes as pointed as arrows. Only in hot weather would they remove their jackets in their offices and they never took off their vests. What stayed on were hats — straw hats in the summer and derbies in the winter. Women dressed differently too. They covered themselves literally in layers from their head clear down to their shoes. For the most part, clothes were dark.

This wasn't the upper-crust New York of Edith Wharton, a world in which the rich cavorted about in parlors behind closed doors. The decade or so leading up to World War I isn't generally remembered as a romantic time — save that for the Jazz Age of the 1920s captured in the fiction of F. Scott Fitzgerald.

It was dynamic all the same. At the turn of the twentieth century, New York was three years removed from consolidation, a sea change of extraordinary importance in which more than 40 municipalities were combined into one. On Jan. 1, 1898, Manhattan, Brooklyn, the Bronx, Queens and Staten Island joined to officially become Greater New York, a city of five boroughs. Its population was 3.4 million, second only to London.

Greater New York's unifying concept behind the consolidation: its harbor, the world's greatest for the next 50 years. The following year, it opened a new zoo — the Bronx Zoo. And the next year — 1900 — when electric lights replaced gas, Broadway became the Great White Way. And theater wasn't the only entertainment available for an emerging middle class; turn-of-the-century New York was a city in the midst of an information revolution. No, there was no Internet, but there were newspapers of every description, vaudeville and the latest news medium, moving-picture "actualities" or "visual newspapers" that the Biograph and Edison companies were exhibiting at those vaudeville halls.

New York was a city of perpetual motion. In 1901, steel magnate Andrew Carnegie gave money to build 65 public library branches throughout the City. Meanwhile, with 83,000 tenements housing 70 percent of New York's population in horrendous conditions, these "old law" buildings were declared substandard by a new Tenement House Law. "New law" buildings were a substantial improvement.

For the most part, New York just after turn of the century was the city of Lewis Hine and Jacob Riis, whose photos are famous for stark displays of life in the raw — child laborers, dark bars, factories and people in poverty. The average work week in those days: 60 hours, compared to 44 today.

Sports-wise, baseball was king, followed by horse racing and boxing. College football was growing in interest but largely the providence of elite Ivy League collegians; pro football was years from the radar screen as was basketball, a sport still played in many circles by using peach buckets for baskets.

In New York, much of the sporting life revolved around Madison Square Garden, the great pleasure palace named for the place where it was built — Madison Square, then a 4½ acre park off 5th Avenue, heading north from 23rd Street. There have been no fewer than four Madison Square Gardens since 1879; this was number two, designed by the famed architect Stanford White, and surely the most lavish of the bunch.

White designed Garden Number Two as the showplace public arena of America. Spires shot off in all directions, topped off by a pantheon with a 320-foot Italianate tower, and that topped by a 30-foot statue of a bare-breasted Diana, the Huntress, dressed in a loincloth and little else.

For his own pleasures, White built himself private living quarters in the tower penthouse and took to relaxing in another apartment-turned pleasure palace nearby. It was there that a teenage showgirl from Pittsburgh named Evelyn Nesbit would entertain by swinging back and forth while sitting naked in another of White's creations, a red velvet swing.

That presented a number of problems. For starters, Nesbit was married. Secondly, her husband was a young man with a temper named Harry Thaw, the heir to a railroad fortune. On June 25, 1906, Thaw approached White, who was watching a musical called "Mamzelle Champagne" at the building's outdoor roof garden, and pumped three bullets into his head, killing him.

The trial of Harry Thaw, 34 and younger than White by 20 years, became the century's first great trial, an O.J. Simpson-style case that riveted the country. In court, Nesbit admitted to swinging naked, but said she'd been slipped a glass of spiked champagne.

Thaw had his alibi, but was no soul of innocence himself. A notorious playboy himself, he was known for whipping women in a room he rented in a brothel. It turned out he whipped Nesbit as well before they were married. Moreover, as the details spewed forth at the trial, Thaw seemed disinterested, spending his hours in his Tombs prison cell by eating squab and sipping champagne, ordered from Delmonico's restaurant.

The newspapers reveled in it all. Thaw's lawyer, Dephin Delmas, argued his client suffered from "dementia Americana," an insanity caused when the sanctity of an American's home or the purity of his wife is violated. The first trial ended in a hung jury. The jury at the second trial found Thaw not guilty by reason of insanity. He died in 1947; twenty years later, Evelyn Nesbit announced as she faced her own death that Stanford White had been her real love all along.

Vintage photos of the New York cityscape reveal a sense of the place. Despite the population density, there aren't yet many cars in these photos — only street cars and horse drawn carriages — making it all seem a bit sparse. Buildings were certainly more compact — there didn't appear to be much zoning — and there were a lot of billboards. A 1909 photo of Herald Square, near Mc-Graw's pool hall, shows perhaps three street-cars per block and long skirted women bustling about, along with a couple of other things that aren't there anymore either: the New York Herald Building, which was torn down in the 1920s, and the Sixth Avenue elevated train or "el," which went the same way in 1938.

Times Square sure looked different. It was — and still is — the heart of the city, where the Great White Way collides with what a 1933 musical labeled "naughty, bawdy, gaudy, sporty 42nd Street." It wasn't even called Times Square at first, but Long-acre Square until 1904 when *The New York Times* built a new headquarters there, topped off in 1928 by the Motogram, which started flashing news bulletins in lights.

The year the *Times* built their head-quarters was also the year a subway station went to Times Square. A year later, 5 million had used it. A 1900 photograph look-ing south from 46th Street reveals the fa-miliar blend of theaters and hotels — the Hotel Cadillac and the Pabst are two that are clearly identified. The difference is in the street itself — seemingly as wide as today, it is sprinkled with trolleys, some pedestri-ans, horse-drawn hacks and thankfully, a street sweeper.

And yet, much of what was new at the turn of the century is still familiar. The Flat-iron Building was new then, going up in 1902. That same year, the Broadway Lim-ited began its New York-Chicago run and the Horn & Hardart Automat debuted at 1557 Broadway, perhaps inaugurating the era of fast-food dining. The following year, Enrico Caruso made his Metropolitan Opera debut in *Rigoletto* and Luna Park opened at Coney Island.

Ah, Coney Island.

"Step right up! Lilliputa, a city of 300 of the world's tiniest people! A city designed to exhibit buildings proportioned to a race of Midgets!

"See the strangest and rarest and most talented entertainers gathered from all over the universe!

"The Blue Man! The Fat Lady! The Human Skeleton! Don't crowd! Come on folks. There's room for all!"

Perhaps no other place showed turn-of-the-century New Yorkers at play and in the midst of developing a leisure-time sen-sibility. Coney Island was a carnival of the strange and a feast for the curious. Facing the Atlantic Ocean in Brooklyn, it was ac-cessible by a subway ride and the nominal admission fee.

There have been other amusement parks and curiosity sideshows have long been a part of the American scene. What made Coney Island different was its sheer volume of the bizarre, such that between 1900 and 1930, it displayed the oddest as-sortment of humanity ever collected in one place.

One reason: the vision of former New York state senator William H. Reynolds who decided to build the world's greatest amusement park. It was called Dreamland, which opened May 15, 1904, and included a double "shoot-the-chutes," an estimated 1 million electric lights and a 375-foot snow-white illuminated tower. Built for the then monumental cost of $3.5 million, Dreamland dwarfed two existing amuse-ment parks there — Steeplechase Park and the brand-new Luna Park.

There was another reason: Reynolds's promoter of promoters, one Samuel W. Gumpertz. Arguably the most relentless seeker of the strange, Gumpertz trekked the globe in search of the *most* bizarre and the *most* unusual. P.T. Barnum may have cov-ered an actor in blackface and passed him off as the Wild Man of Borneo, but Gumpertz went for authenticity, once traveling to Borneo itself and importing not one, but 19 men.

Elsewhere, he went to the Pyrenees for midgets and made five trips to Egypt, five to Asia and two to the heart of Africa, all in search of the exotic. From Africa, he brought back members of the famed Ubangi tribe, whose women enlarged their lips to huge dimensions. From Burma, he brought a remarkable Padaung "giraffe woman" and in France, he found a female midget he named "Little Lady," whom he adopted after paying her parents $4,000. You get the idea.

So it went on the unusually warm late April day in 1903 that the Highlanders opened in New York. On that day, the population of the United States was 75.9 million, compared with 273 million today; the country's median age was nearly 23 as opposed to nearly 36 today; and, perhaps most extraordinarily of all, life expectancy for men was 46.3, compared to 73.6 today.

Divorce in the U.S. was rare just after the turn of the century. Only 0.3 percent of men and 0.5 percent of women were divorced, compared to 8.2 and 10.3 percent today. The number of adults completing high school in 1900: 15 percent, compared to 83 percent today. And the number of paved roads: 10 — yes, 10 in 1900 — compared to 4 million today. The day's most popular song: "Good Bye Dolly Gray."

In St. Louis that day, President Roosevelt — a dyed-in-the-wool New Yorker — kicked off the World's Fair festivities with a military parade and a big fireworks display. Fortunately, most of the dedication ceremonies for the event, organized to celebrate the 100th anniversary of the Louisiana Purchase, took place inside at the Liberal Arts building; the city was gripped by a cold, raw wind that left many in the crowd shivering, including the President who was wrapped in a big Army blanket to fend off the cold.

Fittingly, the President used the occasion to deliver a speech on the virtues of American ideals. As usual, it was a Roosevelt-patented blend of history, sociology and long-winded, old-fashioned U.S. jingoism — in this case, wrapped around the theme of the Louisiana Purchase. And, as usual, only Roosevelt, ever the showman in his bully pulpit, could get away with using words like "indissolubly."

"Our triumph in this process of expansion was indissolubly bound up with the success of our peculiar kind of Federal Government," the President told the packed crowd of 18,000, "and this success has been so complete that because of its very completeness, we now sometimes fail to appreciate not only the all-importance but the tremendous difficulty to the problem with which our Nation was originally faced."

Back in New York, the elegant clothiers John Wanamaker took advantage of the East Coast's unusually warm temperatures that April 30 to break out their new line of spring and summer fashions. At Wanamaker, at the corner of Broadway and 4th Avenue, men's fancy and worsted suits were going for up to $25. And up at the Metropolitan Motor Club on East 57th Street, the new line of "Toledo" gasoline cars ranged in price from the 12-horsepower at $1,000 to 24-horsepower for $4,000.

For those needing lodging, a four-story apartment building on Greenwich Street was theirs for $8,000. Brownstones on Washington Square were $22,000 and an elegant, modern tenement on West 101st Street, near West End Avenue and not far from Grant's Tomb, went for $36,000.

In the headlines that day in New York, a threatened tie-up of all foodstuffs from Southern ports and other places by New York's marine engineers was averted when railroad operators agreed to arbitrate their demands.

Elsewhere, a runaway pony owned by an Italian priest grew excited after a long run in Central Park, sauntered down Lexington Avenue and tried to run up the stairs of 164 East 78th Street, just before dinner. No one was hurt in the incident, but the pony evidently stamped so hard on the floor that plaster fell from the ceiling in the hallway.

Not far away, at the foot of Jackson Street that day, two boys, Eddie Monihan, age 8, and John J. McGinn, age 9, were saved from drowning when their friend, Jack Lynch, jumped in the East River to save them.

It was a decidedly more quaint affair at the Hotel Martha Washington, where 250 members and guests of the Get Together Club joined in the celebration of New York City's 215th birthday. All in all, it was a celebratory crowd, despite the urgings of Hamilton W. Mable, the first speaker, who tried to fire up the proceedings with his thoughts on the importance of public service.

"The trouble with New York is that it has too many residents and not enough citizens," said Mable. "It does not make a man to erect a fine mansion, no matter whether it cost a million or more. He must enter into the life to advance the interests of the city in order to become a citizen."

But Hamilton Mabel wasn't the only one sharing their thoughts this April 30 in New York. At the Girls' Technical School, Mrs. Edward R. Hewitt urged in a speech that young women should mind their manners, sit properly and practice their etiquette. "These things, no one will deny, enter in, a very great deal, to that womanly quality which we call charm," Mrs. Hewitt lectured, "which no one will deny is almost indispensable to the successful, the agreeable and the welcome woman."

Across town, at the southeast corner of 7th Avenue and West 40th Street, George Edwards of 316 West 32nd St. deliberately made bets on the races at Jamaica Track in what was described as a deliberate plan to test the bookmaking outside the racetrack. Wearing a big diamond stickpin in his shirt and with bills of various denominations between the fingers of his left hand, Edwards was arrested after 15 minutes.

But if things weren't going well for George Edwards, they could have been worse, much worse, for a man named Miller. Appearing as a feature attraction in the Military Show at Madison Square Garden, Miller, a trumpeter, fell 25 feet off a signal station built by First Signal Corps. A cry of horror arose as Miller, whose first name is lost to history, toppled headfirst, but fortunately, he was able to grab onto two of the stanchions halfway down, steady himself and go bounding back up the tower. But Miller was a lucky man; he wasn't injured.

In other words, just another day in the most important city in the world.

6

Play Ball!

"You never unpack your suitcases in this business."

— Preston Gomez

Meanwhile, there was a team to put together. That substantial task fell to Clark Griffith, the team's hastily-named manager, and among the big name major leaguers brought in to populate the Highlanders.

Griffith was the right man for the job. In time, he would be recognized as a baseball pioneer — reaching the Hall of Fame in 1946 for his contributions on the field, as a manager and as an executive. He was even the man who thought up the idea of having the President throw out the first ball and start the new season. In 1912, President Taft was the first such President to do the honors in what for decades became an annual tradition in Washington, D.C.

For all his eventual success — most of it with the Senators, which he led for more than 40 years — Griffith's tale started humbly, a classic American tale of getting ahead by brains and drive instead of brawn. It is also a reminder of exactly how long ago it was: Indirectly, it has been written many times, Jesse James was the one who pushed Griffith into the game.

Born in a log cabin in 1869 in Clear Creek, Missouri, Griffith and his family lived in the untamed wilderness, where James and his gang were always stirring up trouble. After Griffith's father was acciden-

tally shot and killed in 1871 while deer hunting, Griffith's mother decided for safety's sake to move her six children to the more urban setting of Normal, Illinois, where the young Clark became interested in baseball.

After pitching for sandlot teams, Griffith turned professional at 17 for Bloomington, Illinois, of the Interstate League. He made his major league debut in 1891, pitching for the St. Browns of the old American Association. Midway through that season, he was sold to Boston, where he finished the year with a combined 14–9 record and helped Boston take the pennant.

Unfortunately, arm trouble followed and Boston cut him loose after the season. In an effort to work out his problems, Griffith signed with Tacoma of the Pacific Northwest League, winning 13 games there in 1892, and the following year with Oakland of the Pacific Coast League, where he pitched in 48 games, winning 30.

Griffith's break came late in the 1893 season when while pitching for Milwaukee, he joined Cap Anson's National League Chicago White Stockings. With the arm trouble behind him, he promptly became the team's biggest winner, posting a 21–14 record in 1894 and for the next six years, winning 20 games in all but one season.

Physically, Griffith wasn't a big man. Standing only 5'8" and listed at 175 pounds, he relied on control and smarts. "They say of him that he never threw a pitch over the heart of the plate," wrote Arthur Daley many years later in *The New York Times*. "He was shooting for the corners and nicking them because his control was unbelievable. It mattered not that his fast ball couldn't splinter a wafer-thin pane of glass."

Helping Griffith too was a taciturn confidence that many perceived as arrogance. He didn't mind crowding batters for intimidation and to keep them off balance. There is the story of the time Griffith, who acquired the nickname "The Old Fox" for his caginess on the mound, so unnerved one opponent that when the batter turned to the umpire to argue a called strike — but without leaving the batter's box — Griffith, sensing an opportunity, threw again, hitting the bat with the ball, fielded the trickler and started a game-winning double play.

Along the way, Griffith served as vice president of the League Protective Players' Association or LPPA, and in 1900, he led the members in baseball's first universal strike. The players wanted the minimum salary raised to $3,000 and their uniforms paid for by the owners. Honorable demands aside, "The Old Fox" had the ulterior motive of helping old friend Ban Johnson establish the rival American League.

In 1901, Griffith became one of the first stars to jump to the A.L. Both his pedigree on the field and his union leadership made him a valuable commodity; Griffith contrived to get every player to pledge not to sign a new contract without LPPA approval, a tactic that crippled the N.L. owners. Eventually, Griffith persuaded 39 N.L. stars to jump leagues, and for his efforts, was rewarded with the leadership of a new franchise, Charles Comiskey's Chicago White Sox. It was another banner year for the "The Old Fox," who went 24–7 on the mound and led the team to the first A.L. pennant, edg-

ing out Boston by four games. It would be another two years before the World Series.

It helped that Griffith was a man of restless ambition, unusual for a baseball man of the era. Back in 1891, when not on the mound for St. Louis of the American Association, he worked the gate to collect tickets. A few years later in Oakland, when Griffith had trouble collecting his salary from the financially-troubled franchise, he took a job singing in a honky-tonk bar.

How fitting then that in 1903, Griffith jumped at the chance to head to New York to lead the Highlanders. It was Ban Johnson's idea since it was important to stock the new team with proven talent; Comiskey agreed and released Griffith for that purpose.

There was another reason Griffith was anxious to hit the big city: his desire to upstage McGraw. The two longtime rivals shared an intense dislike for one another, stemming from an incident when Griffith had plucked the feisty former Oriole from the mound three times in a single at-bat.

McGraw, noted for crowding the plate in his playing days, was the kind of batter who would do most anything to reach base. But in this situation, as Umpire Hank O'Day, the game's lone arbiter that day, headed toward the infield to assume his regular position, Griffith yelled out, "Hank, McGraw just called you a no-good, Irish so-and-so."

McGraw hadn't said a word. But the alleged slur got O'Day fuming. So when Griffith's first pitch clunked McGraw smack on the kneecap, up went the hand for strike one. That got McGraw riled up — and Griffith's next pitch plunked him in the back. Strike two. The third "strike" hit McGraw in the ribs and the story, as retold years later, is that they had to almost put John J. in a straitjacket to restrain him.

The two rivals harbored other grudges from playing days. Pitching for the White Sox in early American League days, Griffith

Clark Griffith, the Highlanders' first manager. (National Baseball Hall of Fame Library, Cooperstown, NY)

was tagged for a single by McGraw, who promptly cussed him out all the way to first base. Big mistake, especially with Joe Cantillon, Griffith's good friend, umpiring.

Both men got angry. "Pick him off the bag," whispered the umpire. Griffith looked over to first and McGraw was too close to the base. "How?" he asked in puzzlement. "Balk him off," said Cantillon. So, the Old Fox balked, caught McGraw cold and Cantillon called him out. Then he had to toss the ballistic McGraw out of the game for using profanity.

But when Griffith tried the same operation on the next base runner, he got into an argument with the umpire and was tossed out too. "Balks only work with McGraw," Cantillon later said.

❖ ❖ ❖

Details of the Highlanders' first spring training are sketchy. Periodic references to warm-up games are sprinkled through the

newspapers of the time, but the team appeared to have no correspondent, unlike the other established major league franchises whose regular beat writers filed lengthy reports in both the local press and *The Sporting News.*

This much is known: Griffith met his team March 17 at Union Station in Washington, D.C., where the season would open the following month. From there, they headed south to Atlanta, where they set up training. Bits and pieces of information about that first spring endure: On March 26, in the first organized game the Highlanders ever played, they beat the Atlanta Crackers of the Southern League 9–0 at Piedmont Park before a crowd of 2,000.

It was a comfortable win. The New Yorkers coasted behind the six-hit pitching of Jack Howell and the wonderfully-named Snake Wiltse. Sadly, *The Baseball Encyclopedia* includes no mention of how 31-year-old Lewis DeWitt Wiltse actually got the name Snake. It must have been in the family; Snake's younger brother by nine years was Hooks, who, the following year, would begin a solid 12-year-major league career as a left-hander, mostly with the Giants. A native of tiny Bouckville, New York, near Utica, Snake had a career that wouldn't go as well. Brought to New York in the move from Baltimore, Snake had a lifetime record of 29–28 and would go only 1–3 with the Highlanders before his brief career in the majors was over.

Even so, "Griffith's men showed up in fine condition," *The Times* wrote of the Americans' first game. "Their sharp, clean fielding, base running and throwing (were) especially noticeable." Indeed, the 1:50 game featured doubles by former Oriole Jimmy Williams, the second baseman, and Keeler, the right fielder, along with a striking catch in foul territory by Wid Conroy, the third baseman, late of the Pirates.

That the popular Keeler was in the line-up at all was another coup for Ban

Johnson. With Griffith, he had landed a big-name manager for the Americans, as people were calling the team; Keeler brought them a big name in the outfield, a guaranteed hit producer and, as a Brooklyn native, a big name drawing card.

Keeler stood all of 5'4" but was one of the game's top stars. He had collected at least 200 hits in each of eight straight seasons, once batted safely in 44 straight games and claimed to have played a whole season without striking out. His batting averages were more astounding, principally the season of 1897, his greatest, when he hit .424 with the Orioles. It was the second highest single-season ever, next to Hugh Duffy's .440 for the N.L.'s Boston Beaneaters in 1894.

Born March 3, 1872 in Brooklyn, Keeler was the son of a horse car driver on the DeKalb Avenue line. Living then and for most his life on Pulaski Street between Stuyvesant and Pulaski streets, Keeler took to the game as a duck to water. As a boy, he played in New York with a team called the Flushings; and, in New Jersey for the Plainfield Crescents. At the time, it took eight balls for a walk and the batter's box was 45 feet from the mound.

Keeler's baseball beginnings took place as the game caught on, particularly in Brooklyn. The game had first been played by teams of upper and middle class gentlemen, but by Keeler's time was securing a big following among the working class, of whom Keeler and his family were a part.

In 1888, at the age of 16, Keeler left school to play semi-pro ball as a pitcher and a third baseman for the Brooklyn Acmes. His salary: $1.50 a game. Continuing to play on the Brooklyn sandlots, Keeler returned to Plainfield in 1892 to play for the Crescents at a 33⅓ percent salary increase — $2 a game. Binghamton of the Eastern League soon called at a salary of $90 per month, and Wee Willie was on his way to a landmark career in baseball.

Keeler was already a rarity: a left-handed third baseman, in addition to playing the outfield, short and second base. But it was his bat that attracted attention. Spraying the ball to all parts of the field, Keeler hit .373 for Binghamton and was brought up to the Giants in 1892.

But it was more than batting statistics than ranked the diminutive Keeler among the game's giants. He played all of 7 games for the Giants in 1893 before heading to Brooklyn, where he was a part of 20 more. But after breaking his leg that season, Keeler was traded to Baltimore. Bad move, for it was there he spent the next five years as a pivotal member of the great Orioles team of the roaring '90s, a team lauded for nailing the basics — the hit-and-run, the bunt, the squeeze play and yes, the patented Baltimore Chop.

Keeler and his teammates, John McGraw, Hughie Jennings and Joe Kelley, weren't big men — of the four, Kelley was the tallest at 5'11". But they were smart, did "whatever was unexpected and put their opponents on edge," as Burt Solomon explains in his wonderful 1999 study of the team, the appropriately titled *Where They Ain't.*

The Orioles brand of baseball depended on what was called scientific or inside baseball. Sometimes, it even got dirty — the cranky McGraw wasn't averse to tripping a base runner or two or flashing his spikes when sliding. Keeler's trademark was more legitimate: using his immense raw talent to hit the ball and reach base in an era when home runs weren't much hit. "No one who ever batted a baseball was more adept at placing a hit than Keeler," said McGraw, who managed more than a few good hitters. "His skill was uncanny. He seemed to sense what the opposing fielders would do, and he had the skill to cross them."

At the plate, Keeler choked almost halfway up his bat, which at 30½ inches, was the shortest in major league history for

Brooklyn-born Willie Keeler was the Highlanders' first bona fide star and first big drawing card. The diminutive Keeler personified the game's Dead Ball Era's reliance on singles and doubles and playing for the single run. Of his team-leading 160 base hits in 1903, all but 21 were singles and none were home runs. His secret? "Hittin' 'em where they ain't," as he put it in what become the game's most-famous quote. Note Keeler's arched collar, wide belt with the buckle on the side and the glove in the back pocket. (National Baseball Hall of Fame Library, Cooperstown, NY)

a frontline player. Choking up was a contrast to most players when he broke in who would hold the bat at the very bottom. Keeler relied on control, for he didn't just hit; he chopped, stabbed and poked at the ball, helping to create a whole new style of play in which runs came sparingly and were punched across. In another few years, players like Ty Cobb and Rabbit Maranville would do the same and the era would go down as one of the dead ball.

All that was accomplished by a man who never married, choosing instead to devote himself to baseball and spend most of his life living with parents, straying only from the New York area when traveling for baseball, and otherwise, only when he absolutely had to. That, plus a friendly, self-effacing demeanor, endeared Keeler to New York baseball cranks long after his prime.

Asked a quarter century into retirement how the players compared to his day, Keeler was characteristically humble. "There are more good players now than there were," he said. "I also think the pitching is better." As for the famous expression Keeler had coined, he was matter of fact: "When I was hitting good with Brooklyn, I was approached by a newspaperman in Boston who asked me to explain the secret of successful hitting," Keeler said. "I told him to hit 'em where they ain't."

When he joined the Highlanders in 1903, Keeler had just finished his fourth season back home in Brooklyn as the Superbas' right fielder. Keeler's '02 season was another solid one — a .333 average and 186 hits — his first sub-200 hit-season in eight years — sparked the team to a surprising second place finish. The Superbas finished 12 games over .500 under manager Ned Hanlon, but a distant 27½ games behind N.L. Champion Pittsburgh.

Such was the baseball resume of a man who, Johnson determined, was needed in New York. Although by 1903, players were repeatedly jumping to the American League, few were of Keeler's stature. On the other hand, as Johnson had shown over and over again, the American League President was a hard man to stop when he had a mission.

Johnson pushed hard to sign Keeler. Willie resisted. So Johnson recruited Griffith for the task, and the Highlanders' new manager got the aid of a friend, Boston manager Jimmy Collins, to help out. The two men arranged a meeting with Keeler, where they presented the Brooklyn rightfielder with a $10,000 contract to jump leagues and play for the Americans. Keeler, who wasn't one to forget his roots nor the $1.50 he had made with the Plainfield Crescents all those years ago, was flabbergasted by the offer, but still said he'd have to give it more thought.

Collins, thinking him ungenerous, was perturbed and said so in front of Keeler.

"Don't depend on Willie," he told Griffith. "Get another man or your right field will be shy a star."

Griffith wasn't so certain that Keeler had turned them down and said in fact, he was confident he'd sign.

"I'll bet $100 that Keeler won't sign the contract you have in your pocket," Collins countered.

Griffith, the "Old Fox," liked his chances. Turning to Keeler, he winked and grinned. "His $100 is easy."

Keeler took the cue. He called Collins back and both men posted $100 with Griffith. The signing deadline was set for March 1, 1903.

Several weeks later, when Keeler was traveling through Chicago with a post-season barnstorming team, Griffith called him at the hotel. Holding up two $100 bills to show him, he called them "the stakes on that bet you made with Collins."

"They'll both belong to me soon," said Keeler.

"Come on over to Johnson's office and earn them. The contract is there."

Keeler went and signed the Americans' contract that afternoon. With that, he was handed $2,000 in advance of his salary — along with a pair of $100 bills.

When Keeler left, Johnson and Griffith remained. Johnson then drew up a $100 check to be mailed to Collins in Boston and smiled. "If we lose a few more bets like this," he said, "there won't be any National League."

Was Keeler being coy? Perhaps. Nonetheless, the episode seemed out of character. More likely that Keeler, at the time, was concealing a potentially-serious injury he had suffered on the barnstorming tour. While in California, he had hurt his left arm near the collarbone in a carriage mishap — or so he thought. Newspapers reported the accident had left him and Umpire Joe Cantillon "severely injured." It wasn't until he was back home in Brooklyn that doctors determined that there was no fracture and the lameness Keeler had felt in his arm was probably the result of a left shoulder injury from two years previous. And with that, Willie Keeler, new contract in his pocket, was free to "hit 'em where they ain't" on the Hilltop in 1903.

Southern League teams supplied most of the opposition in the inaugural spring of the New York Highlanders. Most, like the Atlanta Colonels, were overmatched by the major leaguers. On Saturday, March 28, the Americans shut out the Colonels again, this time 6–0, behind the eight-hit pitching of Griffith and rookie Bill Wolfe. Conroy again drew praise for a difficult catch in foul territory, "after a run that left him breathless," the *Times* said, and Herman Long, the shortstop, had three singles in four at-bats. Meanwhile, "the Americans are showing the effect of the team coaching, which is being given them by Griffith," the paper wrote. "They are beginning to move like clockwork. Their fielding and base running this afternoon were well nigh faultless."

Another game, another triumph: On March 31, the Americans, as the team was also being called, shut out Atlanta for the third straight time — playing again at Piedmont Park and winning again, 9–0. This time, the Crackers managed only four hits, all singles, off Jesse Tannehill and Howell. Things were much the same three days later, when Atlanta finally scored off the New Yorkers, but were drubbed, 12–4, this time the victim of Jack Chesbro, who had arrived just the night before and was starting his first game of the spring.

Taking to the road, the New Yorkers traveled to Mobile, Alabama, where they took on that city's Southern League franchise, winning again on a raw Sunday, April 5, this time 8–0. Again, Tannehill started, working the front five — and was again relieved by Howell, who this time, struck out six.

With the Highlanders' 140-game schedule (actually, the team would play only 134 that season) due to begin April 22 against the Senators in Washington, D.C., the team took one last spring trip, to New Orleans, before heading north. On Saturday, April 11, they beat the New Orleans Pelicans 7–2 at Athletic Park, behind Chesbro, and lost the next day, 5–4. Then it was back the train to head north to Baltimore, where the New Yorkers took two of the last three tune-up games against the now-minor league Orioles.

The idea of heading south before the season was still novel in 1903. Spring training was a little different in those days. Like the origins of the game itself, spring training's roots are a little murky. For years, most writers routinely ascribed an 1886 trip to Arkansas by Cap Anson's Chicago White Stockings as baseball's first team to head south in the pre-season.

Hall of Famer Anson collected 14 players and headed to Hot Springs that year, but not so much to practice baseball as to sweat out a long winter's deluge of boozing and carousing. Ironically, one of those 14 was a weak-hitting utility infielder named Billy Sunday, who left baseball a few years later for the preacher's circuit — most notably in a series of memorable performances in 1920 at the Fairgrounds where a ballpark named the Hilltop once stood.

The 1886 date is as good as any to use as the start of spring training. But in recent years, baseball historians have cited an 1870 trip by an another version of the White Stockings as the true origin of the tradition. Others argue that Tammany Hall's Boss Tweed spearheaded baseball's move south by packing off the New York Mutuals to New Orleans during the 1860s.

Whatever the story, spring training launched a baseball tradition. With Anson, baseball had a Hall of Fame player and manager, and a bit of a showman. To drum up publicity, he had his players dress in outrageous uniforms, appearing sometimes in short, balloon-shaped Dutch pants and other times, in form-fitting Nadji uniforms, the name deriving from a show featuring exotic dancers. While other teams traveled from their hotel to the ballpark by bus, Anson stuffed his men into a barouche — four to a carriage. The result: a healthy dose of publicity back north, conveniently timed to drum up attention, just weeks before the start of the season.

Two years after Anson hit Hot Springs, the Washington Senators became the first professional baseball to make a spring trip to Florida. They went only as south as Jacksonville, where the team stayed in flimsy shacks on the outskirts of town and where reverie ruled the night.

These were ballplayers remember and a class of men not invited to the best parties in town. "By the time we arrived in Jacksonville," remembered Connie Mack, then a young catcher with the Senators. "four of the 14 players were reasonably sober, the rest were totally drunk. There was a fight every night, and the boys broke a lot of furniture. We played exhibitions during the day and drank most of the night."

Despite the promise of working out under sunny skies in Florida, most penny-pinching owners kept their teams away, preferring to ready their ballplayers for the upcoming season by working out in the north. What the concept of spring training needed was a champion, which it got in Baltimore Orioles manager Ned Hanlon, who, in 1894, took his team south for eight weeks in Macon, Georgia and focused on baseball.

The Orioles took things seriously. They held drills twice a day and focused on fundamentals. Some said that's where Willie Keeler, a member of that team, as was John McGraw, perfected his style of hitting the ball to all fields. The Orioles took the pennant that year — starting off with a bang, when they swept the New York Giants. Said Giants manager John Montgomery Ward: "It's a whole new game they're playing, it's not just baseball."

Taking it all in was the crafty McGraw. When he became a manager a few years later, he promptly turned spring training into an institution. His camps were disciplined affairs, seemingly more like boot camp than a way to work off fat from the off season. There were classrooms, visual aid charts, pitching machines and psychologists.

Then there was the dictatorial, street-smart McGraw himself. "His language was salty, punchy and profane," recalled Hall of Famer Frankie Frisch, who played for McGraw in 1920. "He called each Giant by his last name or by a sobriquet, mine being 'Cementhead.' He had little formal education and saw no reason why a man should know more than how to play winning baseball. And to play winning baseball, a man had to hit his peak of physical perfection in the spring."

McGraw dominated the camp. His rages alone could reduce accomplished major leaguers to jelly. He once traded a future 20-game winner when the pitcher showed up in camp wearing tennis whites. Another time, angry at Giants coach Wilbert Robinson about some long-forgotten slight, he loaded a picnic chicken with barnyard droppings, that Robinson unknowingly started to sample during a fishing outing.

Along the way, McGraw kicked off some other spring training traditions. One was barnstorming, which kicked off formally in 1907, when McGraw took his New York Giants on a cross-country training trip, which went as far as Los Angeles and San Francisco.

Another was good accommodations, prompted by his insistence that his ballplayers were professionals, and not carnival riff-raff. When an old friend of McGraw's, circus magnate John Ringling, convinced him to move the team from Texas to Sarasota, Florida, for the 1924 training camp, McGraw went ballistic when he discovered that the team's quarters was a rundown, dirty cement-block building on the edge of town. So he moved the Giants to new quarters — the Mira Mar, a spanking new luxury hotel in Tampa Bay.

That most of what the Highlanders did

that spring isn't recorded wasn't from a lack of interest. Intrigue about these New Yorkers was growing, but most of the interest wasn't focused south, but to a tad north to the spot overlooking the Hudson River, where Hilltop Park was hastily going up.

As an army of workmen tore into the rocky terrain, it became apparent just how remarkable Ban Johnson's coup was, not only in securing the team and quickly finding a couple of owners, but in finding them a place to play.

In the late winter, even before the property was secured, rumors flew of Johnson's triumph. In the February 14 *Sporting News*, a correspondent dropped into a Manhattan tavern, writing of his conversation with a patron. It hardly matters that the patron speaks like a Jay Gatsby wannabe and is probably made up; New Yorkers were clearly impressed.

"Has the American League located a field for a ball park yet?" the dispatch quoted the patron as asking.

"'No, not yet,' I replied.

"'What do you think of this whole business anyway,' was his next query.

"'I do not know what to think of it,' was my reply.

"'Well, it's my opinion those fellows have been dishing up a dose of cod. What takes my time is that Ban Johnson is such a kidder. Had it been Comiskey, it would not have fazed me a bit, as he takes the whole bakery in that specialty, but Johnson? Great Scott! Who would have thought it?' At that moment, a deep respiration escaped from him that reminded one of the rumblings of a junior Mount Pelee.

"However, he soon recovered himself and resumed the conversation by saying:

"''There's no use talking, old sport, those youngsters just threw the scare into those old old chaps — the Nationals — in great shape, didn't they?' He, he, he.

"''The Americans did hand a few jolts out to the old Nationals,' I admitted.

"''Those old fellows just give me a weary feeling,' was his next remark. 'All last summer, they were boasting as to what they would do to Ban Johnson's crowd. Some of their sayings would make the fables of Hercules' cradle exploits with the serpents read like a simple news item. They certainly had all the assurances of the coal barons and showed a swagger in their vocabulary that makes the talk of our recent chief of police (Devery) sound like a rustic.'"

Only a month or so later — March 12 — Johnson finally announced closure of the deal. It was some triumph. He basked in the limelight.

"This latest victory for Ban Johnson over Brush and Freedman is the greatest he has won in his career," *The Sporting News* crowed March 21, "a fact which must be admitted by anyone who peruses his statement and is conversant with the conditions which exist in New York both from a political and a sporting standpoint."

"It would have been a serious enough task to locate a ball club advantageously on Manhattan Island without opposition," the newspaper continued. "But with all the power which Freedman was able to bring to bear in opposition and with this power exerted in underhand and treacherous manner, the task was seemingly impossible, and more than one of the best wishers the American League has were doubtful of the outcome."

A man who never met a reporter's pad he didn't like, Johnson talked about his apparent coup. He spoke of the prolonged negotiations, of the search for a site and provided details on the lease, which was for 10 years. He named Joseph Gordon as President and spoke of the origins of how he had brought a team to New York.

Johnson had kicked off the plot in August 1902 — well before the baseball peace agreement. Making it all possible was his discovery that a number of Pittsburgh Pirates — Leach, Tannehill, Chesbro, Kitty, Bransfield, Conroy, Smith, O'Connor and Davis — were all willing to jump their contracts. Although Leach and Smith eventually returned to the Pirates, several became Highlander mainstays as part of the Peace Agreement. It meant that out of the ashes of the old Baltimore Orioles, New York would have a decent A.L. franchise after all.

But Johnson wasn't yet in the clear. And had the baseball owners who attended Johnson's "victory banquet" that night at the Critereon realized how far away completion of the ballpark really was, they'd had laughed him back home to Cincinnati.

At the time, Opening Day was all of six weeks away and the property secured for the ballpark between 165th and 168th streets still covered by a huge mountain of rock and not looking much like the site for a ballpark. Johnson wrote later that, "we had to use so much dynamite that if unleashed at exactly the same second, it would have blown up half of New York." The apex of the rock rose some 50 feet above the surrounding land, while other parts of the grounds were so low and uneven that fill would have to be carted in.

That Johnson had outmaneuvered the cadre of National Leaguers trying to block his entry into Manhattan was even more remarkable. It turns out that Brush, Freedman and their agents had conducted a block-by-block survey of Manhattan, starting south at the Battery and steadily working their way northward. They were exceedingly comprehensive in their work — obtaining options on any vacant lots they found that could conceivably be used for baseball — but they had made a fatal mistake, which was stopping on reaching 155th Street.

Looking north and seeing little beyond rocky hills, Brush and Freedman figured no person in their right mind would venture to build a ballpark up there. But even after finding that Johnson had secured the spot overlooking the Hudson River, they tried to stop him.

Two moves were considered. First, they mounted a legal challenge against the Institute for the Blind for executing an improper lease. It failed. The other plan — street-cutting — went further. Two weeks after the lease was announced, 125 area property owners presented a petition to the Washington Heights District Governing Board demanding the cutting through of 166th and 167th streets, which dead-ended at Fort Washington Avenue on the eastern edge of the property, to 11th Avenue on the park's eastern boundary. Johnson was unruffled: "When Andy Freedman is elected president of St. Patrick's Society," he said, "our ball grounds may be cut up, but not before."

Moving quickly, Johnson mounted a counter-offensive, engineering a petition before the governing board's next meeting that contained the signatures of just about every other Washington Heights property owner who had not signed the street-cutting petition.

The new document was persuasive. It argued that the street-cutting was unnecessary, that streets in the proposal weren't needed and that baseball in the area was a good idea that would enhance property values. Despite the pressure that Freedman and his Tammany Hall cronies placed on the five-man board, the street-cutting petition was turned down in early April by a 3–2 vote.

Meanwhile, construction of the new park got off to a low key but festive start early on the morning of March 16 when a telegraph lineman working in the neighborhood ran a wire between two trees on the newly-acquired property and fastened an American flag to it.

"This American League grounds should be at all times covered by an American flag," the lineman said. Standing nearby, team President Gordon recognized the historical significance of the situation, and presented him with a crisp dollar bill to commemorate the occasion.

On March 18, Gordon, speaking from the team's new suite of offices on the sixth floor of the Fuller Building at Broadway and 23rd Street, pronounced himself "well-pleased" with the progress the hundreds of laborers had made. Four days later, the *Times* reported that despite a steady rain, "a good deal of rock drilling and blasting," along with news that "the work is being rushed along rapidly, and the contractors as well as the management are perfectly satisfied with the progress made so far."

On March 28, *The Sporting News* weighed in with another construction update. It came in the form of a further interview with the turn-of-the-century equivalent of Joe Sixpack, in this case, "The Man from Up Cedar Creek."

"Rocks and hollows describe (the property), with some trees as a side issue," the Man from Up Cedar Creek said. "Johnson's wild, woolly Western experience sent him into that unexplored region to look for a ball park. No native would have dared to venture into its profundity. Could Mr. Owen Wister only have gotten a peep at this site before he wrote *The Virginian*, he would never have wasted so much time and space in describing such a tame place as the 'Hole in the Wall.'"

"It would be a great stroke of genius if the new club should build its dressing rooms on the banks of the Hudson," the Man says later, "so that its players could take a plunge without using the city's water, and thus avoid coughing up a season pass every time the water was turned on."

But in another write-up that same issue, *The Sporting News* got serious when Henry Chadwick weighed in with his weighty verdict on the new ballpark. No Man from Up Cedar Creek, "Father" Chadwick was one of the most respected minds in the game, a journalist-turned-baseball booster, whose word was taken seriously.

When Chadwick held forth, people listened.

What Babe Ruth was to the playing side of baseball, Father Henry was to the writing end. Striking in his long white beard that gave him a resemblance to Walt Whitman, Chadwick was baseball's greatest writer and its greatest guardian. He even invented the box score, reason enough to suggest that American culture just wouldn't be the same without him.

Born in Great Britain, where he was weaned on cricket, Chadwick came to the U.S. at the age of 13 in 1837. But it was in 1856 while on his way to cover a cricket match at Elysian Fields in Hoboken that Chadwick's attention was attracted to a number of young men wearing long pants and long whiskers and playing a game called baseball. He was hooked — and for the next 52 years, was the game's greatest advocate.

Chadwick became a kind of one-man publicity machine, covering the games and turning in his stories to newspapers throughout the area. Coincidentally, Chadwick's new passion coincided with his first newspaper job, in 1856 with the *Times*. The following year, he joined *The New York Clipper*, then the *Tribune*, *The Brooklyn Eagle* and other publications.

Eventually, Chadwick turned in so much baseball copy that the papers, which once took two or three lines on the sport, expanded their coverage. Chadwick, in turn, talked the ears off city editors — there were no sports editors in those days — in urging them to cover baseball. He also served for a time on rules committees for both the National Association of Baseball Players; and, later, the National Association of Professional Players. In 1894, he became an honorary member of the rules committee for the National League.

Along the way, Chadwick developed

the box score and devised the system for scoring games — essentially the same as used today. He also edited a vast array of baseball guides from his American Sports Publishing Company office at 21 Warren Street, beginning in 1860 with *Beadle's Dime Base Ball Player* and including the well-known *Spalding's Base Ball Guide*, from 1881 to his death in 1908.

Chadwick considered himself a guardian of the developing game's image and well-being. He railed against the drinking and rowdiness of the players as well as persistent threats by gamblers to corrupt the game and reduce baseball to a betting medium.

In 1904, Chadwick was awarded the only medal given to a journalist by the St. Louis World's Fair. Four years later, he died at 84 of heart failure at his home, "The Glen," at 840 Halsey Street, Brooklyn. How fitting that Chadwick's first question after briefly recovering following his stroke was the outcome of that day's Superbas-Giants game.

According to news accounts, the Superbas won. Chadwick expressed his disappointment and promptly died. With the flag at Washington Park flying at half-staff, Chadwick was buried in Green-Wood Cemetery in a tomb adorned with sculptures of baseballs, a catcher's mask and interlocking bats.

"When the grounds are completed, no field in the country will approach the American grounds in its scenic attractions," Chadwick wrote in the March 28 edition of *The Sporting News*. "Looking to the Northwest, the view embraces the Hudson River and the Palisades; while on the other side are the Westchester Hills with the Long Island Sound in sight."

So there would be a nice view from Hilltop Park. But far more important to the team's future is that "Father" Chadwick pronounced himself well-satisfied with the park, the franchise and its prospects for achieving success in New York.

Chadwick described the scene at the rocky terrain that was quickly becoming a new ballpark. "Every fine day from here on will see hundreds of people wending their way to the northern part of Manhattan Island to watch each day's progress made in the work going on at the American league grounds," he wrote.

And he went through the personnel of the club itself, pronouncing it "one of the strongest that will enter the list this year."

But Chadwick wasn't finished. Less than a month later, in a report filed April 8 and published April 18 in *The Sporting News*, he was even more impressed. Chadwick rhapsodized further about the view and even managed to get in a few licks at Freedman and Tammany Hall, and how they'd been outfoxed by Ban Johnson.

"I was no longer left in doubt as to how it was Freedman's inspectors missed discovering the site of President Johnson's new ball grounds, for a more unpromising locality on which to place a ball field I never saw," Chadwick wrote. "Imagine a lot of ground, three blocks wide by as many in length, on which were several rock mounds covered in places by plots of grass and about a dozen old trees; and on looking at it, you would likely to laugh at the idea of selecting such an unpromising spot for a ball grounds. But then go on top of the highest of the rocky hills … and take a look around, and you would enthusiastically exclaim: 'What a lovely view there is from here!'"

"When one comes to consider impartially what an arduous understanding Mr. Johnson entered upon when he resolved to place an American League club on Manhattan Island, and how his task was rendered doubly difficult by the determined opposition of the National League Club; and especially in the face, more recently, of the obstacles to the encroachment on 'National League rights' by the persevering American League magnate placed in his way by (Freedman) the Tammany politician and his cohorts, common justice must award to Mr. Johnson a deserved mood of praise for the spirit of enterprise and perseverance, energy and pluck he has displayed in his very heavy piece of expansion work."

7

Into the Swing

"A wise man once said a baseball takes funny bounces."

— *Bob Gibson*

Cold, rainy skies blanketed the Northeast as the National League kicked off its 1903 season on Thursday April 16, postponing both the Giants-Superbas game at the Polo Grounds, and the Phillies and Braves in Philadelphia. The season's first game was taken by the defending N.L. champion Pittsburgh Pirates, who beat the Reds 7–1 before 12,000 in Cincinnati, behind the two-hit pitching of Charles "Deacon" Phillippe and two hits from their 29-year-old homegrown star shortstop, Honus Wagner.

Like the rest of the American League, the Highlanders got started a few days later, on April 23, against the Senators in Washington, D.C. And as in previous months, the newspapers didn't focus their attention so much on the team as they did the manic, round-the-clock efforts back on the northern fringes of Manhattan to complete Hilltop Park in time for its first game later in the month.

It was going right down to the wire. On April 21, the first carload of chairs for the grandstand arrived. On April 22, relays of mechanics and laborers showed up to begin erecting the open stands. Work would continue night and day until completion.

Ah yes, the opener: "Manager Clark Griffith and his New York Americans will begin their championship race in Washington, D.C. this afternoon," the *Times* reported in rather dignified form April 22, "and their many friends in this city will watch the outcome of the games there with great interest so as to get a line on what they are to expect from the new team when they make their first appearance (in New York)."

At least on paper the New Yorkers had assembled a strong team. Pitching staffs were small in dead ball days — there were no setup men or relievers in those days. In the case of the Highlanders, the staff was all of five men — four starters and a spot starter. But it was a good crew led by Chesbro, late of the Pirates and a workhorse who had developed a spitball along with masterful control.

Chesbro was the ace, having broken in to the big leagues just four years before and quickly become a star. He had gone 21–10 for the '01 Pirates and 28–6 in '02; both teams had won the National League. There was Tannehill, the slight, veteran Kentucky native and a three-time 20 game winner, all with Pittsburgh. Rounding out a solid staff was the veteran Griffith, coming off 15–8 record with the White Sox; "Handsome" Harry Howell, a Brooklyn native and late

51

of Baltimore (9–15 with a 4.12 ERA in '02); and, the rookie Bill Wolfe.

Helping the New York pitchers was an unexpected ace in the hole that spring of 1903. It was among the most significant and enduring changes of the era — a little-noticed rule change, passed by the N.L. in 1901 and the A.L. in 1903. It was the foul-strike rule in which foul balls counted for the first time as strikes until there were two strikes on the batter. Before that, foul balls had not counted at all, giving batters an extraordinary advantage through much of the 1890s, and the regular occurrence of .400-plus hitters like Hugh Duffy, Sam Thompson and Ed Delahanty and whole teams averaging in the .300s.

The rule was intended to speed up the game. And it worked, giving pitchers an unquestionable advantage — far more than its creators had probably ever thought. Just like that, A.L. total run scoring plummeted from 5,407 runs in 1902 to 4,542. The ERA dropped too, from 3.57 to 2.95 and the number of shutouts nearly doubled. Cumulative batting statistics are just as dramatic; runs and extra-base hits fell, and so did the number of singles and stolen bases.

Highlander pitchers needed all the help they could get. That's because the New Yorkers' batting order was, well, really rather average, a team of mostly expendable former Pirates and Orioles, brought in to stock the new franchise. The sole exception was Keeler. But even that was getting a tad worrisome: the Highlander right fielder was getting on for a ballplayer in 1903 at the age of 31 and entering his 12th major league season.

Elsewhere was the first baseman John Ganzel, late of the Giants, whose older brother Charlie had already retired after a solid 14-year major league career, spent entirely with the Boston Braves. There was another old Oriole at second, "Buttons" Jimmy Williams, a .313 hitter in '02; and Conroy, the old Pirate and a Camden, N.J., native at third. Joining Keeler in the outfield

was a '02 Pittsburgher, Lefty Davis, in left; and Herm McFarland, an old Baltimorian in center. The catcher was a rookie, Monte Beville.

Even so, Henry Chadwick liked what he saw, picking the New Yorkers to be contenders, citing in particular, their pitching crew as having "a batting force unequaled." In fact, the only weakness he cited was Griffith, a manager, he said, who was prone to tantrums. "The question is," he said, 'is a player who can not govern his own bad temper fit to govern a team?' I think not."

Things got off well enough on the New York Americans' first day in the major leagues. As was tradition in Washington, D.C., the teams paraded through the streets to the ballpark. There, before an overflow crowd of 10,000 who filled the stands and lined the outfield, were the usual opening day festivities, including the presentation of many pretty floral arrangements. The biggest was the gigantic horseshoe of American Beauty roses presented to Senators star Big Ed Delahanty, back in the fold after nearly jumping to the National League Giants.

For the record, District of Columbia Commissioner H.L. West threw out the ceremonial first ball. The Highlanders struck first — in the first when Keeler, facing Smiling Al Orth, drew a walk, becoming the team's first-ever base runner. He took third on a successful hit and run single by former Brown University football star Dave Fultz — it was the team's first base hit — and scored its first run when he was driven in by Ganzel for the team's first sacrifice and run batted in. Center fielder Fultz later nabbed the team's first double.

Pitching for the New Yorkers, Chesbro walked the first three batters he faced but got out of the first unscathed when he, O'Connor and Ganzel turned a quick double play. Chesbro settled down and pitched well — giving up a run in the fourth and two more in the fifth. That would be it for the game's scoring, with the Senators winning 3–1 in a crisp 1:45 game the *Times* described as "closely contested at every point."

The Highlanders' first win came the next day, 7–2, in a game more notable for how wintry conditions turned infielder fingers into stone. The Senators made five errors and the Highlanders three — all of them by shortstop Herman Long, who after the last mishandling was pulled for Ernie Courtney.

Jack Howell pitched the complete game victory for the New Yorkers, scattering eight hits, all singles, and even smashing the franchise's first triple, a shot off the right field fence. The teams split the series' last two games — the Senators cruising April 24, 7–1 on a day the Highlanders made six errors, two by the third baseman Conroy; and coasting the next day, 11–1, behind Chesbro.

The team then traveled to Philadelphia for a three game series against Connie Mack's powerful A.L. Champion A's. Behind their 20-year-old star rookie pitcher Chief Bender, Philadelphia took the first game 6–0 and then the second, 7–3, before the Highlanders squeezed out a 5–4 victory and headed home to face the Senators for Hilltop Park's debut.

"Yes, the American League grounds were ready for the opening game," William Rankin of *The Sporting News* gushed about the first game at the Hilltop, the 6–2 Highlander win. "To say that I was surprised is but mildly putting the case. I could not help exclaim(ing), 'Well, miracles have not ceased! How was it accomplished?' It looked as if the Count of Monte Cristo had been there the day before and transformed a rocky mountain into — I was going to say a paradise, but it can hardly be called that — but rather a beautiful ball park, probably the finest in the country. It certainly will be when it is completed."

That Ban Johnson and company had pulled it off and put together a picturesque, serviceable park in time — barely — was undeniable. But the Hilltop still needed some work; there was a crater in right field, which would get some attention once the Highlanders took to the road.

News of the new team and the building of the ballpark dominated most of the team's press attention. On the field were bigger questions, principally how to mold a team of high-priced, veteran talent into winners. On May 7 — after all of six home games — the Highlanders left home for the grueling six city, 21-game trip to Boston, Detroit, Cleveland, Chicago, St. Louis and Philadelphia. They wouldn't be home till June 1 for a series against the Pilgrims.

The prospect of an extended road trip was good news for one reason only: It would allow them to fill the gaping hole in right field, such that, as the *Times* reported, "by the time the men get back, three weeks hence, the new grounds will be perfectly level and in first-class condition." Otherwise, the road trip stood to test the mettle of a team that stood with a mediocre 7–6 record after 13 games. Already, there were rumblings that this was a team that just wasn't jelling. This *was* New York, a town where winning was expected, and those who didn't, were ridiculed.

On May 7, the Highlanders opened a series at Huntington Avenue Baseball Grounds in Boston against the Pilgrims, who would change their name to the Red Sox in 1907. That they'd lose 6–2 to "Big" Bill Dinneen wasn't significant. Nor was the fact that every man in the powerful Pilgrims' lineup but pitcher Dinneen would get a base hit that day, including a home run by Hobe Ferris, the second baseman.

The significance was that this was the first game of what would be one of baseball's most famous, fiercest and longest rivalries. Boston's professional baseball heritage went clear back to 1871, with

Dave Fultz — the team's first centerfielder and owner of its first base hit in history. (National Baseball Hall of Fame Library, Cooperstown, NY)

the birth of the National Association Red Stockings. And on hand the day that the New Yorks first took on the Bostons was a particularly rabid fan base, led by a group of Pilgrims cranks billing themselves as the Royal Rooters.

They were baseball's first groupies. Chief Rooter was one Mike "Nuf Said" McGreevy, who ran a saloon by the name of Third Base, a pop fly away from the Huntington Avenue Baseball Grounds. His moniker derived from his stature as Boston's foremost authority on all matters related to baseball. Adding to the legend was a famous billboard inside the ballpark, which posed the question: "How can you get home without reaching third base?" With the support of another Royal Rooter, Boston Mayor John "Honey Fitz" Fitzgerald, John F. Kennedy's future grandfather, club members would arrive at the ballpark, making lots of noise, wearing oversized red badges and flashing plenty of dollars at the Pilgrims' opponents, especially when it came to New York. More than one member of the Pilgrims called the Rooters a legitimate competitive advantage.

Concerns about the Highlanders persisted. "What the local American leaguers will do or where they will stand at the finish is a question that can be asked far easier than answered," *The Sporting News* chimed in its May 9 edition. "There is no denying the fact that it looks like a good team on paper, and should prove a winner.... There are enough high-priced stars in the bunch to land almost any old thing, but — well, you know the old adage about too many cooks. If Clark Griffith has the real thing, it will soon develop itself, and the public will find it out without being told so.... If it is a gold brick, then the fact will soon make itself known."

Then came questions about the short fuse of Griffith himself. On May 7 in the last inning of the last game of the home stand — a 6–1 loss to Eddie Plank of the A's — the Highlanders' manager was tossed by umpire Thomas Connolly after arguing against a Philadelphia batter receiving three bases on a ground rule. Chalk up another first — the Highlanders' first managerial ejection.

With the exception of the Highlanders' home opener, Griffith had been particularly vocal in his umpire baiting, a gigantic no-no in Johnson's fan friendly league. Although the yelling from both dugouts had been on the rise, Griffith was also the first of the American League season to be tossed.

Johnson acted swiftly. On May 8, he suspended Griffith for 10 days, leaving the team in the charge of Keeler, recently named the team's first captain. Ironically, the suspension came on the same day that National League President Pulliam suspended Pirates shortstop Honus Wagner for threatening to hit an umpire. "Rowdyism" and unseemly behavior, as Johnson called it, would simply not be tolerated.

8

Of Wise Guys and Other Matters

"I like going to baseball games with my wife. It is an interesting experience. I also like not going with my wife."

—Arnold Hano

Clark Griffith's ejection spoke to a larger battle that Ban Johnson was waging against rowdyism and its sister vice — gambling — that wreaked havoc on the game as the new century kicked off.

The history of baseball wouldn't be complete if it failed to include the range of wackos, drunks and shady guys who populated its ranks from the start.

Imagine one of those classic "wanted" posters, the kind tacked up to a bulletin board in the post office: "$25,000 Reward ... Dead or Alive." Okay, it's from the 1930s, but you get the idea.

In this case, the subject is one Louis "Lepke" Buchalter — alias Louis Buckhouse, Louis Kawar, Louis Kauver, Louis Cohen, Louis Saffer and Louis Brodsky. Staring out in three photos with cold eyes and a stone-faced expression, Lepke, the poster says, is wanted for conspiracy and extortion. No, not exactly a guy you'd expect to run into at Carvel.

The poster provides pictures of Lepke's fingerprints from both hands. It provides a few fun facts — "is wealthy ... has connections to all important mobs in the United States ... involved in racketeering in unions."

Then, it gets really fun: "Eyes — piercing and shifting ... nose — somewhat large ... somewhat blunt at nostrils ... ears — prominent and close to head ... mouth — large ... slight dimple to left ... suffering from kidney ailment."

And then this: "known to frequent baseball games."

And therein lies one of the more critical links between baseball and wise guys: They liked the game, gambled on it, giving credence to the fact that a rugged world loomed out beyond the batter's box. And oh yes, just after the turn of the century, they were really happy that that New York had an American League baseball team.

From the get-go, baseball and wise guys went together. It followed a time-honored tradition of New Yorkers of all classes who liked betting on just about anything.

For years, that meant betting on shuffleboard, cards, billiards and other games. In colonial times, gambling created diversions for people in taverns and restaurants. By the mid–18th century, English-style lotteries found their way to the city and were used by churches, public corporations and the city government to raise funds for charity and public works.

Gambling became big business in New York in the 1830s, when the city's growing middle class sought new hobbies. Among them was gambling, despite concerns about the morality of it all, triggered in part by a number of scandals in lotteries during the first few decades of the century.

That only heightened the public outcry against gambling. In the 1830s, the state legislature banned lotteries; in the 1840s, it took after gambling halls and other public gambling places. Professional gamblers took advantage of the void and used the opportunity to build businesses linked to city government and political organizations, therefore providing links to organized crime.

They created all sorts of gambling enterprises. In the 1840s, the rage was a card game named faro, in which chips or money were placed on a cloth embossed with a suit of cards and players bet on which card would appear next from a deck turned face down in a dealing box. Players liked faro because of its speed and odds that were more favorable to other card games; gamblers liked it because it meant big profits and used it to build posh "halls," the forerunners of casinos, in spots along Broadway from 24th Street clear to the Battery.

Elsewhere, horse racing, boxing and other spectator sports provided ever-emerging opportunities for gamblers. One was the nation's first racetrack, at Saratoga, in 1864. Just after the Civil War, off-track betting developed in which results from Saratoga were relayed by telegraph to Manhattan poolrooms. And although gambling was technically illegal, it flourished thanks to the intervention of Tammany Hall figures like the "Big" guys — Sullivan and Devery — who made sure that with the right donations to the right people, vice would be protected.

Baseball and gambling were in sync from the start. In its early days, when the game was a largely upper-class diversion for the moneyed set, it was played in private clubs by gentlemen who enjoyed a friendly wager or two. Indeed, the very terms used in the first baseball games were gambling terms, notes Eliot Asinof, author of *Eight Men Out*, the classic study of the 1919 World Series fix: at-bats were "hands" while runs were "aces."

Baseball provided the bettor with all kinds of advantages. It was more civilized than a boxing match or a cockfight, and more easily controllable than a horse race. Things turned the bettor's way even more in the 1860s as players turned professional and admissions were charged.

It was a living. Typically, baseball afforded those first players far more than they could earn working in a store, the mine or the mill. A star would be hired as a company clerk for $40 a week, a job that normally paid $6. The game had become a business.

And with that, the gamblers made a full frontal assault and the game became hopelessly corrupt. Not only had baseball "lost its gentlemanliness," as Asinof puts it, but "most games, it now seems, came adorned with some weird behavior. It might be an outfielder, settling down to make a catch and find himself pelted by a rock thrown by a spectator who stood to lose some money if the catch was made. In one case, a gambler fired a gun at the field to keep a fielder from chasing a long fly ball. "The victims had no chance to appeal," writes Asinof: "there was no nothing in the rules to cover such behavior."

In time, gambling traditions developed. Fans wagered on the final score, but also on segments of the game, like the total number of hits and runs and even the call of the pitch. Certain cities developed reputations for wagering, especially Pittsburgh and Boston, where there was no thoroughbred racing to interest the gambling crew.

Another tradition was the baseball

pool. Dating to 1871, it was the most popular system of baseball wagering. The early form was an auction pool in which the pool manager would sell or "auction" a choice of teams to win a game or the pennant to the highest bidder. That died out in the 1880s and was replaced by bookmaking, more popular because lots more could play from ball parks to barbershops, in which the gambler established odds and people could bet accordingly.

To achieve their desired results, many gamblers resorted to dubious techniques of persuasion: bribery was a time-honored tradition, so much so that in 1878, precisely two years after the start of the National League, the St. Louis weekly paper, *The Spirit of the Times*, editorialized that "the amount of crooked work is indeed startling and the game will undoubtedly meet the same fate elsewhere unless some extra strong means are taken to prevent it."

In 1876, the situation went from bad to worse. That September, when the powerful Louisville Grays, way ahead in the pennant race, went east to play an inferior Hartford club and all but fell apart, all kinds of suspicions were raised. The six-game series, played on a neutral ground in Brooklyn, featured error after error by normally sure-handed Louisville infielders — there were so many that Louisville President Charles Chase began an immediate investigation.

In fact, Chase's doubts had been raised earlier by a series of sloppily-played games in Cincinnati. They were confirmed before one of the Hartford losses when Chase received an anonymous telegram to "Watch Your Men!" The Grays lost badly that day, with errors by slugger George Hall, shortstop Bill Craver and substitute Al Nichols.

Particular suspicions centered on 35-game winning pitcher Jim Devlin, who had been receiving daily telegrams while in Brooklyn. On opening the telegrams, Chase discovered they were coded and repeatedly included the word "sash," the term used for a fixed game. Interrogating his players and playing one off against another, Chase soon found the guilty parties: Devlin, Nichols, Hall and Craver. With the strong backing of National League President William Hulbert, all were banned for life.

The Louisville scandal received enormous attention and contributed to restore confidence in the game's integrity — sort of. Despite the usual amount of strife led by teams coming and going and clashes between labor and management, the game did seem cleaner for a time.

"Perhaps the most important change in baseball after 1877 ... was the lack of gambling scandals and the improvement in the confidence of fans in the integrity of the game," writes Daniel E. Ginsburg in his entertaining book *The Fix Is In* (McFarland, 1995), a study of baseball gambling. "This confidence that the outcome of games had not been predetermined by gamblers and crooked ball players led to the increasing popularity of professional baseball."

Not that the gamblers were on vacation. Periodic incidents popped up, as in May 1881, when Chicago bookmakers tried bribing Cleveland's John Clapp. According to Clapp, a gambler named James Woodruff offered him $5,000 to allow passed balls with men on base. He reported the incident to Chicago police, which led to Woodruff's arrest and the annoying nickname "Honest" John, that stuck through the rest of his career. No wonder Clapp, on his retirement, joined the police force in his hometown of Ithaca, N.Y.

Others weren't so lucky. In September 1881, longtime batting star Lip Pike, playing in center field with Worcester, led Boston 2–1 going into the ninth inning when things quickly become unglued. Blamed was Pike, who made three errors in the inning, which led to two Boston runs and a 3–2 victory. Afterwards, some of the Worcester players accused Pike of tanking it and he was suspended.

Later that month, Pike was among a number of players expelled from the game for what *The Spalding Baseball Guide* labeled "confirmed dissipation and general insubordination."

That seemed excessive. Pike was a popular veteran whose career started back in 1866 with the Philadelphia A's and had included stints in the National Association, with New York, Troy, Baltimore, Hartford, St. Louis, Cincinnati and Providence. But he was also Jewish and may have been a victim of anti–Semitism. No evidence ever emerged that Pike actually threw the game to Boston; at 36, he was near the end of his career anyway, so he announced his retirement at the end of the season and entered the clothing business in Boston.

"Those who knew Pike best appreciated him the most," *The Sporting News* wrote after Pike's death in 1893. "He was one of the baseball players of those days who were always gentlemanly on and off the field — a species that is becoming rarer as the game grows older."

By 1903, gambling was everywhere. "Present-day fans can hardly comprehend how much open gambling there was in those days, both inside the ballpark and out, and how perfectly accepted it was," writes Thomas Gilbert in *Dead Ball*, his study of the major leagues during the years of 1900 to 1919. "Baseball players betting on games — within certain limits, such as not betting on their own teams to lose — is tolerated, professional gamblers own and run teams, and respectable newspapers brag that the hometown fans put down the biggest wagers."

Some cities developed reputations for gambling around the ballparks. Two were Pittsburgh and Boston, where the lack of big-time race tracks tended to lure the gamblers to baseball. In Boston, the most notable gambler was one Joseph "Sport" Sullivan, a dapper, sweet-talking Irishman, who, 16 years later, would be a central figure in the greatest sports scandal of all-time — the 1919 World Series fix in which eight members of the Chicago "Black Sox" would lose on purpose to the Cincinnati Reds.

For the ballplayers, gambling was a way of life. Poker was the game of choice on long train rides. They played craps in their hotel rooms and wagered on ballgames, horse races and just about anything else involving a contest. Hall of Famer Cap Anson was a big-time gambler, wagering large amounts every year for his N.L. Chicago White Stockings to take the pennant.

In 1897, Anson was in the last of his 22 big league seasons and bet the farm — putting down $2,000 for his team to win. The Sox didn't get there that year — they finished a distant ninth of 12 teams — but it didn't really matter in the end. That's because Anson had won big the year before, betting heavily on the Republican candidate, William McKinley, to win the presidential election. McKinley won. And so did Big Ed Delahanty, whose gambling preferences, as with most ballplayers, was the race track, where he once boasted that he had developed a "system" for picking horses that couldn't lose. The way Big Ed told it, he paid the tipping bureau for the inside dope before making the bet, and collected a few minutes later.

It wasn't really that easy at the race track; in reality, Delahanty had just as many losing as winning days. And Harry Pulliam — yes, even the magnates like to bet — enjoyed the ponies so much that in his years as the Pirates' secretary, he would typically arrange for a messenger to arrive at the office each morning with tips from a "friend" on the day's races. When the friend urged Pulliam to put his money on a 60–1 long shot named Tom Middleton, he held back. The horse won, much to Pulliam's surprise and to the delight of his colleagues, who kidded him for months about his reluctance to take the tip.

Back on the field, persistent stories about gambling cropped up well into the 20th century. There were attempts to bribe players in the first two World Series. And there was Hal Chase, "Prince Hal," the Highlander first baseman who hit New York like a thunderbolt in 1905 and stayed for most of the next eight years, soiling the ground he walked by throwing games, getting others to throw games and generally creating a shadow on the game that endured for years. He even managed. More, much more, on him later.

No history of the baseball's dead ball era would be complete without mention of the assorted scandals and dubious characters that continued to drag the game down through the 1890s and early days of the 20th century. Indeed, a chronology of dubious baseball events of the era reads like a World Wrestling Federation promo guide.

Again, John McGraw set the tone. In 1891, in his first major league game, McGraw's Baltimore Orioles teammates shoved him off the team bench and he came up swinging. Two years later, he cursed the manager of the Savannah team in an exhibition game and was knocked down. The next week, McGraw's roughhouse tactics caused a near-riot in Chattanooga.

That same year in Pittsburgh, Pirate fans, upset at a big loss to Boston, stoned the Beaneaters as they left the park in a horse-drawn wagon. Two years after that, in 1895, the Cleveland Spiders were stoned in Baltimore after beating the Orioles in a big game there.

That was the year McGraw harassed rookie umpire Tim O'Keefe into premature retirement, calling him a drunk. In June 1896, O'Keefe was back behind home plate, when he placed eight members of the Spi-

ders under arrest. That July, the strain caught up again to O'Keefe, when upset by abuse from the Giants and the St. Louis Browns, he walked out of the game in the fifth inning. Two players officiated the rest of the game.

Abusing umpires was a fact of life in the turn-of-the-century major leagues. In 1905 in Detroit, umpire Jack Sheridan forfeited a game to the Senators, when, angry that he had allowed the visitors a run on an interference call in the 11th inning, many in the hometown crowd took after the veteran arbiter, forcing him to flee to the center field clubhouse.

While umpires have always found it rough slogging, their lot was still harder in those days than today. There were no umpire schools in those days; if somebody wanted to officiate, they simply signed up, learning their trade on the job in the minor leagues. That meant more than a few still lacked the essential skills by the time they reached the major leagues, making those unruly players and managers even more so.

Baseball officialdom made it doubly tough on umpires. As late as 1908, each major league had all of six umpires; policy was to keep one man in reserve, meaning that on a full day of four games per league, three would have to work their games solo. No matter how talented a lone umpire might be, he could not possibly be in position to make all or most of the calls. The usual case was for the lone umpire to stay behind home plate calling the balls and strikes until a runner reached first base, when he'd take a position behind the pitcher. With runners on second or third, he'd go back behind the plate in the event of a play at the plate. Only with the 1909 World Series did the baseball hierarchy allow more than two umpires to work a game.

One area where turn-of-the-century umpires did shine was in moving games along. Three decades from night baseball, games in those days typically started at 3 p.m. or 3:30 p.m. to begin single games in order to accommodate spectators with jobs. But to get the games completed before dusk meant umpires had to continually strive to keep players hustling. The fact there were few pitching changes or pinch hitters in those days helped too; most games were well under two hours.

Baseball fires were big news in those days too. In 1894, West Side Park in Chicago burst into flames during a game and fans were caught between barbed wire and the burning exits. Only when players used bats to beat down the barbed wire could people escape. That same year, South End Grounds burned in Boston, as two players fought at third base. The players? Boston's Tommy Tucker and one John McGraw.

No wonder a rhyme of the era started with the refrain, "Mother, may I slug the umpire, May I slug him right away? So he cannot be here, mother, When the clubs begin to play?" Just look at some of the era's nicknames: "Rowdy" Jack O'Connor, "Scrappy" Bill Joyce and "Dirty" Jack Doyle are a few.

Why the sleaze? There are many reasons. Whereas the stars of the earlier baseball era — and in later years — tended to be large men who could belt the ball a long way, the 1890s and early 1900s saw the rise of the bantamweights, the little people. They were men like the 5'4", 140-pound Keeler; Jesse "the Crab" Burkett, a three-time .400 hitter and Cleveland mainstay who was 5'8" and 155 pounds; and, McGraw, the Napoleonic foul-mouthed motor-mouth of a baseball genius who stood all of 5'7" and weighed 155 pounds.

Then, there was McGraw himself, the man perhaps most responsible for changing the way baseball was played. His game was scientific, played for the extra base and the run to tip the balance. With the bantamweights came skilled singles hitters, not fence busters, who would score runs, not in bunches, but by scratching their way to a run here and a run there. It was dubbed "inside baseball," and it was personified by people like McGraw and his Orioles. Consider the "Baltimore Chop," in which the batter deliberately chops or hacks downward at the ball, driving it into the ground and gaining a big bounce and a few seconds — usually enough to just beat the throw to first base.

The inside game had other essentials. Players stole bases and ran hard to second to break up double plays, flashing their spikes high to intimidate opposing infielders. Meanwhile, pitchers were growing more sophisticated — developing rising curveballs and other pitches that broke, dropped, dipped and caught the corners. The inside corner was especially popular and bean balls became the norm. In 1899, figures baseball historian Bill James, 91 batters were hit for every 100 games played.

A hard game attracted hard men. Intimidation ruled. When Baltimore shortstop Kid Gleason, who later managed the 1919 Black Sox and received a kindly, paternal portrayal in the 1984 John Sayles film *Eight Men Out*, faced a runner trying to break up the double play, he typically low-balled him — that is, he threw the ball directly at his forehead. McGraw, the Baltimore third baseman, was known for stepping on the feet of sliding base runners with his high-topped spikes; other times, he held runners by grabbing their belts as they rounded the bag.

Dirty tricks by way of the Orioles set the standard. Based on their own "how-to" manual, they'd plow into first basemen, trip base runners and even slip their fans dead balls to throw back onto the field in place of foul balls that in those days had to be returned to the umpire.

As for the players, many of whom were one step from the coal mines, they played hard both on the field and off. Away from the park, they tended to act like boys and imbibe enormous amounts of alcohol, which was hushed by baseball executives and beat writers alike. Take Big Ed Delahanty, one of five Delahanty brothers in the major leagues and perhaps the game's biggest star of the 1890s. From 1893 to 1899, Big Ed batted between .334 and .408 for the Phillies and his future seemed limitless.

Delahanty's exploits — going nine for nine in a doubleheader and clouting four inside-the-park home runs in one game — endeared him as a hero to the sports-reading public. It was off the field that Delahanty ran into problems.

In 1901, the American League's first year, he bolted Philadelphia for the A.L. Senators, rewarding his new team with the A.L. batting title in 1902 with a .376 average. In 1903, a deal was arranged for Delahanty to be shipped back to the National League, to play for the Giants, where he was promised a $500 raise. But the trade was voided after the two leagues made their peace early that year that included the draining bidding for the best players.

Delahanty grew surly. He argued with his manager, Tom Loftus, drank heavily and threatened suicide. Senators executives were so worried for their star player that they called for Delahanty's mother to calm her 35-year-old son down.

Even so, Delahanty continued to play well, batting .333 when he skipped a June game in Cleveland, his hometown, and was suspended. He continued to play on and off but on the night of July 2 after sulking on the bench at a game in Detroit, he decided to jump ship for good.

Fortified by what the conductor said later were five shots of whiskey, Delahanty caught the Michigan Central #6 bound for Buffalo and promptly turned nasty, pulling a razor and threatening passengers and crew alike. Arriving at Fort Erie, Ontario, on the Canadian side of the International Bridge, Delahanty was ordered off the train and then actually began walking across the span, muscling past a night watchman who tried to stop him.

It was the last anyone ever saw of Big Ed. A short while later, he plunged or fell into the raging waters of the Niagara River hundreds of feet below; nobody knows for certain. Tourists found Delahanty's body six days later, 20 miles from the scene of the accident. Missing was his money and jewelry. Also missing was his left leg.

But if this rowdy game of baseball scared off the women and children, the wise guys reveled in it. And in New York, the wise guys and ballplayers had a particular bond, encouraged perhaps by the fact there were so many of each.

The appearance of Highlanders meant there were three teams in the city and always a lot of action to follow. Games typically started at 3 p.m. or 4 p.m. — good timing for the working wise guy who could run with the night crowd, sleep well past noon and still catch the action at the Hilltop or the Polo Grounds. The hours — and the apparent speed of the new subway — also meant that many in the Wall Street crowd could make it to games, which, in turn, meant more money and action for the wise guys.

The era, meantime, was one of tremendous transition for the hoods. These weren't the Mafiosos romanticized by *The Godfather* or even *Billy Bathgate*. The Mob as an organized and efficient corporation was still a thing of the future at the turn of the century. In the streets of New York, mob rule was still the province of old-fashioned ruthless thugs like Monk Eastman. But change was in the air.

Even Monk Eastman was too formal a moniker. Say "The Monk" just after the turn of the century in New York City and people knew who you meant. "Probably no tougher strong-arm man ever existed than Eastman," writes Leo Katcher in *The Big Bankroll*, his classic 1959 study of gambler Arnold Rothstein. Eastman even looked the part, with his bullet-shaped head, a broken nose, heavy jowels and longish, scraggly hair, topped off with a snazzy derby. He also sported numerous knife scars, had ice-water veins, was cruel by nature and was an equal-opportunity fighter, adept with guns, knives and fists. "Intellectually, he was hardly more than a moron, but he didn't need brains for a living," notes Katcher. "Brute force and cunning were enough and he had sufficient of both these."

Eastman was the leader of one of New York's most notorious gangs, the appropriately named "Eastmans." He had another job too as the enforcer of "Big" Tim Sullivan, Tammany Hall's East Side boss. Eastman proved particularly valuable on Election Day, when Sullivan needed some votes.

Born Edward Osterman in the Williamsburg section of Brooklyn in 1873, Eastman was the son of a Jewish restaurant owner, who set him up in a Brooklyn pet shop. But the Monk's restless spirit took over in the mid–1890s when he left to become sheriff, or bouncer, of the New Irving Dance Hall in Manhattan. It was there that Eastman developed a reputation for violence and eccentricity: As his knack for bullying grew, so did his passion for pigeons and cats. The Monk is thought to have owned 500 pigeons and more than 100 cats and used both to open another pet shop — this one on Broome Street — which, in fact, served as a cover for more dastardly doings.

On the other hand, Eastman was the last of a dying breed — the wise guy as a common thug. On a cold day in 1904, the Monk found himself near Times Square when he caught sight of a man lurching unsteadily down the street and being closely observed by a dubious-looking character. It was the age-old scam of lush-roller and lush, he thought, or so it would seem.

Eastman claimed later he went over to the drunken man to help prop him against a wall. Another version has him getting the jump on going through his pockets. In the end, the drunk was a rich young society hot-shot who was being followed by a Pinkerton detective assigned to keep him out of trouble. As Eastman's fingers drew near the pockets of the young man, the detective fired. Eastman ran away — and right into the arms of a policeman stationed in front of the Hotel Knickerbocker at Broadway and 42nd Street. The Monk's luck had run out: He was sentenced to 10 years in Sing Sing.

Why mention that here? Eastman's career as a big-time wise guy was essentially finished. And although there would always be work as bad-guy enforcer types, the old-fashioned way of doing a thug's work was steadily dwindling. To put it another way, make way for the slick gambler types like Sport Sullivan, whose preference for making a buck was doing so in less dangerous ways, like fixing baseball games. In major league baseball of the dead ball era, the wise guys were everywhere.

There was a very legitimate reason the Highlanders needed to have a strong road trip: the National League Giants, which McGraw was quickly turning into winners. Not technically competitors and usually on the road when the American Leaguers were home, the Giants were nevertheless fierce competitors for the hearts and minds of the New York baseball crank.

Already, the Giants had an advantage: there was history and there was pedigree. Founded in 1880, they were bankrolled by a tobacco merchant named John Day and managed by a dapper man with a handle-bar mustache, "Gentleman" Jim Mutrie. They called their team the "Metropolitans" or "Mets," but when a supporter pointed out that the Mets were a collection of unusually large players, Mutrie agreed. "They're giants on the field as well," he said. And Giants they became.

At first, the team played home games at a variety of fields, from New Jersey to Union Grounds and the Capitoline Grounds in Brooklyn, which had once been home to the Mutuals, a notable team from a previous generation. With such parks only accessible by streetcar or ferry — The Brooklyn Bridge wasn't yet built — the team barely drew from Manhattan, the fan base it coveted.

One day, when Day was asked by a shoeshine boy why he headed all the way to Brooklyn and New Jersey to play his games. His only answer was — no room in Manhattan. But when the shoeshine boy mentioned a polo field at 110th Street & 6th Avenue where his team might play, Day was shrewd enough to investigate.

Day found the area was owned by James Gordon Bennett, Jr., the millionaire son of the founder and owner of *The New York Herald*. The scion of the publisher used the field as a polo field for himself and his wealthy friends. Day liked the location and arranged to lease the field from Bennett. His team became the Giants of the Polo Grounds.

Next, Mutrie focused on building a winner. He went to Washington, D.C., where he signed a score of good players and turned the Giants into winners. In fact, they became an immediate success in their new home, taking 16 games, losing seven and tying one of the season's last 24 games. The crowds came and Day and Mutrie, the new tycoons of New York baseball, had themselves a hit.

Not that everything went smoothly; try weird. It turned out that the Polo Grounds — which stood on a rectangular sliver of land from 110th Street to 112th Street, bordered by the block between 5th and 6th avenues — also served as home to another local team of note, the Nationals.

For a time, the park's vast expanse was actually turned into two fields, divided by a canvas fence that essentially separated the two teams. The owner of both teams was John Day.

Mutrie's Giants prospered anyway. In 1882, they joined the American Association and the following year, at about the time they became the Giants, they joined the National League.

See the Giants in those days and you'd catch Mutrie, with his trademark handlebar mustache, topped off by a stovetop hat, frock coat, gloves and spats, as he roamed up and down the grandstand, cheering his team and adding a distinctive presence to the Polo Grounds festivities. No wonder the Giants were soon known by yet another moniker: "The People's Team."

The nucleus of Mutrie's first Giant teams came from raids on the Troy Haymakers, which he brought to New York almost in a body, including catcher Buck Ewing; pitcher "Smiling" Mickey Welch; and, first baseman Roger Connor, all future Hall of Famers. To that group, he added pitcher Tim Keefe, another eventual Cooperstown member.

In 1884, despite that powerful lineup, Mutrie's Mets, the A.A. winners, were defeated in three straight by the Providence Grays, N.L. champions, in the first World Series ever.

A more unfortunate fate awaited the Polo Grounds, which burned down in the spring of 1889. Mutrie left baseball a year later, but not before several more shrewd moves that assured the Giants another solid decade — acquiring two more Hall of Famers, John Montgomery Ward and Amos Rusie. (The father of the Giants died in 1938 at the age of 86.)

Along the way, the Giants got a couple of new ballparks. In 1889, at the request of the city fathers who decided they needed a traffic circle where the ballpark stood, the team headed north, to Manhattan Field on

155th Street. The next year, when the Players League club built its ballpark next door only to have the league crumble, the Giants moved quickly, leasing the superior Brotherhood Field from the Coogan estate. But loyal Giant fans pined so for the old Polo Grounds that the new park took the name.

But with Mutrie gone from the picture, things went sour for the Giants in the late 1890s and just after the start of the new century. Mostly under the tyrannical Freedman, there was a string of managers — Bill Joyce, and, for a spell of 21 games, Cap Anson, in 1898; Fred Hoey and Day, yes, that John Day, in 1899; and, Buck Ewing and George Davis in 1900 — all for teams that finished well down in the second division. Under Davis, the Giants beat out only Cincinnati on 1901; and, in 1902, finished last, 53½ games behind Pittsburgh, under three more managers, Horace Fogel, Heinie Smith and one John McGraw.

McGraw got to New York on July 17, 1902, and things would never quite be the same for baseball in the city. He didn't just arrive; he blew into town with the force of a hurricane. His task: make them winners, which he quickly did by cleaning house in the winter and assembling in 1903 the Giants' strongest team in years.

McGraw was all of 29 years old. Already, he was famous — a tough, competitive and vulgar man whose consuming passion in life was baseball. "Life without baseball had little meaning for him," his wife Blanche once said. "It was his meat, drink, dream, his blood and breath, his very reason for existence."

McGraw was something else too: a master at molding and motivating men to reach their potential and a symbol for the sparkling city on the Hudson. "The Giants of the McGraw era," wrote Harry Golden, "represented New York of the brass cuspidor, that old New York that was still a man's world before the advent of the League of Women's Voters. Those were the days of swinging doors, of sawdust on the barroom floor."

On the field, McGraw built his team in what, a few years later, would be called "inside baseball." Described by a reporter as "merely the outguessing of one team by another," the inside game featured managerial signaling from the dugout for everything of significance on the field, from what pitches to throw and whether a batter should swing to base-stealing attempts, sacrifice bunts, squeeze plays and pitchouts.

Others had managed the inside game before McGraw — Ned Hanlon and Frank Selee had both played the game that way with some success. But no one perfected it as McGraw and none with the adulation and publicity afforded by the nation's media capital. McGraw once said that because his 1904 team contained so many new players, he called every play. His favorite signal: blowing his nose.

It also helped that McGraw also had a couple of aces up his sleeve. Both were pitchers and both are Hall of Famers blessed to be in New York as Giants at the start of glorious careers. Their names: Christy Mathewson and Iron Man McGinnity.

Both pitchers had suffered through difficult seasons in 1902 — Mathewson going 14–17, despite a 2.11 ERA, and McGinnity going 8–8 with a 2.06 ERA. Mathewson, however, did show considerable potential by finishing among the league leaders in both strikeouts (159) and most strikeouts per nine innings (5.17).

There was something else about Mathewson that people noticed. He stood well over 6 feet, was Jack Armstrong–handsome and became so celebrated for clean living that his wife once felt forced to admit that he was "no goody-goody," who — gasp — occasionally played checkers for money.

In other words, Mathewson was about to become the most celebrated pitcher of the era and its first matinee idol, the perfect antidote to baseball's unsavory image.

As a product of a middle class Pennsylvania family, he was different from the start: He went to college, Bucknell University, where he was a pitcher, an All American football player and the class president who married his campus sweetheart. Mathewson didn't need to play baseball for a living and could arguably have chosen a different career path with more lucrative results.

Most startling of all is that he and Mc-Graw were best friends. Call them baseball's Odd Couple, its Mutt 'n' Jeff. In the spring of 1903, the two became such fast friends that they and their wives moved in together to a spacious seven-room walk-up apartment at 76 West 85th St., just off Columbus Avenue and one block to the elevated train that ran uptown to the Polo Grounds.

Just why McGraw and his new wife, Blanche, invited Mathewson and his wife, Jane, to share their new, furnished ground-floor apartment would intrigue a psychiatrist. The rent, $50 a month, was split between the couples; the Mathewsons paid for food and the McGraws, for utilities.

"We led normal lives, fed the men well and left them alone to talk their baseball," Blanche McGraw wrote in her memoirs. "Their happiness was our cause."

Historians suggest that McGraw may have felt protective of his star pitcher, since baseball players of the era could be nasty, even to teammates and especially to rookies. Such a code applied to Mathewson, with his occasional air of superiority and moral pronouncements that some took for arrogance. "Hardly anyone on the team speaks to Mathewson," a teammate said. "He deserves it. He is a pinhead and a conceited fellow who has made himself unpopular."

But not to McGraw, the gambler and racetrack aficionado, who treated Mathewson as an equal — an almost unheard of arrangement between manager and player. Some said that McGraw, whose first wife, Minnie, had died tragically in 1899 of acute appendicitis, and never had children, looked on Mathewson as a surrogate son.

Both men became famous — Mathewson reaching early-deity status by shutting out the Philadelphia A's three times in the 1905 World Series and winning 373 games over his 16-year major league career. Mc-Graw, meanwhile, led the Giants to three World Championships. Both were early Hall of Famers.

And both men, while fiercely competitive, remained lifelong friends, although the McGraws left the apartment in 1906, after the birth of Mathewson's son. The Giant skipper and his wife moved into rooms at the Washington Inn, a residential hotel near the Polo Grounds, where a few years later, they became friendly with another young New York baseball hero named Hal Chase. As a tribute to their great friend, the Mathewsons, who stayed on at West 85th Street, named the boy John Christopher.

Meanwhile, the Highlanders' long road trip did not go well. There were a few firsts to chalk up — on May 17, they played their first ever Sunday game against the Cleveland Blues, but in Columbus since Sunday baseball was banned in Cleveland, as it was in many cities. Addie Joss beat them 9–2.

A lot was riding on a good showing by the Highlanders. Considerable efforts had been made to secure a team in New York, not to mention a whopping expense — Gordon estimated that salaries alone totaled $200,000, an immense amount for the era. The chorus from the second-guessers were growing daily.

"I have always had bad misgivings about the success of Griffith's team of stars," wrote Frank Patterson in the May 30 *Sporting News*. "The infield is too weak in all departments, but the team must surely do better when Keeler and Fultz begin to bat. I do not look to see Chesbro and Tannehill do the great things they did with Pittsburgh by any means — it makes a lot of difference in a pitcher's record whether he has a team behind him that kill base hits, and bat out victories, or whether he has only a fair fielding team that can net him the balls."

That same Memorial Day weekend, Rube Waddell went to a carnival in Philadelphia, shortly before taking on Barney Wolfe and the Highlanders on Saturday.

The "Rube," as he was known, was in his element among the circus performers, trapeze artists and wild animals. There was even a barber, who was offering a free shave to anyone brave enough to join him inside the lion's cage to have his hair cut among the savage beasts.

Waddell thought it over and volunteered. What better way, he figured, than to prep for a meeting with a wolf by sitting among lions? The onlookers cheered as the popular ballplayer ducked into the cage, sat with the barber and got a haircut. As the barber worked, so did the lion tamer who cracked his whip to keep the lions busy.

But even that wasn't enough for the daring Waddell. Pretending he was annoyed at the lions, he fired blanks from a toy gun at them. Then, he strolled over and stroked one lion on the head. Even the tamer was stunned. Loud applause accompanied Waddell as he left the cage.

It worked, for the next day, he went out and beat Wolfe and the Highlanders, 4–3. And with that, the Highlanders limped home. "Weren't they lucky in selecting a spot so remote from the center of civilization?" one journalist wrote with sarcasm. "There is little danger of the Invaders setting the Hudson on fire from any hot work they do in its vicinity."

Others were less blunt. Some called for Griffith's head. Others just stayed away, choosing not to make the long trip to the Hilltop. A jump start was in order.

On June 11, they got it, unloading a couple of veterans, Herman Long, 34, and Ernie Courtney, 37, to the Tigers for the colorful, mercurial Kid Elberfeld. "In spite of the fact that he has not the most pleasant disposition," *The Sporting News* wrote of the trade, "[Elberfeld] is a very fast young man at short, and may take it into his devoted head to come here and play ball that will do something to put a little life into the American League."

On paper at least, the New Yorkers got the better deal. The Tigers would be backup infielder Courtney's fourth team in two years; he was a throw-in. And in sending Long packing, the Americans sent off a player in the twilight of a good career; the 14-year-major league veteran had several years with Boston (N.L.) in which he hit in excess of .300, but the last had come in 1897. Through 22 games with New York, he had hit only .188.

In Elberfeld, the Highlanders were getting a solid fielder and a proven .300 hitter, but a ton of baggage. The Hilltop would be the fiery 28-year-old's fourth team in five major league seasons — the Phillies and Reds came before Detroit. Suffice to say that the 5'7" and 134 lb. Norman "Kid" Elberfeld, long on talent and tough as nails, was one of those players who wore managers out with his grating personality.

A native of Lookout Mountain, Tennessee, Elberfeld was a cattle farmer back home. As was the custom, the cattle tended to roam free, with the owner identified by the brands they carried. Once, when another farmer accused Elberfeld of stealing a calf, which had a brand that had faded and was hard to make out, the dispute went to court, which awarded the other man the calf. But when the calf got ill and died a few weeks later, residents suspected it had been poisoned. Many suspected Elberfeld. But accuse him? No one dared.

It hadn't taken long for Elberfeld to fit right into the rough and tumble world of turn-of-the-century baseball. In 1898, his

How appropriate that the Hunter Whiskey sign in left-center field is in the background of this portrait of Kid Elberfeld. For spike wounds, the Kid had a solution: spit, whiskey and tobacco juice. (National Baseball Hall of Fame Library, Cooperstown, NY)

rookie year with Philadelphia, he smashed a pile of dishes to the floor of hotel restaurants to get the attention of the waiter if the service was too slow for his taste. There is no record of the waiter's reaction.

On the field, Elberfeld once tagged a runner out who was called safe, and got so angry that he threw the ball up the wire netting in front of the grandstand, allowing two men to score. When he was hurt, he'd use a home-made solution and rub not medicine, but whiskey, on an open wound to stop the infection and keep playing.

Elberfeld played well for the Phillies that rookie season, hitting only .237, but exhibiting catlike agility and command in the infielder, mostly at third. But the team

grew weary of this behavior and traded him to Cincinnati. Still, when Elberfeld's old Phillies manager George Stallings took a job managing the Tigers, he scooped up his old shortstop and signed him to a contract.

No question the Kid was talented. A natural left-hander, he had broken his left arm as a boy and taught himself to throw right handed. His ability to use both hands served him well; on pop flies, Elberfeld was noted for roaming deep into center field and throwing away his glove to make a left-handed catch and throw, all in one motion.

Things went reasonably well for Elberfeld in Detroit. But when another strong-willed, no-nonsense baseball man, Ed Barrow, arrived in 1903 to run the Tigers the two clashed. One day, when Barrow showed up at Sportsman's Park in St. Louis and found Elberfeld working out with the Browns, he marched on to the field and accused Browns manager Jimmy McAleer of tampering with his ballplayer.

Barrow then turned on Elberfeld, who glared back. Things got worse when Elberfeld, led to believe he would named the team's captain, saw Barrow give the position instead to second baseman Heinie Smith. That led to some careless play on the Kid's part — his batting average may have been among the league leaders at around .400, but his play in the field grew erratic. The costly errors prompted Barrow to publicly question his work ethic.

The last straw came in a home-and-home series in late May and early June against Elberfeld's old friends, the Browns. Actually, the series started in Detroit for four games, then went to St. Louis for one and a rain out, and then headed back to St. Louis for two more. Clearly, the Kid wasn't trying; he made sloppy plays or errors in three of the games, and overran a playable ball in the last game of the series on June 1, which led to a three-run St. Louis ninth and a come-from-behind 7–6 victory.

It fueled Barrow's anger. He accused Elberfeld of "throwing down" the team. Elberfeld just laughed and bragged that he'd been in negotiations with the Browns about buying out his contract. He announced further that he'd play for only two teams — the Browns and the Giants.

On June 2, The Tigers suspended El-berfeld indefinitely for what it termed was "laxity of training habits and the deliberate throwing of three games during the St. Louis series." He was also fined $200.

Several teams, figuring they could use a hard-nosed player like Elberfeld, inquired to see what the Tigers would take in exchange for his services. The Boston Americans offered their shortstop Freddy Parent in a proposed one-for-one deal. From Charles Comiskey of the White Sox came the offer of George Davis, another holdout shortstop. Cincinnati's Garry Herrmann offered money — a lot of it, at $4,000.

Griffith made an offer as well, traveling June 4 while the Highlanders were at home against Cleveland, to Philadelphia where the Tigers were playing, to talk with Barrow. It was no-go at first, said Barrow, who explained that he had already received several lucrative offers for Elberfeld.

Griffith was offering Courtney and a couple of bench-warmers. Barrow counter-offered, demanding Conroy and Fultz. But Griffith wasn't called the Old Fox for nothing; his next move was masterful. He side-stepped Barrow completely, appealing instead to Tigers President Sam Angus, with the logic that whatever was good for New York was good for the American League.

The argument worked. Angus, a loyal American Leaguer, recognized that a strong franchise was important, agreed to the terms, accepting Courtney and Long in exchange for Elbelfeld. It was a masterful move. So, the Kid would be coming to New York after all.

9

The Good, The Bad and the (Mostly) Ugly

"Be home real soon Mom; they're beginning to throw the curve."
— *Ring Lardner*

Goodness knows, the Highlanders needed something. On June 1, they limped back to the Hilltop after nearly four weeks on the road, with a 15–18 record, seventh in the American League, ahead of only Washington. Even the weather gods were unkind — blue skies and brilliant sunshine had been with them in a doubleheader defeat over Memorial Day weekend in Philadelphia, but when it came time to start a three-game series back home against Boston, the heavens opened.

The New Yorkers were in a funk. To top it off, they couldn't even catch a break with the weather. "The Invaders have not as yet been able to shake off their double hoodoo — rain and defeat," W.M. Rankin opined in *The Sporting News*. "Both follow them with a persistency that makes one think that a Jonah is among them.... According to all kinds of paper and figures, they should be in the lead instead of where they are."

Back home, the New Yorkers lost three in a row to the Pilgrims, the last to 36-year-old Cy Young, still bringing the heat in his 14th big league season. Played under constant rainy skies, the games were a cumula-

tive disaster in which the Highlanders were outscored 27–5. Chesbro, Tannehill and Griffith were all clobbered. Fielding was sloppy and the hits weren't falling. Starting a new series June 4 against Cleveland, the New Yorkers lost again 6–3 — their fourth in a row — with Chesbro again getting hit hard.

But that was the day Griffith went for help to Philadelphia, where the Tigers were playing. After a quick two win series over the White Sox, the deal for Elberfeld was consummated June 10. It was the Kid at shortstop three days later for the start of a three-game series at the Hilltop against — you guessed it — Detroit.

In some ways, the Highlanders game of Saturday, June 13, was just another of the thousands of major league games played in the season of 1903. But in hindsight, it was the game the New Yorkers needed to get on track. That may have been their most pivotal turning point of their first season.

The heavens had let go again that morning, leaving puddles of water here and there around the Hilltop and keeping the crowd down again, this time to 2,100. Sit-

70

ting in the New Yorkers' dugout, Elberfeld looked across the field at Barrow and waved with a sneer.

Elberfeld didn't figure much in the result of the game that day. Batting third, he laid down a sacrifice bunt in his first at-bat in the opening inning and cleanly fielded all three balls hit to him.

But with the score tied 2–2 going into the ninth, Chesbro worked his pitching rival Jack Deering for a walk. Lefty Davis then sacrificed him to second for the first out, bringing up Keeler. With first base open, Barrow, in the Detroit dugout, had to decide whether to walk the talented Keeler and pitch instead to Elberfeld. That would certainly have made sense and Elberfeld, itching for the chance for another turn at the plate against his old team, figured he'd be batting with the game on the line.

Barrow knew that. He had Deering pitch to Keeler, who promptly ripped a ringing double to right. As the ball landed and began heading through the soggy outfield to the fence, Chesbro took off from second and arrived home with the run that pulled the game out, 3–2. Standing at home to greet him was one Kid Elberfeld.

The small crowd whooped it up. Griffith ran onto the field in celebration and two days later, the Highlanders were on a roll and had taken three in a row. Griffith himself shut out his old White Sox teammates 1–0 on six hits in their next game, on June 16 and the team won 1–0 again the next day, behind Bill Wolfe for their fifth in a row. Suddenly, the incessant rains of June didn't seem so bothersome and the tight Philadelphia/Boston race for first didn't seem all that far away.

But in the end, not a great deal changed the rest of the way. The Highlanders had gotten on track — sort of — going above .500 for good in a July 4 sweep of the White Sox at the Hilltop. But by then, Boston had pulled into the lead, as had the Pirates in the National League, the result of which were

two pennant races that were essentially decided by mid-season.

It was an eventful season anyway. On July 2 the great Delahanty disappeared over Niagara Falls in a tragic accident that would cast a pall over the game for quite some time. It would leave Delahanty's widow, Norine, and the couple's young daughter virtually destitute.

Moving in with her sister after the accident, Norine would file suit in 1904 against the Michigan Central Railway, seeking $20,000 in damages. She claimed that the railroad was responsible for her husband's death because it had put him off a train when it was clear he was heavily intoxicated and couldn't take care of himself. The case was heard in the town of Welland, Ontario, in May 1904, when a lot of time was spent recounting Delahanty's heavy binges on the booze. The jury awarded Norine $3,000 and her daughter, $2,000.

A few weeks after Delahanty disappeared, the erratic Rube Waddell did too — walking out on both his wife and his team, the A's, to take up new quarters in a Front Street bar in Philadelphia. A week later, Waddell crossed the Delaware River and got a new job — tending bar in Camden, New Jersey, where he also took some work pitching for the local ball team. The Rube's new idyllic existence lasted a week or so, until he was arrested for bail-jumping and hauled back to Philadelphia. He soon rejoined the A's.

Philadelphia was the scene of further trouble on an otherwise pleasant Saturday in August with 10,000 people at National League Park watching the Phillies play Boston. When a group of neighborhood kids began taunting a couple of drunks as they zig-zagged down 15th Street, just outside the left field bleachers of the ballpark, one of the drunks turned around and hit a little girl, knocking her to the ground. That got the kids angry and started a big, old-fashioned brawl.

The angry shouts from the street attracted the attention of the crowd in the section of the bleachers overlooking the street. As they yelled, more and more people rushed to the top of the stands to check out the commotion. It was too much for the old wooden grandstand, and within seconds, it gave way, sending about 500 spectators hurtling into the street below.

Others inside the park, fearing that the rest of the grandstand was about to give way, ran onto the field, knocking down anyone in their way and causing more fights. On the field, players held up bats to keep themselves from being overrun by the horde. In all, 12 were killed and 232 injured in the collapse of the 150-foot grandstand.

An inspection of the ballpark revealed that the collapse was caused by rotted supporting beams. A coroner's jury put the blame solely on the Phillies' former owners, John Rogers and Albert Reach, the sporting goods magnate. The tragedy, known as "Black Saturday," was the worst event in the history of Philadelphia sports.

Elsewhere in the National League, McGraw's Giants continued to impress. Paced by twin-30-game winners Mathewson (30–13) and Iron Man McGinnity (31–20), the team won 84 games — a dramatic 36-win improvement — to nail down second place, only 6½ games behind the Pirates. Never did a man do more to live up to his nickname than the stocky, 32-year-old McGinnity. Pitching in 55 games, he finished an astounding 44, the third-most in history. Add to that his 48 starts, baseball's fourth-most, along with 434 complete innings, baseball's third-highest in history and 68 innings — about 7½ games worth — more than runner-up Mathewson.

Iron Man McGinnity more than lived up to his nickname in 1903. On August 1, he beat the Boston Braves 4–1 in a com-

plete-game seven-hitter, the first game of a doubleheader. Feeling a particular pop on his fast ball that day, he was sure he could beat the Braves again — the same day.

"Skipper, I'm not tired," he said to McGraw between games. "Why don't you let me pitch the second game too?"

McGraw sized up the offer: with McGinnity going again, the Giants could rest the other pitchers. "Okay," he said. "If you want to, go ahead and pitch."

So he did. There was some trouble in the sixth, with the Braves piecing some base hits together and scoring two runs. But that was it and McGinnity coasted. The result: a six-hit, complete-game 5–2 Giants win.

A week later, the Giants faced the Dodgers in a doubleheader. Again, McGinnity started the opener, winning 6–1 on an eight-hitter. And again, he felt strong and suggested to McGraw that he start the second game as well. The result: another win, this time with drama. Stealing second base, he actually scored the Giants' second run, but trailed Brooklyn 3–2 going into the ninth. As it turned out, the Giants scored two runs and won 4–3.

McGinnity kept pitching his regular turns, piling up the wins and keeping the Giants in contention. Then, on August 31, he did it again — pitching the Giants to a complete game, 5-hit, 4–1 win over Philadelphia in the first game of a doubleheader. Asking for the ball in the second game, he beat the Phillies easily, 9–2.

Three doubleaders, six starts and six wins, all in a single month. From there on, he was no longer Joe, but the "Iron Man." McGinnity wasn't the only man to pitch and win both games of a doubleheader in major league history. Already unusual — McGinnity was one of the few players to actually jump from the A.L to the N.L. when he left the Orioles midway through the 1902 season to join the Giants — his performance only fed the legend.

Iron Man McGinnity would win 35

games in 1904, 21 in '05, and 27 games in '06 before leaving the majors after 1908 with 247 lifetime wins. Then, he joined Newark of the Eastern League and spent 15 more years in the minors — actually pitching and managing for nearly 12 of those years. His career wouldn't end until the Coolidge Administration in 1925, when, at the age of 54, as pitcher, manager and part-owner of Dubuque in the Mississippi Valley League, he went 6–6 and finally put away the spikes. Four years later, he died, legend intact.

Crosstown at the Hilltop, things began clicking for the Highlanders, but because of their poor start, none of it made much difference in the end. Returning home in July after another long western swing, the New Yorkers beat the White Sox behind Chesbro 5–3 for their 29th win and to climb above .500 for the first time since April. Not only that, but the win edged them past Chicago into fourth place, behind only Boston, Philadelphia and Cleveland. They'd win again 5–3 in the second game behind Griffith.

But the reality is that neither the Giants nor the Highlanders nor anyone else would catch Pittsburgh or Boston. Both 1903 pennant races were routs. In the N.L., the Pirates, with the considerable help of Wagner, won their third straight N.L. pennant with a 91–49 record. Nicknamed "The Flying Dutchman," Wagner was everywhere that season — playing first, third, short and the outfield, and winning the batting title at .355.

And in the A.L., the Boston Pilgrims led the league in runs scored and fewest runs allowed, behind the likes of runs-scored leader Patsy Dougherty and long-ball hitter Buck Freeman, who slugged a league-leading 13 home runs and drove in 104; along the likes of the seemingly-ageless Cy Young (28–9), Big Bill Dinneen (21–13) and "Long" Tom Hughes (20–7).

The Pilgrims finished a distant 14½ games up on the second place A's. It was a much-improved performance anyway for Philadelphia, behind the pitching of Eddie Plank, Waddell and Chief Bender. More would be heard from A's pitchers.

Meanwhile, September went quietly for the Highlanders — the ball club that is. On September 1, with the team in Philadelphia for the first of a four game series against the A's, the club's silent owner Big Bill Devery spent an eventful Labor Day sailing, schmoozing and parading his way to what he was hoping would be an eventual nomination for mayor of New York City.

Big Bill's big day kicked off with the annual boat ride up the East River on the iron steamboat *Cygnus* of the association bearing his name. The crowd of admirers who showed up at the 22nd Street Hudson River pier hoping to ride the boat to the noontime picnic at College Point, Queens, was so intense that things didn't get started until 90 minutes after the scheduled 9 a.m. departure.

When the *Cygnus* finally pushed off at 10:30 a.m., the 2,000 or so association members lucky enough to make the boat struck quite a sight in their white yachting caps modeled after Sir Thomas Lipton. With the band striking up "See the Conquering Hero Comes," the boat headed south around the Battery and turned north up the East River to the accompanying toots of respect from the horns of other pleasure and fire boats in the river.

The nautical sounds and salutes continued the length of the course. A group of iron workers, looking like mites far above as they worked on new East River Bridge, saluted Devery by banging their hammers noisily on the steel structure and yelling a greeting. The commotion brought pedestrians to the shore at the river's narrowest point, near Hell Gate. Even the lighthouse keeper saluted by banging his big bell three times and receiving a return salute from the *Cygnus*.

Devery reveled in the love-fest. "This all means that the working men know I am their friend," said the radiant ex-chief. "There was never anything like this before. Did you ever hear every boat in this here big harbor salute a man on an excursion? I never did until today."

Even more remarkable was that despite press reports of kegs being tapped, most of the crowed actually stayed sober. Many had other things on their minds, notably the action in the many on-board poker and craps games. "It was noticeable," the *Times* reported soberly, "that men with their hair cropped short, their eyes close together, their noses pinched in appearance and their jaws very square, who made a pretense of occasionally going to the beer kegs, got much of the money."

The gambling and games continued at the picnic. Then they sailed back to the 22nd Street Pier, arriving just after 9 p.m., where, under calcium lights and riding in a carriage, Devery was the featured attraction of a Labor Day parade. Met by another 1,000 people — wearing their white hats as well — he and the revelers paraded to Devery Clubhouse at the corner of West 28th Street and Eighth Avenue. It was well past midnight when things broke up.

The goodwill didn't last. On September 26, the Citizens Union delivered the findings of their extensive report on the nefarious Devery dealings during the Van Wyck administration. The report, which detailed a police force riddled with corruption and blackmail, was launched by the recent election of Reform Mayor Seth Low.

"Devery was a prince of grafters," the Citizens Union report said. From there, it launched into a detailed analysis of how Devery had been indicted five times for failure to suppress houses of prostitution and how, after he'd once been dismissed from the de-

partment, the courts reinstated him on a technicality.

"This was Tammany's selection as head of the police," the report said. "Under him, vice held high carnival in New York. The right to violate almost any law was regularly peddled. Blackmail flaunted itself before the public eye."

All that, amid the irony that Devery was sponsored for membership to the prestigious Democratic Club of New York. Capping the whole sad spectacle, the report added, was Mayor Van Wyck seconding the nomination by calling Devery "the best Chief of Police New York ever had."

In one respect, Devery never answered his critics: He never came clean nor spent as much as a day in jail. On the other hand, his political fortunes were wrecked. A candidate for Mayor? Thanks to the Citizens Union, he was damaged goods.

About the same time that the Citizens Union was delivering its report, the Highlanders ended their first season on September 29 before a sparse Tuesday crowd at the Hilltop, beating the Tigers 10–4. Only 1,028 people saw the Highlanders finish their season 10 games above .500 at 72–62, good for fourth place, a distant 17 games behind Boston.

For the record, they brought total Highlander attendance that first season to a shade under 212,000 — an average of about 3,200 a game, ahead of only Washington in the A.L. and far behind league-leading Boston, which drew more than 379,000. But more critically for the Highlanders, the attendance was a fraction of the major league-leading Giants at more than 579,000. The good news would come later, when decent Highlander teams and a subway stop to the Hilltop would increase attendance dramatically; the team would surpass the Giants in 1906.

Against the Tigers, those hardy 1,028 saw first baseman Ganzel head the Highlanders hit parade, with two doubles and two singles in five at-bats. He'd finish the season with a .277 batting average.

They saw Ambrose Puttmann, a 23-year-old rookie left-hander getting a long look by Griffith for 1904, go a strong five innings, giving up one run on only two hits. It was a good start for the rangy Ohioan; in three games, Puttmann finished the season 2–0, giving up 16 hits in 19 innings for an 0.95 ERA. Alas, Puttmann would only play parts of three seasons with the New Yorkers, before being shipped to the Cardinals after 1905 and finishing his major league career after four seasons.

And they saw the steady Keeler finish his first season on the Hilltop with a single, a stolen base, two runs scored and several outstanding plays in right field. Despite his shoulder separation earlier in the season, Wee Willie still managed another superior season of hitting to all corners, finishing at .313 — far from his best season, but awfully good anyway. All but 21 of Keeler's 160 base hits were singles. Still, there was hope he'd return to full health in 1904.

It had been a good season for Elbelford too. He finished at .287. Elsewhere, Conroy batted .272, Williams .267 and the oft-injured Fultz .224.

On the mound, the Highlanders were again solid, but not spectacular. Pacing the pack was the spitballing Chesbro (21–16, 2.77 ERA). He was followed by Tannehill (14–14, 3.27), Griffith (14–11, 2.70), Handsome Harry Howell (9–6, 3.53) and Bill Wolfe (6–9, 2.97).

Meanwhile, there was another event that season that very nearly matched the ballpark tragedy in Philadelphia. On the evening of August 28, a train holding both the Cleveland Blues and St. Louis Browns derailed at a crossing and ended up in a ditch. Plowing into the ditch and overturning was the sleeper car, where most of the players slept.

It looked bad — the car was shrouded in smoke and steam — but miraculously, no one was seriously hurt in the accident. After a few minutes, players from both teams alertly began checking on one another, before heading out of the train to safety. Among the Blues, the only significant injury was Larry Lajoie, who suffered a cut on the face and a sprained knee.

Big Larry came back from his mishap to finish the season with a spectacular .344 batting average, strong enough to easily regain the American League batting title he'd lost the year before to Ed Delahanty. It was the first of his three straight A.L. titles — the last coming in 1905, the year he doubled his duties as Blues manager. By the time Lajoie was done in 1916, he would amass more than 3,200 base hits, a lifetime .338 average and recognition as one of the greatest second basemen to don a baseball uniform. Lajoie would be a first-ballot Hall of Famer in 1937.

There was one more piece of business to conclude after the 1903 season that went beyond the usual cross-city or cross-state exhibitions. This one was an exhibition of sorts as well, but between the champions of the two leagues — Boston and Pittsburgh. It would be called the World's (later just the World) Series.

Writers had called for such a series for some time. You might think that relative labor peace would encourage presidents from the two leagues to hammer out the details. But lingering hostility over the Highlanders and other incidents had left neither Johnson or Brush willing to get together on finalizing the series. Instead, when it appeared that both pennant races were going to be lopsided, the owners of the two teams — Barney Dreyfuss of the Pirates and Henry Killilea of the Puritans — agreed to meet in the postseason. In early August, the two men sealed the deal on a handshake and set the format — the best of nine — with receipts to be evenly divided.

So it went in the first modern, yet un-sanctioned World Series. Based on their three straight N.L. pennants and the fast success of new star, Honus Wagner, the Pirates were heavily favored. Opening in Boston, the Pirates roared off to a quick three games-to-one lead, behind their 24-game winner Charles "Deacon" Phillippe — including an historic first-game 7–3 win against the great Cy Young.

Interest was high. Although only about 16,000 turned out for the first game and 9,000 for the second, the third game at Huntington Baseball Grounds on Saturday, October 3, drew a record crowd of 18,801. The crowd spilled out of the stands onto the field and lined the outfield, opening up when a Pilgrim outfielder went back for a fly ball, but closing ranks when the Pirates were in the field. A famous photo of the scene confirms both the scene and the un-usual ground rules.

The Pirates won that game, with Phillippe beating Boston's Young again, this time 4–2. Back at Exposition Park in Pittsburgh for Game Four, Phillippe won again for the third time in four games, returning after a rain delay to outpitch Big Bill Dinneen, 5–4. The win put the Pirates up 3 games to 1 and many of the 7,600 fans at Exposition Park were so confident that they carried Phillippe off the field on their shoulders after the game and then stayed for nearly an hour afterwards to shake hands with the big right-hander.

But three complete game wins in four games wasted Phillippe. Injuries to Pittsburgh starters Sam Leever and Ed Doheny had forced player-manager Fred Clarke to overuse his star. The loss of 16-game winner Doheny, a 28-year-old, nine-year major league veteran, was especially poignant: Late in the season, he suffered an emotional breakdown and was committed to a Massachusetts asylum, ending his career in baseball.

Phillippe was a trouper. He was a star of the Series — going the distance in all five games and winning three with a 3.27 ERA. But with the suspect Pirates pitching and an untimely slump by Wagner, who only batted .222 in the series, the Pilgrims stormed back behind Young to take Game Five. Then, they won the next three to win the first World's Series in eight games. Boston's star was Dinneen, who started four games and won three, including the clinching four-hit, 3–0 shutout at Huntington Baseball Grounds, which ended with a strikeout of Wagner.

That last strikeout sent off a wild celebration by Boston's Royal Rooters. Led by Mike "Nuff Said" McGreevey, the Rooters stormed the field and carried their heroes around the field. For the Pirates and the National League, the defeat was a stunning blow.

"We all felt pretty low after losing," Wagner said years later. "We had expected to win and the letdown was hard to take. I was a Series flop in 1903. After leading the National League in hitting during the regular season, I had only one hit (in the last game), a single. We were big favorites to win the Series, but we let our fans down."

And although the Pirates actually made more per man in the World Series share than the Pilgrims — $1,316 to $1,182 after Pirates owner Barney Dreyfuss threw his share to the players — the A.L. victory was another coup for Ban Johnson. Besides, the first World's Series had been a financial success, despite drawing little attention outside the participating cities because of its unofficial status. The eight games drew more than 100,000 people with receipts of about $50,000.

And with that, the wild, wacky ride of 1903 was finally over. It would be an even wackier 1904.

10

Happy Jack and the Epic Race of 1904

"The hardest thing to do, they say, is to hit a baseball. The reason it's so hard is the people who throw it."

— *Frank Tanana*

"I can make the spit ball drop two inches or a foot and a half," Jack Chesbro once said at the height of his pitching powers.

"The spit ball is worked entirely by the thumb," the Highlander right-hander said, sounding more like a professor than a fun-loving ballplayer who liked nothing more than downing a beer or two during a game. "The saliva one puts on the ball does not affect its course in any way. The saliva is put on the ball for the sole purpose of making the fingers slip off the ball first. Except for the spitball, every ball that goes from the pitcher leaves the fingers last ... by wetting the ball it leaves the fingers first and the thumb last, and the spitball could rightly be called the 'thumb ball.' The ball is gripped the same as if you were throwing a curve."

And so goes another of Chesbro's tutorials on throwing the spitball. Exactly how he controlled the now-forbidden spitter — with his manipulative, sneaky-fast thumb — was something he didn't explain. Such was the element of mystery that surrounded the slippery history of the spitball, a pitch that may have been easy to understand, but few could master.

Chesbro was a frontline major league pitcher who conquered the spitball and become a legend. Chesbro's spitball was his money pitch, the meal ticket, the path to a career in the sunshine and in particular, a season for the ages. That was 1904 when the stocky Highlanders righthander did things with a baseball that mere mortals could not. In doing so, he won more games than any other pitcher in a single season — 41 — a record that still stands. That season, he completed 48 of 51 starts and led the league in winning percentage, games, starts, completions and innings pitched. Of those, 14 came in a row until the Red Sox stopped him.

It was a phenomenal performance. "It appears plain, therefore, that without Chesbro, the New York team would not have been a factor in the race," one rather sober analyst put it after the 1904 season. "And without the spitball, Chesbro would not have been nearly as successful."

And though it was a season that secured Chesbro a spot in Cooperstown, it

Here is "Happy Jack" Chesbro looking uncharacteristically sullen. (National Baseball Hall of Fame Library, Cooperstown, NY)

was also the spitball that cost him — and the Highlanders — dearly on the last day of the season. That's the day when he finally ran out of gas and threw the wild pitch that lost the Highlanders the game and the pennant to Boston. Yes, them again.

The loss capped a season that might have been. Even then, Chesbro didn't get to the Hall of Fame until voted in by the Special Old-Timers Committee in 1946, 37 years after his career had ended and sadly, more than 15 years after his death. The reason: the wild pitch, a stigma that Chesbro's widow, Mabel, tried unsuccessfully for years to have purged from the records and changed to a passed ball. It didn't work: It's still a wild pitch, and because of it, Jack Chesbro is forever remembered as the goat of 1904, a turn-of-the-century Bill Buckner.

He was christened John Dwight Chesbro, a farm boy from the Berkshires town of North Adams, Massachusetts. As with many sports legends, there's a bit of mystery about his early years, principally Ches-

bro's nickname, "Happy Jack." Some say it was owing to his unfailing genial disposition on the mound. Others say he was given his moniker by an inmate of the asylum in Middletown, New York, where he spent the summer of 1894 as an attendant. To Chesbro's boyhood friends in North Adams, he was simply "Chad," his father's name.

It was while playing for the state hospital team in Middletown that Chesbro first attracted attention that summer. Happy Jack was 20 and used his long right fingers for what was noted as an unusually-firm grip of the ball. Having long fingers helped, but big league spitball success was still years away.

Chesbro used the intervening years to become a top-line pitcher anyway. In 1895, he signed his first contract, with Springfield of the Eastern League, in the first stop of an itinerant baseball career. In July that summer, he jumped to Cooperstown, New York, of all places, and in 1896, hooked up with Roanoke, Virginia, in the Atlantic League. Then, it was to Cooperstown for another round, before heading back to the Atlantic League in 1899, this time with Richmond.

Chesbro went 16–18 for Richmond in 1897 and came into his own in 1898, posting a stellar 23–15. In June 1899, he was cruising with a 17–4 record when he was sold to the A.L. Baltimore Orioles. Refusing to report, Chesbro was bought for $1,500 by Pittsburgh, where he went 6–9 the rest of the season.

A year later, Happy Jack had found a home in Pittsburgh, becoming a mainstay of a powerful team. In 1900, he went 15–13 for the N.L. pennant winners. Then, in 1901, he came into his own, going 21–9 for the first of six straight 20–win seasons. The Pirates won pennants the next two years.

Details vary on when Chesbro learned the spitball. Historians credit one Elmer Stricklett, a journeyman pitcher, with being the baseball pioneer who dumped a smidgen of glop on a portion of the ball, held it tight so it slid off the two forefingers as he threw, only to find that it veered and tumbled toward the plate, "like a drunk," as someone put it.

Stricklett needed all the help he could get. Breaking in the White Sox in 1904, he was traded to Brooklyn, where he spent three years, losing more games than he won each season, before finishing his career with a 35–51 record. Some writers say Stricklett taught Chesbro the spitball in a chance meeting at spring training in 1904.

But chances are Big Jack himself may have been baseball's first spitballer. Look at the way he suddenly "arrived" back in 1901 when his record with the Pirates jumped from 15 wins in 1900 to 21 in '01 and 27 in '02. Then, there are those 41 wins in 1904 — a full 20 more wins than in 1903. The stocky Chesbro did report to the Highlanders in 1904 a full 20 pounds lighter, so conditioning may have had a lot to do with his improved performance. But who knows for sure? Ah, the mysteries of baseball.

Just how tough the spitball was to master can be seen by how few pitchers actually used it to achieve success. Among Stricklett's White Sox teammates of that 1904 season was a Chesbro contemporary — a burly right-hander named Ed Walsh, who began throwing a spitball around then and pitched 14 years for a spot in Cooperstown. Walsh had another eerie similarity to Chesbro — four years after Jack won his 40, so did "Big" Ed, winning 40 for the White Sox, before losing the game that decided the pennant on the last day.

But from its start, the spitball attracted controversy. Moisture on the ball meant it could easily slip from control and leave batters exposed. For every pitcher who mastered it, there are perhaps a dozen who tried but found it difficult to control. It took

some years, but in 1920, the spitball was banned from baseball, a ruling that stopped all but the more inventive latter-day spitball pitchers like Gaylord Perry.

With the ruling came an exemption for the 17 legal spitballers authorized to keep throwing the pitch until their careers finished. Nobody else could. The major leagues' last legal spitballer: Hall of Famer Burleigh Grimes, who broke with the Pirates in 1916 and won 20 games six times before his 19-year-career ended in 1934.

But even if nobody knows who really threw the first spitball, there was another thing certain about Chesbro. He, Walsh, and others like Christy Mathewson, Eddie Plank, Chief Bender, Grover Cleveland Alexander and Walter Johnson were among a collection of hard-throwing, rubber-armed and wily front-line pitchers of the era who entered the major leagues around the same time, using a combination of spitballs, cut fastballs and even knuckleballs to dominate batters and in effect, christen the dead ball era.

The spitball was only one of a series of tricks pitchers used by frontline hurlers at the turn of the century. Nothing in the official rules of the time actually restricted pitchers from using any form of moisture to load up the ball. So they did — using spit, sweat, tobacco juice and even dew from the damp grass to apply to the ball and deliver it to the plate. Some of the more cunning pitchers even cut their baseballs with razor blades hidden in gloves or by using belt buckles. Griffith was a notable offender, going so far as to actually step from the mound and knock the ball against his spikes, presumably to pound out the dirt.

Mathewson, as we have seen, reached the National League in 1900 for a cup of coffee and won 20 games a year later. He wouldn't stop for 16 years — and 373 wins. A contemporary was the left-handed Plank, signed by the A's out of Gettysburg College in 1901 and the modern era's first pitcher to win 300 games, mostly with Philadelphia. Bender was Connie Mack's other star pitcher of the era; he'd pitch 16 years and win 210 games.

A few years later came Alexander, the rangy right-hander best remembered for his remarkable relief effort for the Cardinals in Game 7 of the 1926 World Series, when he shut down the Yankees. Alexander debuted with the Phillies in 1911, winning 28 games. Despite a career beset by epilepsy and chronic alcoholism, Alexander won 373 major league games — the same as Mathewson — including three seasons in which he won 30 or more games.

Then there was the flame-throwing Walter Johnson. A native of tiny Humboldt, Kansas, Johnson was the Nolan Ryan of his day, a man born with a rocket for a right arm that he used to compile a remarkable record. Starting in 1907, Johnson spent his 21 major league season with one team — winning 417 games, second only to Cy Young. That included a record 110 shutouts, a dozen 20-win seasons and 56 consecutive scoreless innings, a record unbroken for 55 years. Nicknamed "the Big Train," because his feared fastball was said to travel with the speed of a freight train, Johnson, like Mathewson, was a charter member of the Hall of Fame.

Even cranky, old Cy Young, in the league since 1890, found a way to remain on top. Others may have thrown faster than veteran Young after 1900 and others even had better statistics. But nobody pitched with more consistency, which Young aptly demonstrated by averaging 27 wins and 15 losses a season in the 1890s and the exact match in the 1900s. Never suffering so much as a sore arm helped Young, as did pinpoint control — a big-time curve thrown from a number of arm angles and a variety of off-speed pitches, particularly important after age took its toll on his fastball. Young was the last to admit it: Asked if he changed speeds, Young said, "yes ... fast, faster and fastest."

There were other reasons for the era's dominance of pitchers. The foul-strike rule proved a major help, as did a new five-sided home plate, which created an easier target than the old diamond-shaped, square-foot plate. Ballpark maintenance improved — the best evidence being at the Hilltop, where Highlander President Gordon spent the winter of 1903, repairing that gully in right field.

The ball itself was another factor giving pitchers the upper hand. Supplying the major league with baseballs in those days was the Spalding Sporting Goods Company, which manufactured its baseball with innards composed of a solid rubber core, wrapped with woolen yarn and covered with a horsehide cover. But because the yarn was not wound as tightly as tightly as it was possible to do in future years and because the rubber core wasn't as long-lasting as the cork-rubber center introduced in 1911, turn-of-the-century baseballs just didn't travel very well.

Moreover, when those baseballs were put into play and got dirty, the owners in those days did little about it; Hall of Famer Bill Klem once said that when he started umpiring in the National League in 1905, he was supplied with three new balls at the start of each game. If a ball got lost, the home team would typically get one more ball, not always a new one. Keeping a foul ball was illegal and most teams hired policemen and attendants to force spectators to throw the balls back. The result: more grime and discoloration on the ball as the game wore on, which the wilier pitcher supplemented by scuffing it even more.

Advances in equipment, particularly fielders' gloves, held batters back even more. Still flimsy and looking like oven mitts by current standards, baseball mitts after the turn-of-the-century improved steadily with the addition of a leather strap between the forefinger and the thumb and better padding in the heel, which provided a deeper pocket.

No wonder the average fielding percentages improved by 20 points in the American League between 1901 and 1908. And no wonder the 1906 N.L. Cubs became the first team to commit fewer than 200 errors in a single season.

So if the baseball of those years didn't offer much hitting, base running or scoring, it was still a success — attracting increased attendance every year until 1914. The relative period of baseball peace helped — an era kicked off in September 1903 when the baseball magnates finally ratified still another National Agreement. The new pact, finalized by Ban Johnson and Harry Pulliam, created a three-member National Commission — the two league presidents and a chairman to be elected by the owners — to rule baseball.

Garry Herrmann of the Reds was elected National Commission chairman. In preparation for 1904, the magnates made another significant decision — choosing to return to the more lucrative schedule of 154 games, after three seasons of 140 games in both leagues. Except for 1918 and 1919, the 154-game schedule would remain the major league standard for the next 57 years.

For the ever-restless Griffith, the winter of 1903 would prove eventful as well. Of chief concern was the addition of another front-line pitcher to replace the underachieving, disgruntled Tannehill. There was a hole or two in the infield to patch up and the need for a strong, dependable catcher. Adding to the challenge was the underlying need to keep up with John McGraw, for whom publicity and a strong 1903 created a lot of anticipation about the Giants for 1904.

Tannehill had been a bust in 1903. After winning at least 20 games in four of five seasons with the Pirates, the Kentucky native had struggled to a mediocre 14–14

record with the Highlanders in '03. And it was an open secret that he harbored no love for Griffith, a feud he only fueled in mouthing off to a *Sporting News* reporter in the off-season.

Griffith turned first to his old colleague Barrow. In early January, he hopped on a train for Detroit, ostensibly to see the Gans-Fitzgerald featherweight fight, but also to do some business with the Tigers.

Griffith coveted the promising Tiger righthander, George Mullin. The 23-year-old pitcher known as "Wabash" George, a reference to his hometown in Indiana, was coming off a breakthrough 18-win season with Detroit in 1903. Offering a series of propositions — $10,000 cash; then pitcher Tannehill and $7,500; and finally Tannehill, third baseman Bob Unglaub and a smaller amount — he was turned down each time. For Barrow, it was a good move — Mullin stayed with the Tigers for nearly 10 more years, winning 20 games or more five times.

Very much aware he was trade bait and not wanting to play in Detroit was Tannehill. "Now, there are some places to which I have no objection of going and there are others I wouldn't travel to reach for a bucket of coin," he told *The Sporting News*. "If I'm going to be swapped around like old junk, they've got to give me my share of the junk. I've a two-year contract with New York and would like to remain there. One thing is certain: Clark Griffith can't send me to Detroit. I'll not go. I've too nice a proposition from the Pacific Coast people to be worried about the future. Before anything is done, they've got to talk to Jess."

Griffith did talk to Jess, but only to tell him that he had been unloaded instead to the New Yorkers' A.L. nemesis, the Pilgrims. In return, they got Long Tom Hughes, a 22-year-old righthander, who had broken through in 1903, going 20–7 for Boston, despite a rocky Game Four World Series loss to Pittsburgh.

They also acquired Jack Powell, a well-traveled 29-year-old veteran. The right-hander came over from the hapless Browns, where he had gone 15–19 in 1903, but had won 21 the year before. It was the third time in six years Powell won at least at least 20. In 1898, he won 23 with Cleveland; two years later, he won 23 for the Cardinals.

In place of Davis came another veteran from the Browns — 29-year-old first base-man "Long" John Anderson. Big at 6'2" and 180 pounds, Anderson hit a lot of doubles and triples and even a home run or two on occasion.

A final steadying acquisition was the ageless catcher "Deacon" Jim McGuire. The Highlanders would be the 41-year-old McGuire's 11th major league stop in a career that started way back in 1884 with Toledo of the American Association and would continue until 1912, after 26 major seasons and a .278 lifetime batting average. Said *The Sporting News*: "In Jim McGuire, the New York Americans have the veteran catcher of baseball."

The team set, Griffith again met his team in early March in Washington, D.C., before departing for another spring training in Atlanta. There, the team would remain until March 26, before heading for a barnstorming tour to Mobile, New Orleans, Montgomery and Richmond, before reaching New York to start the new season.

It can be hard to tell where the hype leaves off in spring training. In March, everybody looks to be a contender, but the Highlanders really did look improved in the early going of 1904. Again, they ripped through inferior minor league opposition, including the Atlanta Crackers, as well as New Orleans and Mobile.

And again, Griffith ran a tough, disciplined camp — serving notice on what he expected from his troops and along the way, shedding some perspective on what may have happened last season.

"We have a hard campaign —154

games ahead of us — and we must get in fine shape or be out of the running," Griffith told *The Sporting News* in mid-March. "Next week, I'll send the squad through the hardest kind of practice. Every department of the team will be worked overtime for I intend to have my men ready for the championship work at the start and in condition to stand a driving finish, for that is what any pennant winner must be prepared to face. This thing of a team being in shape for half their games and out of shape the other half doesn't count in a hard race. We'll be ready to deliver the goods in 1904 from April 14 to October 1, or it will be no fault of the training log."

Back north, the coming new season brought with it a New York–style tempest. Baseball peace aside, there were still a number of issues to work out, much of it prompted by the old animosities between Johnson, Farrell, McGraw and Brush. Add to the complicated feud, one Charles Hercules Ebbets of Brooklyn.

You've probably heard of Ebbets. Long before Roy Campanella, Duke Snider, the Dodger Symphony, Hilda Chester and other Dodger-like icons, there was Charles Hercules Ebbets, namesake of the late, great Ebbets Field and a man synonymous with the team that made the borough forever baseball mad.

"It always will be Ebbets and the part he played in the promotion of baseball in Brooklyn that will remain as his greatest monument to the game," the *Times* wrote of him after his death. "Mr. Ebbets was one of the best known and best beloved men in baseball."

When it opened in April 1913, Ebbets Field was the premier ballpark of its time. Built on a site once known as "Pig Town," it housed about 23,000, and later 33,000, when a left field and a center field double deck were added in the early 1930s. Along the way, Ebbets Field became the quirkiest, rowdiest, best-known and best-loved ballpark in baseball.

Several baseball innovations can be traced directly to Ebbets. The *Times* credits him with inventing the raincheck. He was a staunch proponent of Sunday baseball at a time when Sunday Blue Laws ruled the land. He argued hard to establish a permanent schedule for World Series dates. And the system of drafting players in which tail-end teams got first pick and pennant winners got last dibs was also his doing.

Baseball flowed in Ebbets's veins. In his 20s, he sold scorecards at Washington Park for Brooklyn's first professional baseball club, which was a member of the Interstate League, a kind of forerunner to the American Association. In 1889, the Brooklyn club won the last American Association pennant, switched to the National League in 1890 and took that flag too.

Ebbets rose quickly, acquiring stock in the club and becoming president in 1898 on the death of Charles Byrne. Working quickly, he managed the club that first year and bought up star members of the disbanded Baltimore franchise the next year. He was successful, winning pennants in 1899 and 1900.

Alas, Ebbets stopped winning pennants for 16 years. But not even a championship could match the satisfaction of Ebbets' most lasting legacy — the opening of his new ballpark, the aptly named Ebbets Field. It opened April 9, 1913, with a Robins 3–2 exhibition win over their cross-town rivals, the Yankees.

"The day was made to order," gushed the *Times*. "It was one of the nicest little spring days the oldest inhabitant of Flatbush could remember. And the sky … it was the same glorious canopy of pale blue, arched from horizon to horizon and flecked here and there with filmy clouds of white."

Ebbets, who lived at 1466 Glenwood Road in Brooklyn, died in 1925 at age 66 on a day when the Giants beat the Robins at Ebbets Field. As a tribute, both teams lined up around the plate as players and spectators alike paid silent tribute. He is buried in Green-Wood Cemetery in Brooklyn.

But that was far in the future in the spring of 1904. After those pennants in 1899 and 1900, Ebbets had just endured three seasons in which his team was far from contention and was anxious for an edge. You can understand his frustration when he lashed out after Frank Farrell of the Highlanders announced plans for his team to play on Sundays at Ridgewood Park on Long Island.

Arguing against the Highlanders playing games at Ridgewood, Ebbets used arcane logic. He said if the Greater New Yorks, as the Highlanders were now being called, were to play Sunday games at Ridgewood as they proposed to do 14 times over the coming year, it would take valuable revenue from the Superbas. After all, he argued, Ridgewood Park was much closer to his team's home field, Washington Park, than it was to the Hilltop. As long as the Highlanders played in Manhattan, he argued, they should confine their games there.

Just what an explosive issue Sunday baseball was in those days is not easily appreciated a century later. Exhibition Sunday baseball had a long tradition in New York, but blue laws strongly prohibited the playing of league games on the Sabbath. Feelings against Sunday ball was particularly strong in conservative, family-conscious Brooklyn, known as the "Borough of Churches," where adherence to relaxation on the Sabbath ran strong.

In contrast to midwestern cities, blue laws throughout the East Coast dated from colonial times and were feverishly backed

by white, native-born Americans who dominated most state legislatures and argued
that big cities, dominated by immigrants,
were centers of vice and corruption. Heading the blue law brigade in New York was
the New York Sabbath Committee, which
since the 1850s had opposed not only ball
games on Sundays, but mail delivery, newspaper printing and the opening of libraries
and museums.

In particular, the Sabbath Committee
targeted New York City, where in 1900
nearly 77 percent of the population was of
non-U.S. origins, mainly Catholics and
Jews, who tended to oppose a strict Sabbath
observance. That made New York a kind of
test case: "If they could defeat the 'ungodly'
in this un–American metropolis," argues
Steven A. Riess in his book, *Touching Base*,
"then they could succeed elsewhere."

Blue law advocates had battled over
Ridgewood Park for years. In 1889, they organized community opposition to Sunday
games played there by Brooklyn's American
Association team, and even secured a $500
fine against the field's owner for violating
the law.

In support of its large immigrant base,
Tammany Hall supported Sunday baseball.
"Ministers ride their bicycles on Sunday and
find enjoyment in it," said Tammany boss
Richard Croker in 1897. "There are thousands of citizens who would find good, honest enjoyment in a game of baseball, and it
does not make any difference whether it is
played on Sundays or weekdays, as there is
nothing demoralizing in it."

The irony is public opinion generally
sided with Croker. By 1904, Sunday blue
laws were feebly enforced in New York.
Permitted was Sunday semi-pro ball, since
judges rarely enforced the laws against
working class youths who didn't have a
whole host of outlets for their leisure at a
time when the upper classes retreated to
country clubs for golf and tennis.

Generally, promoters escaped prosecu-
tion as long as they didn't charge admission.
That led to a number of colorful ways of
raising a buck — patrons could get in for
free, but might pay $1 for a usual 10-cent
program or be asked to pass the hat for a
"donation."

For his part, Farrell, with Ban Johnson's backing, was looking for an edge. He
knew that Ridgewood Park, right on the
Brooklyn/Queens border at Myrtle and
Wyckoff avenues, with its 10,000-seat capacity, was an attractive spot for a Sunday
getaway from the city. And he recognized
that the issue could generate some welcome
attention on the Highlanders in the middle
of baseball's winter break.

Johnson chimed in, rather diplomati-
cally, in mid-January. "It is an interesting
situation," he wrote to *The Sporting News*.
"Wise baseball men say the decision will be
in favor of the Americans for the simple reason that not a foot of Ridgewood Ground
is in the borough of Brooklyn and that it
cannot be shown the New York American
League Club was to be confined to Manhattan."

Citing a study he had commissioned,
Johnson wrote that Ridgewood Park was, in
fact, closer to the Hilltop in Washington
Park than it was to Washington Park in the
Red Hook section of Brooklyn. By triangu-
lation measurement, he claimed the distance
from the home of the Highlanders to Ridgewood was 6⅛ miles, while it was 6½ miles
from Ridgewood to Washington Park.

He claimed further than Ridgewood
officials had said they drew 60 percent of
their Sunday patrons from Manhattan, and
that, "it would not pay him to open his
gates if he had to depend on Brooklyn people for support."

As January dragged into February, the
issue drew tremendous press interest, much
of it generated by the wily Farrell. In early
February, he scored a major coup, when,
still awaiting a decision on the matter from
Herrmann and the National Commission,

he suggested that the Highlanders share their Sundays in Ridgewood Park with the Superbas.

For Farrell, the pool hall king–turned–baseball magnate, the offer was an olive branch that scored big points in the newspapers. Score one for spin control and chalk up a big step toward respectability.

"How much more sensible and sportsmanlike and reasonable it would have been for Ebbets and company to have accepted Farrell's generous and sensible proposition for both to play Sunday ball at Ridgewood Park," wrote Frank Patterson in the February 6th *Sporting News*. "How vastly more sensible to have said to Farrell, 'We can both cop off a little money here and at the same time, give a large element of baseball-loving people who work all week the chance to see the game on their day of rest. Let us divide dates as best we can. Let us join forces against the puritanical and fanatical preachers who wish to rob the working man of his recreation on his rest day.'"

In the end, none of it mattered very much. On March 2 after weeks of deliberation, Herrmann and the National Commission ruled against the Highlanders playing Sunday league games at Ridgewood Park. Apparently, baseball peace was a more important consideration than doing what the newspapers endorsed.

The tight-lipped Herrmann announced the decision and said nothing more about the matter. Not so the increasingly statesmanlike Farrell, now cast as the noble loser. "While I am greatly disappointed and it means the loss of considerable money to me, I propose to take the defeat philosophically," he told reporters. "I agreed to this course some time ago, and I intend to stick to it."

Still, that wasn't the end of the Sunday baseball controversy in New York that season. Not heeding the advice of Herrmann, Ebbets decided to take his victory over Farrell a step further, when in early April, he decided himself that the Superbas would play a regular season Sunday game at Washington Park.

And so, despite the lack of consent of the other seven National League teams, they played. The date was Sunday, April 17 and the Superbas beat the Boston Braves, 9–1. There were no arrests and no disturbances.

But when they tried again a week later—April 24 against Philadelphia—things didn't go as well. Arrested were three program distributors and as many players—Brooklyn battery mates, pitcher Ed Poole and Fred Jacklitsch, along with catcher Frank Roth of the Phillies. The ballplayers were immediately bailed out by friends, but the message was clear: Sunday league baseball was still out of bounds in New York. Except for occasional fund-raisers—in 1909 for newspaper carriers and in 1912 for survivors of the *Titanic*—Sunday baseball would be off-limits until 1919.

Spring training wore on with prognostications from all angles for maximum Highlander glory in '04. "We will have a grand team this year," Farrell predicted. Griffith, not able to help himself, talked up his infield, calling it simply "the fastest ever."

Also checking in was the great Larry Lajoie of Cleveland. He predicted that only four teams—his Blues, along with Boston, New York and Philadelphia—would be in the running for the A.L. pennant.

"Boston will be just as strong as last year, but no stronger as Hughes in my mind was a trifle better twirler than Jess," Lajoie predicted. "At least he was harder for us to hit than Tanny. New York will be in better shape. Last year, the Highlanders did not get started until they had secured Elberfeld and Griffith had struck his gait. This year, they will start off better as Griffith has practically recovered his health while their infield will have the advantage of having played together for several months. A year ago, Griffith had to start off with an infield that had never played together and naturally, he was handicapped."

Also weighing in were the scribes, the most enthusiastic of whom was W.M. Rankin of *The Sporting News*. "The outfield is certainly a wonder," he wrote. "In Anderson, Fultz and Keeler, the club has a trio of outfielders it may well be proud of. If the team's infield was as strong or in the class of the outfield in fielding and all-round work, there would be no questioning its ability. The pitching department is greatly improved: Powell and Hughes should add great strength.

"As they stand now, I think Jimmy Collins (Pilgrims) will beat them out in the pennant race. Conroy, Fultz, Keeler, Elbelford and Anderson of the New York Americans should keep a good many pitchers guessing when that quintet of bat wielders face them." (Sportswriting was like that then.)

Rankin proved himself remarkably astute. Keeler was indeed the old Keeler again, as he banged the ball again to all corners of southern minor league ballparks, seemingly healthy again and recovered from his dislocated shoulder the year before.

Rankin was right as well about the pitching staff, where he found the greatest improvement. "Griffith, Powell, Hughes and Chesbro should be able to carry any team along if they are in shape all season without mentioning the youngsters who give promise of doing good work," he wrote. "When this season begins, the officials of the Greater New York Club have done good work toward getting together a good team and they are entitled to a good return for the money they have invested."

The key was Chesbro. Armed with his spitball, the star pitcher stayed away from camp well into March to coach the Harvard baseball team. Chesbro's regimen helped him drop some 30 pounds from his 1903

playing weight to a svelte 163 pounds. By the time he reported to Atlanta on March 25 — a little late in the interests of completing his college coaching obligations — he was in regular season form.

The next day, March 26, Griffith sent Chesbro to the mound against Atlanta. It was a promising start: He and Griffith teamed up to shut out the Crackers on three singles as the Highlanders coasted 16–0. On April 6, he and Hughes shut out the Eastern League Montreal Canadians in the first game of a final two-game tune-up in Richmond, the final spring training stop before the New Yorkers came home.

The Highlanders reached Pennsylvania Station in New York on the morning of Friday, April 8. That afternoon, they went to Olympic Field at 136th Street & 5th Avenue in Harlem to play the semi-pro team known as the Murray Hills. Olympic Park? The Highlanders had hoped to play their last few exhibitions at the Hilltop, but had to look elsewhere when Gordon decided to make a number of late winter-break improvements to the ballpark. Again, the opposition was inferior — the Highlanders won this time 19–1— and again Chesbro pitched, this time on two day's notice and with little trouble.

Two more local tune-ups awaited the Highlanders before the season — Saturday in Jersey City and Sunday out at Ridgewood Park against the semi-pro Ridgewood Park Exhibition Co. The games were again lopsided, but served an important purpose: In contrast to 1903, when the Highlanders went straight from southern barnstorming to start the season on the road, Farrell insisted this time that they build up the local interest.

The effort was well-spent. A record breaking crowd met the Highlanders at Ridgewood Park that Sunday. Conservative estimates put the attendance at 10,000, so many that people jammed the elevated trolley cars and long before the preliminary game between Ridgewood and the Negro League Philadelphia Giants even started.

The appearance of Big Bill Devery brought an air of frivolity to the proceedings. Cries of "Hello Bill, how many votes do you want?" met the retired New York police chief. Devery just smiled. Oh yes, the Highlanders took another squeaker, 14–2 behind three hits by Elberfeld, two by Keeler and pitching by Powell and Hughes.

Chesbro was the Highlanders' opening day pitcher — on April 14 against Boston. Despite Brooklyn opening their season at Washington Park against the Giants at the exact same time, the Highlanders attracted more than 15,000 people to the Hilltop for their first season opener at home.

What those spectators got was a still-unfinished subway and blustery conditions with temperatures in the low 40s, making it more like football weather. At least they got the benefits of President Gordon's winter labors — a closed-in grandstand on the Hudson River side to guard against the winds, a fresh coat of paint and an enlarged scoreboard in left field. And for Willie Keeler, there was a special gift in right field — nearly 100 feet of dirt that had filled up the Hilltop's ravine and the big stone wall moved back to 120 feet in the corner.

"Last season, Willie would trot over to the fence in time to see the ball disappear over the top and then turn around the watch the runner make a circuit of the bases because of the short right field fence," wrote Rankin. "It will not be so this year. Willie will have a look in at all high balls that come into his territory."

Just as in the opener the year before, there was pageantry, starting with bunting and flags around the stands, the presentation of small American flags to spectators and music before the game, this time from the 69th Regiment Band. And again there was a parade — both teams emerging from their locker rooms behind the center field

fence and marching toward the grandstand, as the crowd waved their flags.

Then, quite suddenly a new tradition kicked off, one that endures today. With the game set to begin promptly at 3:30 p.m. and home plate umpire Frank Dwyer calling Puritans leftfielder Patsy Dougherty, everybody paused: The band struck up the Spar-Spangled Banner and everybody in the ballpark stood up, snapped to attention and afterwards, waved their flags again. The ceremonial first pitch from former Judge William M.K. Olcott followed, and only then did Chesbro finally deliver the season's first pitch.

It was a good start for Happy Jack. Pitching against Cy Young, he shut down the Puritans until the seventh, when Buck Freeman uncorked a solo home run over the big wall in right. He allowed another run in the ninth on a homer by Parent and coasted 8–2 in a complete game, 10-hitter. Chesbro was handy with the bat himself, socking a home run and a double.

And with that, Chesbro's wondrous season was underway. On April 18, he lost to Bender and the Philadelphia A's, 5–1 at Shibe Park, but that was a relative blip. Four days later in Washington, he beat the Senators 2–0 in a complete game, one-hitter — the only Senator base hit was a clean single to right by Kip Selbach in the first inning.

After several rainouts, Chesbro won again May 7 in Boston, shutting down Dinneen and the Pilgrims 6–3, before a Huntington Grounds crowd of more than 11,000, some 200 of whom traveled from North Adams to see their old hometown friend. Then, back home in New York on May 13, Chesbro went the distance but was rocked by Cleveland, 7–0. The loss, on a delightful summer-like day, evened his record at 2–2 and ran the Highlanders record to 11–8. It would be Chesbro's last loss for nearly two months; in between, he'd amass one of the more remarkable pitching streaks in major league history.

Chesbro's next start was two days later, in the same Cleveland series. Before a festive Saturday crowd of 10,123, the Greater New Yorks, as newspapers were now calling the team, breezed 10–1, taking three of the four games. Their three runs in the third came on four straight singles, with Williams's fly to right breaking open what had been a scoreless game. Elbelfeld and Fultz each had four hits in a balanced New York 17-hit attack. Chesbro pitched a complete game and the streak was underway.

All in all, it was quite a day in New York. With the Highlanders' game letting off about 6 p.m., Coney Island was just springing to life. It was opening day at the seasonal resort and before the night was finished, some 250,000 people had sampled what the *Times* called, "a swaying, rocking, glittering magic city by the sea."

Many went to Coney Island for its usual array of cheap eats, organ grinders and side shows. But the big attraction this time was the glittering open of Luna Park's acres of new attractions, along with Dreamland's ever-increasing array of exotica from all corners of the globe. "Coney Island is regenerated, and almost every trace of Old Coney has been wiped out," reported the *Times*. "Frankfurters, peanuts and popcorn were among the few things left to represent the place as it was in the old days."

Back on the ballfield, Chesbro continued pitching the Highlanders to wins. On May 17, he beat Detroit 5–1. Three days later, he beat Chicago, 3–2. Then, on May 24, he beat St. Louis, 3–0. The streak was at four.

Several other things were happening as well. Chesbro, with his rubber arm was pitching every three days or so, giving new meaning to that old baseball expression, "workhorse." Typical was the May 24 win in which he scattered four hits, all singles. The day before, in the final game against Chicago, New York had lost 6–2, with Griffith pitching. The day after, on May 25, St. Louis beat them again, this time, 7–4, with Powell knocked out after the fourth.

It was indicative of a early-season Highlander pattern — Chesbro's wins, surrounded by a loss here and there from others. He had become not just the team's mainstay, but its ace: Playing on Memorial Day in Philadelphia, the Highlanders lost two to the A's. The next day, in Detroit, Chesbro won 5–3. Then, three days later, he beat them again, 5–1. The streak was six.

Chesbro's pitching meant more than a guaranteed win every third day or so. It was literally keeping the Highlanders in the thick of what was shaping up as the team's first race for the American League flag. On June 7 — the day when Frank Farrell reached out to sign a new pitcher, Walter Clarkson of Harvard — the Highlanders found themselves in a logjam near the top. Boston was first, with the Blues second, three back; and, the New Yorks third, four back. Yup, it was a race.

On June 9 in Cleveland, the fates showed that maybe, just maybe, they were backing the Highlanders. Pitching against Nap Lajoie and the Blues, Chesbro gave up two quick runs in the first on successive singles to Harry Bay and Bill Bradley after which Elmer Flick drove them in with a triple. Then, he shut the door, giving up one more hit and striking out eight.

The problem is so did Blues right-hander Earl Moore. Twice, the Highlanders had a man on third with one out and failed to score. Reaching the top of the ninth, they still hadn't scored as Cleveland clung to its 2–0 lead, with Moore seemingly in control.

After all, he had shut out the Highlanders for eight innings. No wonder many in the crowed of 2,894 began leaving the stands, thinking it would all be over in a few minutes. But leading off the ninth, Moore walked Conroy. After Williams flied out, Ganzel singled, scoring Conroy. It was 2–1 Blues with one out. Then, Anderson singled and scored on a wild throw by Harry Bemis, the catcher. Tie score; still one gone. McGuire then struck out for the second out. So, it was up to Champ Osteen, the second-year back-up third baseman who Griffith had obtained in the off-season from the Senators. He singled and came around to score. Just like that, it was 3–2 New York. Chesbro shut Cleveland down in the bottom of the ninth and the New Yorkers had pulled off a memorable win. Ah yes, the streak: It was Chesbro's seventh straight win, moving New York back into second place.

Decades later, Griffith remembered the game vividly. Holding court with writers, the Old Fox recalled it not only for the comeback, but because it was the first time he recalled that Chesbro was using the spitball. After giving up those early two runs, Chesbro sought Griffith on the bench.

"'Griff, I haven't got my natural stuff today,'" Griffith recalled Chesbro as telling him. "'I'm going to give 'em the spitter the next inning, if it's all right with you.'"

"I told him to go to it," Griffith told him. "And you know what?... They didn't get another run." No, they didn't. The Old Fox had a good memory.

Moving on to Chicago, Chesbro won his eighth in a row June 11, beating the White Sox 6–3. Number nine came June 16 at St. Louis in a 10–3 win over the Browns. Against the Senators in Washington on June 21, Chesbro won 3–0 for his 10th in a row.

The spitball was working. And clearly, having Chesbro on the mound was giving the Highlanders a boost, since they always seemed to find a few extra runs when Happy Jack was on the mound. Even the Highlanders' fielding seemed cleaner and more crisp behind Chesbro, putting to rest the old stories that infielders couldn't handle the balls thrown by spitball pitchers.

Rolling into Boston June 25 to face the defending champions for, oddly, one game only, the Highlanders found themselves with a 33–21 record, percentage points behind the Pilgrims. It was an early litmus test.

After all, the Pilgrims were still the class of the American League. Anchored by a proven, veteran pitching staff, the champion Puritans were again powerful. There was 37-year-old Young, the old battle-ax; Series hero Dinneen, a six-time 20-game winner; ex-New Yorker Tannehill, anxious for revenge against his old mates; and Norwood Gibson, the 17-game winner.

Adding an air of drama to the series was the June 18 trade Griffith had just engineered for Boston's pesky leadoff hitter and left fielder Patsy Dougherty. Gone were back-up infielder Bob Unglaub and cash. The move was a clear advantage for the Highlanders; the talented Dougherty had batted a hefty .331 and led the league in runs scored in 1903, his second season in the big leagues, endearing himself as a particular favorite in the hearts and minds of Royal Rooters. But his average had dropped to .272 at the time of the trade, putting himself in the bad graces of manager Jimmy Collins.

The deal showed how lightly the Pilgrims took the New Yorkers. It ignited the Royal Rooters, who turned their wrath toward Boston owner John Taylor, publisher of *The Boston Globe*, and gave credence to conspiracy theories that Ban Johnson was working in the shadows to secure the pennant for the Highlanders. No grassy knolls were involved, but the theorists had a point: Johnson was still trying to do everything in his power to get back at McGraw and Brush, his longtime adversaries, by building a strong A.L. presence in Manhattan.

It stuck in the Royal Rooters craws that Dougherty, in his first game as a Highlander, stuck it to his former teammates by leading off the game with a single and singling twice more. With 16,000 squeezed that Saturday into Huntington Avenue

Baseball Grounds, many of whom were wildly cheering Dougherty's every move, the Highlanders beat Cy Young, 5–3. His opponent: Jack Chesbro, who went the distance for his 11th win in a row.

After a day off Sunday, the Highlanders served notice that Monday, again beating the Pilgrims and Tannehill 8–4 behind Powell's pitching, four more hits from Dougherty and a home run from Ganzel. The trade was just the tonic Dougherty needed; the new Highlander went on a tear, running the bases with abandon and hitting a solid .283 the rest of the way. Unglaub made it into only nine games for Boston that season, hitting .154.

Meanwhile, Gibson pitched Boston to a 5–2 win in the series' final game—a scheduled fourth game was rained out. The New Yorkers had gone into the home of the defending World Series champions and taken two of three games, before heading home, only percentage points behind. Litmus test: very much passed. These Highlanders were for real.

11

They Might Be Giants

"Some days, you tame the tiger, and some days, the tiger has you for lunch."
— *Tug McGraw*

There was another opponent that year. No, the Highlanders didn't meet them on the field, but they were still formidable, a team whose success was a constant dagger in the side of the Greater New Yorks and one of the more challenging job hazards of setting up shop in Manhattan. "They" were the N.L. Giants, waking up under John McGraw and having a season for the ages.

The 1904 Giants were McGraw's first great team. A veteran ball club, averaging 28-years-of-age, they won a then-record 106 games, losing only 47. Their clear strength was pitching, handled primarily by the twin workhorses, McGinnity and Mathewson, who won 68 games between them. Lacking a big star at the plate, the Giants were "made up of beautifully complementary parts," as Thomas Gilbert puts it, and still led the N.L. in offense. Among those parts were shortstop Bill Dahlen, the league RBI leader, right fielder George Browne, its leader in runs scored; and left fielder Sam Mertes, who was second in doubles.

As a team, the Giants led the N.L. in runs, hits, doubles, home runs, walks and team batting average. They played well against everybody — winning 18 games in both June and July — and feasting in particular against Brooklyn, Boston and Phila-

delphia, all league doormats. Against those three, the Giants' aggregate was 56–9. In some ways, it was a typical McGraw team — one that relied on the hit-and-run, with a touch of brashness, like the old Orioles.

The Giants' most colorful personality was "Turkey" Mike Donlin, a man who lived up to his nickname. Donlin didn't run, he strutted. Turkey Mike's most lasting legacy was off the field: He was a flamboyant, colorful personality who wore $350 suits, wed a vaudeville star and got into more barroom brawls than a crew of sailors on shore leave. Such behavior often got him into hot water with both the law and the baseball hierarchy.

Once a wild-throwing minor league pitcher, the versatile Donlin became a star major league outfielder and sometimes first baseman and shortstop. He had a checkered 12-year career with six teams, but thrived with the Giants as a consistent left-handed batter. Donlin topped .300 in all but two of those seasons and compiled an impressive .333 lifetime average.

Donlin missed most of the 1902 season with the Reds because of a six-month jail sentence for assaulting a live-in girlfriend. McGraw was willing to overlook such behavior, and, in 1904, brought him to New York, where he fit in perfectly with the rowdy Giants.

New York took to Donlin, making him and Mathewson the most popular Giants of all. Turkey Mike returned the favor, serving as team captain from 1906 to 1910, squiring actresses about town and plunging into theater himself. It was during one of his suspensions — this one in 1906 for drunkenly terrorizing a trainload of passengers headed to Troy, New York — that he met and fell in love with Mabel Hite, a leading vaudevillian of the day.

The daughter of an Ashland, Kentucky druggist, Hite had reached the stage as a singer and comedienne, starting at the age of 11. By 1908, Hite and Turkey Mike were starring in their own show — one of the first "talking films" — at Brocker's Bijou Dream on West 23rd Street.

It was a new start for Turkey Mike. He and Hite married and toured in a song and dance review during their honeymoon. And when his contract for the 1908 season arrived, he held out and didn't report that season, nor the following either, choosing the theater instead. Lamented frustrated Giant fans: "If Donlin would only join the Giants, (we) would drink his health in pints."

By 1911, Donlin considered himself an actor and the impatient Giants sold the 33-year-old veteran to the Boston Braves. Donlin returned to the field, played sparingly and retired again, in 1913. Meanwhile, on the stage and in the movies, he landed a few leading roles, one as an ambidextrous pitcher.

The new lifestyle suited him. "Marriage has made a man of Mike Donlin," a newspaper reported. "He is leading a temperate life and inspires confidence in his resolution to continue on the straight and narrow path for the rest of his life."

What could draw him back to baseball? Hite's tragic death, that's what. The 27-year-old actress died October 22, 1912 of cancer, despite claims that she had been completely cured after converting to Christian Science. It was on her deathbed that she read her husband the story of Napoleon's return from Elba and bade him to go back to baseball.

Donlin did go back, but his bat speed was gone. After a cup of coffee with the Pirates, Turkey Mike disappeared into the minors, before closing out his baseball career as a utility infielder in 1914 with the Giants. His batting average that final season: a measly .161.

Another sad part of the Mabel Hite chapter popped up in 1915, when Donlin went to court in the bizarre case of the desecration of his late wife's remains. It seems that one Ray Frye, an undertaker's assistant with Manhattan's Campbell's Funeral Home, had negligently left the urn that contained Hite's ashes in a Broadway restaurant.

The lure of Hollywood endured. Turkey Mike remarried in 1914, and devoted himself entirely to films, appearing in 20 more silent films and talkies. But the hard living caught up to Donlin; he died in 1933 at 55.

Donlin helped the Giants back in 1904, his first season in New York, hitting .329, even though at the time they dealt for him, he was sitting out a month's suspension for drunken behavior in Chicago. Not that they need have worried; by the beginning of September, the Giants had opened up a 15 game lead over Chicago. On September 22, they beat Cincinnati for their 100th win. Their 106 wins would set a single season record.

But for all the Giants' extraordinary success in 1904, the reality is they seemed to lose interest after clinching the National League pennant. After September 22, McGraw would take in the early races at various New York racetracks before heading to the Polo Grounds for the 4 p.m. game.

"They forgot all about their contractual obligations to give the club their very best at all times," wrote Henry Chadwick. Even the crowds weren't interested, dwindling into the hundreds.

There was a reason interest had dwindled. As early as July, Brush and McGraw had decided that under no circumstances would they participate in post-season games against the American League champion, as had been launched the year before in the Boston-Pittsburgh World Series. They became even more obstinate as it appeared that the Giants were running away with the pennant and that their opponent in the World's Series could be the Highlanders.

With both New York ballclubs playing well, pressure mounted on both men to relent. Ban Johnson wrote to Harry Pulliam proposing another American/National championship, but unlike 1903, one with the official sanction and supervision of the National Commission.

Brush remained stubborn. "There is nothing in the constitution or playing rules of the National League," he said, "which requires its victorious club to submit its championship honors to a contest with a victorious club in a minor league."

That last reference — "minor league" — showed the venom in Brush's attitude about the upstart American Leaguers. In later years, McGraw explained their reluctance to play as Brush's concern over the lack of rules on the distribution of receipts, umpire selection and the like. The reality is that the two still mixed a particular loathing for Johnson and his American Leaguers with a fear of losing again, as the Pirates had done to Boston.

On June 30, the Highlanders returned home and kept on winning. First game opponents: the hapless, last-place Senators. First game New York pitcher: Chesbro, who coasted again, this time, 8–3, giving up seven hits on five walks for his 13th straight win. It was the Highlanders at their balanced best — not just pitching, but hitting in abundance, with two hits each from Keeler, Williams and Ganzel. Too bad not too many were around to see it — only 1,500 attended the game.

But New York baseball fever was spreading. On July 4, the traditional halfway point of the season, the Giants took two from the Phillies at the Polo Grounds, drawing 30,000 for their 18th in a row. Back on the road to face the A's in Philadelphia, the Highlanders took their two — Chesbro beating Weldon Henley in the morning game, 9–3, for his 14th straight, and Griffith outdueling Waddell in the afternoon, 5–2. Those games — with fans paying separate admissions — drew more than 41,000. The Giants were in first, the Highlanders, second. Yes, things were going well.

On July 7, the Bostons behind Gibson beat Chesbro 4–1. The chain was broken at 14 wins in a row as the Pilgrims pounded out nine hits on a wet, overcast day when the rain fell steadily all day, stopping only 45 minutes before game time.

Was the great Chesbro overworked? Hardly. The loss fueled him to actually step up the pace. Taking the mound two days later, he lost a tight game to Boston 2–1, largely on four damaging Highlander errors and the baffling delivery of the old master, Cy Young. He pitched in relief July 14 in a laugher of a 16–3 loss in Cleveland, but regained a measure of revenge the following day, going the distance, as the Highlanders won, 21–3.

On September 1, the Highlanders were holding tight, still percentage points behind Boston. Behind Powell, they took Detroit 4–2 at the Hilltop, before a crowd of more than 4,062, some 400 of whom were boys and girls of the Hebrew Orphan Asylum on Amsterdam Avenue at 135th Street. Accompanied by the asylum's fife and drum corps led by a small boy in a tall fur hat that played a number of tunes during batting practice, their appearance lent an air of festivity to the game.

More important, it gave Farrell a chance to demonstrate his benevolent side. After saluting both teams, the band broke ranks and joined their comrades in the stands for the game. It was another way of showing that the one-time pool hall king of New York had crossed the bridge to the big-time, achieving respectability as a legitimate big-shot team owner.

That Farrell suddenly had a big-time team heading into the homestretch was largely due to the right arm of one man: Jack Chesbro. The spitballer had been a workhorse. From April through August, the burly pitcher started 36 games and finished 35. But then came September and he grew even better — making an extraordinary 13 starts, finishing 13 and winning, just winning.

On September 3, Chesbro beat the Tigers 2–1, with the winning run coming in the seventh on a sacrifice to left field by Williams that drove in catcher Red Kleinow. It was a typical Chesbro performance — six hits, all of them singles, except for a triple by Sam Crawford, and six strikeouts. More important, it put the Highlanders into first place, where they'd find themselves a few more times before the season ended.

Two days later, on Labor Day, the Highlanders split a doubleheader with the A's in Philadelphia — why was it always the A's in Philadelphia on holidays? — and fell from first place. Chesbro, though, did his job, beating Andy Coakley in the morning game, 2–1, on a four-hitter. Chief Bender took Griffith in the nightcap, 7–2.

On September 12, Chesbro beat up on the sorry old Senators again, 4–2. He followed that and on two days' rest, beat the Pilgrims and Big Bill Dinneen 6–4. Then, on September 21 in Washington, D.C., he put the Highlanders further up into first place with an extraordinary performance in a doubleheader against the Senators.

In the opener, Chesbro relieved the injured Al Orth in the 10th inning of a scoreless game. Each team then scored twice to send the game into extra innings. The Highlanders won it in the 11th with Keeler singling, advanced by Elberfeld and scoring on Conroy's sacrifice. Chesbro was the winner. And if that didn't comprise a day's work, he went the distance in the nightcap, beating the recently-traded Long Tom Hughes, 5–1 on an eight-hitter. They were wins number 38 and 39.

But the Pilgrims kept winning, so Chesbro did too. With the season down to its final week-and-a-half, Chesbro beat Chicago on October 1— his 39th win — and St. Louis on October 3 for number 40. It kept the Highlanders close, and with the Giants having long clinched their pennant and no World Series on the horizon, interest in New York reached fever pitch.

On October 5, the Highlanders beat the Browns in St. Louis and headed home to begin their final four games of the season. Their record stood at 90–56 for a winning percentage of .613. Boston's record was 92–57 for a winning percentage of .614, all of .001 ahead. Adding to the drama was the opponent for those last games: yup, Boston.

October 6 was a travel day. It was also the day that Brush and McGraw gave Ban Johnson and the Highlanders their final answer about meeting them post-season: a big, fat "no."

Speaking for the Giants, McGraw took the hit, claiming the decision was his and his alone. That their final answer had been left so long was easily explainable, he said; Brush was ill and hadn't been in the office to receive the invitation, mailed six days ago. It was only today, he said, that they had been able to address the situation.

"When I came to New York three years ago, the team was in last place," McGraw began. "Since that time, on and off the field,

I have worked to bring the pennant to New York. The result is known. Now that the New York team has won this honor, I for one will not stand to see it tossed away like a rag. The pennant means something to me. It is the first I have ever won. It means something to our players, and they are with me in my stand. We never stopped until we clinched the pennant, even if it did rob the game of the interest of a pennant race…. If we didn't sacrifice our race in our own league to the box office, we are certainly not going to put in jeopardy, the highest honor in baseball, simply for the box office inducement."

McGraw was wrong on two accounts. His seeming lack of interest in the "box office inducement" was a ruse, for McGraw was a man who never met a business opportunity he didn't like, from race track gambling to real estate speculating in Florida.

His argument that Giants players were behind him was hogwash too. Not playing the series robbed them of a time-honored post-season tradition of major league exhibition games between rival teams from the same city, as took place for years in St. Louis, Chicago and Philadelphia, and between Cleveland and Pittsburgh. In New York, the Giants benefited from a couple of theater benefits and something called "Field Day" at the Polo Grounds, an exhibition game against past team members, an event preceded by wrestling and boxing matches. But neither that nor Brush's personal gift of $5,000 was enough to satisfy the grumpy players for what they thought they could have earned in a World Series or a cross-city championship.

One such grump was Donlin. "There was a sore bunch of ballplayers around the club house when McGraw refused to stand for the post-season games," Turkey Mike told a reporter in Cleveland, on his way home to Erie, Pennsylvania. Brush had made "a barrel of money" that season, Don-

lin said, but had "let McGraw con him" into turning down the chance to make even more. McGinnity was upset too, largely because his contract prohibited him from pitching in California that off-season; Iron Joe claimed that he and his teammates were "sore to the core" at not getting the opportunity to make some extra cash.

The Giants players weren't the only ones favoring a post-season. There was a petition signed by 10,000 New Yorkers urging that the series take place. Boston, in the event that they won the American League, wanted one too. So did a bookmaking syndicate that put up $50,000 cash to make it happen.

But the reality is that McGraw was driven more than anything by a raging hatred of Ban Johnson. "I know the American League and its methods," he said October 10, with the matter already decided. "I ought to…. They still have my money." No way would McGraw ever concede to "a haphazard box-office game with Ban Johnson and company," he said. "No one, not even my bitterest enemy, ever accused me of being a fool."

Back home at the Hilltop, Chesbro went to work, shutting Boston down 3–2 for his 41st win against only 11 defeats, and pushing the Highlanders back into the lead by six percentage points. There were four games to go. It was the closest race in major-league history and New York seemingly having the advantage by only having to split the series to gain the pennant.

What followed is among the more curious quirks of baseball history. On Saturday, October 8, the Highlanders/Boston doubleheader had been scheduled for New York. But a few months earlier, Farrell, never in his wildest dreams thinking the games would be important, had rented the park for a college football game between

Columbia University and Williams College. The games were transferred to Boston.

Something else had happened after the win that Saturday. Knowing the teams would be back in New York for the season's last two games, Griffith, fearing his ace was overworked, told Chesbro to stay there, rest his arm and not accompany the team to Boston. But Chesbro had felt good that Friday and showed up at Grand Central Terminal, urging his manager to reconsider. "I'll pitch and I'll win," he said with conviction.

Standing nearby was Farrell, who urged Griffith to reconsider and let his ace face the Pilgrims. So the Old Fox caved and Chesbro hopped on the train to Boston. Baseball-rabid Bostonians were ready. Reserved tickets to the doubleheader had been sold out for a week. And although 28,040 had managed to squeeze into Huntington Avenue Baseball Grounds for the occasion, thousands more milled about the bulletins around town watching for the returns.

Baseball cranks filled up the bleachers 90 minutes before the first pitch was thrown. They filled several hundred temporary seats in front of the grandstand too, with standees lining the fences. So dense was the crowd on the field that teams agreed to a special ground rule in which a fair ball hit into the crowd would be a two-bagger.

Things started well for the New Yorkers, when Dougherty singled in the first inning off Dinneen and came around to score the game's first run. Things seemed promising: On the mound for the Highlanders was Chesbro, gunning for win 42. But the Highlanders' ace had pitched nine innings the day before, and after 48 complete games and more than 445 innings, seemed to finally have run out of gas. Chesbro held the Pilgrims off until the fourth when the floodgates opened, and the Bostons tallied six runs. Walter Clarkson, the ex-Harvard University prodigy signed in June, relieved

Chesbro. Boston pushed seven more over the last four innings to win 13–2.

The second game was tighter, but the results were similar. Jack Powell, gunning for his 24th win of the season, pitched well for the Highlanders, giving up one run on four hits. But crafty, 37-year-old Cy Young was better, scattering seven hits and walking no one to take the New Yorkers, 1–0 for his 27th win. And just like that the season was down to the end, with the teams returned to New York for the last two games, a Monday doubleheader at the Hilltop. Sweep — and the pennant would belong to New York.

If Bostonians were excited, New Yorkers were downright delirious. The Giants had ended their season that Saturday, beating the Superbas at Washington Park in Brooklyn for their 106th win of the season and leaving the city to focus solely on the important Monday doings at the Hilltop. Fueling the excitement was a long-winded telegram from Governor Odell that urged Griffith "to defeat the wily Boston bean-eaters and achieve the world's championship as well as the American League pennant for the great Empire State and for the City of New York."

On Sunday, the Pilgrims arrived at Grand Central Terminal and checked into the Hotel Marlborough. Accompanying them were about 200 "Royal Rooters," many wearing big red badges with the words "World's Champions" emblazoned on their coats, and carrying, as good luck charms, the same suitcases and satchels they had taken with them to Pittsburgh for the 1903 World's Series.

Boston players told reporters that the drubbing they'd given Chesbro Saturday was a sign that the pitcher was worn out. But he was still the Highlanders' ace and felt he could pitch one more game, even if he'd pitched two of the last three days. That left Griffith with another decision: Should he go with Chesbro or somebody else in the first game Monday? But once again, the pitcher, figuring one more solid game was in his arm, cornered his manager. "I'll trim 'em Monday if it costs an arm," he said. Decision made: Chesbro would get the ball.

This time, more than 28,000 crammed the Hilltop. Seated behind the Boston bench down the first-base line were the "Royal Rooters," accompanied by Dockstander's Band, and with the aid of megaphones and tin horns, kept up a constant din throughout the games. But, the noise was weak compared to the raucous support given the Highlanders.

With one gone in the third, Chesbro rifled a triple to the right field exit gate, and the crowd rose, waving hats, handkerchiefs and canes. But Dinneen bore down and struck out Dougherty and Keeler, ending the threat.

In the fifth, the Highlanders sent eight men to the plate. One was Chesbro, but as he stepped to the plate, the game was temporarily halted so a delegation of New York fans could parade on the field and present him with a fur-lined coat and cap in appreciation for his extraordinary season. As if returning the compliment, Chesbro then lined a hard single off Dinneen's glove and waved his cap to the cheering crowd. The Highlanders very nearly put it away that inning; twice they filled the bases with Kleinow and Dougherty also connecting for singles and two bases on balls. But they managed only two runs.

It remained 2–0 New York until the seventh when Highlander second baseman Jimmy Williams booted a grounder to put a runner on base. And then, one out later, Williams made a poor throw home, and Lou Criger and Hobe Ferris ran home. It was 2–2.

Chesbro was very nearly spent. After returning to the bench, he sought out Griffith to send in a reliever. Now that didn't sound much like the gritty right-hander who'd just won 41 games. Did he have anything left? Griffith asked Kleinow. "He hasn't got anything," replied the Highlanders' catcher, "but he's getting along all right.… It's a toss-up as to whether it would be advisable to send someone else in or not." Griffith's decision: Chesbro had just enough left to continue.

The Pilgrims should have taken the lead in the eighth. They pieced together singles by Chick Stahl, Buck Freeman and Candy LaChance, but when Stahl tried to score, he was nailed at the plate on a pretty relay from Anderson to Elberfeld to Kleinow. The game went into the ninth, still deadlocked.

Lou Criger led off for the Pilgrims and reached base on an infield bloop. He reached second on Dinneen's sacrifice, and third when Elberfeld at short threw out Kip Selbach. Chesbro then got two quick strikes on the next batter, shortstop Freddie Parent, and then uncorked a throw for the ages — a wild pitch that bounced in the dirt, got away from Kleinow and skidded to the backstop. Criger skipped home with the go-ahead run. It was 3–2 Boston.

Versions differ on how wild the pitch really was. It has been described as everything from a shoulder-high fast ball up and away from the right-hand-hitting Parent to a spitball that broke 10 feet, whereas some said the pitch actually struck the grandstand on the fly. In 1942, Kid Elberfeld told *The Sporting News* that "the ball went so far over Jack (Kleinow)'s head that he couldn't have reached it with a crab net."

Whatever the case, Boston took the lead. Chesbro then gave up a hit to Parent before getting the final out. The Highlanders mounted a rally in the 9th, nicking Dinneen for two walks with two out, but Dougherty struck out for the third and final out. Game and pennant, Pilgrims. The Highlanders took the meaningless second game 1–0, before a greatly dispersed and greatly disappointed crowd.

For Chesbro, 1904 included both his greatest triumph and his lowest point in baseball. His powerful right arm had carried the Highlanders and what had made the great American League pennant race possible. But when he threw it away on his wild pitch to Freddie Parent in the ninth on October 10, he became a goat for the ages.

Either way, Chesbro had put together a remarkable season. There were the 41 victories, the 454 innings, the 14 straight wins, the 1.82 E.R.A. and the 48 complete games. But perhaps most astounding of all was Chesbro's work down the stretch in September and October, when he made 15 starts, finishing 13 and winning almost until the end.

But looking back, the Pilgrims may have been right; maybe all the work was catching up to him. Oh, he was still a front-line major league pitcher, but Chesbro was starting to slow down. In 1905, he'd win 20 games and another 22 in 1906. But that was the year he turned 32, and starting in 1907, his career tailed sharply off. In 1909, he was traded to Boston, by then called the Red Sox, of all teams, and retired. He had won 196 major league games in 11 seasons. The numbers were more than adequate for Cooperstown.

After his retirement, it was back to the chicken farm in North Adams for Happy Jack. Baseball still called and he coached at Harvard for a few years and in 1924, returned briefly to the major leagues as a coach for the Washington Senators. As for those 41 wins, except for Ed Walsh's 40 wins in 1908 no one ever came close to breaking his single-season record.

But there was still the question of that wild pitch. Chesbro died in 1931 at the age of 57 while tending to his chickens on the ranch. After his death, his widow, Mabel, took up the cause by submitting many clippings and articles to baseball officials in an effort to show that the fateful pitch had been a passed ball that skipped by Kleinow, who himself had died in 1929.

Then, Griffith jumped into the long-simmering controversy. Holding court before writers at baseball's 1938 winter meetings, he vividly recalled the wild pitch of more than three decades before. "It was a passed ball," the Old Fox said, "and Jack Kleinow … was the man who blew the championship."

"Ordinarily, he would have caught it easily," Griffith said of the pitch that got away. "Kleinow had been out celebrating the night before. His vision was none too keen and he missed the pitch that would have given New York its first American League pennant."

In 1939, Mabel Chesbro formally asked Major League Baseball for a review of the incident and considered the case closed. By then, the Baseball Hall of Fame had been open for three years and had elected 25 members, but not a deserving Chesbro. Election was a bit stingier in those days, and after electing nine members in 1939, only one person, Rogers Hornsby, was elected until 1945. One person in six years was hardly a track record and to put things in context, many worthy candidates were not elected or even came close. Lefty Grove didn't make it to the top ten in his first year of eligibility.

Just as today, there were two blocks of Hall of Fame voters — the Baseball Writers Association of America or BBWAA and an Old-Timers Committee. Why didn't more make it to Cooperstown in those years? For one thing, a rule had been passed that the BBWAA, responsible for considering those players whose careers fell after 1900, would conduct an election every three years rather than annually.

The Old-Timers Committee was another matter. Composed of Ed Barrow, the Yankee president; Bob Quinn, president of the Braves; Sid Mercer, a writer; and Connie Mack, the Committee just couldn't find the time to meet. For the same five-year period in which the BBWAA elected the one player, Hornsby, the Old-Timers Committee elected no one. It never even met.

One person in five years? Loud controversies met the Hall of Fame's reluctance to accept more people. And, as Bill James points out in his 1995 book *Whatever Happened to the Hall of Fame?* no election means no induction ceremony, nothing to report, no news…. The Hall of Fame's administrators were concerned that the Hall of Fame would suffer from the lack of attention."

In August 1944, Judge Kenesaw Mountain Landis changed the rules three months before his death. First, he gave them a clear mission to consider the election of pre–1900 players for the Hall. Then, he expanded the Old-Timers Committee to six and made them a permanent committee. Finally, he did the most important thing — appointed them as Hall of Fame trustees, responsible in turn for dictating the policies and rules of the entire Hall of Fame selection procedure.

That opened things up. In April 1945, with an absurdly high number of qualified candidates unable to gain election, the Old Timers went bananas. Voting in a troop ship full of long ago stars from Ed Delahanty and Fred Clarke to Hugh Duffy and King Kelly, 10 old-timers in all, which set the trend for future elections. Then, on July 3, 1945, they instructed the BBWAA to vote every year and this time, with a greatly expanded process to allow more people to make into Cooperstown.

A year later, the Old Timers Committee elected 11 more people, two of whom were Chesbro and Clark Griffith. Others making it that year were the famous Chicago Cubs double play combo, Joe Tinker, Johnny Evers and Frank Chance, along with Jesse Burkett, Tom McCarthy, Iron Man McGinnity and a trio of A's pitchers, Eddie Plank, Chief Bender and Rube Waddell.

Happy Jack Chesbro was finally in the Hall of Fame, as was the ball he used to throw the famous pockmarked wild pitch. It's dry now, but still pretty nicked up and pockmarked from the day nearly 100 years ago when Chesbro used it for the pitch that would keep the Highlanders out of the World Series.

12

Prince Hal

"There ain't much to being a ballplayer — if you're a ballplayer."
— *Honus Wagner*

Something else of consequence had happened that fateful October of 1904. It seemed like no big deal at the time and it took place a long way from New York, but in the end, its consequences would have far greater impact than any one game or pitch.

On October 4, 1904, eight days before Jack Chesbro uncorked his infamous wild pitch, the Highlanders made another move that in retrospect was huge — purchasing the contract of a young Californian named Hal Chase from the Los Angeles Looloos for $2,700. The reviews were promising. Chase had just completed his first and only season in the Pacific Coast League, where he had hit .279, fielded like a dream and stolen 37 bases. It was a solid deal, or so it seemed.

Years later, no one who ever saw Chase questioned his extraordinary talent as the first great New York Highlander/Yankee, the best until Babe Ruth. "Prince Hal" was his most common nickname, although sometimes it was just "Prince," or simply "fabulous," yes, "fabulous." As the Highlanders' best player, he was personable, gregarious and Hollywood handsome. He was the first major leaguer to star in a feature film and is thought to have had his likeness on more baseball cards than anybody else in the era.

For a few years anyway, Hal Chase was fabulous, a "Fancy Dan" in the lingo of the day. From the minute Chase replaced John Ganzel as the Highlanders' first baseman at the beginning of the 1905 season, sportswriters couldn't contain themselves. "He is a natural ... fast as greased lightning, easily confident and brainy," wrote one, "He seems to know what it meant by inside ball." Added Frank Graham of *The New York Journal-American* on Chase's death years later: "Just as, at shortstop, there was only one Wagner, so, at first base, there was only one Chase, greater than Gehrig or Terry or anyone else you care to name."

Mostly, they gushed about his fielding and his seemingly effortless ability to anticipate the throw and speed in getting to the bag. Those abilities helped Chase achieve things that no other baseball player of the era could dream of doing. "Because of his speed and his agility and quickness, he played better than any first baseman in the business," said longtime A.L. umpire George Moriarty. "Never mind me, just throw to the bag and I'll be there in time to take the throw,' Chase would tell his infielders. Pitcher Nick Altrock said, "He was the greatest first baseman of all-time."

Chase could hit too. In 1906, his second season in the majors, he hit .323. In four other seasons, he would eclipse .300, including his best year, 1916, when he batted .339 for the Cincinnati Reds. His lifetime average on finally retiring in 1919: .291.

Better reserve most of a day to wade through the Hal Chase file at the Baseball Hall of Fame in Cooperstown. It takes awhile, for Chase's long, twisting career is better documented than just about any other player of his era. With his personable, seemingly easy-going persona, he made good copy. But walk down the hallway from the library in Cooperstown and look for his plaque in the Hall of Fame Gallery and there's a surprise: Chase isn't there. He was never elected, and today is all but forgotten.

What happened? As can happen in a complicated life, all kinds of things. Not only was Chase the most crooked player to ever play the game, he pursued his corruption brazenly and openly. For a few years, he was a model citizen and celebrated for it. But starting in 1908, he became the most notorious thrower of games, a night-crawling wise guy and a thoroughly corrupt man who remained the idol of New York, but whose ultimate achievement, baseball researcher Bill James writes, was that "one man could so alter the ethics of the sport."

"Could he really have existed, or was he perhaps invented by Robert Louis Stevenson, along with the Master of Ballantrae, Long John Silver and the good Dr. Jekyll?" writes James, perhaps only slightly sarcastic in his *Historical Baseball Abstract*. "Chase's lost charm is something which can be forever speculated about, but it seems to me fairly safe to say that he was a borderline psychotic, that he was one of those people — you probably have known one or two yourself— to whom lies and truth were all the same, and who eventually was not always certain in his own mind when he was lying and when he was telling the truth."

Chase's shenanigans became an open secret in baseball circles. He did his busi-

Hal Chase from his 1909 baseball card, produced by Piedmont Cigarettes.

ness with gamblers, not only behind closed doors at McGraw's, but right at the office — the ballpark, where his wise guys occupied the best seats, and even in the clubhouse. Yet, baseball did nothing definitive about gambling until after the World Series fix of 1919, in which Chase is alleged to have played a central role. Why the inaction? For one reason, a lot of people were doing it. Another reason was that throughout Chase's tempestuous 8½ years in New York, he was hands-down the best player and biggest drawing card in the league's most important market. Life with Chase was full of "yets" and "buts." To his teammates, he was well-liked, with an edge; there was some dark side that defied description. There was always something about Hal Chase that wasn't quite clear.

Even his personal life became a mess. Married in 1908, Chase had a son in 1910 and two years later, was embroiled in a contentious divorce that was eagerly covered in the papers. Well documented was Chase's flimsy fight against alimony payments, not to mention his extracurricular affairs. Married again, in 1913, he was divorced a few years later and his randy ways became fodder all over again.

James and others go too far. No question Chase was corrupt. And no question he was a complex man, alternately pleasant and cruel and ever so enigmatic. But a borderline psychotic? An amoral, twisted beast? No and no again. The truth was somewhere in the middle. Try incorrigible, undisciplined, irresponsible and spoiled. And try someone with a knack for making a buck and blowing it. Nearly a century later, Hal Chase still makes good copy.

But all that was far in the future at the end of 1904. Chase was 21 at the time, newly signed and already being groomed as the Highlanders first baseman of the future. He was that good.

Chase had come from Los Gatos, California, south of San Francisco and christened either Harold W. or Harold Homer Chase — to this day, nobody really knows for sure. The son of a lumber executive, Chase was the youngest of six children and had what seems to be an idyllic childhood playing baseball. Academics was never an interest — Chase was a high school sophomore dropout — and he developed his talents as a ballplayer by playing on semi-pro teams with a mostly older crowd.

Chase's first break came when Charlie Graham, who had caught for Sacramento in the California League, recommended Chase to the Brothers at Santa Clara University, where he enrolled in 1902. Still not much of a student, Chase later boasted that while he enjoyed his college years and played every inning of every game there, he never even attended a class at Santa Clara.

What Chase did in college was play a lot of baseball, mostly second base, along with some first and pitching. It was at Santa Clara, coached by ex-Baltimore Oriole pitcher Joe Corbett, that Chase perfected his agility in the field, especially at first, along with a strong arm and an ability at the plate to drive the ball hard to all fields.

There, as in the future, it was Chase's unorthodox play at first that drew the most attention. The custom in those days was for the first basemen to be almost stationary and play close to the bag. Not Chase, who used his speed to play far off the bag, so he could charge bunts and throw out runners trying to advance. It was right there and then that Hal Chase created the blueprint for playing first base that is copied to this day.

It was on the West Coast that Chase, like a lot of good collegiate players in those days, he played in various pro leagues — during the summer of 1903, for Victoria, British Columbia of the Southwest Washington League and then with the PCL's Los Angeles in 1904.

Chase's journey to the Pacific Coast League was fast. On March 5, 1904, second baseman Chase went with Santa Clara to Los Angeles to play St. Vincent's College, later Loyola University, where he went three-for-six, with a double and three stolen bases in a 13–8 win — and St. Vincent's first loss in three years. Taking notice was the next day's *Los Angeles Times*, which called him "the fastest ever seen in an amateur game in Los Angeles."

Also taking notice was one Jim Morley, who, in a curious kind of dead ball jobshare, was the day's umpire who doubled as the Looloos owner. On March 12, Chase struck out 10 in pitching Santa Clara to a 4–3 win over Stanford. On St. Patrick's Day, Morley signed him to a contract. Chase's signing bonus: a .22 rifle, bought at a Los Angeles hardware store.

Chase's timing was fortunate. The month before had seen Looloos first baseman Cap Dillon awarded to Brooklyn as part of the Peace Agreement between the P.C.L. and Organized Baseball, leaving a big gap in the team's talent. Again the papers piped up: "Before he had practiced five minutes at first, (he) was solid with the crowd," crowed the *Times* after his debut, March 27 against Oakland. "If Chase isn't a great natural ball player, then Los Angeles never saw one," the *Examiner* added two days later.

Enter Dan Long, the Highlanders' San Francisco-based West Coast scout. With Chase fielding and hitting his way to a respectable season, Long sent glowing reports back to New York. And so, during the winter meetings in October, the Highlanders drafted Hal Chase from Los Angeles for $800.

But like so many things in Hal Chase's life, even that wasn't so simple. Some months later, Morley claimed that the Highlanders' move violated the Peace Agreement, which stipulated that no P.C.L. player could be drafted until November 1. Refusing to let Chase go, Morley made it even more complicated when the following March, he and the P.C.L. signed a new agreement with other high minor leagues, changing the drafting rules for good.

So, on March 20, Chase signed again with the Looloos — three days after he purchased a railroad ticket in Los Angeles for New Orleans, which was presumably the right direction and most of the way toward Natchez, Mississippi, where the Highlanders were spending spring training. In stepped Ban Johnson, who, in a Ban Johnson kind of way, dispatched a sternly-worded wire demanding that Chase be permitted to join New York. And at the urging of Clark Griffith came Dan Long from San Francisco to try to sort things out.

The dual strategy worked. Finally, on March 23, Chase boarded the train for Natchez. Five days later, he arrived in Jackson, Mississippi, and made his spring training debut the following day, March 29, col-

lecting a single in three at-bats, scoring a run and stealing a base in a 5–0 whitewash of Jackson of the Cotton States League.

Chase said he was happy to be in camp, saying the fault wasn't his for "throwing down Griffith," but belonged entirely to Morley, who had him scared. In reality, something else happened: Just prior to leaving, Chase's 23-year-old brother, Edwin, had died after surgery for acute appendicitis. Understandably, the Highlanders prospect had gone home to Los Gatos to be with his family. Once again, twice in the same month and before he'd ever played a regular big league game, Hal Chase had attracted a strange kind of attention.

But all was quickly forgotten as Chase went to work. Quickly inserted in the starting line-up, Chase became part of the Highlanders' traveling cast as they barnstormed north. After two more games against Jackson, the team went to Macon and then Columbus, where they opened up that city's new ballpark and beat up on most of the minor league opposition.

Chase's arrival was the talk of spring training, most of it spent in Montgomery, Alabama. To pave the way, Ganzel had been unloaded back at the winter meetings in February to Detroit. Reporters had conducted a kind of daily countdown in anticipation of his arrival. After he arrived, they marveled at his abilities, gushing in print.

Meanwhile, Griffith ran his usual demanding camp. With his team's hotel a hilly two miles from the ballpark, he had his players walk or run to practice several times. On the morning of March 17, with the grounds too wet for practice, he took his team out for a six-mile run. Everyone went, except for Clarkson, Orth, Anderson and Williams, who lucked out by instead playing basketball at a nearby gym. When the sun came out in the afternoon, it was back to the ball field for a two-hour practice.

One reason for the hard work was the Highlanders themselves — an aging crew by major league standards, and, except for Ganzel going and Chase coming, virtually unchanged from the year before. Among them were Keeler, coming off a .343 batting average, Williams at second and Elberfeld, both of whom hit .263. Other than Chase, the other major addition was 25-year-old rookie pitcher Buffalo Bill Hogg.

Nobody was really watching the others anyway. All eyes were on Chase. Back in New York for a week's worth of exhibition games before the opener, Chase went hitless in a 7–1 thrashing of Jersey City on April 8. But it was the first glimpse many in the New York area had of the future star and they were impressed. Even the musty, old *New York Times*, not given to flattery, was impressed. "The work of Chase, the Californian … was accounted the best in the game," the paper gushed. "His display in the field was the work of an artist, and the opinion of old baseball 'fans' was that he was undoubtedly the greatest 'find' seen on a baseball field in a long time."

Two days later in the Highlanders' final local exhibition — and their first game at the Hilltop since the day Jack Chesbro threw his wild pitch six months ago — the *Times* again waxed poetic about the new guy. "There was much curiosity to see Chase, the Californian, who made a deep impression at first base," the paper said in its summary of the Highlanders 5–1 win over Newark. "The newcomer is young, active and uses excellent judgment, something not often seen in a minor league player. He throws left-handed and unlike most left-handed players, throws fast and accurately. He is lively on the bases, and at the bat stands like a man who should be able to hit."

Five days later, on April 14, the regular season kicked off to the usual grand prognostications that, well, just about everyone was a contender. Ban Johnson,

ever the statesman, was looking forward to a season that would "bring the eight clubs to the chalk line on edge and well fortified." Was he hoping they'd improve their diets? In 1905, the smart money was riding on the prospects of not only the Highlanders, but of Philadelphia behind strong pitching, Cleveland behind Lajoie and Boston, with its consistency.

Adding to the Highlanders' competition was that other New York team, the Giants. On April 14, with the Highlanders opening on the road in Washington, D.C., against the Senators, the defending N.L. champs celebrated their first pennant in 16 years in grand style before that afternoon's opener against the Boston Braves.

Kicking things off was an impromptu parade that carried both the Giants and Braves in cars to the Polo Grounds. Starting from a garage at 1684 Broadway, the uniformed teams wended through the big city, traveling south down 5th Avenue, all the way to Washington Square. Looping around the Square, they turned into 4th Avenue, headed back to Broadway, on to 8th Avenue, and headed north all the way to the Polo Grounds for the 3 p.m. game.

McGraw ensured his Giants played it to maximum dramatic effect. Their vehicle flaunted pennants of yellow bunting bearing the inscription in black letters, "Champion Giants." The only problem was traffic; when 3 p.m. came and went and there was still no sign of the teams, many in the overflow crowd estimated at 40,000 grew restless.

Their concern didn't last long. At 3:01 p.m., a flock of carrier pigeons, released way downtown as a message to the throng that the teams' arrival was imminent, passed over the Polo Grounds. That prompted a big cheer and the delicious irony of a baseball crowd cheering, not the action on the field, but pigeons. Precisely 11 minutes later, the first car arrived, sending up a greater cheer, loud enough that it "might have been heard in Battery Park," as one reporter put it.

The cars headed through the center field gate and onto the field. First out was McGraw — naturally — followed by Mathewson, and then George Browne, Bill Dahlen, Art Devlin, and lastly, Iron Man McGinnity, the day's pitcher. The teams then headed into the clubhouse and quickly filed back to the field for more drama — the ceremonial flag raising. Stretched across home plate, the blue and yellow flag featured the inscription, "Giants, Champion Baseball Club of National League, 1904." And with that, McGraw took hold of the flag as members of the team picked it up en masse, and on to and up the flag pole. The Star Spangled Banner and the first pitch from Mayor George B. McClellan, Jr. followed, and with that the season was underway.

The game itself was anti-climactic. McGinnity gave up one run on three singles and a walk, and even a triple. The Giants cruised 10–1. On a damp, chilly day down in Washington, the Highlanders cruised too, 4–2 behind Chesbro, with a home run from Williams and two hits each from Chase, Dougherty and Anderson, now the starting center fielder. For Chase, batting seventh, a double and a single off Case Patten was hardly a bad day's performance for his first day in the big leagues.

But the success of the Giants demonstrated another reality in New York — the Giants were still very much the main attraction and the Highlanders were still very much the interlopers, or the Invaders, as they were still sometimes derisively labeled. Indeed, the fates seemed against the New Yorkers when, a week later, they tried opening at home themselves. They were rained out.

Frank Farrell and the Highlanders did what they could. For the first time in three seasons, the Hilltop's field was in prime playing condition for an opener — "as level as a billiard table (and) prepared with much

care," a reporter wrote. They got the Senators again and Chesbro on the mound to face them. They got music as well, in this case, the 69th Regiment Band along with the usual player's parade and a lot of dignitaries, like Ban Johnson and Big Tim Sullivan, who took first-pitch honors.

More importantly, they finally got adequate transportation to and from the ballpark. Cranks could now take the subway to the 157th Street station, a five minute walk from the ballpark, thanks to the IRT's new construction, which had opened the extra track and the station the previous November. That, along with express trains from the Brooklyn Bridge to 157th Street — a 25-minute trip — and the Third and Amsterdam avenues' surface cars, all made the journey to northern Manhattan more enticing.

It all helped draw about 15,000 to the Hilltop, despite the rain. Anxious not to disappoint the crowd, Farrell plunged ahead with the festivities. And promptly at 3:30 p.m., Sullivan uncorked his ceremonial pitch and Chesbro got to work on the Senators. But by the time the Highlanders came to bat in the fourth, rain was falling in buckets and the field too soggy to continue. Umpire Thomas Connolly stopped the game and waited the allotted 30 minutes before calling the game for good.

Out of the disappointment, Farrell had a brainstorm. Why not try it again the next day — Saturday, April 22 — and let everyone in for free? Okay, so you don't clear much of a profit, but you earn the gratitude of a lot of New Yorkers and score one for public relations. Farrell had demonstrated yet again his aptitude for building interest in a big league club: About 25,000 of those New Yorkers took his offer on a pleasant, dry day. That's a mob, by most accounts, and 150 policemen on hand, many of them from the 157th Street police station, had their hands full, mostly on account of the army of neighborhood boys trying to enter the ballpark, long before game time.

Quickly, police deduced they had a challenge on their hands: admit all those boys and there wouldn't be room for another soul. After talking to Farrell, police made a quick rule: no boy under 16 would be admitted, unless accompanied by an adult. Wise to the new rule, many of the adolescent crowd quickly lined up, waiting to pick off adults who might vouch for them.

"Only boys accompanied by their fathers were admitted," the *Times* reported. "Many bachelors adopted sons during the afternoon." Incidentally, the Highlanders mysteriously lost nine new baseballs before the afternoon was up and every time a foul ball fell in the stands, it disappeared, contrary to the rule in those days that it must be returned.

The policemen worked throughout the day to keep the clogged aisles as open as possible. In addition to the cops, there were 15 firemen and another 21 club employees, most of whom actually spent the day underneath the stands, with 10 lines of hose for water and buckets in the event that spectators dropped burning cigars and other trash that could start a fire.

In the end, it didn't matter, for the crowd was well-behaved and for the most part, appreciative. One exception, reported in great detail but sounding made-up, was the tale of several women who became upset that the crush of people kept them from seeing much of the game.

"Oh John," shrieked one such woman at her date. "How could you bring me where I can't see the game and have me all crushed up in such a crowd?"

"Mamie, I told you it was a free show and that we ought to be early," said John. "I called at noon and begged you to come. I waited two hours to let you manicure your nails, curl your hair and put on all that finery. Every half hour, I called to you that we would be late."

"You horrid thing," Maggie shot back. "The next time I go anywhere with you, be sure you have reserved seats. Charley would never have treated me so."

Ah yes, the game: Clarkson went the distance and the Highlanders took advantage of Washington errors from their old friend, Bill Wolfe, and second baseman Jim Mullin to coast 5–3. All in all, it was a good start.

For all the optimism, the Highlanders never really got on track in 1905. Most notably flat was Chesbro, who won some and lost some, but really seemed to be showing the effects of a tired arm after all. Gone were the days when Happy Jack pitched on two days' rest; in contrast to 1904, when he pitched in 55 games, good for 454 innings, Chesbro's 41 games and 303 innings in '05 were an output far from his best.

Not that Chesbro's season was exactly a failure: He still went 20–15, posting a 2.20 E.R.A. to lead the staff, but to put it in context, it was less than half the innings he had pitched in '04. Matching him almost inning-for-inning was Al Orth, the 32-year-old former 20-game winner with the Phillies, and acquired from the Senators the year before. Orth pitched 305 innings, going 17–16 with a 2.86 E.R.A.

Nor did the Highlanders get the pitching they needed from others. After 25 games, the team was in a funk, stuck at 11–14 and ahead of only Boston, the defending A.L. champs who, inexplicably, were in more of a funk. On May 17, with the Highlanders on their first western swing of the season, "Buffalo Bill" Hogg lost to the Browns 3–1. Hogg fell behind from the get-go, giving up two runs in the first inning, and the team was a disaster in the field, committing five errors.

So Griffith made a move, sending Clarkson to Jersey City of the Eastern League for more seasoning. The term used was "temporarily released," but the point was clear: Despite what one newspaper called "the careful coaching supervision" of both Griffith and Chesbro, the young former Harvard pitcher was finding it tough slogging in the big leagues. For Clarkson, whose much-older brothers were Dad and the future of Hall of Famer John Clarkson, a right-handed mainstay of the Cubs and Braves during the 1890s, carrying the legacy would have to wait.

So much for the rest of the staff. Hogg would win all of seven games, Griffith seven and Powell seven, before being traded to St. Louis. For Powell, a 23-game winner in 1904, it was a precipitous drop in numbers; the right-hander would labor on seven more years for the Browns, winning 16 games in 1908, and retiring after the 1912 season. Added to the rag-tag staff — one Ambrose Puttmann with a final record of 2–7 and an E.R.A. of 4.27.

Compared to the rest of the league, the Highlanders' pitching was a legitimate breakdown that season of 1905. It was, after all, the year of years for the pitcher, a season, as baseball historian Thomas Gilbert says, when the "dead ball was never deader than in American League."

Only two men — Keeler and Cleveland's Elmer Flick — batted more than .300 in 1905. Wee Willie batted .302, and Flick, .306, pacing the American League. It was the lowest average to win a batting title in either league until Carl Yastrzemski's .301 in 1968, that other "year of the pitcher." The entire league batted only .241, whereas, on the pitchers' side, all eight teams had E.R.A.s under 3.00.

Pitchers had a field day in 1905. Eddie Plank of the A's led the A.L. with 26 wins, followed by Rube Waddell with 24. Waddell also took the E.R.A. title at 1.48, with the next four pitchers on the list — Cy Young, "Doc" White and Nick Altrock of the White Sox, along with another member of the A's, Andy Coakley — all under 1.89. Of all the all-time top pitchers in lifetime E.R.A., 15 pitched in 1905.

For the enigmatic Waddell, it was another successful season amidst personal discord. On February 7, Waddell had escaped serious injury by carrying a burning stove from a store in Peabody, Massachusetts. Three days later, he fled the town to escape charges on assaulting his wife's parents.

Waddell, Plank, Coakley, and Chief Bender were the major reason the Philadelphia A's won the A.L. pennant in '05. Down the stretch in September, Waddell pitched 44 consecutive scoreless innings to help the A's hold off the surging White Sox by two games. The Chicago pitching was actually better on paper with White, Altrock, Frank Owen and Frank Smith combining for a team E.R.A. of 1.99. Add to their staff the continued improvement of Big Ed Walsh, who went 9–4, joining Chesbro on the slim list of big leaguers who could control the spitball. How ironic then that it was the A's offense — paced by first baseman Harry Davis, who led the league in runs scored, RBIs and doubles — that gave them the edge in winning the A.L.

Languishing far down in fifth place with a 71–78 final record and 21½ games off the pace were the Highlanders. There were some bright spots — Keeler's .301 — but overall, it was a mediocre season for the New Yorkers. Elberfeld turned in a .262 average and former Tiger Joe Yeager had perhaps his best major league season, filling in for Conroy at third and batting .267. The versatile Conroy himself spent most of the year filling in for others at five positions.

But for center fielder Dave Fultz, the season came to an abrupt and painful end. On September 30 at the Hilltop, Bill Bradley of the Naps hit a ball to short center field that both Fultz and Elberfeld tried to catch. With Fultz running full-steam ahead and Elberfeld backing up from shortstop, neither called the ball and they collided violently.

It knocked both men cold. Before a packed house of 20,000, three doctors ran out to where they lay and worked over both men for 10 minutes, before Elberfeld, the luckier of the two, walked off the field nursing a nasty gash over his right eye and cuts on the chin, nose and cheek. It took three stitches to close the wounds.

More seriously injured was Fultz. He lay motionless and then went into shock, before being carried to the clubhouse by two teammates on an improvised stretcher. He was sent to Washington Heights Hospital, where he recovered consciousness, but was found to have broken both his jaw and nose.

For the popular Fultz, the injury was ironic — as a star football player at Brown University in the late 1890s, he had never suffered as serious an injury as he did here. The collision not only ended Fultz's season, but forced a career change: After the season, he decided to call it quits, choosing instead to focus on a burgeoning law career. Call him the Yankees' first renaissance man: With an eye to life beyond baseball, Fultz, who was also a noted pianist, had enrolled a few years earlier at Columbia Law School and, in February 1905, passed the New York Bar.

Fultz went into partnership with former Brown football teammate Fred Murphy, the two hanging a shingle at 41 Wall Street. It wouldn't be the last Fultz would be heard from in baseball circles; in 1912, following a players' strike by Detroit, he led the new players' union. Later, he'd become president of the International League. For the record, he would bat .271 lifetime in an injury-plagued seven-year major league career. For the Yankees, he'd be remembered as the team's first center fielder; and the man who had the team's first base hit and scored its first run.

Continuing to impress was the young Chase. He hit only .249, but his fielding opened eyes, and before the season was done, he was being hailed as a star. Chase's defensive play stood out; he developed the now-common tactic of charging bunts and drifting into the outfield for cutoff throws. Never mind his league-leading 31 errors at the position — his miscues in the field would get a bit more attention in future years — Chase was a master of the phenomenal play and rapidly became a crowd favorite.

Typical of Chase's play and telling of the Highlanders' frustrating season was the first trip to the Hilltop of Napoleon Lajoie and the Cleveland Blues. The wily Lajoie had heard all about Chase, particularly about a play, with a man on second and the hitter trying to advance him by bunting toward third, in which the young first baseman broke for the plate with the pitch — and cut across in the front of the pitcher to scoop up the ball and nail the advancing runner at third.

Nowadays, a batter of Lajoie's caliber would swing, hoping to drive the ball into the outfield to drive the runner in. But not so in the dead ball era. Hankering to get at the Highlanders, Lajoie was adamant: "I hope he tries that on me," he said. "If he does, I'll fix him so he won't try it again — on me or anybody else."

He got his chance in that first game, June 8. The scenario was exactly as the Cleveland star and first-year player-manager had surmised: Facing Chesbro with a man on second and nobody out, Lajoie faked a bunt but let it go, hoping to see what Chase would do. Sure enough, the first baseman ran in to a position almost in front of the plate.

Lajoie smiled to himself, thinking of how he'd dismember Chase by driving the next pitch. In came Chesbro's next pitch. And in came Chase. Lajoie swung hard, but Chase, only a few feet away, speared the ball cleanly in his gloved hand, then methodically turned and tossed to Williams at second, doubling up the runner off the bag. Score one for the new guy; the ruse had failed.

Hal Chase wasn't the only promising

newcomer in 1905. So it went on August 30, with the fourth-place Highlanders at Bennett Park in Detroit to face the sixth-place Tigers, and partook in a piece of history. With about 1,200 in attendance, the Tigers got off to a quick start off New York's Jack Chesbro when left fielder Matty McIntyre led off with a double and Pinky Lindsay, the first baseman, singled him home.

Lindsay then went to second on a sacrifice bunt by Germany Schaefer and third on Sam Crawford's tapper back to Chesbro. Up to the plate stepped an 18-year-old native of Augusta, Georgia, playing in his first major league game. Positioning himself in a slight crouch with his feet about a foot apart and knees bent slightly and holding the bat with his hands about three inches apart, the new man swung through Chesbro's first pitch, a high fastball. He took a curveball for strike two. But on the next pitch, he swung again, and laced Chesbro's fastball into the left-center field gap for a double to score Lindsay.

The batter's name was Ty Cobb. And although he walked the next time up and went hitless the rest of the way, his hit helped the Tigers beat the Highlanders 5–3 behind the pitching of George Mullin. Along the way, he watched and absorbed the major league game, where softies weren't tolerated. "Such speed, class, style, speedy maneuvering, lightning thinking!" he would say years later about his first day in the big leagues. "And they went at it with such a red-eyed determination I couldn't believe." In that game alone, Schaefer knocked down Elberfeld when the Highlander shortstop blocked his way on the base path. When Frank Delahanty slid into third, he tore his ankle tendons and was done for the year. And when Tigers third baseman and captain Bill Coughlin argued with umpire Silk O'Loughlin, he was thrown out of the game.

Cobb caught on fast. He appeared in all of the Tigers' remaining 41 games, hit-ting only .240, but helping the Detroits improve from seventh the year before to edge Boston for third. Rough around the edges, he nonetheless showed potential, impressing those who watched him play. "An infant prodigy" and "a sensational fielder and thrower," wrote Paul Bruske of the *Detroit Times* in a *Sporting Life* column.

Their instincts were right. That double off Chesbro was the first of Cobb's 4,189 hits, a record not topped until 1985 by Pete Rose. He continued to learn and became the dead-ball era's greatest hitter, and arguably, the greatest ballplayer in history. In hindsight, it was remarkable that Cobb had made it to the major leagues when he did; his debut came precisely three weeks after a tragedy of mind-numbing proportions — the double-barrel shotgun slaying of his father, a much-loved rural school teacher, by his mother, who, the story goes, had mistaken him for a prowler. His mother, Amanda, was later acquitted, but nobody can ever calculate the emotional damage it must have caused the son.

Proud, intense and already overly-sensitive, Cobb said little of the incident publically. But what demons it must have unleashed both on the field and off. Cobb's tempestuous 24-year career was noted as much for ugly incidents as it was for base hits.

Cobb once pummeled a teammate who had the nerve to jump in the bathtub ahead of him. He beat up a grocery boy and once punched a friend who left him with the restaurant check. Cobb displayed a decided animosity toward Negroes and got into fights at various times with a black elevator operator and a black night watchman. An early Billy Martin? No. Cobb was worse, having even been arrested after an argument with a female cashier over a glass of water. Whatever the reasons, he was a mean, amoral, bigoted racist for whom New Yorkers, as we'll see later, seemed to reserve particular venom.

Other, more quirky events unfolded that season of 1905. On April 30 at a minor league game in Evansville, Indiana, future big league umpire Cy Rigler raised his right arm to indicate strikes for the first time. It was so his friends sitting in the bleachers could distinguish the calls — and it quickly became part of the game.

On September 17, with the Highlanders still in fourth place, they took on the Senators in a doubleheader at the Hilltop. But with Jimmy Williams out of the lineup and finding themselves short of infielders, Griffith took the sure-handed Keeler, a lefty, out of right field and played him in both games at second base. It worked, with Keeler committing only one error. The teams split.

Less than a month later — on October 7 in Boston — the Highlanders' season mercifully ended with a doubleheader loss to the Pilgrims. If it was a poor season for the New Yorkers, it was nearly as bad for Boston, where the great Cy Young, somehow, finished with a stellar 1.82 E.R.A., but a record of 17–19. Things weren't so good in Cleveland either, where, despite Flick's batting title, Lajoie's season ended after a bad spiking led to a case of blood poisoning.

Heading into the World Series, the A's looked invincible behind their powerful starting pitchers. Their N.L. opponents: the Giants of Brush and McGraw, who had somehow come around to the idea of actually agreeing to the league-sanctioned concept of a best-of-seven World's Series.

As if it were a tough choice: the two, still nursing the grudges of Giant players from a year ago, faced the promise of a big payday. As in 1904, the Giants had dominated the N.L. in '05, moving into first place for good on April 23. This time, the Giants won 105 games, nine games up on the Pirates, behind their big mound meal tickets —

Mathewson (32–8 with an astounding 1.27 E.R.A.), McGinnity (21–15, 2.87), and the 23-year-old right-hander Leon "Red" Ames (22–8, 2.74). Elsewhere, Turkey Mike Donlin hit .356, good for third in the more batter-friendly National League.

Small wonder the World Series that year was almost anti-climactic. It took the Giants only five games to completely dominate their A.L. opponents. Their only runs: three in game two. The overwhelming reason: three Series shutouts by Mathewson.

Taking particular notice that fall was a young reporter named Grantland Rice, who covered the Series for *The Atlanta Journal.* "I marvel at what Matty has done," he wrote. "In those few days, he was the greatest pitcher I've ever seen. I believe he could have continued to pitch shutouts until Christmas."

At 25, Rice was the same age as Mathewson and the two became fast friends — golfing together and playing checkers, chess and poker, with the hyper-competitive Mathewson usually winning. It didn't matter; after Rice moved to New York and became syndicated around the country, he wrote often about the pitcher who combined pinpoint control with impeccable habits in the private life. It helped spread the legend of the pitcher who was a gentleman and a matinee idol too.

If Clark Griffith was already tightly-wound, the disappointing '05 Highlanders only hardened him for 1906. The Highlanders of '05 had been an undisciplined bunch, so heading into the New Yorkers' fourth season, Griffith got tough.

You could sense it March 5 as the team departed Penn Station, Jersey City, for spring training in Birmingham. Some 200 Highlander fans gave the team a rousing send-off to Griffith and several of his players — Chesbro; Keeler; Dougherty; catcher

Ira Thomas; Mike Martin, the trainer; and a 26-year-old rookie right-handed pitcher Louis LeRoy, the team's first Native American. In years past, Chesbro would be off coaching baseball at Harvard and didn't arrive at spring training until mid–March. But not this year: Griffith was adamant that every eligible player should report on time.

The players got the message. Meeting the Jersey City contingent on arriving in Birmingham were six more Highlanders who had been resting in Hot Springs before the start of the season. "Boiling out" at the Arkansas resort, as the papers called it, were Elberfeld; Doc Newton; catchers Red Kleinow and Deacon McGuire; along with two new acquisitions named Hahn. That's right, the Highlanders were heading into 1906 with a veteran left-handed pitcher, Frank "Noodles" Hahn, late of the Reds, and a rookie outfielder named Ed "Noodles" Hahn. How fitting that the two, who were not related but shared a nickname, became friends.

Others made it to Birmingham in their own way. Boarding the train in his hometown of Camden, New Jersey was Conroy. And coming in from California was Chase. For the first time, Griffith had a full complement of Highlanders as spring training kicked off March 6. The team seemed pretty strong after all. Said Senators manager Jake Stahl: "If Grif' ever happens to get his bunch working right, and not too many accidents happen, they are a mighty dangerous proposition. If luck breaks right, the New Yorks can win their share of games from any team in the business."

Stahl had a point. Ripping through the usual inferior minor league opposition, the Highlanders did seem a tad more determined this season. Griffith himself seemed pleased, but said little. He declined to predict how the team would do, claiming himself to be the only manager who never proclaimed a pennant before the season got underway. "We will do our best," was all Griffith would say.

But there *was* something different about the Highlanders in 1906. Chase was fielding better than ever and was shaping into a top-notch big-league hitter. And to prepare for their April 14 opener against Boston, the team found the Hilltop looking splendid — freshly painted apple green, covered with bunting and the banners of several nations that flew from flagpoles set atop the fences surrounding the ballpark.

To top it off, the team had new uniforms, with the interlocking "NY" of previous seasons separated, with the "N" on the right breast and the "Y" on the left. It was also the season that the newspaper scribes seemed to finally fix on a consistent nickname — Highlanders for the record, but increasingly the Yankees. Although the team would primarily be called Highlanders, a year or so later, they'd be the Yankees for good.

The team even had a completed subway to look forward to at last. In late-February, the six-year tunneling to Washington Heights was finally done, meaning fans could take the Interborough Company line to the new station at 167th Street and walk the short one block to the ballpark entrance.

To emphasize the positive, the Highlanders were due to open the season for the first time on a Saturday, guaranteeing a good crowd, and also for the first time, ahead of the Giants, who had started the day before on the road. And with the Chesbro getting ready to take on Boston's Cy Young in a match-up of pitching greats, a true wonder-of-wonders happened when Highlander President Joseph Gordon opened his mail. Inside was a telegram wishing the team luck from Giants President John Brush, finally willing perhaps to bury the hatchet. "I wish you luck artistically and financially," it read.

The opener stuck to the script. Despite windy gray weather, some 15,000 journeyed to the Hilltop for action. As usual, the crowd was festive, or as *The New York Press* put it, "The men looked prosperous, and the women were dressed in the height of metropolitan fashion." For the record, the first to arrive for the 4 p.m. game was a small boy — at 11 a.m. By 3:30 p.m., the stands were full, so much so that some spectators chose to watch from the roofs and windows of nearby buildings, with a few more agile types filling the two trees that stood just beyond center field.

Showing that the team's new nickname was catching, a band played the song "Yankee Doodle Dandy," to which a knot of bellicose fans sang along and added their own words in honor of the team's manager: "Yankee Griffith came to town, a ridin' on a bean can," they bellowed. "Collins furnished all the pork — O joy! 'twas a cinch man." Hearing them, Griffith smiled.

Then came the pre-game parade and something else, designed to tug on the New Yorkers' proverbial heartstrings. In strode John Montgomery Ward to throw out the game's first ball. Ward, a one-time Giant and Brooklyn Superba mainstay, was among the most popular players to ever don a uniform in New York and was now a successful lawyer in the city. Standing at home plate, Ward removed his hat, made a short speech and handed the ball to Griffith. The season was underway.

And what a tight, snappy game it was, with Chesbro edging Young 2–1 in 11 innings. The Highlanders broke first, scoring a run in the second on a single by Conroy, now in center field as a replacement for the recently-retired Fultz, and a two-out double to right by Chesbro. The Pilgrims got their run in the fifth, due to errors from new third baseman Frank LaPorte and Elberfeld. The New Yorkers won. When Williams doubled to left with one out, Conroy fouled out and Chase followed with a sharp grounder that bounded off the foot of shortstop Freddy Parent, who ran the ball down and threw home, but too late to catch Williams crossing the plate. The win set off a rowdy celebration with fans, as they were

now being called, doing war dances and tossing their hats in the air.

Chesbro had a more sober reaction. "I'm glad we won, but you are certainly a tough proposition," he told Young after the game.

"No, not tough," replied the great Cyclone. "Just a trifle difficult, you know." But for the good will that the game created for the New Yorkers, it was another bad start to what was becoming tough slogging for the Pilgrims.

Boston would have a dreadful time of it in 1906, losing 105 games and finishing smack-dab last, behind even the Senators. On May 25, they'd beat the White Sox to end a 20-game losing streak. Young would finish 13–21 that season, and Jimmy Collins would be replaced late in the season by Pilgrim outfielder and Royal Rooter icon Chick Stahl, Jake's brother. But the strain of managing would prove too tough for Stahl; on March 28, 1907, during spring training in West Baden, Indiana, he committed suicide by drinking four ounces of carbolic acid. With his body would be a note that read, "Boys, I just couldn't help it. You drove me to it." Chick Stahl was 34 years old.

For the Highlanders, those 200 fans who saw them off to spring training may have been a good sign after all. Behind Newton, the Highlanders beat the Pilgrims April 17 for the second win, and the next day, again, behind Hogg, in Boston's home opener. Make it three wins in their first three games.

The strong play continued. In late May and early June, the Highlanders ripped off 11 wins in a row, all at home. The performance "worked the old town up to a great pitch of enthusiasm," Joe Vila wrote of the streak in *The Sporting News*. On Saturday, June 3, the New Yorkers took on the A's in a doubleheader before an estimated 25,000 fans who filled the grandstand and stood 10 deep behind a rope that ringed the outfield. So the teams split, but the Highlanders left for their first extended western trip of the season — in first place, and a hair in front of the White Sox.

Vila wrote a few other things about the Highlanders in his weekly dispatches in *The Sporting News.* You remember him, the well-connected friend of Ban Johnson who had hooked him up back in the early days of 1903 with Farrell and Devery. Vila, the longstanding correspondent of the *New York Sun*, had started penning his weekly dispatches on the Highlanders for *The Sporting News* in 1904, and had become the team's biggest champion.

"I do not believe there is a team on earth that has played any faster ball than that shown by the Yankees in the last three weeks," he wrote in the June 9 *Sporting News.* "The team has been hitting the ball in a phenomenal manner and better still the fielding and base-running have been superb. The pitching has been fairly good, but the other departments of the game have been so powerful that all opponents have been swept off the map."

Vila reserved particular praise for Kid Elberfeld. Along with Griffith, the Tabasco Kid was the team's inspiration, whose batting, base-running and fielding "have been the talk of the town," Vila wrote. Chase came in for the usual praise — "hitting the ball on the nose, in addition to playing first base in brilliant style." There was equal praise for Williams at second, for the potent lead-off trio of Keeler, Elberfeld and Chase, and for the team's overall speed.

Having Vila on their side was a good omen. He had been with the *Sun* since 1893, after leaving Harvard, where he played baseball and football, and working as a brakeman on the Baltimore & Ohio Railroad. By the time he starting filing dispatches for *The Sporting News*, Vila was a man known for

using his legion of sources to break the big story.

Vila failed to hide neither his enthusiasm for the American League nor his disdain for the Giants, "If the Yankees can win the championship, I hope they will be able to tackle the Giants in the World's Series next fall, for Grif and his great team of hustlers will put it all over Brush's gang of kickers as sure as the sun rises and sets in the East."

Vila's reports spoke to a larger truth — that in their fourth year of life, the Highlanders were having a breakthrough season. Not only were they outplaying the Giants, but in drawing big, enthusiastic crowds to the Hilltop, they were making a full frontal assault on the Giants' longstanding hold of the affections of the New York sporting public.

Not only were the Yankees finally drawing well, but the crowds were enthusiastic and vocal in their support. On July 17, they mounted a sensational rally to beat the White Sox in the ninth inning, and spectators were so excited that several hundred burst on to the field, hoisting Chase to their shoulders and lugging him to the clubhouse. Two days later, after another improbable last-inning victory sparked by Williams's clutch hit, hundreds again surged on the field, with Williams getting the star treatment, borne away by adoring fans. "Never before at Highland Park were such wild demonstrations seen," wrote Vila. "The Giants formerly monopolized this mobbing business, but now the scenes have shifted. No wonder Freedman and Brush are shaking in their shoes."

Further evidence of a shift in the affections of New Yorkers were demonstrated downtown on Park Row, the section of lower Manhattan where the offices of Vila's *Mirror* and other major New York newspapers such as the *Globe, Commercial Advertiser* and the *Recorder* were housed. The custom in those days was to post information from the telegraph office on oversized news bulletins. Proving especially popular were the baseball scoreboards, and from what Vila observed, "you hear the crowds … in Park Row talking about Chesbro … Hal Chase, Elberfeld, Orth, Griffith, Keeler, Conroy and all of the men who are making history here for the American League."

The western swing went well and the Highlanders traded the A.L. lead with Cleveland and Philadelphia. But then Elberfeld went down and so did Newton. Still, with solid pitching from Chesbro and Orth, the team kept pace and sustained the interest of New Yorkers. It helped that in the National League, the Giants were not their invincible selves of the previous year and were being matched game-for-game by the Pirates and the surprising Cubs, led by Frank Chance and Johnny Evers.

"The swelling of the head in Harlem in going down slowly," Vila wrote of the Giants in the July 7 *Sporting News*. "When the Yankees win the pennant — and it looks like a cinch now — you'll never hear of the bumptious Giants and the Jay Hawk League. As I've said before in these columns, it will be all American League here by next year…. Here's to Clark Griffith, the best manager in the country, and to the fastest ball team in the world, the Yankees!"

Vila looked to Cleveland and Philadelphia as the New Yorkers' main opposition to win the American League. Nobody considered the White Sox, hovering about harmlessly in fourth place most of the season until early August, when they reeled off 19 straight wins to secure the pennant. The team would go down in history labeled as "the Hitless Wonders," which sounds nice, but hardly described the team's true make-up — adequate hitters backed by a strong starting pitching foursome of Nick Altrock (21 wins), Ed Walsh and Frank Owen, each with 19 and Doc White, with 18. The 25-year-old Walsh was showing continuing signs of the dominant pitcher he would

shortly become; on August 18, he struck Keeler out for only the second time in the season. The other strikeout? Yup, Walsh.

The Highlanders still managed to make things interesting. On August 30 at the Hilltop they faced the A.L. opponent now known as the Washington Nationals. They took both games — the first won 5–0 by a quirky 24-year-old rookie right-hander named Joe Doyle from Clay Center, Kansas. Purchased from the Wheeling, West Virginia, club for $2,500, Doyle had a herky-jerky pitching motion, a baffling, underhand delivery and a hardened composure.

All in all, it was quite a beginning for the man nicknamed "Slow" Joe for his time-consuming pace on the mound; five days before, he shut out Cleveland at the Hilltop in his first start. In doing so, Doyle became the first player in American League history to begin his career with two shutouts. Of his 24 lifetime victories in five big league seasons, seven would be shutouts.

Game two was a nailbiter, won by the Yanks, 9–8, on a run in the bottom of the 10th on a single by Wid Conroy. Scoring two for the Yankees was Chase, who spent an exhausting day by following his two hits in game one, with, of all things, three triples in the second. Three triples in a single game! It was a Yankee record that endures today. For good measure, the Prince added a double for four hits and eleven total bases in the game.

A day later, the New Yorkers, behind Chesbro and Orth, beat the Nationals in another doubleheader sweep, their second in two days and fourth and fifth wins in a row. It would have been a really good day, except that Elberfeld punched Conroy smack dab in the face and had to be separated by teammates, team officials and even a policeman or two. In the third inning of game two, with the Highlanders comfortably ahead 10–0, Elberfeld slid into first base and hurt his ankle. A bit excessive thought

Conroy, with such a lopsided score. He addressed his concern to Elberfeld, who promptly decked him. In the end though, it was all chalked up as a case of boys being boys: Conroy kept playing, collecting two singles and a triple in a lopsided 20–5 win.

The Highlanders did it again the next day — beating Washington in a doubleheader back at the Hilltop, behind Orth and Hogg. It was six in a row against the Nationals and seven straight altogether.

After the off day Sunday, the Philadelphia A's came to the Hilltop for a Labor Day twin bill, which the Highlanders swept, but again with some damage involving the hotheaded Kid Elberfeld. With the score knotted at 3–3 in game one, Danny Murphy of the A's stole third in a close play, quickly protested by the Yankees, many of whom quickly gathered around umpire Silk O'Loughlin, who had made the call from his position behind home plate. O'Loughlin just brushed them off and the argument seemed over, except for Elberfeld, who seemed incensed by the call and rushed the umpire, attempting to spike him.

Six times the enraged Elberfeld tried to gouge the umpire. Trying to protect himself, O'Loughlin threw up his hands, which Elberfeld grabbed, throwing him back. Three policemen rushed to home plate to protect the umpire and ushered the irate ballplayer toward the bench. The shaken O'Loughlin refused to allow the game to continue until Elberfeld had left the ballpark. But when the ballplayer reached the gate, he turned around and leaned on the fence, refusing to budge. Only when Griffith, fearing that the game would have be forfeited, went out to talk with Elberfeld did the testy ballplayer leave.

The disgraceful episode was among the most blatant exhibitions of baseball rowdyism ever witnessed. It took away from an otherwise banner day in which the Highlanders scored a run in the ninth inning of the first game to win 4–3, behind Slow Joe

Doyle, and beat Waddell, behind Chesbro, in the second game, to go back into the A.L. lead by percentage points.

That second game spelled more trouble for the beleaguered Silk O'Loughlin. With the A's ahead 3–1 in the ninth, Conroy singled to lead off and advanced when shortstop Lave Cross fumbled Keeler's hard smash. The runners advanced to second and third on Elberfeld's out, and when the next batter, Williams, sent the ball to short again, Keeler ran into Cross and the ball rolled into the outfield. Both runners scored, knotting the score. This time, it was the A's, led by their captain Harry Davis, who were incensed. Claiming that Keeler interfered with Cross, they argued long and hard, but to no avail. Twice O'Loughlin ordered the A's to leave the field and twice they refused. So he awarded the game to Highlanders by a forfeit, 9–0. They had won their fourth doubleheader in as many days and eighth and ninth games in a row.

Looking back, you wonder what the American League schedule maker was thinking. That night, the Highlanders piled into a train at Grand Central and journeyed to Boston for yet another doubleheader the next day — their fifth in as many playing days. And again they won both games, behind shutouts from Clarkson and Orth. It was their 10th and 11th straight wins and kept them in first place.

But in between games, the Highlanders got some bad, but expected news. Ban Johnson suspended Elberfeld for good, removing the team's captain and spiritual leader in the middle of a pennant race. Between injuries and suspensions, it had been a frustrating season for the Tabasco Kid; playing in only 99 games, he still managed to hit .306. Utility infielder Joe Yeager replaced him the rest of the way and performed admirably — batting .301 — by far his best of a 10-year-career with four teams.

The Highlanders bore on. They won four more in a row — taking two more to sweep the pitiful Pilgrims and then, back at the Hilltop, two from the A's. That 15th win in a row was an 11–4 laugher with Chesbro and Griffith combining to beat Jim Holmes. That it drew 11,000 on a day when the Giants drew fewer than 5,000 in a double-header in Brooklyn was cited by Vila as further evidence that the city's allegiances were tuning in to these upstarts.

But the Elberfeld suspension had removed their sparkplug and even after the testy shortstop returned, the team faded down the stretch. With two weeks to go, they took three of four from the White Sox in Chicago, including the last game, a crisp 1–0 three-hitter by Bill Hogg over Walsh before a record crowd at American League Park of 25,000.

With the Yankees percentage points up on the White Sox, the team went on to Detroit for a three game series, whereupon they fell apart, lost all three and squandered the pennant. Nothing went right in Detroit. Balls were fumbled, pitchers failed to find the plate and batters couldn't find the holes. Even injuries took their toll, with Chase having to miss the second Detroit game for the removal of corns from the bottom of his feet, of all things.

Chesbro was chased in game one after a six-run seventh to pace the Tigers, 7–4. Things got downright painful the next afternoon when the Tigers staged an improbable two-run rally off Orth with two in the ninth to steal another win, 6–5. Sparking the rally was Tiger pitcher Ed Killian, a .170 hitter that year, who singled with two down in the ninth, went to second on a walk and scored the winning run on Coughlin's double.

Then, in the final game of the series, left-hander John Eubank, of all people, with exactly three lifetime wins to his credit, was the day's Highlander-slayer — shutting out the New Yorkers 2–0. At the same time, the White Sox were beating up the hapless Pilgrims three straight in Chi-

cago to regain the league lead. They'd hold on for the pennant.

So blowing the pennant this time wasn't as dramatic as Chesbro's wild pitch two years before, but years later, that series continued to torment Elberfeld. Reminiscing to a reporter as an elderly man, the Tabasco Kid called it among his most frustrating times as a ballplayer.

"Everybody seemed to think that (winning the) Chicago series settled it," he told *The Sporting News* in 1942. "We had one more series in the west, with Detroit, a sixth-place team that season. In all my experience in baseball, I don't remember another week in which so many things went wrong on a club as happened to us that week when were losing steadily.... Grounders were taking bad hops, poor hitters were hitting balls they never hit before, we were misjudging flies, running into each other, until the club was almost off its head."

On October 5 in Boston, the Highlanders closed out their best, but perhaps most frustrating season yet, beating Boston 5–4 for their 90th win. Combined with the Chicago loss to Cleveland, it put them three games behind the champion White Sox, who were about to face their crosstown rival Cubs in the World Series.

Sure, it was disappointing, but it had been a whopper of a season for the Yankees. Farrell made money and although the team drew 434,700, some 4,000 less than in '04, they had outdrawn the Giants for the first time. As for McGraw's team, the Giants had also finished second, but a distant 20 games behind the powerhouse Cubs. That's good on paper, but it had been a trying year, with Mathewson having a subpar (for him) 21-win season and Donlin breaking his leg and missing most of the year.

As if to highlight the shifting currents in the New York baseball power structure, this time it was Brush who tried to arrange a post-season intra-city series. And this time, it was the Yankees — mindful of the slight from two years before — who nixed the idea.

Despite the disappointment in New York, baseball's first one-city World Series matchup was attractive. For the record, baseball would experience 14 more one-city Series — 13 in New York and no more in Chicago. Heavily favored were the Cubs, thanks to their stupendous 116 wins against only 36 losses, and the steady leadership of their first baseman and manager Frank Chance.

Chance was all of 27 years old when he was handed the Cubs' managerial reigns the previous season. Wise beyond his years, Chance had already assumed the nickname of "The Peerless Leader," shortened to "P.L." by the time he arrived a decade or so later in New York. In 1906, Chance's .319 batting average paced the Cubs' offense that outscored its nearest rival by 80 runs. In the field, his play anchored the league's best defensive infield comprised of third baseman Harry Steinfeldt and a notable couple of names, shortstop Joe Tinker and second baseman Johnny Evers. It was the infield immortalized by Franklin Adams' poem, "Baseball's Sad Lexicon," published in the New York *Evening Mail* in 1910.

"These are the saddest of possible words," Adams' tribute begins. "Tinker to Evers to Chance." How ironic that the trio should be immortalized for their teamwork — Tinker and Evers were bitter enemies, who played together for 11 years, uttering no more words to one another than was needed.

Helping the Cubs as well was a potent pitching staff, led by Three Finger Brown, whose 25 wins were second in the league, behind only McGinnity's 26. Even better was his microscopic 1.04 ERA, the second lowest ever. Balancing the pitching staff were 20-game winner Ed Reulbach, 19-game winner Jack Pfiester and the curiously-named Orval "Orvie" Overall, all of whom had ERAs below 2.00.

Bitterly cold weather greeted the teams for the October 9 first game at the Cubs' West Side Grounds, giving a decided advantage to pitchers. Altrock edged Brown 2–1 in the opener and Walsh took Game Three, 3–0. Then, with the Series tied at two games each, the White Sox' bats got going, beating up Reulbach 8–6 in Game Five and Brown and Overall 8–3 in Game Six to take the Series. Leading the hitting barrage was the unlikely George Rohe, a utility third baseman. Even so, the Series was vintage dead ball; the White Sox outhit the Cubs .198 to .196, while clearly outpitching them in ERA, 1.50 to 3.40.

Back in New York, the Highlanders looked forward to 1907, still basking in their most successful season yet. It had been a year of continued improvement for young Chase, who batted .323, third in the league, which only solidified his position as a star and the opinion of *The Sporting Life*, which, on January 26, 1907, called him "perhaps the biggest drawing card in baseball … modest in the extreme, (a) well-balanced, level-headed, educated youth whose habits are above reproach."

From the dependable Keeler, now 34, had came another solid season with a .304 batting average. Sure, all but 13 of his 180 hits had been singles, but he hadn't struck out until the season's 106th game. And nobody was considered smarter in terms of baseball instincts than Keeler. "Solid" could describe Chesbro, not as effective in '06 as his wondrous season of 1904, but ever the workhorse with 22 wins, second in the league, and a league-leading 49 games. And it was the year that Orth finally put everything together — his 25 wins led the league, as did his 36 complete games and 338 innings pitched.

But performances from the mainstays had also been ever so deceptive. Keeler wasn't getting any younger. And could Griffith depend yet again on Chesbro and Orth, the men with rubber arms? Even Chase may have been basking in all the press clippings, as he began to show signs of becoming the dead ball era's greatest head case.

As he had done the previous year, Chase went home to San Jose after the season to play Sunday ball in the California State League, where good salaries and a season that extended well into November drew many major leaguers of the day.

But when he showed no signs of intending to meet up with the Highlanders for the start of spring training in Atlanta, Griffith put on a brave front. "There is about as much truth in the story that Chase will not play with the Greater New Yorks this year, as there is that I will not be with the same team," he joked to reporters March 1, 1907, a few days before leaving for the south. "Chase will be at first base for the New York team next year just as sure as he is alive. He had received a contract and a railroad ticket for his passage from his home, at San Jose, to Atlanta, by way of New Orleans, and I expect to meet him when the New York contingent gets to the Georgia capital."

As usual, Chase was headed in several directions at once. He was a holdout, demanding that the Yankees pay him $5,500 instead of their $3,500 offer — that, a $1,000 raise. At the same time, he had signed on as coach at St. Mary's College and was in the midst of leading them to a 26–0–1 record when the call came to head to Atlanta.

Chase was a good coach; connecting with people was never a problem for him. It didn't hurt that St. Mary's happened to have a very good team, with future major leaguers Harry Hooper, Harry Krause and Eddie Burns. And it was there that Chase helped to develop the first successful attempt of the double squeeze play.

But when the college season ended,

Chase signed on with San Jose of the California League. At Highlander headquarters at the Aragon Hotel in Atlanta, Griffith was compelled to say again how confident he was that Chase would be back in the fold by the time the season was to start April 11. For New York baseball fans that spring, Chase's holdout marred an otherwise uneventful spring training and matched the news of another notable holdout — Turkey Mike Donlin of the Giants. For the first of many times, Chase was one very large distraction.

"Both New York teams are at sea over refractory players," the *Times* wrote March 10. "Donlin persistently maintains that he will not again play for the Giants unless salary differences are adjusted to his satisfaction.... Donlin would unquestionably be missed for his skill, but the team might be the better for his absence for all that. The loss of Chase — if Chase be lost — would be much more serious to the Americans for Chase is one player in a hundred in skill and an easy man to handle."

Ever the trooper, Griffith tried to ignore the fuss and focus on the season ahead. Having spent much of the winter at his second home in Montana, he had gone to spring training after tacking 35 pounds on to his frail frame and feeling refreshed, or as he put it to reporters, like "a two-year-old."

He had seen little reason to tinker with the Highlander lineup that nearly won the pennant in 1906. "There will be no trades made by this club," he had said, before departing for Atlanta. "Before I ever make another trade, they'll have to show me the goods and then let me take my pick. Why, some of these fellows want to give you a two-cent piece for a $20 gold piece. They've got no idea that you've got any brains or common sense in your head at all, and as a result, they just make you sick with their idle chatter. Trades? Never again!"

But there was the Chase problem. And

then there were two other holdouts — one of them, Frank Delahanty, a .238 hitter in '06 and not a big deal since he wasn't expected to challenge Keeler, Hoffman or Conroy for a starting position. More critical was Chesbro, still on his Massachusetts farm and refusing to travel to Atlanta.

Meantime, Griffith had nine pitchers in camp, several of whom, said Joe Vila, should work out to be front-line major leaguers. Getting a good look in particular were a couple of rookie right handers, Lew Brockett and Tom Hughes — not "Long Tom" of a couple of years before, but a hard-throwing 33-year-old Coal Creek, Colorado, native who had pitched in three games with the Yankees the year before.

Facing more of a do-or-die situation was Walter Clarkson, starting his fourth season for the Yankees and coming off a respectable 1906 season in which he went 9–4 with a 2.32 ERA. Vila was optimistic, writing in the March 16 *Sporting News* that Clarkson seemed to be "in better physical condition than ever before."

"The former Harvard man is bigger and heavier than last year, and when he cut loose the other day, he made the other men open their eyes with his wonderful speed and puzzling benders," wrote Vila. "If Clarkson does not make good this season, I shall be very surprised, for I have all along held the belief that he has the skill of his famous brother, John, and has only needed time and experience to develop."

Nothing else much happened until, quite suddenly, Chase sent a telegram April 1, stating that he'd report just as the team was breaking camp and starting north. While it had always been expected he'd play in 1907, his decision caught Frank Farrell by surprise, especially since the Highlander owner had never offered him a penny more than the original $3,500 offer. As often happened with Chase, there was an element of mystery about the whole episode; one report had him playing in the California State

League, while opening a café in San Jose. Then, Chase himself spoke up, saying he'd have been there earlier if he hadn't caught a bad cold while coaching St. Mary's.

Uh-huh, sure. Even after he said he'd show up, the unpredictable Chase decided to go home first to San Francisco and then report. So there was utility third baseman George Moriarty on first base when the Highlanders opened the season on a frigid April 11 in Washington, D.C., against the Nationals. Moriarty had joined the Yanks the year before from the Cubs; a good fielder but sometime hitter, Moriarty would play another 10 years in the majors, mostly with the Tigers. He'd manage the Tigers in 1927 and '28, retire, and then spend a long second career as an American League umpire.

Things seemed okay at the start at least. Getting the ball as the opening day pitcher was Orth, a nod to his magnificent season of 1906 and a decision made easier because Chesbro still hadn't reported. There was even the surprise of surprises — Kid Elberfeld actually promising to "lay off the umpires." That's baseball in April, where anything seems possible.

Despite the weather, the Highlanders played a crisp opener, scoring two in the fourth to hold off the Nationals 3–2. Orth went the distance, scattering 10 hits and third baseman Frank LaPorte had three hits and drove in one. Taking the loss for the Nats was Tom Hughes — Long Tom, the former Highlander. And yes, Elberfeld behaved himself, not getting thrown out, although there was still a long season ahead.

Four days later, the Yankees opened at home against the A's amidst the usual ceremony. As always, there was musical entertainment, this time from the Old Guard Band. There was a flag raising and the teams marched in from center field to home plate, where each team was presented with an oversized bouquet of flowers. Only Kleinow was singled out; he got a big horseshoe of roses, with an attached card bearing the inscription, "From the Bunch," whoever they were. Then Diamond Jim Brady, the gambler, but described in newspaper accounts of the day as a "horseman," threw out the first ball and the Yankees' fifth season was underway.

The home opener pitted Orth against Chief Bender. It was an omen of things to come. On another cold day, Orth was roughed up early, hurt, wrote Vila, by the cold. The A's scored twice in the first, four times in the second and twice more in the fourth, and although the Highlanders made a game of it, held on to win 9–6. The Highlanders used three pitchers — unusual in those days — bringing in Hughes and rookie left hander Roy Castleton in his big league debut. And their fielding was even worse, with Chase, in his first game, along with Elberfeld, Hoffman and Kleinow, committed errors that the *Times* attributed to "over-anxiety."

That only 10,000 — a good 7,000 or so below capacity — journeyed north to Washington Heights for the game and the festivities was attributed to the wintry conditions. But could part of it have been Harry Thaw? Remember him? Just three days before, the murder trial of the eccentric millionaire who shot and killed architect Stanford White for having an affair with his wife, Evelyn Nesbit, had ended in a hung jury. It was the day's "Trial of the Century," and about the only item of interest to outdo New Yorkers' growing obsession with baseball. The jury had gone 49 hours without reaching a verdict, when the judge dismissed the case and sent Thaw back to a mental institution.

The Highlanders were suffering from more than over-anxiety. The pitching was spotty and the hitting worse. Not getting on track for the first time in his illustrious career was Keeler, who missed a half dozen games after mashing a finger and getting the flu.

The schedulers didn't help either, and in May, the Highlanders went on the road for more than a month, visiting every A.L. city and Boston twice. Even the elements were stacked against the New Yorkers — Chesbro finally reported May 1, but didn't get to pitch much because of a severe cold spell that plagued the Northeast that spring. And when Lew Brockett, known as a warm weather pitcher, threw May 14 on a cold day against Detroit, he wrenched his arm and was lost for more than two weeks.

The excuses flew. "The Yankees have fallen off with the stick to an alarming degree," wrote Vila in the June 8 *Sporting News*. "But I think you'll find that it is due to the fact that the team has been jumping around the circuit with no chance to practice batting in the morning, and a general lack of energy because of the long strain that the men have undergone since going West."

Injuries were a greater problem than a lack of energy. By early June, the Yankees were decimated. There was Keeler's finger. There was Kleinow's split hand in April that caused him to miss a week. There was Hoffman and LaPorte, who both injured ankles. There was Clarkson, who injured a hand, got better and then got hurt again. There was Williams' sprained back and Elberfeld's flu.

Then, there were the weirder ailments. Pitching against Boston May 2, Hogg left the game when he injured his arm. In fact, he was suffering from a floating kidney, which kept him out five weeks, during which he lost his conditioning. Then, there was the case of a cerebral young catcher, acquired that February from the St. Louis named Branch Rickey.

The 25-year-old Rickey had just 65 major league games to his credit, but Griffith was high on him, thinking he had a good chance to become one of the league's premier catchers and traded Yeager even-up to get him. But Rickey came with a catch — he was the baseball coach at Ohio Wesleyan University and didn't actually join the Yankees until May 8. Then, his arm went lame and he played in only 52 games, including one dubious performance June 28, when he let 13 Washington Nationals steal bases.

In time, Rickey would be hailed as the Mahatma, a baseball architect of innovation and genius, who built the Brooklyn Dodgers, the Pirates and the Cardinals into championship teams and signed Jackie Robinson, the big leagues' first African American. But all that was far in the future from the spring day in 1907 that Branch Rickey, being groomed as the eventual successor to Red Kleinow, got a bum arm.

Clearly something was wrong. By early May, the team was in a funk, mired in fifth place, way behind defending champion Chicago. But when the flagpole at the White Sox ballpark, South Side Park, broke May 14 during pennant-raising ceremonies honoring the 1906 A.L. flag, it was perhaps a sign that their chances weren't so good. Just behind were the surprising Tigers, led by a potent hitting combination of Ty Cobb and Sam Crawford.

So, Griffith went to work. Forgetting his spring training pledge to not trade anyone, he unloaded the unhappy holdout Delahanty, along with Clarkson, to Cleveland on May 8 for the veteran right-handed pitcher Earl Moore. The 28-year-old Moore had been with the Blues since 1901 and had chalked up some good numbers — winning 17 games in 1902 and 18 in '03. But he wouldn't do much with the Highlanders, going 2–6, before being sent to the Phillies after the season. With Delahanty and Clarkson, two players trying to live up to famous older brothers, Griffith had clearly run out of patience.

Delahanty wouldn't do much for the Blues that season, appearing in all of 15 games and hitting .173. Ironically, he'd return to the Highlanders in 1908 as a utility man and hit .256 before being let loose. His career would end in 1915, after two years in the Federal League. Nor would Clarkson ever get on track, going 4–6 with Cleveland and retiring in 1908 with 20 lifetime wins, a good ways below his brother John, who had retired in 1894 with 327 lifetime wins. Sometimes, it just doesn't pay to try to outdo an older sibling.

Griffith wasn't panicking, at least publicly. "The boys are doing the best they can under the circumstances," he said in mid–June. "They have been overanxious and because of a string of defeats due to a slump in hitting, they have gone to pieces. But all teams experience those kinds of setbacks only to get into their proper stride later on. I do not attempt to cry 'hard luck' or 'the umpire,' for that would not be fair. I simply say that the team has not played good ball."

On Memorial Day, the Yankees were mired in fifth place. On July 4, the traditional mid-season point, things hadn't improved much, with the team still in fifth place, behind a tightly bunch top four of Chicago, Cleveland, Philadelphia and the surprising Detroit Tigers. Their record was a mediocre 31–32, as they readied to meet the A's in a 2 p.m. doubleheader at the Hilltop. It would be the third and fourth games of the series that the teams had split to date and bring an end to the Highlander home stand. That night, they'd depart for Cleveland.

13

A Closer Look

"No matter what I talk about, I always get back to baseball."

— Connie Mack

Why focus on July 4, 1907? There is a well-known Brown Brothers photograph that gives a sweeping vista of both the day's crowd and game. The photo (*opposite*), reproduced in a number of books, and the day's doubleheader are as good a chance as any to give a sense of what it was like to see the Yankees play at the Hilltop at the height of the dead ball era.

The photo's most noticeable aspect is the crowd. It is big, too big for the grandstand and spills on to the foul territories and outfield. Newspapers the next day estimated that 25,000 had the Hilltop bursting at the seams in what was said to be the rickety little ballpark's greatest crowd ever.

Taken from behind home plate, and a few feet down the third base line, the photo shows the crowd packing the first base side of the grandstand and spilling out, perhaps 20 or 30 deep, onto foul territory from behind home and clear to the right field wall. Indeed, the crowd is so thick that from first base toward the outfield, it can be seen encroaching within a few feet of the playing field. More spectators, perhaps four deep, stand and sit in the outfield, along the outfield wall.

There doesn't appear to be a great deal of comfort in the grandstand. Spectators are crammed together. If there are aisles, they're clogged. And those at the top of the grandstand are standing; somebody holds an umbrella aloft, not to guard against rain, but against the sun that bathed the field on that pleasant, long-ago 78-degree holiday.

Another panoramic shot, appearing in the next day's *Post*, shows the ballpark from the third base side. That shot shows the spillover crowd along the third base line, which is every bit as close to the playing field, but much more orderly. For some curious reason, spectators along the third base line have acquired a line of benches that they use to stand. Where would the benches have come from? Dragged in from the street? As on the other side of the field, the crowd is perhaps five or 10 deep.

The overcrowding demonstrates one of the ironies of the dead ball era: the steadfast unwillingness on the part of major league owners to build ballparks big enough to accommodate the growing number of fans. The result was crowds that for holiday and weekend games typically spilled out onto the field, prompting all kinds of funny ground rules — balls hit into the outfield crowd were generally considered doubles — and putting spectators at the peril of sharp foul balls. That was the case for one unfor-

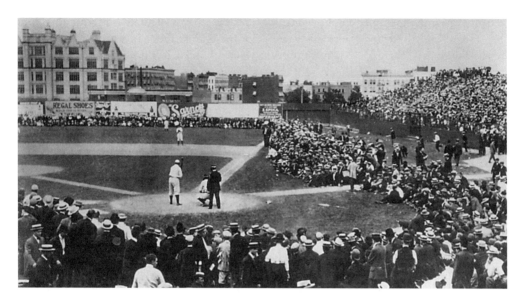

It is July 4, 1907, and the Highlanders are taking on the Philadelphia A's before a big double-header crowd at Hilltop Park. (Brown Brothers)

tunate soul on July 4 at the Hilltop, when he, as the *Post* put it, "lost several teeth by colliding with a foul ball."

A further irony is how close the fans are to the players — a couple of nattily-dressed women in long skirts actually appear to hanging on the first-base dugout steps. Baseball in those days wasn't front and center the way it is these days. Long before ESPN and decades before television and radio, baseball was accessible mostly through the newspapers.

Most of those who journeyed north to the Hilltop that warm holiday would have read about the games in that day's newspaper. They'd have had a lot to choose from — general circulation papers in 1907 included the *Times*, the *Post*, the *Journal*, the *World*, the *Herald*, the *Tribune*, the *Evening News*, the *Daily Mirror*, the *American* and the *Press*. That enough? Then as now, New York was the media capital of the world and the Highlanders were well-covered.

Baseball coverage had kicked off back in the mid–1890s with publication of big league box scores by William Randolph Hearst's *Journal*, then in a deadly competi-

tion with Joseph Pulitzer's *World* for the hearts and minds — and readership — of the city's working classes. All kinds of measures were tried in this protracted, costly newspaper war, from slicing the price of the daily paper in half to a penny to beefing up the Sunday feature pages and sensationalizing and embellishing the crime coverage. Hearst saw baseball coverage as another avenue to capture working class readers and their growing interest in entertainment. Other papers soon followed.

A decade or so later, papers varied in their baseball coverage. Most listed that day's opponent and the starting time — in this case, 2 p.m. — along with the standings and the previous day's game summary and box score. (Most single games in New York in those days started at 4 p.m., to allow workers to attend but early enough, in the era before lights, to get the game in before dusk.) But while there may have been a lot more papers in those days, the coverage wasn't necessarily as comprehensive as that of today.

For the most part, the game reports were strictly that — summaries of who got the hits, drove in the runs and did the pitching. It was baseball treated as a titanic game of chess with little context, no player quotes and only an occasional comment from the manager. All in all, the coverage was a little pedestrian.

Chances are most of the crowd had journeyed north to the subway's 168th Street station and walked the short one block to the ballpark, where most paid 75 cents for a grandstand seat. For those taking in their first game of the season, the Hilltop looked a little different from previous years. For a time, owner Frank Farrell had promised there would be no advertising at the Hilltop, but that pledge had lasted until 1907, when ads for just about everything plastered the outfield fence. Most noticeable in the photo is an ad in right field for Regal shoes. Other ads peddled Morocco cigarettes at 15 cents a package and F.C. Rye. Two years later, the biggest sign of all would arrive — a Bull Durham tobacco sign, shaped like a bull and twice the size of the right-center field where it was positioned.

Keeping the crowd orderly was too big a job for the six Pinkertons hired that day by the Yankees. Six guards for 25,000 people? Even so, the crowd made do as best they could, behaving generally well through the first game at least, as the A's, behind the powerful Chief Bender beat the Highlanders' Al Orth 3–1.

Clearly visible in the famous photo are a few players, notably the battery and right side of the infield. It's all enough to get a quick look at how the overall look of the players and their equipment have changed considerably since then. Wearing high collars and plain uniforms — white for home and gray for the road, with script on the front chest — gives these dead ball ballplayers more the look of bellhops than lords of the diamond.

Numbers? They weren't wearing them as yet — as far as anyone knows, the first numbers wouldn't be worn until 1916, when the Cleveland Indians starting wearing them

on the sleeves of their uniforms in a June game against the White Sox. The numbers corresponded to numbers set opposite the players' names on the scorecards.

Really different were the players' mitts, flimsy bits of leather that look more like oven mitts than protection geared to stop a baseball. Only the catcher wore anything that resembled the gear of a modern day player of the same position.

Catchers of the dead ball era wore masks made of a buffer of doeskin or dog skin stuffed with horsehair or cotton to insulate them from the solid steel grill. Since 1900, they had worn chest protectors made of leather or canvas filled with cotton felt or kapok. Their gloves, unencumbered by today's size restrictions, were big, bulky and pillow-like, and even bulkier when stuffed with straw, grass or horsehair. And it was just about then that catchers began wearing shin guards, introduced by Roger Bresnahan of the Giants. The invention prompted criticism from fans and players, but replaced the custom of some catchers wearing padding under the socks.

Umpires looked somewhat similar as well. If anything, umpires of the dead ball era were a tad more natty than those of today, largely because they were dressed somewhat formally, in black suits, ties and caps, making them look like a cross between a mortician and a chauffeur.

Regardless of Ban Johnson's dream for a rowdy-free league, those umpires faced a tough road during the dead ball era. For all the stern talk that managers and players needed to behave themselves, there was a good deal of rowdyism that seemed to go unchecked in dead ball days. One way that big time baseball would stem the nonsense somewhat was to hire umpires who had been respected players and knew the game upwards and sideways — people like George Moriarty and Big Big Dinneen, the old Boston pitcher — but that was still a decade or so away.

Dead ball umps did what they could. The perception of them you get today is that they were a dictatorial lot, not given to reasoning with disagreeing players — which just may have incited them even more. The personification of the dead ball umpire was Silk O'Loughlin, Elberfeld's nemesis and the autocrat of the baseball world, as Christy Mathewson once said. "There are no close plays," Silk liked to say. "A man is always out or safe, or it is a ball or a strike, and the umpire, if he is a good man and knows his business, is always right." For the record, Silk said he was "always right" — refusing to let players discuss a call. Trying was futile; Silk tossed 'em.

Behind such bluster was a man who was a bit of a dude. In 1904, when, of all things, Silk ran for the State Assembly as a Democrat and soundly lost, he was asked for a statement. "I think," he said, "that the public made a rotten decision." He was the first umpire to toss Ty Cobb. And in 1907, he demonstrated his trademark strike call for a Coca-Cola ad.

Silk invented creased pants for umpires, and it is said with a grain of salt that some players were afraid to slide when he was close down to make a call for fear that they would bump the crease and cut themselves. At all times on Silk's right hand was a large diamond that glistened in the sunlight every time he called a man out. A 1908 Charles Conlin photograph of Silk reveals a handsome, 30-something face, but ever so stern. Maybe Kid Elberfeld was on his mind.

On that July 4, as throughout the dead ball era, the majority of those spectators are men, dressed in button-down shirts, dark pants, and boaters. Some stand. Others sit. Next in predominance appear to be adolescent boys, dressed in knickers and caps. Women seem far and few between; two of

them sit behind home plate, wearing long, flowing dresses and substantial, flowery hats.

Chances are those boys were learning about the players courtesy of a new hobby catching on around the country. It was baseball card collecting, an interest that had kicked off a decade or so before when the first cards were introduced with cigarettes in the 1890s and dominated the trading card field through the early part of the century.

Those early cards were crude by today's sleek standards — most of the photographs were taken in an artist's studio with the action simulated to resemble game conditions. Indeed, it wasn't unusual to see players catching or hitting a ball suspended from a string or sliding into a base on a wooden floor.

Particularly memorable at the turn of the century were the T-205 and T-210 sets, including the famous T-210 Honus Wagner card, which sold for nearly $500,000 in the 1990s. Included in packs of cigarettes, the cards were notable for their superior colors and were the product of German inks. World War I put a stop to the ink supply and the sets were discontinued. It wouldn't be until 1933 that Goudey (Big League Gum Co.) introduced cards with bubble gum, not to mention more realistic poses and heavier cardboard, and the hobby grew to resemble the more modern hobby.

The Brown Brothers photograph is conspicuous as well for a crowd you don't see — African Americans, who didn't venture much to major league games in those days. It would be 40 years — 1947 to be exact — before a black man, Jackie Robinson, would reach the big leagues, the result of a longstanding color ban that had gone into existence in the late 19th century.

As a result, black baseball at the turn of the century was a separate world, set off by the Jim Crow dictums of the times. More recent history has romanticized teams like the New York Black Yankees, Pittsburgh Crawfords and Kansas City Monarchs. But those names were still far in the future at a time when there appeared to be a handful of major black teams — several each from New York and Philadelphia, Chicago's Leland Giants and another, the Norfolk Red Stockings. They earned their keep, not in leagues, but in a kind of barnstorming sandlot format, playing among themselves and against white teams.

Excluding African American players from the big leagues in those days was policy — accepted by magnates, players and fans alike without too many questions or complaints. When a really good player like John Henry Lloyd would pop up, it didn't matter; bringing a black player into the major leagues was prohibited. It was what society wanted.

When America's first baseball league, the amateur National Association of Base Ball Players, was established way back in 1867 with more than 100 teams in the northern U.S., there was fear that black players would apply. So they were excluded, a policy that was extended four years later when the first pro league, the National Association of Professional Ball Players, formed. By then, there was no need for a clause against African Americans. The rule was unwritten and clearly understood.

So, blacks formed their own teams, the earliest of which played out of Philadelphia with intriguing names like the Uniques and the Excelsiors. And the first notable black player: one John "Bud" Fowler, born of all places in Cooperstown, New York, and an itinerant ballplayer of sorts, who played with semi-pro teams, some of them white, throughout the Northeast in the 1870s.

Fowler's career was followed with considerable interest in *The Sporting News*, which called him "the crack colored player." In time, they picked up on the career of

another notable black player — Moses Fleetwood Walker, known as "Fleet." An honors graduate of Oberlin College, Walker latched on with Toledo of the major league American Association. But when Toledo headed south for a series of games, Walker endured a torrent of abuse, including lynch threats. Toledo released him for his own well-being and Walker took to bouncing around the minor leagues, most notably the International League, which employed a number of black players

But Walker's reception in the South was a sign of trouble ahead. When, in 1887, Chicago's Cap Anson — yes, him again — began threatening not to play a series of exhibition games against International League teams, a trend was started. That July, he refused to take the field against Newark, which had a black pitcher named George Stovey. In September, the National League's St. Louis Browns did the same — refusing to play an exhibition game against the all-black Cuban Giants and leaving the crowd of 7,000 in the stands.

The policy stuck, and by the end of 1887 season, had become the big leagues' unwritten law. The reasons, according to the odd logic of the time: leagues, including the International League, as *Sporting Life* put it, feared an exodus of white players "on account of the colored element." And so did baseball descend into the racism of the times — barring not just blacks, but Native Americans and Latinos. Sadly, black players like Stovey, and others like Frank Grant and Bob Higgins, were released — and the long, disgraceful era of league-sanctioned racism was underway.

That people should be spilling out of the grandstand and onto the field gives this notable dead ball photograph a kind of sandlot atmosphere. For the most part, those spectators were left largely to fend for

themselves — there were no scoreboards or public address announcers. And both inside and outside the ballpark was the kind of open gambling that the magnates talked about ending, made periodic, ballyhooed efforts to stop, but did little about.

For the vice, the spectators weren't even allowed to keep foul balls hit into the stands. That tradition of keeping the balls — the time-honored tradition of the lout knocking the little kid out of the way to get a baseball — wouldn't start until 1921 in Pittsburgh. Not from benevolence did baseball start the practice either; it only happened after three fans at Forbes Field threatened to sue the police department after being arrested for refusing to throw the balls back onto the diamond.

At least there were some comforts — hot dogs and a lemonade stand or two. It was among the first rudimentary efforts at concessions and New York had one Harry M. Stevens to thank for that. Legend has it that the story of Stevens started at the Polo Grounds on a cold April day in 1900, when Stevens, the ballpark's head caterer, wasn't selling too much ice cream and soda water.

Calling his vendors together, Stevens told them to go to neighborhood markets and buy all the dachshund sausages they could find and an equal number of long rolls. Frankfurters — so named for their Frankfurt, Germany birthplace — were called "dachshund sausages" because of their shape. Stevens heated the sausages, placed them in the rolls and sent his vendors through the stands with a cry, "Get your red hot dachshunds!" The verdict: an immediate hit.

Legend, act two: Sitting in the press box that day was Tad Dorgan, America's most successful cartoonist, searching for an idea to meet a deadline. Seeing the vendors roaming through the stands, he sketched them selling "red hots" and then stopped because he couldn't spell "dachshunds." The next day, Dorgan's cartoon appeared show-

ing the dachshund sausages in rolls, barking at one another. And for "hot dachshunds," the lousy-spelling Dorgan had substituted, "hot dogs."

It was just the beginning for the Hot Dog King. In time, Stevens expanded his food selection to include not just hot dogs, but soft drinks and scorecards at sporting events. And just like that, a new industry was born.

An English immigrant, Stevens came to the U.S. in 1882 and found work in an Ohio steel factory. One day, while watching a baseball game, he hit on the idea of selling scorecards. He sought and obtained the concession, first in the Tri-State League and then among big league teams in Boston, Brooklyn, Pittsburgh, Washington and Milwaukee.

Stevens didn't actually create the scorecard; his genius was in perfecting it by accurately printing the players' names. "I made it a business to find out just how the teams batted and gave fans a card on which they could keep score," he said. "It was a selling campaign. I had to convince them that a game could not be really enjoyed without a scorecard."

Stevens's marketing aptitude was already evident, as in his profitable idea to sell scorecards printed in German in Milwaukee. It was also there that he met John Montgomery Ward, manager of the New York Giants, who advised him to go to New York for a shot at a truly big market. Stevens did, arriving there around 1894 with exactly $8.40 in his pocket.

His first New York catering job were bicycle races at the Garden and baseball at the Polo Grounds. In time, he was selling sandwiches and lemonade and hit it big with hot dogs, peanuts and soft drinks. Stevens soon had concessions at all three major league parks in New York, Belmont Park and Aqueduct racetracks, as well as polo matches at Westbury, Long Island.

Stevens's gentle charm, prodigious

work habits and energy — he kept offices first at 320 5th Ave., before the company moved to 521 5th Ave. and ultimately to its current locale in New Jersey — masked a surprising breadth of education and erudition. Much was made of Stevens's knowledge of Shakespeare, and it is said he could quote almost any line from the bard's plays.

Stevens's four sons, one of whom was actually named Frank — really — followed their father into the business. Today, the thousands of vendors selling those "red hots" would do well to raise a ceremonial toast — make that a hot dog with relish and mustard, no ketchup — to Harry M. Stevens.

Back at the Hilltop, the mob managed to behave themselves through the first game. But when the crowd swarmed onto the field at the final out, things started to unravel. "The spectators on the field flocked around the players and inspected the diamond as if they had never seen them at close range," the *Times* reported.

When Yankees game two starter Doc Newton, just up from the Montreal farm club, warmed up on the sidelines to face the A's Rube Waddell, the crowd was pressed so tight that he needed to be extra careful to reach his target and try not to nail a spectator.

By game time, the crowd was pressing so much that umpire John Stafford appealed to Griffith to ask the fans to keep back. He tried but it didn't work. "Griffith told the crowd what was what, but they wouldn't move back," reported the *Post*, a bit tongue and cheek. "'Nay, nay,' quoth the foolish herd, 'We want this one chance to stand here and touch with our own fingers the uniforms of Hal Chase and Rube Waddell and our other heroes. We know of no better way to celebrate the Fourth and bother those blokes who had 75 cents for a seat in the grandstand.'"

They tried to play anyway. Nobody seemed all that concerned by the situation, with the exception of the "blokes" in the first few rows of the grandstand, who had plucked down their coins for good seats and couldn't see over the mob on the field. So they yelled, cursed and threw a lot of bottles and cushions at the instigators.

Throw something these days and you'd be tossed from the park and prosecuted. So goes another difference with baseball of the dead ball era, where guards were generally overwhelmed and for the most part, looked the other way when the errant missile came tumbling from the stands.

After all, it had been less than three months since the Giants' home opener at the Polo Grounds, where on a cold day against the Phillies with piles of snow built up around the park, fans kept a barrage of snowballs directed at players throughout the game. Even with New York's Frank Corridon pitching a shutout, the fans by the eighth inning took to running around the field. With no police on duty, the game was forfeited to Philadelphia.

And it would only be four days until another ugly incident at Washington Park, Brooklyn. Bombarded by soda bottles, Cubs manager Frank Chance would throw one back into the stands, where it cut a boy on the leg. This time, there were police: they helped Chance leave the park after the Cubs' 5–0 victory, under escort and in an armored car.

Fortunately back at the Hilltop, nobody was seriously injured, and luckily, the Yankees got to Waddell in the third, scoring six runs to put the game on ice and thin the crowd out considerably.

Making the rally possible were several pop fouls that Philadelphia infielders would have normally run down, but couldn't because of the crowd. Helping them too was Doc Newton, suspended the previous September by Griffith for training infractions, but back in the fold after his stint of solid citizenship in Montreal. The game was called after seven innings, with the New Yorkers on top 7–3.

Receiving a scant few lines in the next day's papers was the appearance in game two of a young A's infielder named Eddie Collins, recently the baseball captain at Columbia University and trying to make an impression in the big leagues. "After Connie Mack had given up the game as lost, the youngster was sent to the short field and accepted the two chances he had with the ease of confidence of a veteran," the *Post* wrote. "He ought to make good."

It was a case of the proverbial baseball "cup of coffee," a wonderful expression for a short stay in the bigs. Actually, Collins had come up the previous September while still a Columbia junior. Playing as Ed Sullivan — go ahead, look it up — Collins got a hit and struck out twice against Ed Walsh of the White Sox. And yes, he'd make good — Collins would come up for keeps in 1908, play another 23 years, hit .333 and join the Hall of Fame as a charter member.

14

Going Nowhere

"It's not the winters that bother me. It's the summers."

—Walter Alston

The July 4 doubleheader mirrored the flow of the Highlander season: a win here, a loss there and never climbing much above .500 or out of fifth place. With the team's mediocre performance came the inevitable front office turmoil and rumors. And then came something really strange — a touch of scandal and a dash of the bizarre that didn't have much to do directly with baseball. As was increasingly the case with most things odd on the Highlanders, it involved Chase. And as was the case with most things Chase, things weren't quite on the level.

Actually, the controversy involved Chase's wife, Nellie, or so it seemed. Nellie was Nellie Heffernan, whom Chase had met two years before when playing an exhibition game in her hometown of Bayonne, New Jersey. The two weren't really married — yet — as the newspapers reported, but lived together in Suffern, New York as common-law husband and wife.

As Suffern residents, they were part of a Highlander enclave of sorts that included Kid Elberfeld and his family, along with team trainer Mike Martin and his wife, Ethel. It just may have been the most tranquil period of Chase's increasingly erratic tenure in New York; he commuted to Hilltop Park each day on the train, where he

quickly became known as the ballplayer who told great stories and did card tricks for other passengers.

But on July 26, the suburban tranquility was shattered when Heffernan and Ethel Martin were arrested on charges they had concealed the death of the Martins' week-old son after burying the infant in their backyard and a stray dog had dug up the body. Neighbors had alerted police, who found the body and arrested the two women.

Ethel Martin later broke down and confessed to police that the child had been dead for several days and she had indeed buried the body in the yard. With both women held on $1,000 bond each, Elberfeld posted bond and they were released. Charges against Heffernan were later dropped.

Back in baseball circles, the shenanigans continued. With the Highlanders going nowhere, Frank Farrell fired team President Joseph Gordon, stating that he too should "get some of the glory."

In reality, it was an old-fashioned power grab. "I had put up the money and done a lot of the work," Farrell added impetuously.

Then came rumors that Griffith would be next to go, to be replaced by George

Stallings, the hard-drinking former Detroit manager who lived in New York and had taken to hanging around the Yankees office at the Flatiron Building. Farrell denied the report, this time responding with a tone of self-righteousness.

"I'd give a great deal to know who started this latest knock at my club," Farrell said. "Why, Stallings has never had a chance to be the manager of the Yankees and never will have! Griffith has been loyal to me through all kinds of adversity and hard luck and it would be a piece of gross injustice on my part to relieve him of the management of the team at this stage of the proceedings."

After all, sympathies were with Griffith. "It looks as if everything is working bad for a first-class team which has hoodwinked for years," Vila wrote in the July 25 *Sporting News*. "No wonder Griffith is worried. He is a hard loser and the failure of the team to be up with the leaders must be a terrible blow to him."

The leaders were the surprising Tigers, managed by former Orioles shortstop Hughie Jennings, who with one shrewd move was responsible for making the team a contender. When Jennings saw Ty Cobb, he knew he was a star in the making so he put the young Georgia native in the starting line-up. Detroit made a 21-game leap in 1907, moving clear from sixth place to the American League pennant.

Cobb was on fire in 1907. He batted .350 and won the American League batting title. He drove in 116 runs, collected 212 hits, and stole 49 bases, all A.L. leading figures. He had become the leader in a potent Tiger batting order that started with lead-off man Davy Jones, who scored 102 runs and continued with Sam Crawford, who hit .323 and slugged .460, both second in the league. Cobb's numbers were so good

in part because he spent most of the season knocking in Crawford and Jones.

The kind of batting was more than enough to support a solid Tiger pitching staff anchored by "Wild" Bill Donovan, with a 26–4 record and a 2.19 ERA and followed by Ed Killian (24–12, 1.78) and George Mullin (21–20, 2.59) in his third straight 20-win season. And it was just enough to outlast the second-place A's and their great pitching staff by a scant 1½ games. Taking third were the White Sox, 5½ games out.

As in 1906, the N.L. race in '07 was decided virtually from the start. The Cubs dominated again, only winning 107 games (107!) and outpacing second place Pittsburgh by 17 games. It was more of the same for Chicago, with their five strong starting pitchers and a staff ERA of 1.73 (1.73!), balanced by tight defense, clutch hitting and the heart of the Tinker to Evers to Chance double play combination.

The Tigers-Cubs World Series started October 8 at West Side Park in Chicago. The Series itself was anti-climactic. As the year before, pitching again dominated, but this time it was all Cubs, whose combined 0.75 ERA held Detroit to a team batting average of .209, including a disappointing .200 from Ty Cobb. Along the way, they ran the bases with abandon, stealing a then-Series record of 18 bases, all of which contributed to a four-game sweep after a tie in the opener.

The Series had kicked off two days after the Highlanders' season mercifully ended at the Hilltop against Boston, with, of all things, a 3–3 tie in the second game of a scheduled doubleheader. It was a day in which the somewhat curious rules of the dead ball era took effect; game one was a tie as well, an 8-all, 10-inning affair that was rained out. But instead of resuming the first game, umpire Silk O'Loughlin started the second, which ended in the third on account of darkness. A doubleheader had been scheduled, but was washed out by rain.

In a sense, the second game was a microcosm of the Highlanders' second half of the season. Griffith, realizing his team was headed nowhere and thinking ahead to 1908, used a makeshift line-up to give the up-and-comers a look. Getting the look in game two was a rookie pitcher, 25-year-old right-handed Brooklyn native Joe Lake, purchased from Jersey City. Lake did okay in his three innings of work, giving up four hits but showing some grit in ending a Boston threat with consecutive strikeouts of Harry Lord and Charley Wagner, the Pilgrim shortstop.

Wagner, by the way, was the subject of some attention that day. Amidst the raindrops, just after the first game had been called, a delegation head by Senator Thomas McManus tumbled out of the stands to present Wagner, a New Yorker, with a handsome diamond ring. Wagner, known as Heinie, had come up briefly with the Giants back in '02, and had just joined Boston for the tail end of the '07 season and seemed to have found a home. Wagner did; he'd play 10 more big league seasons, retiring in 1918 with a .250 career batting average. In 1930, he'd manage Boston, by then called the Red Sox.

Nobody in the stands seemed to realize what was happening as McManus droned on with his speech about Wagner. It didn't matter much; the few who were there cheered lustfully anyway, according to the newspapers. Nobody seemed to mind that either of the day's two games ended without results. And so the Highlanders' fifth season ended with a whimper: their final record was a forgettable 70–78, good for fifth place and 21 games behind the Tigers.

If the season had been disappointing for the New Yorkers, they were positively horrid for the Pilgrims. The team managed only 59 wins, ahead of only Washington. Amazing they got that far, considering the team had started the season with the suicide of their manager Chick Stahl. Four

others — Cy Young, George Huff and a couple of old Highlanders, Bob Unglaub, and Deacon McGuire — managed Boston in that year of upheaval. About the only bright spot was Young's 19 wins and 1.99 ERA.

The Highlanders' last weeks of the season had been particularly rough. The mercurial Elberfeld didn't last, suspended without pay by Farrell on July 26 after the Yankee president watched him play with seeming indifference in a doubleheader loss at the Hilltop against the Cleveland Naps. His replacement: Wid Conroy, who had the flu.

Farrell had been hearing reports of Elberfeld's erratic play for weeks. So he went to see for himself and took immediate action, suspending him after the Tabasco Kid made three errors in game one and sent Chase diving after several errant throws. "For more than two weeks past, he has refused to talk with the other members of the team," said Farrell of his erratic shortstop. "He has declined to be rubbed by the trainer. He has refused to try to play his best, as the public well knows. In short, he has acted in such a queer manner that if he has not been tampered with, he has gone daffy."

Yankee fans backed Farrell. The announcement of his suspension right after the first game was cheered heartily by the 8,000 or so spectators at the Hilltop. All in all, the Cleveland series was the weekend that sank the Highlanders for the '07 season; when the bats woke up, the pitching fell apart. The series' final game was an 11–10 loss to give the Naps four of the five games.

"Elberfeld has never been a consistently good player for the New York club," opined the *Times*. "His quick temper spoils his work, and when crossed he has proven a stubborn and sulky individual in the game. Time and time, he has been banished from games for breaches of rules and umpire baiting, and has never been on the best terms with several members of his team."

The next week, with the New Yorkers

back on the road, the hoodoo set in again. Facing the White Sox on August 3, Chase went down, badly spiked on the arm by George Davis. And for the first time in more than a decade, Keeler just couldn't get on track. His average hovered below .250 and nobody could say for certain exactly why. Keeler himself didn't say much of anything; the newspapers editorialized that he was worried about the poor health of his father, Pat, a Brooklyn train conductor on the DeKalb Avenue line.

At the end of his longest season in 15 years of major league baseball, Keeler finished with a .234 batting average, a tremendous falloff and a bitter disappointment for a player whose average sometime exceeded .400 and had never fallen below .300. Retirement? Keeler thought about it, but withheld a final decision. He just went home to Pulaski Street in Brooklyn, his lips sealed, to spend the winter with Pat and his brother Tom.

On the pages of *The Sporting News*, Vila summed up another lost season. "It is the same old hoodoo that is at work and the fans are seriously thinking of offering a large reward for his apprehension," he wrote. "The police department will not be notified, for that would be a useless waste of time in these days of crime waves. But seriously, the Yankees have been up against some sort of Jonah ever since the American League came to the Big Town, and the end is not yet. Griffith has done his best, only to be discouraged again and again."

15

Hoodoo Reigns

"Stay away from firearms and don't room higher than the second floor."
— *Frankie Frisch on advice*
he'd give young managers

A lot more than hoodoo had sunk the Highlanders in 1907. The fact is that Griffith had lost control of his players. Late in the season came ominous reports of his players partying at Harlem jazz joints and giving half-hearted efforts at the ballpark. And there was irony in Elberfeld's suspension since he and Griffith were good friends. And when Farrell suspended the errant shortstop, the sign was clear: Not only was the Yankee president serving notice on Elberfeld, but he was sending his manager a clear sign that more was expected of the Yanks.

Griffith knew that all too well. He had managed five years in the big town, come close to pennants twice but failed. Intense to start with, he was 38 years old and prematurely gray. At times, Griffith seemed to be swallowed up by his baseball uniform, seemingly smaller than his 5'6" and 156-pound frame would indicate, due perhaps to a diet of raw eggs and olive oil during the season. After 1906, Griffith didn't pitch much anymore — with 236 lifetime big league wins behind him, he focused on managing.

So was the disappointment of 1907 an illusion? Griffith thought so, but he decided to retool anyway. It didn't work. In fact, not much of anything worked in 1908, a year when hitting and pitching broke down, players bolted and near-mutiny reigned supreme. But what about the Bronx Zoo Yankees of the late 1970s? At least they won. By comparison, 1908 would be among the strangest, most disillusioning seasons in Yankee history.

Looking back, there had been other letdowns in '07. After holding out, Chesbro had never gotten back on track, pitching through a miserable 10–9 season. The team's biggest winner had again been Orth, but he too suffered through a lost season, going 13–21 with a 2.61 ERA. About the only player to have a good season had been Chase, who batted .287, although his average had plummeted 33 percentage points from the year before.

Chase didn't seem to mind. In three short seasons, he had become the Yankees' best player, its first bona fide homegrown star, and he was beginning to act like it. The influx of rookies that Griffith had tried out over the last couple of months of 1907 clearly fed Chase's ego. Many was a night that Prince Hal could be found regaling those young impressionable ballplayers at Gallagher's Steakhouse, where he dined several times a week and enjoyed playing the big shot in springing for the check. "They don't make enough money to afford a place like this," Chase would say.

Basically, Hal Chase was rounding into the Hal Chase of legend — a raffish, cocky young man who liked a drink, liked the action of a high-stakes game of poker and although he was engaged to Nellie, always seemed to have a woman from the Ziegfeld Follies on his arm. In little time at all, he had established a reputation both on and off the field. When a Boston newspaper reported on the off-the-field talents of contemporary players, Frank Chance of the Cubs was voted the best boxer; Frank Hahn, a piano player bar none; Jake Beckley, a great cook; Honus Wagner, tops at pinochle; and, Chase, the big leagues' best at pool. New Yorkers just ate it up. Chase's fan mail doubled that received by the rest of the club. His charisma had particular appeal to two groups: young boys, who would tag along after him following the games, and women. It was for him that Ladies Day was dusted off and brought back to the Hilltop.

It was a given that Chase would be in the lineup in 1908. But little else was set, a fact set in motion by Griffith when he started making moves at the end of 1907 and in the early winter. In the last weeks of 1907 came pitcher Joe Lake from Newark of the Eastern League. From Williamsport, PA, of the Tri-State League came Rube Manning, a right-hander with a 14–7 record and Walter Blair, a catcher.

There were more. From Atlanta of the Southern League came the 17-game winning pitcher Rube Zeller — what is it about the name Rube? — and 19-year-old catcher Ed Sweeney. Then came Neal Ball, a shortstop from Montgomery of the Southern League; Bill "Baldy" Louden, a third baseman from Dallas of the Texas League; and, at the recommendation of Chase, pitcher Frank Arellanes from the California League. Most

would have journeyman major league careers.

In early November, just before he took off for his annual pilgrimage to Montana, Griffith pulled off a trade he hoped would lay a real foundation for the Yankees in 1908. Swapping Jimmy Williams, Danny Hoffman and Hobe Ferris even-up to the St. Louis Browns, Griffith picked up right-hander Fred Glade, the winner of 53 games in five big-league seasons, most of them spent with lousy teams; second baseman Harry Niles; and veteran outfielder Charlie Hemphill. Then he signed Washington first baseman Jake Stahl, the old Pilgrim and Chick's brother.

The flurry of moves had the pre-season pundits talking flag. "The team, as it will be constituted, will be one of the fastest ever gotten together," Vila gushed in *The Sporting News*. "In hitting, base running, fielding and other departments, there will be greater strength and skill than ever before."

Elsewhere on the pages of *The Sporting News*, W.M. Rankin chose to focus on the pitching, citing Slow Joe Doyle, who dallied his way to an 11–11 record in 1907, Glade, and several of the promising minor leaguers like Lake, a Brooklyn native, and Zeller.

The optimism carried over into spring training. On March 6, off they went — 16 players on the train headed south from Jersey City's Pennsylvania Station to Atlanta, where the team would once again set up at the Piedmont Hotel. And what a camp: there was sunny weather and only one holdout — not Chase this time, but infielder George Moriarty. An added bonus, for Griffith anyway, was the new state law that made Georgia a non-alcoholic state. "It's pretty odd to not to able to buy a drink," said the Yankee skipper, known to enjoy a stiff one now and again himself. "However, as a manager, I rather like it. I won't have much trouble keeping the boys straight."

Brightness and sunshine continued all around. On March 12, in their first exhibition game, the New Yorkers lost to the Atlanta Crackers, but no need to worry. In three innings of work, Jack Chesbro appeared to be in old-time form, giving up all of two base hits in three scoreless innings. Could Happy Jack be back to his form of four years before? Fingers were crossed.

Keeler too was back, convinced by Farrell to sign for another year. He had thought about retiring and moving to Baltimore to buy a tiling business. But in his heart, he knew all along he'd be staying in Brooklyn with his sick father and wanting in the spring to start his 17th big league season. Besides, writes Burt Solomon in *Where They Ain't*, "Willie was the financially fluctuating ball club's biggest draw, an institution really, the little man embodying the nation's mightiest city."

"Among the Yankees will be found some old favorites and others who fandom will adopt as idols if they demonstrate their fitness for the honor," wrote the *Times*, once again demonstrating its knack for innocuous baseball prose. "Few of the Yankees are strangers here.... With a fair share of luck coming their way, the Yankees have as good chance to win the pennant as any other club."

Behind surprising first-day starter Slow Joe Doyle, the Yankees took their opener April 14 in front of 20,000 at the Hilltop, beating the A's in a 12-inning, 1–0 nailbiter. Even more surprising was Connie Mack's choice as the opening day starter: Eddie Plank? Chief Bender? Nope and nope again. It was Nick Carter, a 28-year-old rookie right-hander who had pitched for Syracuse Stars of the New York State League in 1907 and was appearing in his first major league game. He pitched magnificently and went the distance. It was the high spot of

his season and of his career for that matter; Carter would pitch 14 games, go 1–5 in 1908 and never again reach the big leagues.

The A's sole threat came in the 10th when Doyle hit ex–Highlander Rube Olding with a pitch and gave up a double to catcher Syd Smith who, like Carter, was making his big league debut. Then, with runners on first and third, Carter sent a fly deep to right that Keeler, running at full steam, caught and immediately turned and made a perfect peg to the plate to nail Olding for the third out. The Yankees then pieced together hits by Kleinow, Doyle and Niles to take the game in the 12th.

The next day, an off day for the teams, ballplayers from both sides attended en masse a play at the Casino Theatre at Broadway and 39th Street. Back on Washington Heights the next afternoon, the Yankees with Doc Newton pitching outdueled the A's again, this time 2–1.

Just like that, the Yankees were winning and in the A.L. lead. On April 17, Chesbro shut down the Pilgrims on eight hits and the New Yorkers won 1–0. A month later, they were still in first place, but by then had lost both Kid Elberfeld to an injury and pitcher Bill Hogg to a bad mood.

Elberfeld went down when he was badly spiked on the leg in Washington by the Nationals' Bob Ganley, an injury that caused a cut clear from the knee to the ankle. Hogg was another matter; thinking he hadn't been pitching enough, Buffalo Bill complained about it to Farrell and was promptly sent out to face the Browns. He was lit up and Farrell ordered him suspended without pay. Griffith was opposed on his belief that a ballplayer shouldn't have his salary docked and refused to enforce the suspension.

There were whispers that Griffith, gaunt to begin with, wasn't healthy. Clearly, the strain was catching up to him. On May 4, in the Washington series, Griffith was tossed from the park after protesting violently against a call by umpire Tom Connolly. But he refused to leave and retired to the grandstand behind third base, where he was later joined by third baseman George Moriarty, who was also tossed. The two of them then started to argue with a spectator, and nearly incited the crowd to riot. The next day, Ban Johnson suspended Griffith.

Griffith, though, retained his sense of humor. On the day he was suspended, he and 11 members of the team went to the White House to met President Roosevelt, amidst reports that the two-term President was mulling over a run for a third. "Here's a bunch of mighty handy voters," said Griffith, indicating his players with a backward jerk of his thumb, "and if you'll only get out and run again, we'll also hustle for you to beat the band."

Roosevelt flashed his famous toothy grin and said nothing to indicate his intentions. He only regretted that his son, Quentin, the true ball fan of the Roosevelt family, couldn't be there to meet the Yanks. Roosevelt also regretted he couldn't attend that day's game, saying he had "a tremendous fight on his hands," whatever that was. Just as well: the day's game was rained out.

Rumors flew that Griffith was on thin ice. But thanks to the mound performances of Manning, Lake and Chesbro — sounds like the name of a law firm, doesn't it? — the Yankees doggedly stuck to their lead through May. What good news that Chesbro seemed back and in shape after a winter spent chopping wood on his Massachusetts farm. It didn't hurt that Elberfeld's replacement, speedy Neal Ball, was fielding and batting with aplomb. "The more we see of this lad's work," the *Times* wrote of Ball, "the more we become reconciled to the protracted convalescence of Kiddo Elberfeld."

Not that it hurt all that much either on June 2, when the Yankees dropped a doubleheader to Boston at the Hilltop. Keeler lost the game with two gone in the last of the ninth of the second game when he uncharacteristically muffed a routine fly that let three runs and secured a come-from-behind 6–5 Pilgrims win. More significant was that the loss knocked the Yankees out of the lead for the first time after 37 games. Their record: 20–17, two games behind Cleveland. Who would have thought that the Yankees would then descend the most complete free fall of their history?

16

Rock Bottom

"I came into this game sane, and I want to leave it sane."

— Don Baylor

The Yankees' fortunes went sour very fast that June. "The Yankees took a tumble last week — played poor ball, in fact," Vila wrote in the June 4 *Sporting News*. "They fell off in hitting and fielding, while the pitching was not up to the mark. But that happens to all good ball clubs, and we are not worried at all."

But the fact is the Yankees were, quite literally and suddenly, a terrible ball club. Everything fell apart at once. Hogg, back in the saddle, had a sore arm. So did Doyle. Glade was in bed with malaria. These were not good signs as the team headed west for a tough six-stop, 20-game western swing. They started June 4 in Cleveland and were bombed 10–1, with Manning somehow going the distance. They lost again the next day, then won two behind Chesbro and Orth, before heading to Detroit, where they dropped three of four. By the time they left Detroit for five games in Chicago, they were at .500 and in fifth place.

The White Sox, winners of nine in a row, were hot. Four straight wins over the Yankees later, they had won 13 in a row, during which the New Yorkers fell into sixth. Thank goodness for Manning who took the series' final game to push the Yan-

kees back into fifth, ahead the struggling A's.

Things really unraveled in St. Louis. On June 18, the Yankees were ugly, making eight errors and even losing Harry Niles in the fifth inning from heat exhaustion. They lost 12–6. They lost again June 19, 4–0, and on June 20, 2–1 to, of all people, Rube Waddell, briefly resurrected as a Brown.

The eccentric right hander had been banished to St. Louis for $5,000 the previous winter after Mack had finally tired of his antics and absences, most of which involved the substantial intake of alcohol. Waddell would help the Browns, keeping them in the race and winning 19 games, before announcing that manager Jimmy McAleer knew "as much about baseball as a hog knows about skating" and walking out on the team. It would be his last effective season; booze and age were catching up to the eccentric 31-year-old left-hander. Two years later, he'd be gone from the big leagues.

On June 21, the Browns completed their four-game sweep of the Yankees, 5–1. The New Yorkers had played 17 games on their western swing and lost 13. They were in fifth place, seven games under .500 and ahead of only Boston and Washington. As the team headed east for the road trip's final

138

four games in Philadelphia, Griffith headed off on a scouting trip for new players.

Meeting the team in Philadelphia was Frank Farrell. Earlier in the road trip, the Yankees boss conferred with Griffith in Detroit and returned to New York confident that the team had turned the corner. Brightening his mood was the team's $5,000 purchase of a 20-year-old 6'4" left handed pitching prospect with a wonderful nickname — Jim "Hippo" Vaughn. A Texan, Vaughn was said to throw smoke like Rube Waddell.

But even Vaughn, who would go on to win 176 major league games, couldn't win here. In 1908 for the Yankees, he'd pitch all of 2.1 innings in only two games. Success would have to wait. So, with the team losing like never before, there was Farrell again, waiting for the Yanks in Philadelphia, where they'd play the last four games of the road trip.

On June 23, the Yanks lost again. They hit well, in particular Chase, who had two doubles, a single and scored two runs. But the pitching fell apart and behind Chesbro, then Orth and finally Newton, and the A's won 9–6. On June 24, they tied up all things when darkness ended the game. It was all too much for Griffith, who called reporters together after the game and quit.

At least that was the official version. "It was simply useless for me to continue as manager, and in justice to Mr. Farrell, I resigned," Griffith said. "I grew disenchanted. I was fighting against fate and I knew when I had enough." In five plus years, he had gone 419–370, nearly 50 games above .500. It was awfully good, but he had won no pennants, which in New York just wasn't good enough.

The post-mortems were numerous. One of the newspapers said he had been fired. Others said he had resigned out of (a)

frustration, (b) health and/or (c) a sudden, overwhelming desire to head for his ranch in Montana. The truth was probably somewhere in between, with Griffith having feuded with Farrell and Devery throughout the spring.

The beginning of the end had been set in motion a week earlier, when Griffith wrote to Farrell asking that he be relieved of his contract. The manager had asserted that there was no team dissension and the players were still trying. Rather, it was the old "hoodoo" — his words — that had reared its head. Said Griffith after his resignation: "I hope my successor will pull the team out of the rut and place them where they belong."

But no successor was in place. Elberfeld's name came up. The hard-nosed shortstop, still injured, was known to covet a managerial position, and he and Griffith were good friends. Keeler's name emerged as well and was thought to be Farrell's choice. Catching wind that Farrell was looking for him, Keeler took off, not wanting to even be asked. Hittin' 'em where they ain't was one thing, but inspiring a group of under-achieving ballplayers was quite another. When Farrell came looking for him at the hotel, Keeler was gone, not wanting to even be confronted with the opportunity to just say "no."

The choice was Elberfeld. On June 24, before their doubleheader in Philadelphia with the A's, he was named the team's second manager. Then, the Yankees, now ahead of only Washington, went out and split. The next day they lost again, 6–2, and also lost Chase, when he was badly spiked on the ankle by Jimmy Collins. And with that, the Yankees' 6–14 road trip from hell was done. Back home, it was reasoned, things might get better.

17

Evolution and Other Weighty Things

"Baseball is a lot like life. The line drives are caught, the squibblers go for base hits. It's an unfair game."

— *Rod Kanehl*

The Yankee swoon added to an already-eventful baseball spring in New York. On April 2, after a two-year investigation, a commission headed by former National League President Abraham G. Mills declared that despite overwhelming evidence to the contrary, baseball had been started in tiny Cooperstown, New York, in 1839.

The report was nativist hogwash. Throughout most of the 19th century, the origins of baseball were not even debated. The game had evolved from a variety of ball games played by children and especially the English game of rounders. The theory was air-tight, considering its strongest advocate was the eminent Henry Chadwick, who even used the argument to claim that baseball was the American national game.

But by the end of the century, the idea that the game had been influenced, even slightly, had started to offend many, most notably Albert Spalding, the famous pitcher turned sporting good magnate. Jumping on the bandwagon was Mills, who used the occasion of a banquet in honor of Spalding to make a public rejection of the rounders theory.

It was baseball's version of creationism. "Patriotism and research had established the fact that the game ... was American in origin," said Mills, not bothering to specify either his research or his facts. The debate picked up steam in 1905 when Spalding, in reaction to a letter from Chadwick, decided something should be done to resolve the debate. He formed the commission to investigate, and sent word they'd be willing to look at information from anyone interested in helping.

The debate raged for two years. Spalding favored an evolutionary theory of baseball's origins, but believed it started, not with rounders, but with the American colonial game of "One Old Cat," a game played by three boys consisting of a thrower, a batter and a catcher. A similar game, "Two Old Cat" and so forth, would add extra players with the ground laid out around a square. His theory was that the game started here: "Some ingenious American lad naturally suggested that one thrower be placed in the center of the square," which brought more players into the game and made it possible to change sides.

Arguing that "boys do not make records of the rules of their boyish game," Chadwick countered that rounders was the logical origin of baseball. After all, he wrote,

"America has no Stonehenge and therefore we are handicapped in any discussion of this nature by the entire absence of contemporary data."

The points and counterpoints rolled on. How happy the Mills Commission must have been when it received a letter in 1907 from one Abner Graves of Cooperstown, New York, who claimed he'd been a boyhood playmate and fellow student of Abner Doubleday in 1839 at Green's Elementary School in Cooperstown, New York. It was there, Graves wrote, that Doubleday outlined with a stick in the dirt the diamond-shaped field, complete with the number of players specified and the rules of what he called "Base Ball." Graves claimed to have been one of the boys recruited to play in that first game.

It didn't hurt the theory that Doubleday had become an American hero, later graduating from West Point and guiding the Union Army in 1861 at Fort Sumter at the outbreak of the Civil War. Nor did it hurt that Graves claimed to have opened a trunk in nearby Fly Creek, New York, and found what is reputed to have the first known baseball, a mangled little thing that stands as a centerpiece to the Baseball Hall of Fame collection in Cooperstown. Doubleday himself is never known to have even mentioned baseball; he retired from the service in 1873 and died in 1893, his lips sealed to the end.

Others piped up. But Graves had captured the attention of the Mills Commission, which declared finally that baseball had been Doubleday's doing way back in 1839. In the end, it didn't make a difference. Their most lasting legacy wasn't on the place of origin since most people considered their findings hooey, it was designating that Cooperstown was the most likely site for a possible baseball Hall of Fame and museum. That, in fact, happened, 30 years later.

Then, quite suddenly, Chadwick died of heart failure at his home in Brooklyn. The end for baseball's august promoter at the age of 85 came only 18 days after the Mills Commission issued its report.

How fitting that Chadwick's first question after briefly recovering following his stroke was the outcome of that day's Brooklyn-Giants game. And how fitting it was that his home of Brooklyn later became the symbol of a population made for its team. Yes, baseball owes a lot to Henry Chadwick.

Elsewhere in baseball circles, that spring of 1908, baseball's anthem was born. The National Anthem? No. Try that schmaltzy, waltzy little ballad "Take Me Out to the Ballgame," the most popular baseball song of all time.

Every red-blooded baseball fan knows at least the first verse of the song, sung for generations at most seventh-inning stretches at the old ballyard. But how this song, written from language taken from a subway ad, became an American folk classic is an intriguing tale.

There are more than 100 recorded versions of the song. In the 1949 MGM musical "Take Me Out to the Ballgame," the title song got the attention of some real all-stars, as Frank Sinatra sang it, Gene Kelly tap-danced to it and Esther Williams swam to it. In the updated 1950 version, the Dodgers' Roy Campanella and Ralph Branca, along with Phil Rizzuto and Tommy Henrich of the Yankees, teamed with Mitch Miller and the Sandpipers.

There are lots of other, better songs about baseball. What is particularly ironic about this one is that the song's composers, Jack Norworth and Albert Von Tilzer, had never even seen a major league game, nor had any interest in the sport when they composed their ode to baseball. That they composed *the* song that became the National Pastime's National Anthem is about as unlikely as Hal Chase clerking at the Christian Science Reading Room.

Norworth wrote the lyrics to "Ballgame" on a 1908 subway ride, getting the idea from an ad promoting baseball at the Polo Grounds. Norworth gave the lyrics to Broadway show tune producer Albert Von Tilzer — he of the five famous Tin Pan Alley composing brother brood — who promptly composed the memorable music. But when he introduced the song to his act at the Amphion Theater in Brooklyn, it bombed.

Figuring he had a dud on his hands, Norworth forgot all about it, until three months later when he reintroduced the song during the ninth act at Hammerstein's Victoria Theatre vaudeville show in Brooklyn and the crowd went wild. So what happened? The positioning of the galaxy perhaps — and good timing.

Actually, the song's sudden popularity may have had something to do with the exciting National League pennant race of that year, won by the Cubs over the Giants and Pirates by a single game. Another craze of the era — the spread of popular music through nickelodeons — may also have contributed to its popularity as well. Indeed, when Norworth discovered he had a hit that night at the Victoria, he found the song had already proven so popular that several acts before him had blended it into their acts.

So Norworth had a hit — one of many, including "Shine on Harvest Moon" — in a prolific career of some 3,000 songs. Actually, "Ballgame" was more than a simple chorus we all sing at the ballpark. It includes more verses than the standard ditty and tells the tale of one Katie Crosby, a baseball-mad young woman who turns down her beau's invitation to a show, insisting instead he "take me out to the ballgame."

The song would inspire a virtual "golden age" of baseball songs, which is hard to fathom since most appeared to be forgettable imitations of the Norworth/Von Tilzer classic. Even George M. Cohan tried by co-writing a suspiciously like-sounding song called "Take Your Girl to the Ballgame." Said Norworth of that effort: "Who ever heard of a baseball song with, 'in the stands it's so grand if you're holding her hand at the old ball game?' Nobody holds hands at a baseball game.'"

Then again, how would Norworth know? Both he and Von Tilzer lived long and artistically productive lives, but never showed the slightest interest in baseball. It took Von Tilzer more than 20 years to see his first game. Norworth wasn't in much of a hurry either, finally making it to Ebbets Field on June 27, 1942, when the Dodgers had a day for him.

So how could these two men who could care less about the game write the baseball song that is embedded on the consciousness of America? Explained Norworth years later: "A friend of mine, Harry Williams, wrote 'In the Shade of the Old Apple Tree,' and he never saw an apple tree."

Headed home after the road trip, the Yankees had a glimmer of hope that things might improve. Back on the Hilltop June 27 for the first game of a homestand against Boston were 6,000 fans, along with Farrell and even Griffith present to see how things turned out. It was a decent crowd, considering that Christy Mathewson was on the hill for the Giants in Brooklyn and that there was an Ivy League rowing championship down on the Hudson all on the same afternoon.

And for a day at least, the tide was stemmed. Out rolled a giant floral tribute to wish Elberfeld luck before the game. And although the Pilgrims roughed up Orth for four runs in the first, the Yanks humbly fought back to make it 6-all, that made possible with a three-run outburst in the eighth. Then, in the ninth, Lake, the Yanks' third pitcher of the day, laced a double, scoring Conroy who had walked, and Hemphill dropped a single, scoring Lake. The pitcher then stopped Boston in bottom of the ninth to leave the Yanks with a satisfying 7–6 win.

Three days later, it was back into the tank for the New Yorkers when they were no-hit by Cy Young, 8–0. It was the third career no-hitter for the legend and the first time the Yanks had ever been no-hit. At 41, Young became the oldest man to throw a no-hitter, a record that endured until 1990, when Nolan Ryan threw one at 43. The performance came amidst Young's last of 14 seasons with 20 or more wins. He'd be sold for the '09 season to the Cleveland Naps and retire two years later.

Meanwhile, Chase was still hurt and hobbling about on a cane, Slow Joe Doyle had a bum arm and Niles had yet to lick his problems from the heat. But even with all the injuries, the big question wasn't whether Elberfeld could manage, but manage to behave himself. "The new manager has the support of everybody who likes aggressive baseball," wrote Vila, "but he should restrain himself in his troubles with the umpires, if only to avoid being placed out of commission by President Johnson."

Elberfeld did what he could. He moved Jake Stahl to replace Chase and then changed his mind and sold him back to Boston, and then reacquired Frank Delahanty. He tried Moriarty in the outfield and Kleinow at second of all places. Still, he couldn't help himself and got suspended for arguing in the Boston series with who else but Silk O'Loughlin? Then, he went to Washington and eventually got suspended again. Really.

In the first game of the July 4 doubleheader against the Nationals, Elberfeld, watching the game from the grandstand, tried to make a pitching change by jumping up and down and yelling for Doc Newton to take the place of Manning in the seventh. He did so and the Yankees won, but Elberfeld was banned again, this time to the center field clubhouse.

Nothing worked. Finally, on July 23 with a doubleheader loss to the White Sox at the Hilltop, the Yankees officially hit rock bottom — last place behind even the Nationals, 23 games under .500. Then Kleinow broke his finger and was lost for the season, Keeler got sick and so did Conroy. "The team is sadly crippled and disorganized and nobody seems to care what happens to it," Vila wrote in the August 6 *Sporting News*.

Clearly, the Yankees were not responding to the hard-nosed Elberfeld, himself still out with a bad leg from the spiking back in the glory days of May. Attendance was falling so sharply that *Globe* beat writer Mark Roth wondered, "If it gets any smaller, they'll have to put fractions on the turnstiles." There were reports of team dissension, divided into those who liked Elberfeld, and others who didn't and were loafing as a result.

One such loafer was Chase. "There is only one Chase and he has an array of followers here," wrote Vila. "But he acts at times as if his heart were not in his work." That was putting it mildly, for not only did Chase not like Elberfeld, but he'd become inflated by his own press clippings, so much so that he thought he should be manager. It only inflated his feelings of hostility about the Tabasco Kid.

So Chase sulked. He pouted. He mouthed off about Elberfeld, further dividing the team into factions. He lollygagged in chasing down errant throws, ones he would have reached a year earlier, and he swung at pitches that before he would let go. And when he was finally replaced by Moriarty in mid–August for what the Yankees said was an ulcerated tooth, Vila figured "it was more a case of a sore head than anything else."

When Farrell fired trainer Mike Martin, Chase went into a real funk. It was a move of desperation for the Yankee president, who figured that Martin had become too friendly with Chase and was a bad influence. Actually, the move was at the insistence of Elberfeld, which alienated Chase even more. Could it have been around then that Prince Hal first started picking up a few extra dollars to work with the gamblers? Considering it was in 1908 that Chase firmly established his pattern of erratic behavior on the field, it's entirely probable.

"Perhaps Chase wants to be traded?" wondered Vila. "Perhaps he has a chance to get more money? In either case, it is a sure bet that the great first baseman is disgruntled. If I had a say in the management, I'd trade Mr. Chase so quickly it would make his hair stand on end. A player who, for petty reasons, does not give his full value to his employer is not fit to remain in professional baseball."

If Chase wanted to be traded, he didn't let on. On Friday, August 21, Farrell, hearing rumors that Chase was about to quit and leave for California, was assured by his first baseman that yes, he was committed to New York and wanted to stay. At the same time, he added that Elberfeld's temper and frequent tongue-lashings of players were a cancer on the team.

Chase had a point. With every loss, Elberfeld's rage, and particularly his wrath against umpires, boiled nearly to the breaking point. Chase noted one recent incident when Elberfeld went after umpire John McCarthy by spitting tobacco juice in his face and punching him. Farrell excused the behavior, meekly saying that Elberfeld was committed to winning. McCarthy suffered permanent damage to his right eye from the incident. All the Kid got was a two-day suspension.

"Gee, Frank, we all want to win,"

Chase said. "But after all, we are playing a kid's game and getting paid to do it. You can call it what you will, but as far as I'm concerned, Kid Elberfeld is definitely unbalanced."

On Sunday August 23, New Yorkers woke up to headlines in *The Evening Journal* in which Chase announced he was quitting. He said some other things too that turned the tumultuous Yankee season into a soap opera, that nobody on the team liked or respected Elberfeld and that the management of the team was a joke. Then Chase said more, that he'd disrupt the team if he was forced to keep on playing and he'd never again suit up as long as Farrell was in charge.

Farrell was stunned. Then, just like that, Chase said he had been misquoted and it was all a big misunderstanding. The article in question, it was said, was planted by a scribe who hated the Yankees and was looking to trash them as a way of supporting the National League Giants. Chase even went to the ballfield and resumed his duties at first base. So, he didn't bolt after all. As with most things Chase, fingers were pointed and things were murky.

Rumors flew that Chase was negotiating with the outlaw California State League and was about to leave town. On September 1, he received his salary and had another chat with Farrell, assuring him. The Yankee president said a few days later, "that he was more than satisfied with the treatment that he had received ... and (giving) me his word of honor as a man that he had no intention of leaving the New York Club."

Two days later, Chase reported for morning practice before that afternoon's game against Chief Bender and the A's. He lasted through the practice, packed his trunks and really did quit, still stewing over the August 23 article in *The Evening Journal*. This time, he said, it was Yankee management that had planted the story to discredit him.

"I am not satisfied to play under a management that sees fit to give out a story detrimental to my character and questions my integrity and honesty," Chase said before leaving. He went on to say that he was quitting to return to California, and oh, by the way, that he never had managerial aspirations.

Farrell was stunned all over again. "He has repeatedly defied organized baseball, and in this way, has caused more trouble than any other ball player in the league," he said. "Regarding Chase's published threat to disrupt baseball in this city, I would welcome any statement he may see fit to make."

But Chase had signed with Stockton and really was gone. There were no further statements and Moriarty replaced him at first. Later in the day, the Yankees beat the great Bender, 2–1, and "Oh, by the way, Chase wasn't among those present," wrote the *Times*. "Don't everybody get excited. It's been sort of a futile Chase anyway, for the last few weeks. And we won yesterday without him."

But then the Yankees went right back in the tank. On September 7, Nationals pitcher Walter Johnson shut out the New Yorkers for the third time in four days, 4–0. At least with the Big Train, working on a 14–14 record that season and still two years away from stardom, they had an excuse. The shutout would become a specialty for Johnson, who would pitch a record 110 of them during his 21-year-career — 20 more than runner-up Grover Cleveland Alexander.

Amidst the wreckage, Elberfeld did his best — trying to fire up his ballplayers from the dugout and tinkering with the lineup. Harry Niles, hitting .248, was traded to the Red Sox for Jimmy O' Rourke, son of the former Giant and future Hall of Famer "Orator" Jim O'Rourke, a hero of the Giants from a decade before. The genes didn't help.

O'Rourke, the younger one played a few games for the Yankees for the proverbial "cup of coffee" — baseball-speak for a short big-league stay — and then was gone.

Faring somewhat better was Jack Warhop, a Native American by the way of West Virginia, who had been pitching well for Williamsport of the Tri-States League. The right-hander stuck with the Yankees and would last eight years with the team, winning 11 games in 1909, 14 in 1910 and 13 in 1911, before retiring in 1915 with 68 big league wins to his credit.

Having a hand in most of the new player moves was former Phillies and Giants manager Arthur Irwin, hired by Farrell as general manager and head scout. On the surface at least, it was a good move. This former shortstop and 13-year big league veteran who had piloted six clubs in eight big league seasons was considered one of the shrewdest baseball minds in the business.

Sure, Irwin's acquisitions would help the Yankees. But it was actually off the field that Irwin had true creative talent. For him, just getting to the ballpark every day was an accomplishment.

Cooperstown recognition isn't given for Irwin's brand of unusual extracurricular talents. Away from the park, the former shortstop and 13-year major league veteran, had a wife, Edna, who he had married in 1883 while playing for Providence of the National League. Edna and the couple's two daughters and son lived in Boston. So?

Irwin's story gets interesting around 1890, when he became a bigamist — this time, marrying a New York woman, with whom he had a son, while continuing to manage in Philadelphia. Neither woman was aware of the other, although for a time, Edna and the couple's three children from family number one lived with him at the Grand Hotel. Meanwhile, wife number two and their son, whose names are lost to history, resided nearby. Both wives considered Irwin a devoted husband and family man.

Maybe it all did catch up to him after all. Baseball's original ramblin' guy died in 1921 at the age of 63, an assumed suicide. *The Baseball Encyclopedia* says he died in the Atlantic Ocean, bringing an odd close to an odd life. No further word on Edna.

More galling to Farrell was that the Giants were having another year for the ages — not just playing well, but challenging the Cubs and the Pirates for what was one of the great pennant races in history.

The National League race was a summer-long dogfight, so marvelous that it obscured the race in the American League, which itself was a good race. In the end, both races came down to the final day of the season and both ended with three teams separated in the standings by a game or less. "To non-baseball fans, 1908 was the year that nobody talked about the presidential election until November," writes Thomas Gilbert in *Dead Ball: Major League Baseball Before Babe Ruth*.

Gilbert writes that the baseball events of 1908 would be so seared into people's mind that decades later, dead ball notables like Three Finger Brown, Christy Mathewson, Honus Wagner and Ty Cobb would be asked over and over again about that season.

Thanks to another sensational season from Cobb and a quirk in the rules, the Tigers took their second straight American League title. Detroit won 90 games to edge Cleveland by a half game and the White Sox by 1½ games. Cobb and Crawford again placed 1–2 in the A.L. batting race and a 33-year-old rookie right hander named Ed Summers won 24 games to go with a glittering 1.64 ERA.

Helping out was an antiquated rule specifying that teams did not have to make up rain-outs or postponements, even if they might affect the standings. As a result, the Tigers defended the flag by playing only 153 games — one less than the schedule and Cleveland, which played all 154. Such a scenario wouldn't happen today; they'd have to make up the extra game and if they lost, would have to go to a playoff.

Thanks to Walsh, the White Sox made the race interesting. Similar to Chesbro four years before, the big right-handed spitballer came into his own in 1908, going 40–15 and pitching an astounding 464 innings. Of those wins, 12 were shutouts. And of the White Sox's final nine games, Walsh started seven, one of them a memorable October 2 duel against Addie Joss of Cleveland. Walsh was tough, giving up four hits and striking out 15 in eight innings. But Joss was perfect, retiring all 27 Sox batters in a 1–0 victory.

Three days later, Walsh won his 40th game of the season, topping the Tigers 6–1. But he'd rest the next day — October 6 — in the final game of the season and Doc White shelled in a 7–0 loss that gave the pennant to Detroit. A footnote to the season's last game is that Crawford would finish with a league-leading seven home runs; having led the N.L. in 1901 with 16, he became the first player to lead both leagues in homers.

Over in the National League, the race was every bit as epic. In another year of pitching dominance, Mathewson stood head and shoulders above the crowd, keeping the Giants at or near the top and the turnstiles clicking by leading the league in wins — 35 — as well as complete games, strikeouts and ERA. It didn't hurt that Hooks Wiltse won 23 games for the Giants, and that Donlin, a reclamation project in progress, had another sensational year, hitting .334 when he wasn't squiring actresses around Broadway.

Keeping things interesting were Fred Clarke's Pirates, who combined their superstar, Wagner, who hit .354 for another batting title, and the steady pitching of Vic Willis (24 wins) and Nick Maddox (23 wins). After winning 90 games in '07 and

93 in '06, all the Pirates had to show for their efforts was a distant second place finish.

The reason: The Cubs were again the team to beat. Chicago was led by the usual cast of characters, including Frank Chance, the Evers-Tinker double play combo and the pitching of Brown (27 wins) and Reulbach (24 wins).

You probably know the rest of that season's National League story — starting with how on September 23, in a climactic Giants-Cubs matchup at the Polo Grounds, 19-year-old Fred Merkle of the Giants failed to touch second base with the score tied 1–1 in the ninth inning after Al Bridwell had singled home Moose McCormick for the apparent game-winning run. But with the crowd milling about on the field and Merkle and the other Giants headed toward the clubhouse, Umpire Hank O'Day ruled that the ball was still in play. When Johnny Evers retrieved what the Cubs said was the game ball and touched second, Merkle was ruled out and the run voided. The game needed to be replayed.

And if you know baseball, you probably know the aftermath. The next day, N.L. President Harry Pulliam upheld O'Day's weird delayed decision, plunging the race into a playoff. In the playoff, the Cubs won and beat the Tigers in an anti-climactic World Series, topped off by the smallest crowd in Series history — 6,210 — who watched the fifth and final game in Detroit.

No, the Giants hadn't won the pennant. But they had won 98 games for McGraw and played to a major league record 910,000 fans, a figure that would stand until 1920 when the Yankees of Babe Ruth became the first team to draw more than one million. But these Yankees of 1908? After the mid-season swoon, attendance fell off dramatically to hit only 305,500, ahead of only the lowly Senators in the A.L. The decline in attendance — more than 44,000 from 1907 — matched the team's depleted fortunes.

The Yanks had gone bad quickly. On June 1, the Yanks were in first place with a 20–15 record. When their season mercifully ended October 8 with a 7–5 loss in Washington, its final record was 51–103. The Yanks had won 31 games over its final four months, had finished 39½ games behind, a distant 17 games behind the next-to-last Nationals. The .331 percentage would be the Yankees' second worst in its history, eclipsed only by the 1912 team that would win 50 games for a .329 percentage.

In the end, Kid Elberfeld won only 27 of his 98 games managed. The Yankees' breakdown was most apparent on the mound — they were the major leagues' only team in that year of the pitcher to have a team ERA of more than 3.00, far above the A.L. average of 2.38. And the records were abysmal, with Rube Manning as the team's big winner with 14 wins (and 16 losses). Meanwhile, Chesbro went 12–20, Lake 9–22, Hogg 4–15 and Orth a sad 2–13. Shades of the 1962 Mets.

Things were just as sour for the position players, with Conroy hitting only .237, Moriarty, .236 and Kleinow, a measly .168, his worst season ever. By the end of the season, there was no Chase, although Prince Hal still managed to hit a respectable .257 in 106 games. Nor was Keeler there at the end, having returned home to Brooklyn and boycotting the season's last six weeks in protest to Elberfeld's surly managing style. Keeler left the team with six weeks to go, having returned to the team after an illness and costing the Yankees a game when he muffed a fly ball in left field. Keeler left, telling Farrell that "I cannot give you a run for your money." He quit without pay.

Even so, Keeler managed to have a respectable season — batting .263 in only 323 at bats, his most limited action since way back in 1894, a millennium in baseball circles and his first full season in the bigs. That winter, Keeler's real reason for leaving would become clear: his complete disillusionment with losing. "When I saw game after game lost by rank playing," he told Vila in February 1909, "I became so disgusted that I couldn't play myself a little bit."

Only center fielder Charlie Hemphill managed to have a solid season, hitting .297, good for fourth place in the A.L. batting race in the year of the pitcher. It would be a career year of sorts for the journeyman 32-year-old outfielder. He'd play three more seasons with the Yankees, mostly as a fourth outfielder and a pinch-hitter.

By season's end, it was all but certain that Elberfeld would be back as an infielder but not as a manager. Irwin gave the Yankees some certainty in the front office. What they needed more than anything was a manager who could discipline and keep the players in line. The search didn't take long: By late October, Farrell had found his man.

18

Nowhere to Go But Up

"Don't forget to swing hard in case you hit the ball."

—*Woodie Held*

Farrell's choice was right under his nose. He was 41-year-old George Stallings, who had been managing Newark in the Eastern League and was a first-rate baseball mind in the making. An Augusta, Georgia, native, Stallings had reached the major leagues 19 years before, as a catcher with Brooklyn. In 1897, he turned to managing in the old 12-team National League for the Phillies, where he stayed for two seasons, before jumping to Detroit late in 1898 and managing until 1901, the American League's inaugural season. But it wasn't until he reached Buffalo of the Eastern League that Stallings carved his reputation, winning two pennants in five years, before heading to Newark for a year.

Stallings' hallmarks were supreme confidence, a good rapport with his players and iron discipline. Born to a Georgia family with an aristocratic past — his father was a Confederate general who used his friendship with William Tecumseh Sherman to spare their property from destruction — Stallings was an anomaly in the dead era of largely uneducated ballplayers. A graduate of Virginia Military Institute who had attended medical school, he was an intriguing blend of the military mindset and the dapper Southerner.

Stallings was intense, hot-tempered and spectacularly foul-mouthed on the diamond. "Dunce," "bonehead," "simpleton" and "clown" were among the printable nicknames he reserved for his ballplayers. "Bonehead," he once screamed while managing the Boston Braves, "get up there and hit!" Six players grabbed bats. Said catcher Bubbles Hargrave: "He was the cussingest man I ever knew."

But Stallings was far from the baseball ruffian. Off the field, he was a charmer, a good interview with reporters, popular with fans, a sharp, snazzy dresser and the owner of perhaps the most unusual middle name in baseball history — "Tweedy." He was also an innovator and smart about it — the first man to regularly play platoon ball by using left-handed pitchers against mostly left-handed lineups and other lefty/righty combinations in the outfield.

Stallings was quirky, a profoundly superstitious man who was convinced that litter in and around the dugout would bring bad luck. On lots of days, he could be found bending over and picking up scraps of paper and peanut shells. He would maintain whatever position he was in when his team got a hit. There is the story of how Stallings, managing the Braves to their

149

George Stallings (National Baseball Hall of Fame Library, Cooperstown, NY)

"miracle" pennant in 1914, bent over to pick up a peanut shell, right as a Boston batter scorched a base hit. So there Stallings remained hunched over as the next batter did the same, and on it went. By the time the rally was over, the Braves had compiled 10 hits. And Stallings's back ... well, there's no word of how he felt.

For the record, Stallings was also a shrewd businessman. In an age before agents and money managers, he and his fellow Georgian and close friend, Ty Cobb, were two baseball men who invested well and enjoyed the proceeds. Stallings's off-season home even had a name — Haddocks — which was actually the name of the small town outside Macon, where he built a 4,000-acre plantation where 50 black people produced cotton. It was there that Stallings liked to bring his baseball friends — Cobb and Honus Wagner among others — for some post-season duck-hunting.

The new man faced formidable odds. "Stallings will have a hard task on his hands

to build up a team that finished the (1908) season completely disorganized," wrote Vila in the October 26, 1908, *Sporting News*. "But he will have some excellent material to work with and the fans expect to see the Yankees well up in the list."

Stallings didn't actually sign a contract until November 5 — two days after William Howard Taft, the first true ball fan in the White House, was elected President. In making the announcement, Farrell said Stallings would have "absolute control" of the team, which he described as ready to "do its utmost to provide winning ball at American League Park."

Farrell had a point. Around the same time, he had given Irwin the green light to scour the land for talent and $30,000 in which to do it. Stallings went right to work, announcing he was spending the winter, not in Georgia, but at the Yankees offices at the Flatiron Building, working in tandem with Irwin to rebuild the team. Concerned that Wid Conroy was injury-prone, particularly as the season wore on, he sold the popular infielder and original Yankee to Washington. That deal solved a couple of other things — freeing up space in the crowded Yankee infield, while securing a spot for Elberfeld at third, assuming he could prove that he was fit enough to come back from the serious leg injury that had held him to 19 games in 1908. Conroy would play three years for the Nationals — retiring after 1911 with an 11-year, .248 lifetime batting average.

There were other big decisions to make. One concerned Keeler, the aging star who had finished the 1908 season demoralized and contemplating retirement. Not that Keeler needed the money; he had invested in a dozen or more apartment buildings in Brooklyn and could certainly have lived off the income. So in January, Keeler did the honorable thing by going to Farrell and saying he was no longer of use to the Yankees. "Yes, I am going to quit baseball," he said, "but it won't be until the wrinkles choke me to death." But Farrell talked him out of it, securing Keeler's services for another year. Feeling rejuvenated, Keeler relented, writing in January to *Sporting Life* that he was feeling fine and would be hitting 'em "where they ain't" again come springtime.

Then there was the question of what to do about Chase. There was always, it seemed, the question of Chase. After bolting New York the previous September, he had arrived in California three days later to — guess what?— more controversy. This time, the question was what outlaw California League team had actually signed him; Stockton claimed him, as did San Jose, his previous employer that argued it still owned his contract. The League sent Chase to Stockton, with whom he played September 9 in a doubleheader at Sacramento. The next day, Chase received what was termed a "substantial" offer from the Red Sox, pending completion of a trade that the Yankees would accept. But Chase was saying he'd never again play ball in the east.

In fact, Chase's jumping to California was part of a trend that consumed organized baseball that winter, so much so that both major league presidents felt compelled to attend a series of December "peace" meetings in San Francisco between the Pacific Coast and the California Leagues. But even with Pulliam and Johnson both in attendance, the meetings failed to stem the raids by the Californians. On January 1, 1909, the *Los Angeles Times'* Stockton correspondent "guaranteed" that Chase would be playing on the West Coast in 1909. By then, however, Chase was of another opinion; on January 9, he applied to the National Commission for reinstatement. That came February 3 on payment of a $200 fine. So Chase — the man who said months before that he was finished with big league baseball — signed with the Yanks for $4,500.

Getting Chase and Elberfeld in line went a long way to securing an infield that

would otherwise have several new faces in 1909. Starting at short would be smooth-fielding John Knight, big at 6'2" and known as "Schoolboy." The 23-year-old Knight had come from the Red Sox after a couple of years with the Phillies. He'd play three years with the Yanks, be traded to Washington, before going back to New York and retiring after the 1913 season. His .239 lifetime average would epitomize the "good field, no hit" shortstop of the times.

Getting a look at third should Elberfeld not recover was 29-year-old rookie Jimmy Austin, an Omaha native. He would end up playing a lot of games for the Yankees for two seasons, before being traded to the Browns in 1911 and enjoying a fruitful 18-year-career. Austin died in 1965 but not before being interviewed and immortalized in *The Glory of Their Times*, Lawrence Ritter's classic pantheon to baseball of the dead ball era.

Then there was Joe Ward, acquired from the Phillies, who would start the season at first, play eight more games and hit .179 before being shipped back to the Phillies on May 20. Ward's biggest baseball contribution? Sharing a page in *The Baseball Encyclopedia* with Hall of Famer John Montgomery Ward.

Joining the outfield would be Birdie Cree, an Irwin find who had joined the Yanks in 1908, played 21 games and did well, hitting .321. He'd be playing behind Keeler, Hemphill and Clyde Engle. On the mound, with the exception of rookie left-hander Jack Quinn, was pretty much the same cast of characters who had been shell-shocked in 1908. The difference was Warhop, Lake, Doyle, Manning and Newton had another collective year's experience under their belts.

Gone was the erratic Hogg, 36–48 in four Yankee years, released to Louisville of the American Association. That was good riddance as far as Stallings was concerned, for Buffalo Bill never was one for training very hard. Gone too were Delahanty, to Louisville, Moriarty to the Tigers, and young Jimmy O'Rourke to Columbus.

Boarding the Southern Flyer in Jersey City for the trip south to Macon, where the Yanks would be spending their spring, there was hope at least that the team wouldn't be the disaster it was in 1908. "President Frank J. Farrell, while not the most optimistic man in the world because of past sad experiences, is mildly enthusiastic on the subject of the team's future," wrote Vila, ever the optimist. "He is banking on Stallings' management and the talent secured by Arthur Irwin, and without trying to flatter either of these men, it looks as if Mr. Farrell's confidence had not been misplaced. I can say that the affairs of the Yankees, for the first time since the American League invaded New York, are now handled with some degree of business judgment."

That went for Stallings' field stewardship. The Georgian ran a tight camp, dividing the team into starters and "colts," who played one another and then other teams. Next door to the ballpark, Stallings was happy to discover a mile-long trotting track, where he sent several of his veterans to help run off their winter bellies. But he also found time to let loose, when during a mid–March rainout, he took off for his plantation at Haddock, with Chase and prospect Clyde Engle joining him for the weekend.

Unlike some previous years, Chase sauntered into camp, radiating joy and peace to all. Much was anticipated about the words he was expected to say to Elberfeld when the two hooked up, their first meeting since the previous fall when Chase had stormed to California, complaining of his old manager's high-strung tactics. But not a bit of it; he and Slow Joe Doyle arrived early the morning of March 5, had breakfast, donned their uniforms and went straight to the ballpark, with Chase making a beeline for Elberfeld and greeting him

with an exuberant handshake. "If there has been any friction between the two, it has all disappeared apparently," reported the *Times*. Reports of ill-feeling between them, Chase said, were simply "dope."

It helped that Elberfeld seemed to be healthy for the first time in quite awhile. He was "gingery" in his step, the newspapers reported, as he tackled third base like a veteran. It was even suggested there was an extra bounce in his step because he was relieved to just be playing again without managerial responsibilities. A more logical explanation was that the 33-year-old Elberfeld found that after years of having to cover a lot of ground at short, he was, in fact, a pretty decent third baseman too. "He is quick as a cat in handling bunts and can make the long throw over to first base like a rifle shot," an admiring Vila wrote. "Stallings made no mistake when he kept Elberfeld for the third corner."

All in all, it was a spring of surprising calm and harmony. Particularly revealing all these years later are Austin's comments to Lawrence Ritter in *The Glory of Their Times*. It is a piece of baseball lore that veterans of the dead ball era, resentful of those trying to take their jobs away, were hard on rookies. Not so, said Austin.

"There were real old-timers on that club when I got there: Willie Keeler, Kid Elberfeld and Jack Chesbro," Austin said of that 1909 spring. "Gee, they were great fellows ... You know, you hear all that stuff about the old-timers being so rough on rookies ... You can't prove it by me. Those guys were swell to me.

"Wee Willie Keeler was still a pretty good ballplayer, even then. He could loop 'em over the infield better than anybody I ever saw. Wonderful fellow. I was too shy to say anything to him, but he came to me one day and said, 'Jim, you've got a great career ahead of you. If I can help you in any way, you just say the word.'" How about that?

"And Kid Elberfeld. Golly, I was out there after the Kid's third-base job, but he always treated me fine." Later that season after Elberfeld was injured and Austin replaced him, the Kid went to the club secretary and demanded that the rookie be given the lower berth on the train. Berths were reserved for veterans. "'Put the youngster down in a lower berth,'" Elberfeld said. "'Take mine if you have to. He's playing every day, hustling like the devil out there, and he needs his rest.' That's the way the old-timers treated a rookie in those days."

But then, in about as much time as it took for Austin to charge a bunt, things started unraveling for Elberfeld, Chase and the rest of the Yankees. It was sudden and it plunged the team into that old, familiar "hoodoo." First to feel it was Elberfeld, called home in mid–March by the illness of his six-month-old daughter who was suffering from diphtheria. The little girl, Nan, would recover and one day become a star athlete in her own right as the Arkansas singles tennis champion.

Then things got weird. Nobody thought very much about it on April 3 when Chase went down with what was described at first as an "ailment." It came just as the Yankees were breaking camp to begin the long northward trek barnstorming to Washington, where they were set to open the season April 12 against the Nationals. Chase stayed behind, vowing to catch up in a few days.

On April 4, the Yanks played their last southern tune-up — against Augusta — and Chase was said to still be hurting and suffering from what teammates described as "a touch of malaria." A day later, with the team set to board the sleeper train for Anderson, South Carolina, for some Carolina League tune-ups, several Yankees visited Chase in the Augusta hospital, leaving a big supply of fruit, flowers and books. The ailing first baseman vowed to rejoin them May 1.

On April 7, however, Chase was confirmed to be undergoing treatment for smallpox and the Yankees had a full-grown health scare on the hands. Evidently, he had contracted the disease from two bellboys at the Macon Hotel where the team had stayed. All three had been reported to the Augusta Board of Health and were being detained in area hospitals. To top it off, two members of Macon's South Atlantic League team — Eddie Barrett and William Brunner — also had contracted smallpox. Headed south to join her husband was Nellie Chase, despite the fact she wouldn't be able to actually see him.

Heading the other way was the rest of the Yankee baseball party, all of whom were immediately vaccinated on getting confirmation of Chase's disease. Traveling through Charlotte to Lynchburg, Virginia, where they were set to play a few games against the city's Carolina League team, they learned that Chase was in fact suffering from varioloid, a mild case of smallpox. Back on the train, Stallings received a telegram from the Lynchburg Board of Health stating the team would not be allowed to leave the train on arrival.

Through nobody's fault, the Yankee spring training had again become a combination of soap opera and life in the twilight zone, not to mention a national news story, prompted in part by banner headlines about it back home in the New York newspapers. Meanwhile, Stallings wondered just what to do. Arriving in Lynchburg at 1:30 a.m. on April 8, he did the only logical thing he could do: reason with the authorities. But there were no authorities to talk with, and a policeman told him to keep his men on the train.

So Stallings flashed a letter from the Augusta physician who had vaccinated the ballplayers. It didn't work. Then, he called the local Board of Health physician and explained that Chase's case was in fact, mild and that yes, most of the players had been vaccinated. It worked and the team was allowed to exit the train and go to their hotel.

No one has died from smallpox in the U.S. since 1978. Today, powerful vaccines have relegated the disease to the history books, making it difficult to fathom just how feared even a mild form of smallpox was just after the turn of the century.

In the 20th century alone, smallpox killed up to 500 million people, more than all the century's wars and epidemics combined. But smallpox was more than just a killer a century ago; the high fevers, deep rashes, aching muscles and oozing pustules that characterize the disease wove a gruesome pattern of disfigurement and pockmarks on its survivors.

Its scars run deep. As many as 3,000 years ago, Chinese records tell of slow deaths and disfigurements from smallpox. There are signs of pockmarks on the mummified heads of the Egyptian Pharoah Ramses V. In the middle ages, smallpox ravaged Europe and came to the Americas with colonists, who spread to virus to Native Americans by giving them blankets infected with the disease.

In 18th century Europe, smallpox killed 400,000 people a year, a toll proportionately equivalent to more than a million deaths today. And unlike some diseases that went after a particular demographic or ethnic group, smallpox's path was indiscriminate, affecting peasants to presidents. One such president, Abraham Lincoln, is thought to have been suffering from the early stages of smallpox as he delivered the Gettysburg Address.

And although vaccinations were common by the early 20th century, outbreaks still occurred like the one in Macon, spreading fear through the populace that a full-scale epidemic was around the corner. So what exactly was varioloid from which

Chase was suffering? It was a mild form of smallpox, to be sure, but don't let that fool you; it was still a disease characterized by an intense fever and pustular eruptions that often left pitted scars or pockmarks when healed.

Several writers have traced the truly malevolent portions of Chase's personality to his 1909 bout with smallpox. They suggest that the scarring from the illness left him a bitter, vengeful man, and trace the crookedness and deceit in his character to the illness. There is, in fact, little evidence of that for if any of the newspaper reports are to be believed, Chase retained a real optimism and humor through his ordeal and handled himself with true dignity and character. If anything, it made him even cockier for he actually seemed to be enjoying the attention.

The same day the Yankees played in Lynchburg, Chase appeared to be improving back at the hospital in Augusta. If the ballplayer was depressed about his illness, he wasn't showing it. For one reason, Chase was delighted his wife was headed south to see him, although he was quarantined, and the two would only be able to chat over the telephone. He was said to be chatting to a lot of others on the phone as well and, in a Chasian kind of way, actually *wanted* to be photographed with his pockmarks. One of the doctors actually complied; no word on what ever happened to the pictures.

Back in Lynchburg, the doctors weren't finished with the rest of the Yankees. They beat Lynchburg 9–3 that day, but before they left, showed their arms to a local physician and only then were allowed to board their train to Richmond. That's where the team was met April 9 at the railroad station by—you guessed it—two more doctors from the city health board, who ordered

Stallings and his men to the hotel to be examined all over again.

Their arms bared, each man was closely examined for evidence they had been vaccinated. Heading up the search was yet another physician — Dr. J. Goldberger, directed by the Surgeon General from the U.S. Public Health and Marine Hospital Service in Richmond. Goldberger and the two doctors from the health board questioned the traveling party — players, team officials and newspapermen alike — about previous vaccinations and the itching of new ones.

Six people, including Newton, Ball and Hemphill, were vaccinated again. So was Elberfeld, still back home in Lynchburg. It was the second vaccination for all. For Elberfeld in particular, it had been a heck of a week of poking and prodding. He had also received a couple of incisions in a carbuncle on his cheek. "The Kid is pretty well carved up," the *Times* wrote.

The good news is the Yankees got a clean bill of health and were cleared to cross the Potomac, where they opened in three days against the Nats. That afternoon, they took their frustrations out on the city's minor league team, 5–1, behind Quinn, before heading home for a quick couple of tune-ups in New Jersey against Jersey City and Newark.

In Jersey City on April 10, they faced the authorities all over again. On a cold, blustery Saturday at West Side Park in Jersey City, the Yankee players were examined to satisfy the skeptics back home. Six more players — Ward, Warhop, Russ Ford, Engle and Austin — were vaccinated for a second time. They wanted to get Elberfeld again as well, but saw the number of incisions on his body and left him alone. Even so, the Kid had a tough day, getting drilled in the eighth by a pitch that landed with surprising accuracy on the very spot of his arm where he'd just been vaccinated. The Yanks managed to win 3–2, losing the next day in a final tune-up to Newark.

It had been a spring of trial and tribulation. Poor Elberfeld, for whom March had started so upbeat, had since undergone the illness of his daughter, a bad cheek, two vaccinations and a sore arm. Ouch. Chase was still in Augusta, recuperating. And several players were said to still have sore arms, owing to the vaccinations. For Stallings and his players, the start of the season was a relief. Playing the games would be the easy part.

Yet there was Elberfeld in the lineup for the Yankees opener — the team's first to be played without Clark Griffith, now in the National League managing the Reds. And there was Stallings sending left-hander Doc Newton to the mound, not as the team's ace, but because the Nats had been particularly lame batting against lefties. It was a last gasp for the 31-year-old Newton who had won 17 games for Brooklyn in 1902, and in 1905 joined the Yanks, but hadn't since won more than seven games in a season. He'd soon be gone — released with an 0–3 record in only four starts.

Lucky that the new-look Yanks were facing the Nationals. "In one respect, the Yankees are fortunate in meeting Washington, as the latter team is by no means a formidable one," opined the *Times*.

One person not attending the opener was President Taft. A 300-pounder who loved baseball, the new president would show his penchant for the game later in the season by attending the April 19 Nats game against Boston. Later that season, he would have a special seat made for him when seeing the Cubs play in Chicago, and meet the champion Tigers at the White House. That December, Taft's sister-in-law, Annie Taft of Cincinnati, bought Shibe Park in Philadelphia.

Quite by coincidence, it was the year that Washington officially seemed to wake up and discover baseball. Also that year, the U.S. Congress would play its first game, with one John Tener, a Pennsylvania Republican, as the center of attention. Tener, an Irish immigrant, was as Bill James puts it, "The Vinegar Bend Mizell of his time," having pitched three seasons in the big leagues and won 25 games. The word was that Tener still had some pop in the old soupbone, but the Democrats won just the same. Tener later became governor of Pennsylvania and National League president at the same time.

For the record, Taft would wait until 1910 to attend the Nationals' opener against Philadelphia and in doing so, inaugurate the pleasant tradition of Presidents throwing out the season's ceremonial first pitch. That would endure for 61 years until baseball deserted Washington after the 1971 season.

Chase, still recuperating down in Augusta, wasn't there either, replaced by Ward. Nor was Chesbro, a hold-out up north on his Massachusetts farm and seemingly near the end of the road at 34-years-old. Also gone were the old Yankee uniforms — the former "N" and "Y" on the shirt fronts of both the road-grays and home-whites by the now familiar interlocking blue "NY" on the left sleeve and at bicep level. The interlocking "NY" made its first appearance on Yankee caps as well, although the lettering was in red and not in white, as today. Also added were two thick horizontal stripes to their blue stockings.

Elberfeld got two hits. But so did Conroy, now playing for Washington, who also scored two runs and helped his new team beat the New Yorkers 4–1, on three runs in the first. Going the distance on the mound for the Nats was veteran right-hander Charley Smith, who'd be traded later in the season to the Red Sox. That it was not the 20-year-old Washington flame-thrower Walter Johnson disappointed many in the crowd of 15,000; the Kansas native, who

had attracted notice the previous September by shutting out the New Yorkers three times in four days, was ill and not yet ready for game action.

It didn't matter for Stallings had his team been playing heads-up ball. The Yankees recovered to take six of their first eight games, seven of the first 10, and bring a glimmer of excitement back to the Hilltop. At the home opener April 22, the New Yorkers returned the favor to Washington, beating up Smith this time, 8–1. Even the Hilltop was looking particularly spiffy, with Farrell having touched it up with a fresh coat of green paint. Meanwhile, the Yankees donned their spanking new home whites and Sheriff Tom Foley followed a pre-game selection of opera music (?!) by throwing out the ceremonial first pitch.

Two days later, the Yankees showed why they were already a better team under Stallings. The *Times* offered sober analysis of the proceedings against Washington, "Yankees Do Things with Baseball Bats," it wrote. True, they did do things, collecting 15 hits and sending an ineffective Johnson to the dugout after only 2⅓ innings. In his first start of the season, Johnson had nothing, walking five and giving up nine runs. Ball had three hits and Keeler, Elberfeld and Kleinow had two each. Lake, meanwhile, scattered five hits and coasted. Final score: 17–0 Yanks.

That Saturday was an eventful day all around. Chase was discharged from the Augusta smallpox hospital and left that afternoon for New York, vowing to be back in the lineup within a week. For the record, the Yanks-Nats game started at 3:30 p.m., drew 10,000 and ended promptly two hours later. That evening, another 10,000 flocked to the ballpark for, of all things, a track meet featuring a 15-mile race between an English runner, the grandly-named Alfred Shrubb, and the Frenchman, Henri St. Yves. Round and round the runners ran the 300-yard or so track — six laps to the mile — that were lit by acetylene gas lamps. Call it, in essence, New York's first night game, won, not by the Yankees, but by an Englishman named Shrubb in one hour, 26 minutes.

Stallings appeared to be a good fit for the Yanks. Sure, he could cuss up a storm. "No man, not even John McGraw or Leo Durocher, ever reached the heights of invectiveness stormed by George," Tom Meany wrote years later. "He could fly into a schizophrenic rage at the drop of a pop fly." But his keen baseball instincts had people talking and talking up the team people started to call "the young Turks."

On May 3, the most important Turk of all made his return. It was Chase, back for his first game, inserted into the day's lineup against the A's at the Hilltop. Batting fifth and stepping to the plate in the first inning, Chase was welcomed back with a flourish, receiving both a warm ovation from the crowd of 10,000 and a $600 silver loving cup from Elberfeld on behalf of the team. "It was a gift on the level," wrote Vila, "and showed just what the Yankees thought of this mild-mannered, modest base ball star."

The Yankees took that game, 9–6 with Chase belting a hit off Biff Schlitzer. How's that for a tongue-twister of a name? Better yet, Schlitzer was part of the best-named pitcher/catcher combo in baseball history — the A's so-called "pretzel battery" of Schlitzer and Ossee Schreckengost, the catcher.

Schreckengost's claim to baseball history? Early in his career, he was the roommate of Rube Waddell, that's what. And it was Schreckengost whom the erratic Waddell blamed when he once refused to sign a new contract.

"You mean you don't think I'm paying you enough?" asked Connie Mack. "No," said Waddell, "It ain't the salary that's bothering me. I won't sign no contract 'less it says that damn Schreckengost quits eatin' them damn crackers in bed."

So that was it. Schreckengost ate crackers in bed and Waddell didn't like the crumbs. He'd not sign a contract unless it contained a clause that said if Schreckengost ate crackers in bed, Waddell would receive a change of quarters. Mack added the clause and Waddell signed.

Back on the baseball field, the Yankees beat the A's again the next day and won the next, this time against Boston. They had taken 10 of their first 15.

Stallings was one important ingredient. So was Austin's play at short and timely hitting from Keeler, Cree and Hemphill. "I know there are a lot of cheap knockers who think the Yankee will tumble to the bottom, just as they did last year, but this time there is a different manager at the helm," wrote Vila May 27 in *The Sporting News*. "Stallings has Griffith beaten in all ways when it comes to shrewd handling and aggressiveness. The players respect Stallings and know that his word is law."

The Yankees' modest success was taking place amidst a sea of change in baseball circles. For the magnates, it had already been a horrid year with more to come. On January 12, Charles Morton, the former President of the Ohio and Pennsylvania Baseball League, disappeared while traveling from his home in Akron to a league meeting in Cleveland.

It was said that Morton was despondent that he was about to be turned out as head of the league and so he disappeared, only to turn up two months later wandering aimlessly about the streets of Chicago. Morton was later determined to have suffered from acute dementia and had wandered around Mexico and Texas during his long, strange journey. When he was picked up March 17, he was found to be muttering incoherently about Corpus Christi. League affairs, meanwhile, was in a hopeless tangle.

It was also the year that the long, sad decline of N.L. President Harry Pulliam came to a tragic end at his apartment in the New York Athletic Club. Severely depressed at his rough handling by N.L. team owners in the rough and tumble world of baseball trench warfare, Pulliam hadn't conducted much business in 1909. Convinced that the owners were plotting against him, Pulliam had taken a long trip west late in 1908, but even that didn't help. He returned more depressed than ever in mid–June 1909 to his office in the St. James Building and committed suicide in July.

An NYAC bellboy found the gravely-wounded Pulliam. He had attracted attention when a club telephone operator noticed that the receiver in his room had been off the hook for quite some time. Dr. J.J. Higgins of 46 West 55th St. was quickly summoned and was working on the body when the coroner leaned over to ask the baseball executive a question:

"How were you shot?" he asked.

Pulliam moaned and said with considerable pain, "I am not shot," whereupon his head fell back and he lost consciousness. Too severely injured to be transferred to a hospital, the 40-year-old Pulliam died at 7:40 a.m. the next day. When he died, Pulliam "had been in a highly nervous state for some time," the *Times* reported, "and some of his friends said ... that his mind had given way under the strain." He was buried August 2 in Louisville.

It was a more progressive year on other accounts. Simply put, it was the year of the ballpark. Both the A's and the Pirates opened new parks in 1909, and not just any ballparks, but showcases for baseball. Both were built with steel and concrete to guard against fire. Both were significantly roomier than the old parks, and both were adorned with architectural flourishes not seen before on ballparks. Shortly after, the White Sox would announce plans for their new baseball palace, set to open in 1910.

Philadelphia's $300,000 Shibe Park opened first, and in April, the Yankees got an early look. What they saw was a new kind of ballpark designed with the fan in mind. It had a classical exterior designed in the French Renaissance style and seated 23,000.

Forbes Field in Pittsburgh opened in June and featured innovations such as elevators for the third-tier luxury boxes and a roomy promenade under the grandstand, where fans could keep dry when it rained. To maintain the purity of the architecture, Pirates owner Barney Dreyfuss barred advertising.

The fireproofing measures started a trend. Within six years, seven more major league teams constructed fireproof ballparks, and others remodeled using fire-resistant materials. By 1915, the Phillies' Baker Bowl was the only unimproved big league park.

There were several reasons behind the rush to build new parks. Many were safety hazards, the most recent evidence happening back in 1903 in the Philadelphia tragedy. Between 1900 and 1911, there were at least six major fires in big league ballparks and countless others in minor league parks. Adding to the woes was flimsy construction of many parks. In New York, it had only been 12 years since a platform at the Polo Grounds had given way to fans scampering for cover from a rainstorm.

On the other hand, baseball was enjoying a boom in the years just prior to World War I and the magnates, conscious that the fans liked the new parks, were anxious to reciprocate. The magnates recognized that they had better offer the public more comfort to meet the growing competition for the entertainment dollar introduced by movie theaters, vaudeville palaces and amusement parks from Coney Island to White City in Chicago.

"Fans were no longer satisfied with uncomfortable benches in ramshackle grandstands and bleachers surrounded by unsightly wooden fences," writes Steven Riess in *Touching Base: Professional Baseball and American Culture in the Progressive Era*. "Owners believed they needed their own comfortable, stylishly designed buildings to compete for the consumer's fifty cents."

Such trends weren't lost on either John Brush of the Giants or Frank Farrell of the Yankees. The Giants, in fact, had spent $100,000 the previous winter to spruce up the Polo Grounds. Among the improvements were extending the grandstand down both lines and rebuilding the ballpark's restaurant, bar and bathrooms. Under the grandstand, Brush had even added an alley where Giant pitchers could warm up and McGraw could manage on days he was kicked out of a game. In McGraw-like fashion, no such accommodations were built for visitors.

The improvements earned the grudging respect of Giant-loather Vila. "It can be said that the new arena is a hummer," he wrote, "and that those who engineered the scheme have the combined thanks of thousands of ball fans who have seen the Giants play in years gone by, standing up in a mob behind the center field ropes." Translation: howling mob, yes, but comfortably seated.

Upgrading the Polo Grounds had another effect. Suddenly, Farrell's little ballpark overlooking the Hudson didn't seem like such a bargain — and he began itching for a new home to put his Yankees. "Farrell does not believe in being outdone and has often told his friends that some time he hoped to own a ball park that would be the finest in America," wrote Vila. "If the Yankees can make a real good, hard fight for the pennant this year, and win it next, Farrell may be compelled to build a stadium something after the plan of the one named for the good Mr. Brush."

A good, hard fight it was for awhile. But a pennant? That would have to wait, for while the Yankees were a vastly improved team under Stallings, there were gaps like a lack of pitching depth and the tendency of the Yankees to lose games late. Their success was still modest, with the young infielders and pitchers developing well, but old mainstays like Chesbro and Orth finally running out of gas — as well as patience on the part of their manager. Then there was Elberfeld, up to the old tricks when he got into another of his patented fits.

The 1909 version of Kid Elberfeld's wars came June 19 at the Hilltop against Cleveland. Once again, it was directed at the play calling of Silk O'Loughlin. Once again, it featured the obligatory bottle throwing and hooting and hollering on the part of the fans, 6,500 of whom had journeyed to the Friday game. And once again, Elberfeld was suspended for his actions, which proved a monumental distraction.

It all started in the fourth when Elberfeld took umbrage when O'Loughlin ruled he had failed to tag Terry Turner on a steal of third base. Up leapt the Kid, barking that the Cleveland second baseman had in fact slid past the bag when he applied the tag. So did a good portion of the third-base side of the crowd, who continued to razz the umpire throughout the game.

Virtually the same thing happened in the eighth when former Yankee Neal Ball opened with a double and tried taking third on a sharp hit by Ted Easterly. But when Chase speared the ball and threw it to third to get the runner, Ball was ruled safe. Elberfeld again protested, as did the crowd. Elberfeld was ordered out of the game and as he stalked off, a bottle came flying out of the stands toward the umpire, missing by a hair. "It didn't hit anybody, but it was the lute that ultimately breaks down the band wagon," the *Times* wrote.

It is June 15, 1909, and the White Sox are beating the Yankees 7–3 at the Hilltop before 10,000. That's Rube Bressler on the mound, Red Kleinow catching and Hal Chase at first base. And that's Bobby Vaughn at second and Ray Demmitt in right — both up for the proverbial big league "cup of coffee" with Silk O'Loughlin umpiring behind the plate. The photo gives a sweeping view of right field and features the big Bull Durham sign, which went up in 1908. (National Baseball Hall of Fame Library, Cooperstown, NY)

After the game, a gang of hotheads ran out of the stands, menacingly heading toward O'Loughlin. Also heading toward poor old Silk were, fortunately, several policeman and Frank Farrell himself, who quickly surrounded the umpire and escorted him toward the clubhouse. Fighting their way through the mob and more debris thrown from the stands — a bottle and a plank of wood this time — they made it safely. O'Loughlin changed quickly and slipped out of the ballpark, thankfully unnoticed.

For all the ugliness of the incident, worse for the Yankees was the timing. At the time, the Yankees were slumping, having lost six of eight games. The argument and ensuing ugliness seemed to throw the team off balance; after Elberfeld was banned, the Naps, clinging to a narrow one-run lead at the time, erupted for five runs in the eighth to win 10–4. The loss dropped the Yanks into fifth place with a 26–26 record. The next day, they'd dip below .500 and not recover the rest of the season. Fifth it would be the rest of the way.

The next day, June 19, in a doubleheader against Washington, the Yankees split. Game one was Chesbro's first start of the season and he got clocked for four runs in the ninth for the loss. There was a time when Happy Jack could be counted on to stem a Yankee losing streak, but those days were quickly coming to an end, and Stallings was losing his patience.

He didn't have to wait long. On August 27 in Detroit, with the Yankees in sixth place, 10 games under .500, Jack Chesbro, the one-time hero of the Hilltop, pitched his last game as a New York Yankee. Entering the game in the third as a mop-up man to left-hander Pete Wilson, who was already behind 5–0, Chesbro pitched himself out of a job. He made it through the third, but then got smoked in the fourth, giving up 10 runs. The game hopelessly out of reach by then, Stallings just kept him in and the Tigers scored two more runs in the seventh. The final score was painful: Tigers 17, Yanks 6.

On September 11, the Yanks twice beat the Nationals in Washington, with Lew Brockett coasting in the opener, 3–0, on a one-hitter. That same day, Chesbro, with an 0–3 record in nine games, was sold to the Red Sox. It was the end of an era: Discounting 1909, Jack Chesbro was the Highlanders/Yankees' first great pitcher — winning 126 games in the team's first six years, an average of 21 a year.

Chesbro wouldn't prolong the inevitable. He'd pitch exactly one game for the Red Sox, starting on the season's last day against his old New York teammates in the first game of a season-ending doubleheader October 2 at Huntington Grounds in Boston. And with that, he retired, heading back to his Massachusetts chicken ranch.

But no Yankee season in that first decade or so was complete without its obligatory dose of dead-ball wackiness. A sliver came April 19, not at the Hilltop, but across the Hudson back at West Side Park in Jersey City in a Sunday exhibition tussle against the city's Eastern League team. It was a most genteel affair: There was no jeering the opposition, no razzing of the umpire and nobody yelling for drunks in the front row to stop standing and blocking their view.

In fact, there was virtually no sound at all. It was a baseball game played in almost total silence as a way of mollifying New Jersey authorities for adopting legislation to ban Sunday baseball. Basically, New Jersey legislators were considering adopting the same law that forbade Sunday ball in New York, and there was a strong possibility that state officials would step in and serve some warrants, once that game had started.

So management devised a plan to avoid trouble. Spectators entering the ballpark were handed a printed card asking that they keep quiet. Yell, clap or hoot and holler, it was explained, and the law might swoop down at any moment to shut things down. As remarkable as it sounds, they kept quiet and a person passing by the park during the game would never have known that a game was in progress. The Yankees did their part, with a patched-up line-up and neither team scoring until the fifth. The final score: 6–3 Yankees, but please, no boisterous celebrating.

The Yankee game had come at a particularly tender time in the ongoing debate about Sunday baseball. Games were still played Sundays, but in constant fear of a raid, so much so that managers typically led off the game with their lowest of the lowest substitutes. The reason: When the authorities arrived, it was customary to arrest everyone in and around the battery, including the umpire and the batter. Losing a substitute was no big deal.

But the game in Jersey City was the only documented case of a big-league team playing in silence. Back in 1905, they'd tried something different to get around the statute at Washington Park, which was playing Sunday, but not charging admission. So more than 11,000 fans showed up and got into Washington Park free of charge — and then paid anywhere from a quarter to a dollar for a scorecard.

Late in the season came the somewhat more demonstrative Great Hilltop Scoreboard Buzzer Caper. With his team mired in fifth and feeling increasing amounts of pressure from Farrell and Devery, Stallings was looking to win by any means possible. It started when opponents noticed the Yankees bats that appeared listless on the road seemed to catch fire back at the Hilltop.

Was it the celestial alignment? The drinking water back home? Or, could somebody be stealing the pitching signs and relaying to Yankee batters? Nonsense, said the Yankees, explaining that the background at the ballpark suited their hitters perfectly. Tiger pitchers like Mullin, Ed Willett and Summers, all on the way to strong seasons, thought otherwise: Why was it they mowed down the Yankees back in Detroit, but the bats mysteriously woke up in New York? Leave it to one Harry Tuthill, the sleuth-like trainer of the Tigers, to investigate.

The Tigers suspected the New Yorkers of an old baseball trick. The most common method was the "sentry-box" in which some kind of shanty or structure would be erected against the outside of the fence, usually in center field, and through the hole, a hidden man would train his binoculars on the catcher, stealing the signs. Then he would signal what pitch was coming to the batter by operating some small portion of an advertising sign on the fence.

So when the Tigers, about to clinch their third straight American League pennant, came calling, Tuthill got cracking. In the midst of a late–September Tigers-Yankees series, he made a lone raid to the bowels of the Hilltop, specifically a spot close to the scoreboard in center field. The way Tuthill told it, somebody heard him coming and scrambled away, even leaving a half-eaten sandwich and freshly-opened bottle of beer. The evidence: On a small platform just below the scoreboard was a handle that

the Yankee sign stealer used to manipulate the crossbar on the letter "H" in the word "Hat." When he turned the crossbar a certain way, the batter knew a fast ball was coming, another way meant a curve.

Certain of his evidence, Tuthill reported his suspicions to Tiger manager Hughie Jennings, who charged the New Yorkers with chicanery. The Yankees were indignant, saying that if any such thing were happening, management knew nothing about it. It quickly became a tempest. In *The Sporting News*, Vila blamed Nats manager Joe Cantillon for starting the trouble and sharing it with Jennings. "What did he find?" Vila wrote of Tuthill's discovery. "Nothing. Absolutely nothing and the lie was quickly nailed. President Frank Navin of the Detroit Club knows this to be a fact and so does Jennings, while President Farrell is ready to prove the assertion beyond the question of a doubt. So Cantillon's scheme to secure revenge has fallen flat."

Had it? Asked about the half-eaten sandwich and bottle of beer, Farrell said they had undoubtedly been left behind by a painter at work on the fences back in the spring. "Some bread and some beer," Tuthill countered. "The bread was as fresh as if it had come out of the oven the day before, and the foam was still on the beer. If I could make bread and beer like that, I'd be richer than Rockefeller in no time."

It seems funny in retrospect. But it speaks to the pressure that the Yankee owners had put on Stallings to win. Sure, fifth place seemed mediocre in hindsight, but it was a sea of change in improvement from the disastrous '08 season and Hilltop attendance was at an all-time high. But it was no irony that Farrell, in early August, had announced he was permanently retiring from horse racing, all in an effort to plow his earnings back into baseball. For years each spring, Farrell had customarily spent $25,000 on yearlings. But the flip side of Farrell's decision to focus solely on baseball was its effect on Stallings: Tightly-wound to start with, the Yankee manager was being driven to distraction by the incessant suggestions from the meddling owners, both before and after games.

The late September series against the Tigers was significant for another reason — it brought to an end the career of another original Yankee. That would be Keeler, who, on September 27 at the Hilltop would go 0-for-4 on a muddy, rainy day 4–1 win against the Tigers. There was supposed to be a doubleheader, but it was so wet and the rain so steady that the second game was called and the Tigers, led again by Cobb and Crawford and about to sew up their third straight A.L. pennant, had to wait another day to clinch.

There were no brass bands nor presentations of loving cups when Willie Keeler reached the end. The understated ballplayer preferred it that way: He sat for the last few meaningless games and then went home to Brooklyn to once again contemplate life after baseball. Injuries had again limited his effectiveness; early in the season, he suffered a charley horse and after returning was headed for the clubhouse after a game when he was spiked, of all things, on the right foot by Bill Hinchman, the Cleveland center fielder. The freakish injury severed Keeler's tendon. He made it into only 99 games and hit .264 in his last season in the big leagues — a decent season for most, but subpar for the greatest batsman of his day.

As usual, Keeler made no announcement about his plans. As usual, he took stock of how he'd make it without baseball. No, it wouldn't be a financial burden, for Keeler had invested well — in Brooklyn apartment buildings, land on Long Island, and along with Farrell and Clark Griffith, ownership of the Eastern League's Montreal Canadians. And, as in previous years, he

waited awhile — but this time announcing February 22 that he was indeed hanging it up.

Farrell made the announcement, saying he'd turned down substantial offers for Keeler's services from two other American League clubs and granted the right fielder his unconditional release. That was considered a high honor and left Keeler with the option to sign with whatever club he wished.

That evening, people made about the only fuss that Keeler would allow. It was a banquet in his honor, held at the Iroquois Hotel in Plainfield, New Jersey, where he had broken in back in 1892 with the Crescents. The 75 admirers there that night presented Keeler with a silver loving cup — what is about loving cups in the early 20th century?— after which the newly retired ballplayer made a speech in which he thanked everyone for attending and recalled he'd enjoyed his time in Plainfield, nearly two decades before.

But it wasn't an American League team calling. It was a National League and it was in New York. Yup, John McGraw of the Giants, nasty and competitive on the field but downright sentimental toward old players off it, signed Keeler up as a pinch hitter and a batting coach. Call it a gesture for an old friend and a bit of a publicity coup — McGraw knew Keeler was still a draw. He would be, sort of, in 1910, but at 38, he wasn't so effective anymore.

So, Keeler pinch-ran and pinch-hit. He taught Fred Snodgrass, the Giants' new center fielder, how to use his wrists when batting. But it would be late June for his first base hit to fall and before he really was finished, he'd bat 10 times and have three hits. For the record, it was his 15th .300 season in 19 big-league seasons.

Then, on September 5, 1910, Keeler pinch hit in the ninth inning for Hooks Wiltse, the Giants' pitcher, but didn't reach base. It was his 2,123rd big league game and his last. Afterwards, McGraw gave him his release and Keeler's career really was over. He finished with 2,932 hits for an astounding .341 lifetime average. But beyond the records, Keeler had changed baseball, becoming personification of the skilled, contact batsman of the dead ball era. "He had modified the prevailing notion of the correct way to bat," writes Burt Solomon in *Where They Ain't*. "Instead of swinging from the very end, ballplayers now commonly gripped the bat farther up. Instead of swinging with all their might, they might take a short chop at the ball." Yes, Keeler's impact had been immense.

Ty Cobb's impact was also quite immense. The tempestuous 23-year-old Tiger superstar and main disciple of Keeler's philosophy had enjoyed another monster season. Not that Cobb seemed to enjoy much of anything; disliked by his teammates and taunted by fans, particularly at the Hilltop, where they habitually pelted him with vegetables, he was a brooding, anti-social loner, driven by an overwhelming desire to show people up.

By 1909, Cobb was revealing his dark side in an escalating number of ugly incidents on the field and off. Late in August against the A's, Cobb spiked third baseman and fan favorite Frank "Home Run" Baker on his right arm, earning the eternal wrath of Philadelphians. Even mild-mannered Connie Mack called Cobb the dirtiest player in the game's history and threatened to take up the issue of Cobb's behavior with Ban Johnson. The A.L. President agreed, saying that Cobb "must stop the sort of playing or he will have to quit the game."

A week later, the Baker incident was still brewing when Cobb got into an argument at the Hotel Euclid in Cleveland with the hotel's black elevator operator whom he later described as "insolent." Cobb slapped the man and was later subdued by the hotel's night watchman, also black. There was an argument and after a struggle, the watchman, George Stanfield, subdued Cobb with his nightstick. In retaliation, Cobb pulled a knife and slashed Stanfield, who then knocked the ballplayer to his knees with another blow to the head. Stanfield later filed charges.

There was other ugliness. Reserving particular venom for African Americans, Cobb once pistol whipped a black construction worker in Detroit for asking him to stay off a stretch of drying asphalt. He did the same to a butcher's assistant in Detroit after an argument about a cut of meat. Guaranteed to turn Cobb venomous were catcalls from the stands of northern ballparks suggesting that Cobb was part African American. Looking ahead, racial heckling at the Hilltop would provide the sorriest of Cobb's many sorry incidents.

Maybe it all served to drive Cobb harder. Nobody came too close to him in 1909. Cobb hit .377 to win the batting title by 31 points. He batted in 107 runs, 10 more than his closer competitor — teammate Sam Crawford — and led the league in hits, with 216, slugging average and even home runs, with nine. Likewise, Crawford had continued to dominate pitchers — hitting .314, fourth in the league.

And once again, the Tigers fielded a line-up balanced by good, but not dominant, pitching. Again leading the way were Mullin with a 29–8 record; and Willett at 21–11 and Summers at 19–9. It was enough to hold off the Philadelphia A's and their phenomenal pitching staff anchored by Eddie Plank and Chief Bender, both 19-game winners with microscopic ERAs by 3½ games. The vastly-improved Red Sox — yes, it was finally the Red Sox and no longer the Pilgrims — took third without Cy Young but helped by a new manager, Fred Lake, and a rookie outfielder named Harry Hooper.

In the N.L., it was another powerful season for the Cubs. Anchored by Three Finger Brown's 26–9 record and 1.31 ERA and the usual suspects — Tinker, Evers and Chance — Chicago won 104 games. But alas, here were the Pirates, in the new home of Forbes Field, who won 110 games and the N.L. pennant. The Giants took third.

The main reason was Honus Wagner. The barrel-chested shortstop hit .339 in 1909, the seventh of his eight N.L. batting titles. And no, he still didn't look much like a ballplayer, but was rounding into arguably the best position player of the dead ball era. No fires of hatred burned in the jovial Wagner; he was everybody's friend, a great interview and a baseball ambassador, who was just happy to be playing ball for his hometown team, the Pirates.

Much was made of his confrontation with Cobb in the World Series. Wagner emerged as the clear winner, batting .333 to Cobb's .231, had eight hits to Cobb's six, and stole six bases to the Detroit star's two. Receiving the most attention was a story told by Wagner — perhaps apocryphal for he was a great story teller in later years — in which Cobb got on base in the opening game and yelled down to short, "Hey Krauthead, I'm coming down on the next pitch."

So when he did, as the story goes, Pittsburgh catcher George Gibson threw a perfect strike down to second, where Wagner laid his glove to make the catch and tag Cobb — smack on the mouth, which needed three stitches to sew up the wound.

But in the end it was pitching that gave the Pirates their first World Series championship. They had an iron man staff that year in Howard Camnitz, a 24-game winner; Vic Willis, who won 23; and Lefty Leifield, who won 17, yet none of those men won a single game in the Series. The hero of the 1909 Series was a 20-year-old rookie named Babe Adams, 12–3 during the regular season, who beat the Tigers three times, including the decisive seventh game. Wagner called it his greatest baseball thrill.

19

Not Bad, Not So Good Either

> "If you know how to cheat, start now."
> — *Earl Weaver, on the mound to a struggling pitcher*

Jack Chesbro and Willie Keeler weren't the only Yankees to depart as the team looked ahead to 1910. The same day Keeler left, 37-year-old Al Orth did too, sold to Indianapolis of the American Association and ending a 15-year major league career that stretched clear back to 1895.

That was the year Orth joined the Philadelphia Phillies from Lynchburg, Virginia, where he lived. Orth pitched seven years there and slightly more than two with Washington before joining the Highlanders in 1904. Orth had contributed, winning 17 games in '05 and another 25 in '06, before struggling his last two seasons, particularly during the quagmire of '08 when he was 2–13. That last season of '09 was a lost one for Orth; he pitched exactly three innings.

On the positive side, call it another sign that Stallings was molding the team the way he wanted. Another mainstay to leave during the winter was Elberfeld, perhaps finally acknowledged to be more of a detriment in his errant behavior than anything. Suspensions had meant another shortened season for the Tabasco Kid who played in only 106 games in '09, hitting .237. He was shipped to Washington to carry on his disagreements with umpires.

Still, 1909 had been a season of modest improvement for the Yanks. Sure, they'd gone 74–77 to finish fifth — a distant 23½ games out of contention — but they'd improved a whopping 23 wins from '08. It had also been another solid season for Chase who hit .283, despite making a league-leading 28 errors at first base. Along the way, Stallings had secured a decent fielding infield, anchored by Austin at third and Knight at short. And his crop of young pitchers had respectable seasons, including Lake (15–11), Warhop (11–16), Manning (10–11) and a bunch of others like Brockett (9–8) and Doyle (9–6) with single-digit win seasons. No, these young "Turks" hadn't set the world aflame, but they were coming along just fine, thank you.

Indeed, the 1910 season would, on paper, be among the Yankees' best. They'd continue to improve, finishing second. They'd hit, run with abandon, and play tight disciplined baseball. In particular, a young pitcher would debut and use a trick pitch to win an astounding number of games and be heralded as a phenom. Crowds would flock to the Hilltop. So why was 1910 so painful and downright dysfunctional for the Yankees? It was the same problem that had plagued them two years before; Hal Chase was feeling his oats.

Things started off normally enough. There was the usual Yankees trainload headed south — this time, not to Macon, but to nearby Athens, Georgia, where the Yankees would set up shop at the Georgian Hotel and train with the hometown University of Georgia baseball team.

With several positions on the team up for grabs, most players reported in good shape. Among them was Slow Joe Doyle, who had spent several weeks at the baths in Hot Springs and was hoping to recapture the magic of his 11 wins back in '07. Sadly, Slow Joe would last only three games with the Yankees before being traded to Clark Griffith in Cincinnati and not winning there either. It would be his last year in baseball.

An intriguing storyline was developing elsewhere on the Yankee pitching staff that spring. The origin of the story dated to 1908 during a spring training session in Atlanta, where two former teammates from that city's minor league Crackers were warming up under the grandstand in an effort to stay dry and out of the rain. They were right-hander Russ Ford, 15–10 the previous year for the Southern League champion Crackers, and his former battery mate, catcher Ed Sweeney. That season, Sweeney, a Chicago fireman during the off-season, would advance to the Yankees, where he'd remain until 1915.

When one of Ford's pitches got away and struck a wooden upright, Sweeney retrieved the ball and tossed it back. Ford threw again and the ball broke, sailing sideways some five feet. Wondering what had happened, Ford examined the ball and found it had developed a scuff mark where it must have struck the upright. Then, as now, throwing scuffed pitches was blatantly illegal.

So he threw the ball again, this time holding it in exactly the opposite way from the previous pitch. And again the ball broke four or five feet, but this time the other way.

"Where did you get that curve ball?" a mystified Sweeney asked. "You never had a good curve when I caught you last year."

"Oh, that's just a funny one I learned how to throw Ed," said Ford. "Forget it."

Sweeney did forget it and went north with the Yankees. Ford forgot it too and himself went north a few weeks later with the Yankees, making a forgettable debut as a mop-up man April 28, 1909 in a one-sided 12–2 loss to Boston. That year, Ford fought a sore arm, pitching mostly for Jersey City in the Eastern League.

But one day in 1909 while warming up at West Side Park, Ford remembered that day in Atlanta where his pitches had broken big-time. Picking up a broken soda bottle, he roughed the surface of the ball and walked out to pitch batting practice.

Ford lobbed the first four or five pitches over and nothing happened. Then, he decided to put some mustard on his pitches and, as he put years later in *The Sporting News*, "the dizzy contortions that ball cut made me doubt my own eyes."

The difference was remarkable. The scuffed-up ball dipped. Other pitches sank and skipped. Cutting loose with an overhand fastball, Ford could see the ball take a hop and then sail sideways, a kind of double curve. Finishing off the day's batting practice, he threw to his Jersey City teammates, Earl Gardner, Dan Moeller and Kid Foster, none of whom could hit him. "Later, they told me that it was their belief I either was a flash for the day, or else they were losing their vision," Ford said years later. "I never took them into my confidence."

Quite by accident with a slight nod to skullduggery Russ Ford, the mild-mannered Canadian, had discovered the pitch that would make him a star. Whether to come clean or continue to conceal his secret and strike batters out became, as he later put it, "the biggest problem of my young life." Keep it quiet and stardom was certain. Spill the beans and, well, it was fun while it lasted.

Ford told no one. Thinking it over back in his Jersey City boardinghouse, he sat down on his bed and pondered his baseball future. "Somewhat selfish, perhaps, I felt that the discovery belonged to me and if anything came of it, I should benefit through its use."

His decision made, Ford set about preparing. Before his next start for Jersey City, he found a piece of emery paper and cut it into small pieces, three-quarters of an inch square. It was just enough to rub the gloss off a new ball, and Ford sewed the small paper onto his glove. And unlike the era's other players who left their gloves in the field when they returned to the dugout, Ford carried his glove with him or stuck it in his back pocket when on the bench. It was best not to have anyone come across the emery paper.

At first, Ford confused players and fans alike with what he called his "freak delivery." Catcher Larry Spahr caught his first emery ball game, thinking it was a spitball that made the ball break so sharply. That was fine with Ford; he did his theatrical best to conceal the reality by going through the all the motions of wetting the ball before delivering the pitch.

Ford threw the emery ball the way any pitcher throws a fastball. Instantly, he became a strikeout pitcher, averaging 10 to 12 strikeouts a game, and once, 16. It might have gone higher had Ford not been spiked by Newark shortstop Baldy Louden. As it happened, he finished with a 13–13 record and tied for second in Eastern League strikeouts that season with Rube Dessau of Baltimore. Taking the 1909 Eastern League strikeout crown: the old Giant, Iron Man McGinnity.

Tracking his progress from across the Hudson was Stallings, who in July, pur-chased Ford's contract for the Yankees. Despite missing more action when the spike wound got infected, Ford continued to experiment with the scuff ball. He took the emery paper from outside his glove and sewed it on the web between the thumb and the index finger. Then, he placed a tiny disc of the emery paper, one inch in diameter, on a ring and cut out the center of his glove. To rub the disc against a new ball to roughen its surface, Ford loosened the glove and let it drop so that the ring finger rubbed against the ball through the opening. People assumed Ford was merely applying saliva to the ball as he held the glove before his face.

So here was Ford getting the nod as a starter in the Yankees' first organized game of the year—a March 10 six-inning intrasquad between the Regulars, under Chase, and his team, "the second stringers" or "Yannigans," managed by Stallings. No one is really certain about the origins of the term "yannigan." Its first use appears to be in a benefit for victims of the 1906 San Francisco Earthquake that divided Brooklyn's Superbas into regulars and substitutes. As a Yankee Yanningan, Ford gave up a run in the second, another in the third and pitched well in a 4–3 game that the Regulars only won with two runs in their last-at-bat. He'd keep pitching well, so much so that a month later, he was the starter everyone was talking about.

People were talking about Chase too. It was shaping into a fine spring for the Yankee star. That spring, he and his wife, Nellie, became the parents of a boy, Hal Jr. In early March, he was named the Yanks' second-ever team captain—Keeler had been the first way back in '03—and it seemed to motivate him. A week or so later, he had sweated off 10 winter pounds, was working hard and enjoying himself on the field more than ever.

Two days after the intra-squad game, the Yanks took on the University of Georgia at Herty's Field on the campus and Chase was clearly the center attraction. With Farrell in camp taking in the game, Chase had two hits and drove in a run in an easy 8–2 win. The gregarious Chase was turning into a true showman, actually taking off his shoes and holding them in his hand, while helping retire the side in the last, scoreless inning.

What a difference a year makes. In an apparent sea change from the smallpox ravaged, sore-armed spring of the previous year, Chase and the Yankees roared through the early part of 1910. Not that major leaguers of the era didn't beat their minor league opponents of the spring with regularity; the difference was these Yankees were doing it with crushing success and a bit of bravado. A case in point: Back home, as tune-ups to the start of the regular season, they beat Jersey City 6–1; Newark 3–2; and then Princeton University 5–2. Also winning were the second stringers, no longer Yannigans, but now called "Americans Number 2," as they wended their way north toward New York, sweeping three games from Lancaster, the 1909 Tri-State League champs.

Then the next evening with everyone back in New York and accounted for, the entire team put on suits and went to the Fifth Avenue Theatre for an "opening welcome" array of songs and jokes. That same night, the Giants attended a performance of "Alias Jimmy Valentine" at Wallack's.

"At the season's start, it is the expected prediction of every manager that his team has been strengthened," wrote the *Times*. True, but there was something about these Yankees as they prepared to kick off their eighth season. At least on paper, there were several reasons to be optimistic, starting with the emergence of Ford and a more seasoned crop of young pitchers like Vaughn, back after a year in the minors, along with

Quinn and Warhop. Another new face was Harry Wolter, a versatile veteran outfielder acquired from Boston for the $1,500 waiver price as Keeler's replacement. Wolter was a throwback of sorts, having played the outfield, at first base, hitting .244 and going 3–3 on the mound for Boston, all in '09. He even showed occasional power, having hit four home runs.

Then, right from central casting came the opener. What a day! On a sun-drenched April 14 afternoon against Boston — now called the Red Sox — the Hilltop was at its finest. Some 25,000 were there, dressed to the nines and "jam(ming) every inch of space in the enclosure (and) root(ing) to their hearts' delight," opined the *Times*. "Mr. and Mrs. Fan and all the little Fans and Fannies were there and said it was the greatest opening ever."

It was all a good omen. Ceremonial flags fluttered in the breeze. The early-arriving crowd filled the stands, as well as the outfield — this time not on foot but in temporary bleachers that lined the wall, obscuring the ads. Then, in a bit of pomp, shortly before 3 p.m., the right field gate popped open and out streamed the Yanks. Led by Captain Chase, the team wore strapping new cream-colored uniforms with the old fold-down collars giving way to new, shorter, stand-up "cadet-style" collars in blue. Even the caps were different, and now sported a red bill instead of blue.

In changing their collars, the Yankees were following the major league styles of the day. It left the Red Sox as the only big-league team still wearing the laced collar, which they'd change for the following year.

At least the Bostons had been a little more aggressive in choosing their new nickname. It had come about after Fred Tenney, manager of the N.L. Boston Doves, decided to switch his team's stockings from red to white, thinking that red would make his players more injury-prone. But when the Boston papers criticized the move, saying that the Doves had always worn red stockings and were making a serious break with tradition, Pilgrims owner John Taylor jumped on the case and announced that his club would from now on wear the red stockings and along with it be called "Red Sox."

Along with the name change came an improving Red Sox team — a young set of players with the makings of a future powerhouse. Under another new manager, Patsy Donovan, who most recently had skippered Brooklyn, there was Hooper in right and in center, 22-year-old Tris Speaker, coming off an impressive rookie season in which he'd batted .309. On the mound were a pair of young right-handers with solid '09 credentials: Eddie Cicotte, 25, nicknamed "Knuckles" for obvious reasons and a 13-game winner; and 20-year-old Smokey Joe Wood, an 11-game winner. Each would reach the record books in his own way — Cicotte as a member of the notorious World Series-throwing 1919 Chicago Black Sox and Wood as a 21-game winner in '11 and a 34-game winner in '12, before developing a sore arm that essentially ended his career. In later years, Wood became the longtime baseball coach at Yale.

Surprisingly, the Yankee lineup was a lot more different than anyone had expected. With Keeler, Chesbro and Elberfeld departed, there were no members of that first '03 Highlanders team left in New York. As expected, Wolter was in right, but there was a new shortstop, Eddie Foster, and catcher Ed Sweeney, the fireman and Ford's former battery-mate. All but two of the players who had started the opener a year earlier — Clyde Engle, the left fielder in place of the injured Birdie Cree, and Charlie Hemphill, the right fielder — were in the lineup this time. And on the mound: big Jim Vaughn, just five days after his 22nd birthday, and still the youngest Yankee pitcher in history to start an opener. Stallings's choice was a surprise, but Vaughn had impressed the New York skipper in that

exhibition tune-up against Princeton, where he'd struck out eight batters.

It was Vaughn's first big-league start and he pitched well. So did Cicotte, the Red Sox starter, and Wood, who replaced him in the eighth. The Yankees scored first, in the bottom of the third, when Sweeney doubled and came home on Hemphill's single. The Red Sox scored in the fifth and the Yanks again in the sixth. Back and forth it went to the ninth, with the score knotted at 4. And that's where it ended after darkness forced the teams to stop after nearly three hours. The game was the first of a record 19 ties that American League teams played in 1910.

That the teams tied didn't matter. It had been a festive, crowded beginning and got the Yankees off to a good start. Two days later on a windswept Saturday against those same Red Sox before 15,000, many in fur coats at the Hilltop, Wolter stepped to the plate. Facing the gloriously-named Sea Lion Hall in the seventh with the score tied at 2, Wolter sent a pitch whistling into the deep crevices of left field. Red Sox left fielder Duffy Lewis made a stab at the ball, "but it shot by him like an express train traveling past a flag station," the *Times* wrote. Thump went the ball against the wall and around the bases rocketed Wolter. When he touched home with the game-winning run, "one could almost hear the tumult and the shouting down in Times Square," the *Times* said. The Yanks had pieced together a gritty win.

Five days later at Shibe Park in Philadelphia, Wolter delivered again. This time, in the first, he doubled, stole third and slid home on Chase's ground out to short. It was all the Yanks needed in their 1–0 win over the A's, for on the mound was the remarkable young Russ Ford and his baffling flutter ball. It was an impressive first start in the big-leagues: Ford scattered five hits, all singles and walked no one. He also struck out eight — four of them the normally-hard hitting Harry Davis.

In beating the powerful A's, the Yankees won their third in five games. Six days later, Ford won again, and then took two more. Ford still hadn't lost on May 11 when he faced the A.L champion Tigers at the Hilltop. Up came serious hitters like Ty Cobb and Sam Crawford and down they went. "Ford shot the moist slant at the slugging Tigers with great speed and judicious control," the *Times* wrote. "The bulb suddenly took a tantalizing little tumble just as Detroit bats threatened it." Translation: Ford was on the money, giving up four hits, walking one. It was in many ways a classic dead ball match-up, with Ford shutting out the Tigers with his emery ball, and big Tiger right-hander Ed Summers practically matching him, inning after inning, with his knuckleball. The Tigers didn't score at all. The Yankees couldn't until the seventh when LaPorte bunted for a single, was sacrificed by rookie shortstop Roxy Roach and scored on a sacrifice by Austin. Backup left fielder Les Channell scored on a hit by Sweeney and the score was 2–0. That was the final and the 8,000 in attendance went home happy.

Far more satisfied was Stallings. With Ford, he had a bona fide big league winner and a phenom. One bit of evidence: The Detroit win gave the Yankees their 10th in 17 games. More evidence: the debut of an unusual ground rule in which umpire Silk O'Loughlin, annoyed at the number of photographers who would position themselves near the edge of the playing field to get their shots, announced grandly that if a ball smashed a camera, base runners would be entitled to an extra base. Leave it to Silk to make decisions to stir up the Hilltop faithful.

Ford and the Yankees were still winning on Memorial Day when they faced the Nationals, but not Walter Johnson, who was in between starts. Ford set down Washington in the morning game 3–1 before a crowd of 7,000, including Silk O'Loughlin and a stray dog. Once again, weirdness seemed to find Silk, when in the seventh, the dog ambled on to the field in the vicinity of home plate and deftly eluded just about everyone who tried catching it. Sweeney tried and missed, then Ford, followed by a crowd of six peanut vendors and Pinkerton detectives. Still it got away. Leave it to sure-handed Jimmy Austin who swooped down, "just as he would a hot grounder," as one eyewitness put it, gathered up Fido in his glove hand and presented it to the detectives. The afternoon game, played before a full house and more at 23,000, featured no dogs and big Jim Vaughn setting down the Nats again, this time, 3–0 on a five-hitter and no stray dogs. His success pushed the Yankee record to 23–10.

Ford kept rolling. On July 14 at the Hilltop, the rookie beat 43-year-old Cy Young of Cleveland 4–1 and kept the legendary pitcher from winning his 500th game. "It was age vs. youth and youth, aided by the emery ball, won out," Ford would say years later, understanding the significance of the event. Young would have to wait five more days to get that 500th win, in Washington, D.C. He'd close out his remarkable year in 1911, pitching for both Cleveland and finally, the Boston Braves, with 511 lifetime victories. In the end, it wasn't his arm that failed him; he had become too fat to field bunts. As for the Yankees, Ford's victory made the Yanks a solid second. Life was good, or so it seemed.

Gnawing just below the surface were some big obstacles. One was obvious: Connie Mack's Philadelphia A's, which were establishing from the get-go that they were headed for the American League pennant. Again, pitching was the difference. On May 12 against Cleveland, Chief Bender threw a 4–0 no-hitter, missing a perfect game with one walk. Bender would go 23–5, which

was ironically one of only two 20-win seasons in 15 years for the future Hall of Famer.
Having an even better year was "Colby"
Jack Coombs, who, with little rest, would
win 18 of 19 starts in July, August and September. Coombs, so named because he had
attended Colby College, would go 30–9
with a 1.30 ERA in 1910. His 13 shutouts are
the A.L. record.

The other was less obvious. Call it
more of a festering sore that wouldn't go
away. It was Hal Chase, again, and his
knack for playing well, but not leaving well
enough alone. Visit the Hilltop as a spectator in those days and you were bound to
like Chase, clearly the most popular Yankee
of his time. That went for covering him;
Chase could be gracious with the press and
good copy. Play with him and you'd probably like him as well. But manage him, or
try to, and you'd probably consider the great
first baseman a pain in the neck.

The first evidence that something was
amiss came courtesy of one Ernest J. Lanigan from an April 7 dispatch in *The Sporting News*. Lanigan was the longtime *New
York Press* baseball writer who took over *The
Sporting News* beat from Joe Vila. Set to retire at the end of the season, Lanigan was
the cousin of *Sporting News* owner Taylor
Spink and a blunt wordsmith without the
pro–American League sentiments of Vila.

Lanigan wrote of rumors that the Yankee camp had fallen into dissension when
Chase had disagreed with Stallings's decision to play Clyde Engle in left instead of
Charlie Hemphill. Was the Yankee captain
trying to manage? Had he started by then
to throw games and deliberately miss a play
here and there, which became his pattern in
later years? Chase vehemently denied it, as
he usually did with any unpleasantness in
which he was involved. But it is ironic that
the story had come out with Farrell in
Athens and close to the controversy.

Was Chase's disagreement, in fact, a
ploy for attention from the Yankees owner?

It may very well have been so; much like
Mathewson's relationship with McGraw on
the Giants, Chase was, in some ways, the
son that Farrell never had.

After all, it was well known that Farrell and Devery had taken a particular lik-
ing to Chase. The three moved in the same
circles and it is likely that the two owners
were the ones who introduced and immersed the young ballplayer into the world
of gambling halls and wise guys. Meanwhile, others were growing wise to Chase's
growing eccentricities. When, during the
season, Jack Knight got a new bat and
went on a hitting tear, Chase asked to use
it too.

"Hal Chase had a thousand bats himself, but he always wanted the other guy's,
especially if it was somebody's who was hitting good," Jimmy Austin said in *The Glory
of Their Times*. "So Hal says, 'You don't
mind if I use your bat, do you Jack?'

'I'd rather you didn't,' Knight said, 'because it's the only one I've got.'" And with
that, Chase got so mad that he took
Knight's bat and slammed it up against the
dugout wall as hard as he could. "That's the
kind of guy he was," said Austin.

That was more than a bat thing. It was
weird. Baseball players of the dead ball era
were to be forgiven for their special feelings
and superstitions about bats — woe to the
batboy who accidentally crossed two bats
while lining them up in front of the dugout.
But Chase's feelings about bats reveal a genuine eccentricity.

It was around then that Chase one
morning placed a call to a doctor to remove
a splinter in his tongue. The doctor removed
the sliver but the question endured: How
exactly had Chase gotten a splinter there, of
all places? He was, well, a bat biter, a man
who'd chew on bats as a test of its wood
quality. No scribe quite had the nerve to
approach Chase about it, so one intrepid
soul asked the Yankee mascot instead. "Yes
sir," the mascot said, "it's true. Almost every

bat we have around our bench has Mr. Chase's teeth marks on it. He just gnaws on them." So what, the reporter persisted, could he tell about a bat by chewing on it? "Mr. Chase," the mascot dutifully reported without a trace of irony, "never lets anybody know what he finds out by biting the bats."

Around then, it was also becoming clear to the writers covering baseball in New York that there were just enough peculiar happenings in Chase's play to cause suspicions. When 23-year-old Fred Lieb arrived on the scene in 1911 from Philadelphia as the new baseball writer at *The Press*, replacing the retiring Lanigan, he was told to keep a wary eye attuned to the suspicion that Chase was throwing games. "Hal was too big to bounce without proof positive," wrote Lieb in his 1977 memoir, *Baseball as I Have Known It*, "and too slick to nail down."

"(Chase) is a remarkable fielder," Lieb's new editor Jim Price told him. "I don't think anyone ever played first base as well as Hal Chase can play it — if he wants to play it. But he has a corkscrew brain."

"I don't want to tell you all I know," Price told Lieb. "I'll just say he can be the greatest player in the world if he wishes. Some days, he doesn't want to be. He isn't a man I would trust."

Growing suspicious, Lieb consulted the record books and discovered that for all the attention extended to Chase for his extraordinary fielding, he had averaged 29 errors in each of his first six seasons in New York, ranking nearly at the top almost every season. Compared to other first basemen, Chase's errors were numerous; in 1909 for instance, he led A.L. first baseman with 28 errors, far outdistancing other established ballplayers at the same position. In contrast, Detroit's Claude Rossman had 18, Harry Davis of the A's had 19 and Boston's Jake Stahl had 20. George Stovall of the Blues had 19 and the White Sox's Frank Isbell had eight. Nobody was even close. For two of

the next three years, Chase would continue to lead the league. Despite playing only 9½ years in the A.L., he remains the league's all-time leader for errors at first base with 285.

Lieb studied Chase hard and was still impressed. Who wouldn't be? "As a glove man, when the mood was on him, only [George] Sisler and [Bill] Terry have come close to him," he wrote. "His range was incredible because of his speed. No other first baseman played so far off the bag. As a man charging in on a bunt, he was fantastic. I have seen him field bunts on the third-base side of an imaginary line between home plate and the pitching rubber, and make his left-handed whip-like throws to third, to second, or to first as the occasion required, all in one apparently seamless motion. He was speed and grace personified."

How exactly Chase was laying down, as throwing games was referred to then, was a subject the writers stepped gingerly around, but was nonetheless a subject of endless intrigue. His most common technique, Lieb believed, was to arrive at first base for a throw from another infielder just a fraction of a second too late. A third baseman, for example, typically throws to the bag, whether the first baseman is there or not. Sure, Chase, playing far off the bag, usually got there. On the other hand, writes Lieb, "If he wanted to let one get away ... maybe if he moved just a bit lazily toward first for a step or two?"

Lieb again: "He would then speed up and seem to be trying hard. But it would be difficult — and it would take a suspicious person ... to charge him with anything but an error if a well-thrown peg slipped off the end of his glove."

Playing with Chase two years later, Yankee shortstop Roger Peckinpaugh would have similar suspicions. "I remember a few times I threw a ball over to first base, and it went by him to the stands and a couple of runs scored," Peckinpaugh told writer

Stephen Fox. "It really surprised me. I'd stand there looking, sighting the flight of that ball in my mind, and I'd think, 'Geez, that throw wasn't that bad.' Then I'd tell myself that he was the greatest there was, so maybe the throw was bad ... What he was doing ... was tangling up in his feet and then making it look like a wild throw."

Years later when playing with the Reds, Chase would be studied carefully by his manager Christy Mathewson, who too concluded that Chase was corrupt. For the great Mathewson, it was Chase's subtle inconsistency that triggered suspicions and led to his dismissal from the big leagues. More on that later.

Making Chase's shenanigans more difficult to detect was the fact that he didn't necessarily have to be on the losing side in his game-fixing plots. If the Yankees had played poorly the previous few games, the logic went, then the "honest" gamblers would favor the opponent to win the game. But since a Yankee win wouldn't net as much of a profit for Chase and his conspiring gamblers, he could reverse his usual routine and try to arrange a New York victory. Instead of catering to his teammates, it's likely that Chase paid off key opponents, even when he played hard to help the Yankees win. So once again, the underdog would win and Chase would enjoy a healthy payday.

It is unlikely that Chase fixed plays in games the Yankees won, and since his play would be normal on those days, there is little reason to suspect him of any deliberate miscues. But judging by later evidence showing that Chase often used opponents to help rally his team to defeat, it is likely he pulled in the occasional teammate to help him as well.

So it went in the gambling-infested ways of dead ball baseball. Gamblers often occupied the best box seats at ballparks of the era, sitting so close to the field that they could signal key players to alter the action as they saw fit. It wasn't difficult to arrange for a certain player here and there to boot a key grounder or give up a long ball and lose every now and then. Everyone would profit, with gamblers taking in a healthy amount from their bets, and the players getting paid off for their trouble. The secret was keeping it low key and spacing out their activities.

Tales of dissension continued. But by the end of the July, there was a new story to occupy the scribes: the long-awaited possibility of a post-season exhibition match up of the Yankees and the Giants. Could the first Subway Series, the first mythical championship of Manhattan, be close at hand? With both teams holding down second, but with few hopes of winning pennants — like the A's in the A.L., the Cubs were running away with the N.L. pennant — talk of such a series was at least a nice distraction. Finally, it appeared New York would get the kind of post-season series that had been a staple of dead-ball baseball for Philadelphia, St. Louis and Chicago, the cities with two major league teams, where October exhibitions between the Phillies and A's, Browns and Cards, and Cubs and Sox could be as heated as games deciding the pennant races.

"John T. Brush and Frank J. Farrell are both wealthy, but they don't dispute that which is the root of all evil and they are passing up a great chance to get a lot of it," Lanigan wrote in the July 28 *Sporting News*. "A series between the two New York teams is bound to come some day, and the sooner it arrives, the better." A more likely scenario is that McGraw, after years of resisting the series with the argument that the upstart Highlanders-turned-Yanks didn't belong on the same field as his Giants, finally figured it could be a profitable venture.

But then the soap opera of previous

years returned to the Hilltop with a vengeance. Actually, the Stallings-Chase disagreement had never gone away and only grown more intense with Chase, more eccentric with each day, and Stallings becoming more frustrated in his inability to motivate his corrupt star.

On July 19, Chase took his regular turn at the Hilltop against the Browns, going 0-for-4 with an error in a 5–1, one-hit victory by Ford. He was in the lineup July 20 for another Yankee win — this one a 2–1, 10 inning nail-biter over the Browns, won with a hit by Frank LaPorte — as Chase again went hitless with an error. But the next day when the Yanks gathered for the last game of the series, Chase wasn't among them, due to what the papers called an "unavoidable absence." His replacement: John Knight.

It set a precedent. Chase accompanied the club for the August 1 start of a series in Cleveland, playing a little, but making more errors than hits. He was still there when the club moved on to Detroit, where the Yankees lost all four games — the last coming August 8, with Chase going 2-for-4, with another error. But when the team hit St. Louis August 9, he was gone, with Knight pretty much taking over the full-time first base duties. It wasn't until the Yanks got back to the Hilltop August 19 to face St. Louis that Chase rejoined the team.

What was going on? Chase claimed he didn't go to St. Louis because he was feeling dizzy, asked for and received a leave of absence from Stallings and returned home to New York. Then he claimed the papers had cooked up a story that he had given Stallings all of a half-hour's notice before leaving. Unnamed teammates added that Chase had used his time off wisely, playing for Andy Coakley's semi-pro team under an assumed name.

Tensons escalated. Once back, Chase sounded off about a tongue-lashing he'd gotten from Stallings. "One day, I dropped a ball, a thing which any player might do,

and I drew a 'roast' from Mr. Stallings," he told the *Tribune*. "If the roast had been brought on by a bone-headed play, I would have felt that I deserved it."

Stallings certainly felt Chase deserved it — and more. On Sunday, September 18 while on a last western swing through St. Louis, the Yankees dropped a sloppy, six-error game to the last-place Browns, 6–3. It was one the Yankees could have used in their increasingly tenuous hold on second place. No New Yorker had it that day, with Vaughn, rookie right-hander Ray Fisher and Warhop getting tattooed for six runs. Meanwhile, the Yankees were able to muster only three runs on five hits against rookie Red Nelson, looking like Walter Johnson that day. Chase went hitless and in the two-run second let a crucial ball get away from him; Fisher took the error.

For Stallings, it confirmed what he'd suspected for weeks: Chase was losing on purpose with the idea that he would replace him as the Yankees manager. After the game, Stallings tore into his first baseman, accusing him of laying down. The two went after one another, but were kept apart by other Yankees. The papers reported the heightened tensions in vague ways, writing that most players had sided with their manager in the ongoing feud.

Things got more dysfunctional the next day — Monday, September 19 — in Chicago. The Yankees dropped the first of a three-game series against the White Sox, 1–0. Again the team lost ground to the Tigers, and again, Stallings seethed. This time, Chase went 1-for-4, but missed Stallings's hit and run sign and fouled out to catcher Bruno Block, who then nailed Bert Daniels steaming into third. It was an unfortunate double play and ended the Yankees' only legitimate scoring chance.

The irony is that Stallings' future was by then all but sealed. Later, it was revealed where exactly Chase had gone while not accompanying the Yankees in early August to

Detroit. He'd taken the train home to New York all right, but made a beeline to Farrell, to whom he'd complained long and loudly about Stallings. As the Yankee drawing card and as the favorite of the owner, he was heard. More than that, he convinced his boss to find a way to fire Stallings and name him as manager.

The real story took years to come out. True to form, Chase went into a dead ball version of spin control in taking a "gee wiz" approach to the controversy, minimizing things and saying that Stallings's remarks stemmed from an unfortunate misunderstanding. There was the missed sign and the illness back in August. But there was no mention of his secret rendezvous with Farrell back in New York or the near-fight in St. Louis. All Chase would say is the evening of the first game in Chicago, he attended the theater and on his return to the hotel, met up with one of the New York baseball writers who repeated Stallings's accusation that he was throwing games.

"Of course, such events could not put one in a pleasant frame of mind," Chase said a few days later, sounding very much the victim. "Stallings has always shown a tendency to go behind a man's back. I feel and know that in this trouble, I have the support of every member of the New York team."

On that he clearly didn't. The Yankees hung tight with Stallings and several went after Chase after the loss in Chicago. The next day — Tuesday, September 21 — the Yankees lost again to the White Sox. Again, it was a meek, listless performance, this time with the team managing only two hits in a 3–0 loss that dropped them to third, percentage points behind Detroit. Considering the turmoil, it was remarkable the team was still 19 games above .500.

It had come down to a question of whether Chase or Stallings would stay. Telegrams flew between Chicago and New York and there were even a few long distance telephone calls placed. Farrell was said to be on his way from New York to find out for himself, as the *Tribune* said, "why Stallings and most of the players on one side and arrayed against Captain Hal Chase." Finally, Stallings was summoned to New York for a meeting with Farrell, to whom he'd demand that a choice be made. Would it be him? Or would it be Chase?

Back in New York that Thursday, Stallings met with Farrell for two hours at the Flatiron Building, where he again accused Chase of losing on purpose. Farrell went through the motions of saying he needed to travel to the Yankees' next destination, Cleveland, in order to conduct a thorough investigation of the matter.

"If Chase is guilty of such Stallings' charges, there is no place on the New York American League team for him or any other team, in my judgment," Farrell said before leaving for Cleveland on the 6:30 p.m. train from Grand Central. "If he is not guilty, he should be promptly cleared of the charges, that he may stand vindicated before the public."

It was all a bit of a charade, a way of delaying the inevitable. Stallings stayed in New York. Managing the team for their final game in Chicago, a 6–4 Wednesday loss, was ... Hal Chase. Rolling into Cleveland on Thursday, September 22, the remarkable Russ Ford used his emery ball and beat the Naps 2–1 for his ninth win in a row and 25th of the season. "The New York men played with more heart, to all appearances, than they did in Chicago," reported the *Tribune*, "but the strife between Stallings and Chase is still uppermost in the minds of all, and little else is being talked about by the players."

Meanwhile, the newspapers had a field day with the story, reporting from midweek on that Chase had indeed already signed a contract to manage through 1911, all for a hefty pay raise to $6,000. Their source: Chase, who was only saying he had

The Yankees in 1911, believed to be the team's earliest known photo. Manager Hal Chase sits in the front middle. Note how the playeres are aligned in an "N.Y." pattern. (Brown Brothers)

the full support of his teammates, but that they all knew he was to manage them the rest of the '10 season and into '11.

Farrell and Yankee Secretary Thomas Davis remained mum. They investigated quickly, interviewed the players and sided with Chase. No surprise there. "Stallings has utterly failed in his accusations against Chase," Farrell said. "He tried to besmirch the character of a sterling player. Anybody who knows Hal Chase knows that he is not guilty of the accusations against him."

But in Cleveland, the real story of Stallings's departure came hurtling to the forefront. It turns out that Stallings's last stand had in fact come the previous Monday in Chicago, directly after the St. Louis blow-up. It came courtesy of A.L. President Ban Johnson, of all people, who quite to Stallings's surprise, summoned him to A.L. headquarters and demanded he resign. Stunned, Stallings went to the ballpark, where he told the team.

Johnson had been looking for a way of getting rid of Stallings and the accusa-

tion against Chase was his answer. "Johnson has had it in for me for years," said Stallings. He was right, for the foul-mouthed, intense Yankee skipper was too much the ruffian for Johnson, who didn't think such behavior fit into his vision of a more fan-friendly league. What had clinched Johnson's dislike for Stallings was the Hilltop buzzer scheme of the year before. It was then, the whisperings went, that the A.L. President vowed to make him toast.

Finally, on Monday, September 26, the news became official. Stallings, paid through the end of the year, was officially let go and 27-year-old Hal Chase was named the Yankees' fourth manager, still the youngest ever. Surprisingly, the sentiment went both ways. "Chase is a big asset to the New York club outside his ability as a player and outside also of the fact that he is a big drawing card, whereas Stallings is not," the *Tribune* wrote. "First basemen like Chase are born, not made, and not born very often either, while managers like

Stallings, so successful as he has been, can be replaced."

On the pages of *The Sporting News*, Lanigan took a more diplomatic view. "As the safe and same here view the matter, it is too bad to see Stallings canned, but hope is entertained that Chase, elevated to the management, will now take the national pastime more seriously and will not be so ready to get peeved on slight provocation," he wrote. "He had a distinct right to get mad at the charges Stallings brought against him, but there are many persons here who will never forget his actions when he jumped the club two years ago at the time his services were badly needed. The less said about the Stallings-Chase incident the better it will be for base ball in Manhattan."

If the controversy upset Chase, he didn't show it. Despite the distractions and the absences, he somehow led the Yankees in at-bats and hit a solid .290. It had been a good year for a couple of others as well — principally Knight who batted a team-high .312 and Birdie Cree who hit .287 and tied Chase for the team lead in runs-batted-in with 73. Wolter batted .267 and led the team with four home runs.

Lanigan was right. Not only had Chase suddenly inherited a team with 12 games left to play, but it was on the eve of about the biggest intra-city baseball happening of the era. On the same day that headlines blared the Yankee managerial shakeup, John Brush of the Giants finally agreed to the long-awaited post-season series between the Yankees and the Giants. Maybe Brush was still smarting from the player backlash after refusing to have played the World Series back in '04? This time, with both teams headed for strong second place finishes, the timing was superb and fan interest was assured to be intense. "So keen is the interest that in all probability the huge stands at the

Polo Grounds and American League Park will be packed to overflowing and the world's championship series between Philadelphia and Chicago will fade, almost into insignificance," wrote the *Tribune*.

It would be a seven-game series, split between the ballparks. In Brooklyn, Charles Ebbets of the Superbas raised a fuss for a day, saying his team should be included in this mythical baseball battle of New York, but was told gruffly that his team needed to establish a reputation. "It is hardly necessary to say that the fans are looking toward the games with great joy, as each Manhattan team has its own set of rooters and roasters," Lanigan wrote.

It had taken seven years for New York's first Subway Series to happen and people were excited, and frankly, more interested in handicapping the delicious merits of a match-up between Mathewson and Ford — the wily veteran against the young turk — than talking about Hal Chase. The series would be significant for another reason in that it would go a long way to burying the grudge between Brush and Farrell; that the two owners would find that by working together, they could make a good buck would play a big role the following spring.

Meantime, there was still a season to finish. The Yankees responded well to Chase, beating the Tigers three straight in Detroit and winning nine of their last 11 to nail down a second for their "boy manager," as the newspapers had taken to calling him. In fact, Chase's first defeat didn't come until the Yanks were back home September 30 at the Hilltop for their first game following their eventful western swing.

Any concern that Chase would receive a rough reception was quickly dispelled in the first inning when, as he stepped to the plate, a large floral arrangement of two horseshoes and two baskets of flowers — there goes that dead ball flower thing again — was deposited in front of the new skipper in a good luck gesture. Yankees and Nationals both streamed out of their dugouts to be photographed and the fans, according to the *Times*, gave Chase a "rousing reception." Then the shrubbery was hauled away, the players went to their respective dugouts and the game resumed, with Chase lining a bullet to Nats shortstop Kid Elberfeld. Note the irony of one Yankee manager sending a bullet to a former one. The only problem was the final score: Washington 6, New York 3.

Conspicuously absent from the season's final two weeks was Ford. As the Yankees' best pitcher by a long shot, he was all but assured of facing Mathewson in Game One of the Yanks-Giants series. But big game pitchers need to stay on regular schedules, a reality that Chase chose to ignore. When Ford found out why, it rattled him that if the manager chose to pitch him, there wasn't much he could do. In an interview a quarter-century later in *The Sporting News*, it still rattled him.

Ford had pitched his way to a wondrous season. Going into the season's final week, he had pitched eight shutouts, second in the A.L. only to Coombs. His record was 26–6 and his ERA was 1.65. Ford had been a workhorse as well — pitching one-third of an inning short of 300 innings and finishing all but three of the 36 games he'd started. Even more important, his pitching had one of the few constants in another season of Yankee turmoil, particularly as the Stallings-Chase episode moved into high gear. In August, he actually threw three shutouts in a row, beating the Browns 8–0 on August 9; the White Sox August 9, 1–0; and the Browns again on August 19, 6–0.

With the Yankees set to take on the A's in a three-game series starting October 5, Connie Mack approached Chase with a proposition for an unusual gentleman's agreement. On the surface, the series was meaningless, with the A's having long clinched the A.L. pennant. So with Mack's attention shifted to the upcoming World Series against Chicago, he asked Chase as a favor that he not be forced to use Chief Bender, who he was hoping to save up for the start of the Series. Chase knew that if Mack were to go with Bender, he'd have to use Ford.

Chase agreed to Mack's request — shocking today but common in the days of the dead ball era. Never mind that Ford was only percentage points behind Bender in the race for A.L. pitching supremacy. He didn't pitch and the percentages remained — Ford at .813 and Bender, with a 23–5 record, microscopically higher at .815. The record made the other Yankee starters solid but mortal — there was Quinn at 17–12, Warhop at 14–14 and Vaughn at 12–11, with a stellar 1.83 ERA.

At least Ford would be fresh for the series against the Giants. Approaching the start of the seven game series, set to start October 13 at the Polo Grounds, New York was hit by a heavy dose of bona fide baseball fever. "No game in recent years has excited the fans to the high tension now evident in baseball circles, except the memorable play-off with the Cubs at the close of the 1908 season," the *Times* wrote. Of some surprise was the lack of big bets on the games — yes, the odds in those days tended to get as much attention as the pitching rotations — owing perhaps to what people were calling the relative even strength of both teams.

There was considerably less mystery about what pitchers McGraw and Chase were planning to use. For the Yankees, it would indeed be Ford in Game One, followed by a solid starting rotation of Quinn, who had gone 17–12, Warhop (14–14) and Vaughn (12–11). For the Giants, McGraw would throw as much Mathewson as possible at his crosstown rivals. The Big Six had been stellar again, going a league-leading 27–9 with a 1.89 ERA, the eighth of his 12 straight 20-or-more-win seasons. Doc Crandall (18–4) and Hooks Wiltse (15–12) were also expected to be ready. It would be Mathewson in Game One.

Thursday, October 13 dawned cold and gray, but it did little to dampen the enthusiasm of New York fans in a day that had all the excitement of epic Yankee-Giant World Series struggles of future years. "The banker, the broker, the clergyman, the butcher, the baker and the candlestick maker, and all their office boys began a rush to the ballpark early," the *Times* reported. "It was mostly a stag gathering. Few women were there, perhaps because they knew there was going to be such a jam, with no bargains in sight."

Finally, the Giants felt they had something to prove. No question the Giants were still the darlings of New York. They had the heritage, along with Christy Mathewson and John McGraw, and had won a World Series. Their massive ballpark was considered a jewel and fitting for the size of New York. They even had the Broadway crowd in their pockets, and an afternoon at the Polo Grounds was considered a worthy day's out for everyone from George M. Cohan to Will Rogers, Lillian Russell and DeWolf Hopper, master storyteller of the epic poem "Casey at the Bat." All were big baseball fans, mad for the Giants and anxious that their team beat the upstart Yanks.

The Polo Grounds gates were thrown open at 11 a.m., three hours before game time. Plenty of youngsters streamed in, claiming the best seats in the bleachers. By 1 p.m., the bulk of the crowd was on its way, crowding the elevated trains and subways around the Polo Grounds. McGraw appeared shortly after 1:30 p.m., walking through the center field clubhouse gate and slowly making his way toward the dugout, as the crowd shook with applause. Others from both teams appeared and did the same.

Last to appear was Chase, who, with some drama, loped toward the infield and made a beeline for McGraw, whose hand he grasped for the benefit of photographers. A photo from the National Baseball Library preserves the moment, revealing a lot of

their personalities in the process. On the right is the paunchy McGraw, only 37 but looking a decade older. He is poker-faced and grim and half-turned toward the camera and probably thinking more about the task ahead. Then, there is Chase, who, at 27, is five inches taller than McGraw, lean in frame and facing his rival manager, with his head cocked slightly and wearing a sly grin. The old western stereotype of gunslinger comes to mind.

After all, McGraw had more on his mind than Chase. He had just finished a pre-game meeting with his team in the clubhouse, where he had discussed the day's pitching opponent, Russell Ford, and what he suspected was a fatal flaw in his game.

The wily McGraw was on to something. Shortly before the series, he watched Ford pitch and saw something in a hard, jerking pitching motion that the Giants could exploit. The key he figured was to take a lot of pitches and make the young Yankee ace tire himself out. Do that and he could be hit hard toward the late innings.

In his 1912 ghost-written book, *Pitching in a Pinch*, Mathewson recalled McGraw's logic. "(With Ford) wait everything out to the last minute," McGraw told his charges in the clubhouse before the game. "Make him pitch every ball you can."

"McGraw knew that the strain on Ford's arm would get him toward the end of the game," Mathewson figured. For the Giants, it didn't hurt things that the Big Six was in command from the get-go, striking out the opening batter, Bert Daniels, on a called third strike, and sending the partisan Giant crowd of more than 24,000 into roars of delight.

It was the beginning of a long afternoon for the Yankees, who managed a run in the second when Knight singled and scored on an error by Merkle. But that was it: Mathewson and his fade away mowed down the Yankees. He struck out 14 in all, and walked no one. The lone run, manu-

Hal Chase (left) certainly looks happier than stone-faced John McGraw at thir meeting at the Polo Grounds prior to the start of the 1910 Yankee/Giants post-season series. (National Baseball Hall of Fame Library, Cooperstown, NY)

factured by two errors from Merkle, was unearned.

But Ford hung tough, so with the score 1–1 in the eighth, McGraw put his team to work. Heading to the plate stalked Josh Devore, whom McGraw stopped and whispered in his ear, "Now go ahead and get him."

"No crack in Ford was perceptible to the rest of us," wrote Mathewson, "but McGraw must have detected some slight sign of weakening." As usual, the skipper was right, and by the time the inning had ended, the Giants had scored four runs to

cruise 5–1. "McGraw just played for this flaw in Ford's pitching and hung his whole plan of battle on the chance of showing it."

Moving to the Hilltop, the Yankees took the next day's game, scoring two in the eighth and two more in the ninth, with the winning run coming in when Wiltse walked Chase with the bases loaded, driving home Austin. Final score: 5–4. Final crowd: a disappointing 10,363, many of them Giants fans making themselves heard.

Back at the Polo Grounds on Saturday, October 15, Mathewson went back to work, winning his second game of the series 6–4 before more than 37,766, the largest baseball crowd ever in New York. With his second win in the series' first three games, Mathewson was looking to match his extraordinary performance in the 1905 World Series when he singlehandedly beat the A's. That the series was in New York against their crosstown rivals gave the Giants something to prove.

Game Four at the Hilltop went 10 innings and was tied at 5 when the game was called due to darkness. At the Polo Grounds for Game Five, Mathewson again went to the mound and again won, this time, 5–1. It gave the Giants a 3–1 series lead. But back stormed the Yanks in Game Six with "a fusillade of ... wallops," as the *Times* put it, in a 10–2 laugher in which the Hilltoppers pounded Red Ames and then Wiltse for 15 hits, three each from Hemphill and Austin. The Giants led 3 games to 2.

The next day — Thursday, October 20 — it rained and the game was postponed. Advantage: Giants, for it gave the great Mathewson another day of rest. So there he was on the mound at the Polo Grounds for Game Seven, a sore site for the Yankees. And there he proved himself again as the great Big Six, the greatest pitcher of his generation. This time, Mathewson took his and the Giants' fourth game of the series, 6–3, as he struck out eight. In doing so, he again beat Warhop, who was touched up in the third by a three-run home run by Larry Doyle. Thanks to Mathewson and his four complete-game wins in four starts, the Giants took the series, 4–2. It was a glimpse of a team molding itself into dynasty form.

But for all the excitement the series had generated, only 4,439 spectators paid their way into the Polo Grounds for the seventh game in what was a curiously anti-climactic end to a tight, dramatic series. Weather had something to do with that — it was cold, wet and more like late November for virtually every game. Even so, the series had attracted more than 103,000 in total attendance and meant a nice bit of spare change for the players heading into the off-season. Each Giant pocketed $1,100, each Yankee $706.

Virtually unnoticed in New York throughout the battle for baseball supremacy there was a controversial A.L. race for the batting title and the A's-Cubs World Series. Three guesses on who sparked the controversy for the batting crown? If you guessed Cobb, you earn a Ballantine break. Cobb led the A.L. again in just about everything — from batting average to runs scored and slugging average. About the only mark on which he was challenged was in batting average, where Larry Lajoie was having the season of his life. With a .385 average on the season's final day, it appeared at first as though he had narrowly beaten out Cobb for the title by a single point.

Things got complicated after the Chalmers Motor Car Company, in a promotion that later inspired the Most Valuable Player award, announced it would give one of its roadsters to the batting champion. On the season's final day however, the race ended in scandal when St. Louis Browns third baseman Red Corriden was purposely positioned deep in both games of a doubleheader against Lajoie. Fueled by their hatred of Cobb, the Browns gave up eight "gift" hits, six on bunts to the Cleveland star, which appeared to be enough for the title.

Ban Johnson quickly voided the results, giving the title to Cobb, and Browns manager Jack O'Connor was fired for his actions. To prevent corruption in the future, the Chalmers award was allowed to continue, but only if it be given to the "most important and useful" player in each league, as chosen by sportswriters and not to a statistical leader. The Chalmers Motor Company, by the way, did the right thing too, awarding roadsters to both Cobb and Lajoie.

The World Series of 1910 started four days after the Yankees-Giants series and ended only six days later. It didn't take long for the A's to dust off the Cubs in only five games. Under Frank Chance, the Cubs had another spectacular season, winning 104 games, but lost their pitching touch during the season as the A's batted a decidedly un-deadball-like .316, while having their way with Three Finger Brown, who lost two of the games and got rocked for 23 hits in 18 innings. For the A's, Coombs won three games and Bender the other. It was a fitting end to a memorable season.

20

East Side, West Side, All Around the Town

"We may lose again tomorrow, but not with the same guys."
— *Rocky Bridges*

The Manhattan that Hal Chase found in his year as manager of the Yankees was a restless city on the verge of becoming modern.

The city center was pushing northward. No longer was the hub in and around the Madison Square area at 23rd Street, right near the Flatiron Building, where Frank Farrell kept his office. A decade or so after the start of the new century, it was a big city growing bigger, to the point where it seemed like one big construction site. Large, important structures — ones that would stand the test of time — were going up everywhere, aided in part by the ease in which the new subway allowed people to get around.

In the previous six years alone, New Yorkers had seen the once dingy area around Broadway and 42nd Street re-christened as Times Square, so named for the growing stature of the once-struggling newspaper of that name that moved there in 1904. Overseeing the moving was the newspaper's ambitious young publisher, Adolph S. Ochs, who bought the triangular right at Long Acre Square, a center for the manufacture and repair of carriages. He took the new name from a section of London dedicated to the same business. Ochs torn down the nine-story Pabst Building, and up went the new Times Building, along with the circulation of a newspaper destined to become among the greatest in the world (but not based certainly on its early baseball coverage).

The Times Building opened for business in 1905. Three years later, the paper started its annual custom of saluting the new year by lowering an electronically-lighted ball down the tower's 70-foot flagpole. When the ball reached the base at the stroke of midnight, its lights went out, fireworks shot skyward and a cherished New York tradition was born. So fast did the *Times* grow in circulation and stature that in 1913, it moved into the location it occupies today — 229 West 43rd St. But back on Times Square, the movement that the newspaper had helped bring to the area — the relocation of theaters, movie palaces and restaurants to the area — continued. The area would change, going from pleasant to seedy and now, Disney and wholesome fun. Some might long for nostalgia and the days of pimps and vice, but through it all, one quality would endure: Times Square as the Crossroads of the World.

Eight blocks south, near John Mc-Graw's pool hall on Herald Square, was the construction dig to take the breath away from even the most jaded New Yorker. For years, the New York Central Railroad monopoly had kept other railroads from entering Manhattan except by tunnel. There was a catch: No tunnel existed under the either the East or the Hudson River. Taking advantage, the rival Pennsylvania Railroad authorized $100 million of stock, bought the Long Island Railroad to tunnel under both rivers, and to build a tremendous station. It would be called Pennsylvania Station, and to build it, the railroad pulled down 500 buildings in an eight-acre area bounded by 31st and 32nd streets and 7th and 8th avenues.

Opening in September 1910, it was one of the great monuments of the age, with its sky-lighted concourse, 150-foot ceilings, and richly detailed columns. Entering the station, passengers passed through a spectacular portal adorned by six stone eagles, weighing 5,700 pounds each. The station, as the *Times* once wrote, "set the stamp of excellence on the city."

Moving slightly west and uptown, another magnificent structure opened just a few months later. It was at the corner of 5th Avenue and 42nd Street, and it involved another big dig, this time for the main branch of the New York Public Library. Once the site of a reservoir, the library was the project of several wealthy benefactors, principally Andrew Carnegie, who donated $5 million to the project. The building itself is said to come closer to any other in America to the epitome of Beaux-arts design; inside are 80 miles of bookshelves and 50-some centuries of scholarly thought. And just outside at the library's main 5th Avenue entrance: the two famous stone lions. Said President Taft who attended the May 1911 dedication of the library, "This day crowns a work of national importance."

All the buildings symbolized a restless city that was constantly changing, pushing and evolving. If this was progress, there was also a flip side, a price to pay for prosperity. Immigration to the U.S. was near its all-time high in 1911—the peak had actually come four years before—as people from everywhere continued to pour into the U.S. and pass mostly through Ellis Island. Many stayed right in New York, where they could always find work tunneling the remaining parts of the subway or working on new skyscrapers that seemed to be going up daily. Still others got jobs in the New York garment industry, where men, women and children alike toiled at all hours in overcrowded, dank, Dickensian factories.

The President had no speeches to address the openings of New York factories. Despite the growing outcry of liberals and muckrakers alike, factory inspections were virtually non-existent and conditions remained abominable. It was in the gathering twilight of Saturday, March 25, 1911, that the situation turned tragic; that early evening, on the top three floors of the 10-story Asch Building, a brick loft at 22 Washington Place, more than 600 employees of the Triangle Shirtwaist Company were packed elbow-to-elbow at sewing machines.

Most were young Italian and Jewish women, between the ages of 13 and 23; virtually all were residents of the Lower East Side. Their employers were typical of the most New York garment-manufacturers of the era. The Triangle Shirtwaist Company was owned by Max Blanck and Isaac Harris, the very symbols of exploitative sweatshop bosses: They billed their employees for supplies, taxed them for the chairs where they worked and even charged for the lockers they used for clothing.

To this day, no one knows the cause of the fire that broke out in the southeastern corner of the factory's eighth floor. It may have come from a cigarette tossed in the trash. Within seconds, it gathered force and with a sudden gust of wind, and burst into a flash fire that shot skyward to the top floor — transforming the Asch Building to a raging inferno of death.

It was a horror of mammoth proportions. Flames burst from windows, shooting slivers of glass to the street below. Women on the eighth floor ran to the stairway exit but the door was locked. Some leaned from windows, trying to gulp the outside air. Others were so panic-stricken that they jumped and died from the impact. Many who didn't get that far suffocated from the smoke and died inside. Firemen responded quickly to the four-alarm fire, but were powerless to do much. Their ladders reached to the sixth floor only and their hoses directed water only as high as the seventh floor.

The fire took all of 10 minutes to do its damage. When it ended, the Triangle fire claimed 141 lives, 125 of them young women. New York stared in rapt horror and then sorrow at the headlines the next day. Jewish labor organizations established a fund for the injured and many city workmen donated a day's pay. Nine months later, the outrage continued as Max Blanck and Isaac Harris were tried on charges of manslaughter. Unbelievably, they were acquitted. Wrote Franklin P. Adams of *The Evening Mail*, "Read that (they) are not to suffer at all for their so dreadful negligence I am grieved, and at odds with those that did acquit them, albeit my heart is soft as any melon."

So it went in the real world of New York City, circa 1911. Another fire, this one in the baseball world, would strike less than two weeks later.

Say this much for Hal Chase that winter of 1910 & '11: He tried. "The Boy Leader isn't making many predictions about the American League pennant race of 1911, but he is putting in six or seven hours of work each day arranging for the trek Southward of the Farrellites," Lanigan wrote in an early March edition of *The Sporting News*. "Chase's foreign critics who asserted that the managerial position would be too much for 'King Hal' will find that they are mistaken if the Golden Gater's present activities are to be considered as a criterion. Chase is as busy as a bee and intends to earn every cent of the large salary that is paid him by Frank Farrell."

Once again, the Yankees headed to Athens for spring training, but that was where the similarities with previous sessions ended. Actually, Chase's first destination was creative. It was Hot Springs, Virginia, where for 15 days he had his first team do just about everything needed to work off the winter girth, from tramping over the Appalachians to gym work, golf and even horse back riding. Meanwhile, Irwin took the second team — the Yannigans — to Athens for an extended camp.

The 17 Yankees in Hot Springs made the most of things. Despite a wintry tinge in the air, they took long morning hikes of up to eight miles and cooled off in the baths. "The bathhouse is a particularly busy place," the *Times* wrote in one of many slow news days that spring. "Each of the … players goes to the bathhouse at a set hour and takes the form prescribed by the resident physician."

After four days, the team got down to baseball at morning workouts that still left plenty of time for activities. On March 4, Chase debuted as a golfer. When, on March 6, a storm dropped five inches of snow on the area, most of the players ran back to the baths, with Chase going horseback riding of all things. It turned out that the native Californian was an accomplished rider and had the leather puttees, khaki breeches and cavalryman's shirt to prove it. The next day, with the weather still poor, he, Daniels and Hemphill went swimming. And of course,

Chase proved to be an accomplished swimmer and threw in some long-distance diving to prove it.

Chase's creative approach to spring training helped him become even more the center of attention, as always. But there was a method to his madness — by getting his team in shape early, Chase was hoping to avoid many of the injuries that plagued the team in previous years. Along the way, he was hoping to build the unity that his fight with Stallings had taken away from the previous year's team. "Discipline and harmony among the men are the things that Chase will have to work for, and the players as a body may make the task easy or hard," the *Times* wrote. "His standing among his teammates is high, and it is believed by Yankee enthusiasts that Chase will make a name for himself this season."

Some of those former teammates were already gone. Traded to the Browns in January had been Jimmy Austin and Frank La-Porte — two who hadn't hidden their sympathies for Stallings the previous summer. In return came Roy Hartzell, who had played second and batted only .218 for the Browns in 1910. Clearly, Chase saw something in the 29-year-old Colorado native: Hartzell would bat a career-high .296 in 1911 and drive in 91 runs. On July 12, he'd drive in eight runs against his old teammates, the Browns, and set an A.L. record that stood until 1933, when Jimmie Foxx knocked in nine.

By the time the Yanks opened the season April 12 in Philadelphia, nobody was calling Chase "the boy leader" anymore. Spring training had been a relative success. Pitted in a two-game series in Cincinnati against the Reds and his old manager, Clark Griffith, Chase had swept. Back in New York, he had beaten the Jersey City Indians and seemed to have his charges and particularly his pitching staff — intact from 1910 — in good shape.

"The men are in fine condition and full of go and are delighted to have the season open," Chase said on the eve of the opener, sounding like a Broadway publicist. "We have, I believe, the best pitching staff in the league, a fast fielding and a hard-hitting team, and I expect we will finish either first or second."

Vaughn pitched the Yanks to a 2–1 win over Bender in the opener. So when Chase's team took the next game and the next, sweeping the World Champion A's on the road, New Yorkers should have paid attention. That they didn't was understandable considering the latest tragedy in the city that had unfolded crosstown from the Hilltop at the Polo Grounds.

As at the Triangle Shirtwaist Company back on March 25, nobody could say for certain how the fire had started. By the time the first fire brigade reached the Polo Grounds just after midnight on the morning of Friday, April 14, a stiff wind had spread the flames from under the right center-field stands clear around the expanse of the old wooden horseshoe of a grandstand. An hour later, the whole park resembled a big bonfire, with flames leaping nearly 100 feet in the air, and the fire threatening the storage yards of the next-door 9th and 6th Avenue elevated lines to the north. By 2 a.m., the fire was contained, but had consumed 30 railroad cars. Damage to the ballpark was worse; the fire had destroyed everything within the grounds, except for the left field bleachers and the clubhouse.

Fires didn't get much more spectacular than the great Polo Grounds catastrophe of 1911. With the towering walls of flames lighting up the night sky throughout upper Manhattan and into the Bronx and eastern Queens, citizens flocked to watch the show. "Get your fresh roasted peanuts," yelled a group of young boys, enjoying the proceedings. Firemen did what they could, but were driven back by the intense heat. "It was a fascinating and awe-inspiring sight," wrote Lanigan in *The Sporting News.*

John McGraw rushed to the scene and said he was told that there had been an explosion that preceded the fire. A peanut roaster owned by Harry Stevens, the caterer, was suspected. But Stevens said he had roasted the peanuts downtown and brought them to the ballpark. Besides, he said the roaster didn't use gasoline.

A more likely reason, never proven, was that the fire was triggered by mounds of peanut shells under the grandstand. The pitcher, Bugs Raymond, said later that before the previous day's game against the Phillies, he had discovered a small fire that was feeding on dried peanut shells. That fire was put out by groundskeepers. Years later, Fred Lieb wrote that the big fire was started by a lighted cigarette dropped by a fan into some papers that smoldered for some 30 hours before spreading.

The great Polo Grounds fire was another black eye for baseball's ongoing safety problems. Lanigan was more blunt, writing that the burning of the grandstand was "a red-hot argument in favor of steel and concrete construction." Bad fire seemed just about everywhere, as at the Washington, D.C. ballpark, where less than a month before, plumbers working on the drain pipes started a fire that burned down that grandstand, which was hastily rebuilt for the opener.

The blaze was particularly unfortunate for the Giants, which had started their 1911 season only two days previous with a wonderful buzz that only they could create. Sure, the New Yorkers had lost to the Phillies, but a great crowd of 30,000 or so had cheered them on, showing once again that however hard the Yankees tried, the Giants were still number one in the hearts of metropolitan baseball fans. From the rafters hung red, white and blue bunting. In the stands sat the usual theatrical contingent

like DeWolf Hopper and the heavy-wagering George M. Cohan. Johnny Murphy, the groundskeeper, had even stuck Irish flags at the positions played by second baseman and captain Larry Doyle and rightfielder Red Murray.

But with the speed it took the flames to shoot around nearly the entire circumference of the Polo Grounds, the Giants had quite become destitute. That day's game against the Phillies was quickly postponed. But what to do the following day — Saturday — in a scheduled home game against Boston? And the day after? It was bad enough that the fire had cost John Brush $250,000, and his players' entire bat supply, many of which had been used for years. His Giants needed a home — and quickly.

Sitting in an Atlantic City hotel that Friday morning, Frank Farrell opened his newspaper, read about the fire, and knew right away what to do. Dashing off a quick telegram to Brush, he offered Hilltop Park to the Giants for as long as needed. Charles Ebbets offered Washington Park in Brooklyn as well, but the National League presidents who quickly concurred on the matter figured the neutral A.L. park would be better. So the Hilltop it would be, and in one magnanimous move, Farrell had made a bold stroke for sportsmanship. And just like that, the Yankees owner swept aside years of animosity between the teams, ushering in a new era of good feeling.

So that afternoon, the Giants and their new bats traveled cross-town to the Hilltop, where they peppered the Superbas 6-3. Some questioned whether the Giant loyalists would actually show up in the American League park, owing to the healthy disdain each New York team had built up for one another. "Would their own rooters follow them there, or would the crowds be the regular American League patrons, with many against the McGraw clan?" the *Times* wondered. In the end, it wasn't an issue, when a crowd of 15,000, mostly Giant fans, attended the game, letting their feelings be loudly known.

Reverberations from the great fire continued. The next day was Easter Sunday, and crowds of New Yorkers took advantage of the pleasant weather to gaze at the ruins of the hulking Polo Grounds, with the thoroughfare along Coogan's Bluff taking on the appearance of a downtown street during business hours.

After all, this was more than a ballpark to many. "In the crowds which pass in almost unending procession daily, there can be detected many traces of feelings quite akin to those with which one would view the wreck of an old home," the *Times* opined. "New York without its Polo Grounds would not seem the same to the vast army of baseball fans."

The Hilltop didn't exactly render the same gushy sentiment. That it was significantly smaller and less grand than the Polo Grounds were facts the newspaper keyed on as the 1911 season got started. There wasn't the shade that the gigantic grandstand at the Polo Grounds had offered. Others complained about the transportation, saying the elevated trains that dumped the crowds off at the Polo Grounds were much more efficient than the subway followed by the crush of elevators that led to the Hilltop. There was even moaning about the positioning of the diamond; at the Hilltop, it faced northeast, as opposed to southeast, as at the Polo Grounds, forcing the first baseman and right fielder to contend directly with the sun.

For Farrell, the debate underscored what had been apparent for several years — the Hilltop, hastily thrown up in the late winter of 1903, was, by 1911, simply too small and thoroughly outdated. By then, it was an open secret that Farrell was hoping to build

a fireproof, steel and concrete structure of his own. Back in 1909, he had secretly bought lots in the Spuyten Duyvil section around 225th Street of the Bronx near the Harlem River for that very purpose.

Pressing team officials to find a new home was the prospect of the Hilltop's lease that was due to expire in just two years. With the character of the neighborhood becoming more residential, there was a growing question whether the team's landlords, the New York Institute for the Blind, would rather keep the ballpark or level it for more lucrative profits by subdividing the land for apartment buildings.

"For several seasons past, I have realized that the club was outgrowing its old home," Farrell would write the following April in a *Leslie's Weekly* article, "Why I Am Building a New Park." "The Saturday and holiday crowds taxed the park to a degree never intended when the present structure was built. With every seat in stands and bleachers occupied, it was necessary to open the gates and permit the overflow out on the field. This was a hardship to both spectators and players. The crowds, great as their interest is in baseball, cannot be expected to stand through a long and exciting game."

Farrell called his quest for a new park an effort to "keep step with the popularity of baseball." Writing as if it were only a matter of time before his club secured a park, he wrote that "I have secured an excellent location, and I shall erect a series of stands that will afford the spectators every comfort and convenience that the up-to-date baseball fan has learned to expect as his right." Was Farrell counting chickens? Time would tell.

Back on the field, the Yankees, the winners of four of their first six games, played their home opener Friday, April 21. Threatening skies kept the crowd down to a tad above 14,000, but the Hilltop still looked festive. Strung across the roof of the grandstand were enough flags to fill a

Hilltop Park from beyond right field. Note the sign for 25-cent bleacher seats. (National Baseball Hall of Fame Library, Cooperstown, NY)

warehouse. The U.S., Irish and British flags were there. Others were too — "strange-looking pennants representing Zanzibar, Homoko, the Flu Islands, East Houston Street and way stations," the *Times* joked. Meanwhile, bands played rousing pre-game tunes and Chase got another big floral tribute, this one wheeled in by six burly men on a caravan from the outfield. The only downside was the game itself: Russell Ford lost to the Senators 1–0.

But for all the optimism of a solid start, 1911 would prove an oddly unmemorable season, one in which a talented team just never seemed to get on track. There were some pleasant surprises, like Ray Caldwell, a powerful 6'2" righthander — an Irwin find the previous August while toiling for McKeesport in the Ohio-Pennsylvania League, who would be a workhorse and go 16–14. And there was Ford, scuffing his way to another 21 wins against 11 losses in what, sadly, would be his last successful season in the A.L.

And although Chase would get a lot of credit for experimenting through most of the season's first half, the team would hold it together for much of the season in third, tightly bunched with Cleveland and De-

troit — before falling apart late and finishing sixth at 76–76. As late as Labor Day, the Yanks still held third, tied with the Naps at six games above .500; afterwards, they'd go 6-16 to place a distant 25½ games behind the pennant winning A's. In the end, the Yanks were trailed by only two teams — Washington and St. Louis, the usual suspects.

A parade of Yankee recruits came and went. One was the 21-year-old Chester "Red" Hoff, the native of the nearby Westchester County of Ossining. Hoff had landed with the Yanks after an Ossining semipro team owner got him a tryout. More than 80 years later, Hoff, by then more than 100 years old, would spend a handful of years being lionized as the oldest living ex-big leaguer.

Hoff's debut was a pleasant footnote to a mediocre season. It came September 18 at the Hilltop in the finale of a three-game series against Cobb, Crawford and the rest of the second-place Tigers, who had touched up Ford for eight runs in five innings. In from the bullpen for the sixth trudged Hoff. And up to the plate stepped Ty Cobb, who had already doubled and always relished the opportunity to feast on young pitchers like Hoff.

But it was Hoff's moment. Cobb lunged at his first big league pitch and fouled it off. Strike one. He swung at Hoff's second pitch and fouled that one off as well. Suddenly, he was in an 0–2 hole, and Hoff came back with a big roundhouse curve that went down the middle of the plate to freeze the Detroit batter. And just like that, the great Ty Cobb was gone on three pitches, and worst of all, a called third strike. Hoff would give up a run and four hits in four innings for a credible debut.

Hoff pitched five games for the Yanks that year, compiling a respectable 2.18 ERA. His big league career would span 23 games in four years, in which he was 2–4 with a 2.49 ERA. He would pitch sporadically with the Yanks for two more years, before playing for Rochester in 1914 and drawing a last call with the Browns the following year.

Years later, after all the interviews surrounding his status as the oldest living ex-big leaguer, Hoff would call the Cobb strikeout his finest baseball moment. Helping to fortify the moment, the old ballplayer recalled, had been a *New York Journal* headline the next morning that read, "Hoff Strikes Out Ty Cobb." Shades of David vs. Goliath and the local guy showing up the legend. "I didn't know (it was Cobb) until the next morning I picked up *The Journal,*" Hoff said years later. "It was the biggest thrill I ever had."

On the field, Chase had his best year yet at the plate — batting .315. But as manager, Chase clearly wasn't the man for the job, despite his best efforts to fit in and be one of the boys. "Were it not for the fact that every one of his men swears by Chase as the best fellow in the world, there would be good reason to scent internal discord," Lanigan wrote in the July 31 edition of *The Sporting News.* "But it is quite unlikely that

there are any malcontents on Frank Farrell's payroll. Perhaps the trouble is summarized in a nutshell in the words of the players. Chase may be too good a fellow."

Lanigan had it mostly right. Erratic as Chase's behavior had become, he simply did not have the hard-headed character to be a good manager. Good managing didn't mean being popular. After all, good managers were seldom liked by their players, and the best, like McGraw, could be downright cantankerous. "Occasionally, a much petted child needs a dose of sprouts," Lanigan wrote. "Chase is naturally of a retiring disposition. He shuns the limelight and even when he goes out on the coaching lines his reserve follows him. If he would only make a noise, or threaten an umpire, or spike somebody, he might put some ginger into his clan."

Yes, but retiring? As Yankee skipper, maybe. Otherwise, hardly. In 1911, Chase's natural ebullience and movie-star looks helped make him, well, a movie star. That year, he became the first major leaguer to star in a feature film — the silent, one reel *Hal Chase's Home Run.* Despite the star billing, Chase's role in the film was relatively minor; it's about his baseball-crazy friend courting a woman who resents her man's fanatical passion for the game. In a fit, the woman demands that the New York club win the pennant or the engagement is off. Enter Chase, to whom the friend turns in desperation. Predictably, the Prince hits a home run in the bottom of the ninth to bag both the pennant and his friend's girl as well. Don't go looking for the remake.

Yet, Chase's performance on the silver screen helped pave the way for other big leaguers to tackle the movies. It was a new genre: Later that year, Frank Chance starred in *Baseball's Peerless Leader.* In 1913, Home Run Baker of the A's starred in *A Short-Stop's Double,* and, in 1914, in *Home Run Baker's Double.* Even Ty Cobb stopped snarling long enough to star in the 1916 melodramatic romance, *Somewhere in Georgia*, written by Grantland Rice. To critic Ward Morehouse, it was "absolutely the worst movie I ever saw." No word on whether Cobb beat him for up for his comments.

It hardly mattered that Chase's short-lived film career was so forgettable. It was a pleasant distraction for the Yankee manager, who by mid-season was being acknowledged for a good try and not much more. By mid-season, the New York scribes were still being kind, crediting him with playing hard and, as Lanigan wrote, "virtually carry(ing) a whole team on his shoulders," but simply not having the goods to be a good manager.

Why not? The psychoanalysis of Hal Chase was something that fascinated the Yankee beat writers as the season wore on. There was Lanigan's "good fellow" theory. Another reason was that Chase was simply too self-centered to be an effective manager — a fact that manifested itself most acutely in his mismanagement of the team's pitchers. "What was universally regarded as the grandest pitching staff in either major league at the start of the season dwindled away into mediocrity long before the middle post of the race had been reached," William MacBeth, the *Morning-Sun* correspondent, wrote in *The Sporting News*. "Maybe it was partly the fault of these same pitchers. Certainly they did not always seem to have their hearts in their work. It looked, however, as if the boy manager showed lack of the initiative in singling out some four or five tossers and working them into top form instead of trying to utilize all his staff."

No question that the season was among Chase's best at the plate. And no question he tried as manager. But the fact was Chase was a man unfit for the job, a lax man for a job with serious duties. He headed a team that simply had no discipline, essentially no training rules and had no clue how to win. "His men simply did as they pleased," Mac-

Beth wrote nearly a year later. "Morning practice was practically unheard of. Chase was no disciplinarian. He was too lax.... His charges could not be expected to take the game seriously when their manager set such an example of unconcern."

The thin-skinned Chase found the criticism especially hard going. He had been a big star in New York since 1905, lauded for his innovative play and solid hitting, and adored in frequent newspaper headlines. He was also vain and had the thin skin to underscore that. Remember 1908, when he had been criticized and just quit? And remember the previous year, when Chase had argued with Stallings and his response was tattle to Farrell? Being an effective manager in the major leagues, then as now, requires a particular ability to motivate players and withstand the second-guessing and sniping by fans and the press alike. You have to swallow and take it; that wasn't Chase.

By 1911, the stress of managing and playing was eating into Chase's preferred life as "the Prince" — man about town. Still the life of the party, he was a man who loved to play the big shot and splurge on teammates when he had the cash to do so. His favorite spot: McGraw's pool hall, where he'd drink and play cards with his teammates and the gamblers with whom he continued to do on-the-field business in the back room. The arrangement was similar to New York clubs of the future, like the Stork Club, where Chase would hang in the back room with other stars of the sporting, stage and gambling set and play cards. Awestruck Yankee teammates, new to the big town, were frequent companions.

Forever charming, Chase was becoming increasingly raffish, his dishonesty spreading to all facets of his life. A particular specialty was cheating a teammate of money and then presenting him with some of the cash as a gift, with the teammates never realized that the culprit had been Chase all along. Never mind that Chase's wife, Nellie, and baby son, Hal Jr. were back home, near the Hilltop, in their apartment at 601 West 172nd St. The nightlife beckoned, and out stepped the Prince.

"During these years, Hal Chase fully immersed himself in the corrupt side of the baseball world," writes baseball historian Greg Beston. "He had become an extremely popular figure in the New York gambling community, and at the same time gained respect and trust from his teammates. The game of baseball had turned into a money-making expedition for him, where he could earn both an honest salary and rake in large amounts of money fixing games while betting on them. Some believe that Chase actually doubled his baseball salary in many years with his gambling winnings. Many baseball fans believe that players of yesteryear played the game for the love of it, and were not overtaken by the lust by the lust for money. But Chase was a man before his time."

Not that the Yankees really had much of a chance at the flag anyway; the 1911 season was another rout for the A's, who took their second straight A.L. pennant by 13½ games behind 28 wins from Coombs. In a distant second came the Tigers, with Cobb compiling another remarkable season with a league-leading .420 (!) batting average. Along the way, Cobb led the league in hits, runs, runs batted in, doubles and triples, and even threw in a forty-game hitting streak that ended July 4 against Ed Walsh and the White Sox.

It should have been a hard year for Cleveland, but the Naps, as they had become known, did well, taking third. In April, the team had endured a devastating tragedy, when their darkly-handsome star right-hander, Addie Joss, a favorite among players and fans alike, who had collapsed before an exhibition game, died at 31. The four-time 20-game winner, nicknamed the "Human Hairpin" for his 6'3" frame and herky-jerky delivery, would become a Hall of Famer. It turns out that Joss had been withholding a terrible secret: He had meningitis, a reality underscored by a sub-par 1910 season despite pitching a no-hitter. Holding forth at Joss's April 17 funeral before a throng in his hometown of Toledo was Billy Sunday, the ballplayer-turned-evangelist. His teammates insisted on being there, forcing postponement of the Naps' opener.

The major reason for the Naps' surprising third place finish was a 22-year-old South Carolinian named Joe Jackson. Nicknamed "Shoeless Joe," Jackson was a Southerner who endured many of the same regional insults as Cobb, the Georgian. But unlike Cobb, the semi-literate Jackson slid into a shell, preferring to play ball and stick to himself. In his first full major league season, Jackson hit .408, only slightly less remarkable than his .468 on-base percentage. Jackson would play three more full seasons for the Naps — hitting .395, .373 and .338 — before going to the White Sox in 1915. His legend lived on, but with a sad ending.

Like the Naps, the Giants recovered from their tragic start as well. McGraw's men played at the Hilltop until June 28, when the team returned to a hastily-rebuilt, steel-and-concrete Polo Grounds and enjoyed a resurgent season. For much of the season, the Giants battled for the lead in the National League with the Cubs, the Pirates and — thanks to a hard-throwing rookie named Grover Cleveland Alexander — the surprising Phillies. Late in July, McGraw made a move that critics later said made a big difference in bringing the New Yorkers the pennant. Leaving New York for Boston were Al Bridwell and rookie catcher Henry Gowdy. In return came one Charles "Buck" Herzog, a cranky Kid Elberfeld clone who played third with a hot glove and enjoyed a career-high year at the plate, batting .290.

There were other reasons. Up from Dallas came another smooth fielder with a hot bat named Art Fletcher, whom McGraw installed at short, where he hit .319, also a career high. But more than anything, what got McGraw his second pennant was the emergence of a slender lefthander named Rube Marquard. Back in 1908, McGraw had paid a then-phenomenal price of $11,000 for Marquard after he had won 28 games for Indianapolis in the American Association. Marquard—nicknamed Rube, not because he was a hick, but because his blazer of a fastball reminded people of Rube Waddell—had endured a rough debut, winning only nine games over his first three seasons. To headline writers, he was "McGraw's $11,000 lemon."

But that spring in Marlin, Texas, Giants coach Wilbert Robinson made Marquard his project. Teaching him to start off hitters with strikes, mix up his pitches and throw to location, Robinson made him a star. Out of the doghouse, Marquard won 24 games; he and Mathewson combined for 51 Giants wins.

The Giants nailed down the pennant in grand style October 4 in Brooklyn as Mathewson shut out the Superbas, 2–0 for his 27th win of the season. Nothing shows the contrast with the Yankees as the scene back at the Hilltop that day, where the Yankees lost to the Red Sox 6–4 in their last home game of the season before a crowd of *fewer than 200*. How embarrassing for Farrell, who had started the season with such optimism, only to see his hopes again dashed. "The crowd was as noiseless as the latest model Maxim," wrote the *Times*, its prose getting snappier. "The only real rooter in the crowd was little Hal Chase, Jr., who was calling out to his illustrious papa. The other 143 members of the loyal legion may have had sore throats."

Across town, the question became how to score tickets for the upcoming Giants-A's World Series, a rematch of the 1905 tussle won by the Giants in five. Both teams still had pitching mainstays from six years before—the Giants with Mathewson and Ames, and the A's with Plank and Bender. As in 1905, pitching was again the difference, but this time with Bender winning two games, and Plank and Coombs, the others. This time, the A's won in six—their team ERA of 1.29, less than half that of the Giants. Philadelphia batters contributed as well, with Baker living up to his nickname by hitting .375 including two home runs, the first of which won Game Two.

Across town, the Yankees' collapse prompted the usual discussions of what lay ahead. With the end of the season came the inevitable post-mortems, most of them increasingly critical of Chase. Would he stay on as skipper? Did Farrell even want him to? The Prince wasn't talking, letting "close friends," whoever they were, do his talking. Farrell said time and time again that Chase could manage in 1912 if he wanted to, but many doubted that the Yankee owner really meant it. Actually dumping him would be awkward because the two were still close. By November, rumors swirled.

"Close friends of Chase declare that the boy leader has no great love for his present billet," MacBeth wrote in the November 23 edition of *The Sporting News*. "While he has declared himself confident of doing better things in 1912 if he is in charge of the Yankees, he also realizes that his 1911 managerial form was about as disappointing as could be. Chase is of a very sensitive nature, and the slams that the press has handed him by whose sales allotments, it is whispered around, has him thinking considerably."

What may have had him thinking especially was the persistent rumor that Farrell was thinking about hiring a new manager named Harry Wolverton. Said to be a tough-talking disciplinarian of the McGraw mold, the 37-year-old Wolverton had spent eight major league seasons as a journeyman third baseman before turning to managing, most recently with the Pacific Coast League's Oakland Oaks.

Finally, on November 21, Chase spared Farrell the inevitable when he resigned, clearing the way for Wolverton. "I have found out that a star ballplayer who can get a big salary is foolish to take up the responsibilities of leading a ballclub," he said with genuine candor. "I have been regarded as a joke when I was manager. Perhaps I was. They tell me I was too soft, and did not have the right temperament for a leader of a ballclub. Perhaps that's right too. It would be better for me to lose that part of the game and attend to my duty at first base."

Chase said he'd been trying to summon the courage to step down for several days, adding he wanted to stay with the Yankees at first base, provided he be paid his managerial salary. Farrell, saved from what would have been considerable embarrassment at having to fire his friend, was only too happy to comply. "Chase is the greatest first baseman in the country," he said, "but he is too big-hearted to make a good executive, and I am sure he will be of more value to the team without the duties of manager to bother him."

So the choice was Harry Wolverton. As the third Yankee manager in as many years and the fourth in the previous six years, Wolverton hit New York a few weeks later. He talked tough and seemed, on the surface at least, to be the Yankees' answer to a club in dire need of discipline. "If there is one thing I hate to hear said in baseball, it is that a pitcher has a team beaten before he steps into the box," Wolverton told New York reporters. "It gets my goat whenever I hear it. Let me tell you one thing: No pitcher will have the Highlanders whipped next season before he pitches his first ball. I'd like to hear one of my players tell me the team is beaten before the game starts. I'll bet he wouldn't tell it to me the second time."

Wolverton spent the winter saying a lot of tough-guy things. "Do you know," he said in another oration, "that the team which makes a decided hit is the one which is full of pepper and all keyed up from the time it leaves the clubhouse into the time the game is over?" They were Wolvertonisms and the newspapers ate them up. The new Yankee skipper was a throwback of sorts — he even took to re-christening the team as the "Highlanders," the first such person to call them that in years — and he was good copy. Wolverton was also an eccentric of sorts — not in the dude-like Stallings tradition, but in his choice of apparel, which was an ever-present sombrero on his head and a cigar in his mouth.

The hawk-faced, heavyset Wolverton had blown into baseball, literally. A Mount Vernon, Ohio, native, he had been a student of nearby Kenyon College in 1895 when, upset at not being given a choice dorm room, he and two companions wrapped a ball of binding around a sizable charge of gun powder and rammed the contraption into a pipe stem. Leaving the bomb at the door of the dorm room he coveted, Wolverton intended only to scare the student into giving up the room. Then the bomb went off, tearing out the door, leaving a gaping hole in both the floor and a good chunk of the building. The explosion was heard for miles, drawing such a crowd that Wolverton and his companions in crime made a detour to watch the proceedings, lest they draw suspicion.

"Did the bomb work?" Sid Mercer asked Wolverton in the winter of 1912. "I can only hope that I get as good results next year for Mr. Farrell," Wolverton said with a sly grin. "We were quite overwhelmed with the success of the thing. So were the college authorities." A few days, Wolverton and his cronies were asked to leave Kenyon.

And with that ended the academic career of Harry Wolverton. Baseball was next. A good pitcher, he hooked up with minor league Columbus, and three years later, reached the majors as a third baseman with the NL's Chicago Colts. Early in 1900, Wolverton was traded to the Phillies, where he joined a hard-hitting band of sluggers including Napoleon Lajoie, Ed Delahanty and Elmer Flick, all future Hall of Famers. Wolverton held down third, hit around .300 and developed a reputation for scrappy, heads-up play. Later, playing for Washington and back in the NL with Boston, Wolverton left the majors in a salary dispute and in 1907, began managing at Williamsport in the Tri-State League.

Managing suited him. Wolverton took two straight Tri-State League pennants and developed a reputation for developing good players, among them Jack Warhop and Walter Blair, along with Cardinal left-hander Harry Sallee. So when Stallings left Newark for the Yankees in 1909, Wolverton was the choice, and helped lead the Indians to a second place finish in the Eastern League. Make that "helped" because shortly after Wolverton signed on, the team was bought by Iron Man McGinnity, leaving Wolverton to play third and act more as team captain than as manager. So, Wolverton jumped again, this time for the 1910 season, to Oakland of the Pacific Coast League, guiding his Oaks to second in '10 and third in '11.

It took a few weeks for Wolverton to sign with the Yanks. The stumbling block was Oakland owner C.A. Wollers who agreed to release his manager from the Oaks only after he received a healthy chunk of change. Finally, the deed was done and Wolverton inked a contract at the Hotel Astor. First to congratulate him was A.L. President Ban Johnson; finally, he thought, the New Yorkers were in competent hands.

After all, expectations were high that Wolverton would prove the answer to the Yankees' nearly decade-long string of hoodoo. "Wolverton will make good if any-

one can," said his old friend Stallings, now manager at Buffalo. "He knows every angle of baseball, and is a natural leader who will get every ounce of energy out of his charges."

One reason for optimism was that the core of players Stallings had rounded up back in 1910 was still intact. Chase was there, as were Earl Gardner, Ed Sweeney of course and Birdie Cree. Jimmy Austin was of course gone, traded by Chase to the Browns for Roy Hartzell. And in December, John Knight and Roxy Roach were unloaded to the Nationals for veteran catcher Gabby Street, who seldom hit beyond the low .200s, but was dependable behind the plate. Gone too was Charlie Hemphill, retired after 11 years in the majors, four of them on the Hilltop, with a .271 lifetime average.

Pitching-wise came a solid staff with more seasoning—mainstays Russell Ford and Hippo Vaughn, along with Ray Caldwell, Jack Warhop, Jack Quinn and the promising 23-year right-hander, Ray Fisher, a nine-game winner in '11. The *St. Louis Republic* called the New York pitching staff "the greatest ... in the American League," adding the Yankees were "strong in every department."

Some were predicting Wolverton would be another Hughie Jennings, the Tiger skipper who had taken over a fifth-place team from '06, and steering them to the pennant in '07. The *Republic* again, "There is no denying that on paper Wolverton has a great team."

Early in spring training in Atlanta, Yankees players got a sense of their new skipper's no-nonsense style. It hardly mattered that the weather that spring in Georgia was particularly rough; Wolverton had his players work, even in the rains that pounded the camp that March. More often than not that miserable spring, the Yankees retreated to quarters under the grandstand at Ponce de Leon Park, practically the same place where three years before, Russell Ford had developed his trick pitch. Training with the Yankees, by the way, were the hometown Atlanta Crackers, now managed by an old friend—Charlie Hemphill.

Wolverton talked tough, but seemed fair. When Sweeney, now involved in the auto business back in Chicago, demanded a $6,000 contract, Wolverton called it exorbitant, saying "there are not very many businesses or professions that would return him a clean profit equal to the salary that I have offered." After a year when he batted .231, Sweeney was showing some moxie. Eventually, he reported, sharing the catching duties with Street, and improving his average to a respectable .268.

And when Happy Jack Chesbro, now 37 and the owner of a Massachusetts lumber yard turned up at Yankee headquarters and announced that his arm was lively and he intended to pitch again for the Yanks, Wolverton said he was welcome to join the team at spring training. It had been three years since Chesbro had been in a Yankee uniform and he appeared lighter than the 180 pounds he had carried for most of his baseball career. But then, quite suddenly, all plans were off and the Yankees announced tersely that Chesbro would not be going south. It was back to the lumber yard for Happy Jack.

Wolverton also showed a practical side in his several heart-to-heart talks with Chase. The Yankee first baseman was said to be happy in hindsight to have shorn his managerial responsibilities as well as the captaincy of the team. Captaincy was still a relatively new phenomenon at the time in baseball and the Yanks made Chase the captain anyway.

The baseball scribes enjoyed it all. So did Wolverton, who quickly took to issuing lengthy treatises of the rah-rah variety. "(What) makes an impression with the fans is the lively work in practice," Wolverton said March 21 of his training methods. "I never did like the ball club that went about their practice as though they were in there just because they had to be. I like to have men who will be yelling in the infield and the outfield. I have always had a ball club of that description, and I think I will have one in the Highlanders."

A week or so before leaving for spring training, the Yankees front office made an announcement that still has relevance today. When Wolverton's men sprinted from the dugout on opening day April at the Hilltop against Boston, they'd be wearing spanking new uniforms with the spiffy pinstripes introduced a few years back by the Cubs and since adopted by other teams, including the Giants.

The home uniform would consist of a white shirt and pants, with a black pinstripe down the side and the famous interlocking "NY" on the left breast. The caps, which still resembled the pillbox hats favored by bellboys in Marx Brothers films, would be white with a blue monogram. On the road, the New Yorkers would be wearing plain gray uniforms, with "NY" in blue letters on the left side of the shirt. Road caps would be gray, with a blue monogram. And in all cases, stockings would be blue with a maroon stripe down the side. Meanwhile, the sweater coat for both uniforms would be navy blue with maroon trimmings.

The big deal? Although other teams had worn pinstripes earlier, 1912 was the year that the Yankees acquired the look that in time became the most famous uniform in American sports and endures to this day. How nice that the team would look so snazzy; looking back, it may just have been the Yankee high spot in an otherwise disaster of a season.

The Yankees did in fact sprint from their dugout on April 11 to open the campaign. Actually, festivities had kicked off 90 minutes before when the Yankees emerged from their dugout for batting practice. Captain Chase was late, arriving 15 minutes later. Maybe it was an omen. More likely, Chase just didn't care. On a raw day before only 12,000 fans, their lowest crowd for a home opener in history, the Yankees lost 5–3 to the Red Sox. Only the 25 cent seats in the right-field corner of the Hilltop were filled, with several sections of the park's outer reaches relatively empty of fans. In contrast, the stands at Washington Park, Brooklyn, were overflowing for the Superbas-Giants tussle, giving credence once again that despite the inroads made by the Yankees, New York was still a National League city.

The Hilltop was adorned with the usual opening day trappings. There was bunting and flags. Assemblyman Al Smith gave Wolverton a loving cup donated by the Board of Trade in Oakland, where he'd been managing. Dominating the pre-game hoopla was Farrell's contribution, another of those enormous floral wreaths with the world "Success" written in a silk ribbon running across its front. The problem is the florist had mounted the entire contraption upside down, "letting all the day's luck run out of the ends," as the *Press* put it. Another omen perhaps?

Yankee ace Russ Ford took to the mound the next day against the Red Sox and was roughed up for three runs in the first, which was all the Bostons needed in a 5–2 win. The New Yorkers lost again the following day, with Vaughn again absorbing the loss — 8–4 to the Red Sox. The Yankees were 0–3. They hit 0–4 in Washington, where Walter Johnson shut them out 5–0 on four hits. Ford was drubbed again the next day 10–4 with the Yankees making five errors. The record was 0–5.

Actually, the omen of a real tragedy was unleashed three days later, in Boston, precisely one week after the White Star liner *Titanic* left Southampton, Great Britain, on its maiden voyage. Word that the massive ship had struck an iceberg and sunk, killing more than 1,200 passengers, was sinking in just as the Yankees were helping the Red Sox inaugurate Fenway Park before more than 27,000 in Boston. The New Yorkers lost again, this time an exciting see-saw 7–6 contest, their sixth straight loss. But in hindsight, the sinking of the *Titanic* may have been more of an omen for the Red Sox, which last won a World Series more than 80 years ago.

Then, the Yankees won, beating the World Champion A's 3–0 on a crisp four-hitter by Vaughn on a cold day back at the Hilltop. They won their first game but had already lost six. Then they lost to the A's twice to go 1–8, before finally putting everything together April 25 back in Washington against the Nationals. Behind Quinn and belting out 10 hits, they won 10–2 as Wolverton proclaimed with a giant sigh of relief that "our losing streak hoodoo is broken at last … watch us climb from now on." Too bad he hadn't been around to see most of it; Wolverton had been tossed in the second after calling Umpire Thomas Connolly a "leather-head mutt."

That set the tone. All in all, it was an ugly spring just about everywhere in and around the Hilltop. But even when you think it couldn't get any worse, it did for the Yankees against the Tigers on the otherwise pleasant Wednesday afternoon of May 15. That's the day Ty Cobb got into it with a spectator, adding one of the biggest black marks in his long litany of black marks.

The Tigers arrived in New York May 11 in sixth place with a 10–13 record and not much better off than the Yankees. A big Saturday crowd had politely applauded Cobb before the game when he received his fourth silver loving cup for winning the previous year's batting title. But the crowd turned nasty, hurling invectives at Cobb when he almost got into it with Yankees third baseman Cozy Dolan after a steal attempt. Later, Wolverton was ejected and the crowd turned uglier still, showering umpire Silk O'Loughlin — who else? — with glasses and bottles.

Detroit took that game, then split the next two. Cobb, meanwhile, continued to endure a steady stream of abuse from Hilltop patrons, particularly from those seated in the third-base grandstand behind the Tiger dugout. Most was clearly audible to everyone in the area, including those in the press. Years later in his memoirs, Cobb recalled that of all the fans who yelled unpleasant things at him, those at the Hilltop tended to dish out perhaps the most vile.

The verbal onslaught continued that Wednesday. From the moment Cobb hit the field, he traded insults with a man named Claude Lueker, dressed in a spiffy alpaca coat, which helped the tempestuous Detroit outfielder identify him. For the first two innings, the two swore at one another, which only subsided somewhat for an inning or two, when Cobb remained between innings in the carriage area of deepest center field to escape at least some of the nastiness.

But at the end of the third, when Cobb returned to the dugout because he had to bat, he detoured first to Frank Farrell to ask the Yankee owner if security could remove Lueker. Unable to find Farrell, he went back to the dugout, yelling an insult about Lueker's sister along the way. Lueker's response: Cobb was a "half-nigger."

For the racist Cobb, that was the last straw. In the dugout, Sam Crawford asked him if he was going to take that, whereupon Cobb bolted from the dugout and jumped into the grandstand to find Lueker. He did so by vaulting the wall and stalking toward the third row near the dugout, where Lueker was sitting. Cobb struck him on the forehead above the left eye, knocked him down and spiked him on the left leg, before kicking him repeatedly in the side. Keeping the onlookers at bay were Cobb's Detroit teammates, who grabbed bats and quickly followed him into the stands, creating space for their teammate to carry on.

The incident takes on a particular twist since Lueker was handicapped, having lost a hand and three fingers of his other hand in a printing press accident the previous year. Someone in the crowd shouted, "Don't kick him, he had no hands." Cobb's response: "I don't care if he has no feet."

Lueker later emphatically claimed he had never heckled Cobb, but the tempestuous Detroit star argued otherwise, insisting that Lueker, an assistant in the 112 Centre Street law office of Tammany Hall leader "Big Tom" Foley, the former Sheriff of New York County, had directed a stream of abuse his way for several days.

Cobb insisted that Lueker's taunts had left him no alternative but to attack. "A great injustice has been done," he said. "When a spectator calls me a 'half-nigger,' I think it is about time to fight."

The *Times* took a bemused view of the festivities. "Everything was very pleasant at the Detroit-Yankee game on the Hilltop," the paper reported, "until Ty Cobb johnnykilbaned a spectator right on the place where he talks ... led with a jab and countered with a right kick to Mr. Spectator's left Weisbach, which made his peeper look as if some one had drawn a curtain over it."

For Cobb, it was another in a long line of ugly altercations. After the incident at Hilltop, Lueker's boss, Foley, leapt to the defense of his injured employee. "If a great baseball player like Ty Cobb can't resist the catcalls and ragging of the bleachers without climbing over the rail and assaulting a cripple with one hand gone and three fingers of the other hand missing, then it is time for the public to stay away from the game." Foley called Lueker a diehard Yankees rooter, but an "unusually quiet fan," never known to utter an insulting phrase.

That Cobb's teammates stood with him, literally, was surprising considering so many of them disliked their temperamental teammate. During the melee, they had grabbed bats and quickly followed him into the stands and stood guard, daring New Yorkers to try to intervene. After it was over and Cobb was suspended, the incident became an odd baseball footnote when the rest of the Tigers protested by calling the game's first-ever strike.

Three days later in Philadelphia, the Tigers refused to take the field against the World Champion Athletics. So manager Hughie Jennings put together a team of college and semipro players, paying them $10 each. With the regulars watching from the stands, the makeshift Tigers lost 24–2, behind the pitching of one Aloysius S. Travers, a St. Joseph's College seminary student who became a Roman Catholic priest.

The strike ended a day later when Cobb thanked his teammates and asked them to return, which they did. Cobb himself returned May 26 in a series against the White Sox — two weeks after the incident at Hilltop Park. Nothing more was ever heard from Claude Lueker.

Maybe the Yankees should have gone on strike. "The Yankees are bumping the rough places with the jinx apparently holding a grasp that cannot be shaken," Mac-Beth wrote in the May 23 *Sporting News*. Injuries were creating a flood of misfortune. On May 20, Wolter went down with a broken ankle. Then, Guy Zinn cracked his elbow and Chase went down, as did Hartzell, Daniels, Cree, Gardner, Hack Simmons, Martin and Street.

Even the weather didn't cooperate. It was the coldest, wettest spring in New York that anyone could remember, and it kept Farrell from at least experiencing some nice gates. "Mr. Farrell has had unusually bad luck as a baseball magnate, but nothing of the past has compared to wholesale disappointment of the present short campaign,"

MacBeth wrote July 3 in *The Sporting News*. "Whatever is the matter with the Yankees would require the services of an ancient prophet."

But it hardly took a prophet to tell that the pitching was abysmal. Ford fretted when Ed Sweeney, his favorite catcher, held out. Then, he fretted some more when he developed a sore arm on his way to a 20-loss season; he would finish 13–22. Vaughn had yet to regain his form from two years before and was 2–8 with a decidedly un-deadball-ish 5.14 ERA when he was unloaded to the Nationals in early July. Caldwell, headed toward a 7–16 record, was suspended for breaking training rules and fined $250.

Connie Mack didn't get it. "I picked the Highlanders to have the greatest pitching staff in the country this year," he said in New York during the Memorial Day series. "I thought it would top my own, which is pretty good I can tell you. But instead of proving the best, Wolverton's corps has proven the very worst in the league. Why, the Lord only knows. His team has made enough runs to win with ordinary pitching. If his twirlers had delivered the ball they showed last spring, the Highlanders would now be up among the leaders."

Nothing worked. Gardner was traded to Cleveland. Dolan, a backup infielder who found it hard to field, was sold to Rochester. In came Ray Keating, a righthanded pitcher and minor league sensation from nearby Bridgeport, Connecticut, but he pitched in all of six games, going 0–3. In came another righthander, the heralded Tommy Thompson, who had struck out 22 men in 9 innings earlier in the spring while at the University of Georgia; he would pitch seven games, go 0–2 and never again pitch in the majors.

The revolving door continued with a lot of people, most of whom weren't around very long. Replacing Wolter was Pat Maloney, purchased from the New England League's Brockton team, where he was hitting above .400; in 22 games with the Yankees, he'd hit .215. When Chase went down, as he did throughout 1911 with a series of real and imagined injuries, his replacement was a 21-year-old Princetonian, Dutch Sterrett. He did well at first, hitting .265 in 66 games, which made reporters think for five minutes or so that Chase was expendable. But when Sterrett pounded out a hefty .171 average the following year, the erratic Prince Hal seemed okay after all.

There were others. From Brockton came shortstop John Dowd, pegged by *The Sporting News* as "a lightning fielder to either side of him (and) possessed of a fine pair of hands." Sure. Dowd too was soon gone after hitting .194 in only 10 games, never to reach the majors again. In mid–July, by way of Williams College came George Davis, who pitched in 10 games and went 1–4 with a 6.50 ERA, after which he was unloaded to the Boston Bees. By season's end, the Yankees had used 44 players, a big number for dead ball days.

That few players stuck revealed a deeper problem. Super scout Arthur Irwin had dropped off the map, confined by illness to stick around the Hilltop and serve as the team's business manager. That left no one in the Yankees front office who could comb the countryside looking for talent, as Irwin had been doing in the Griffith, Elberfeld and Stallings days. The Yankee scouting system had broken down and the talent was simply not being found.

For Irwin, a 13-year major veteran and the inventor of both the padded fielder's glove and the football scorecard — and oh yes, the guy with two families — it was the beginning of a tragic demise. In 1921, he leaped from a steamer into the Atlantic Ocean while on a trip from New York to Boston. At the time of his death, he was 63; his body was never found.

By July 4, the season's traditional halfway point, New York scribes were already well into their post-mortems. "No

manager was handicapped worse to begin with," wrote MacBeth in the July 18 *Sporting News*. "Wolverton has been on the Coast for two years, way out of touch with big league affairs, big league strength and big league conditions. He took hold of a club that was absolutely demoralized as anything that ever played for major league patronage. Hal Chase in his short major league tenure of office as manager had wrecked a pennant possibility. The completeness of that wreck Wolverton had no means of determining, alas, until it was too late. Nature conspired with the toughest luck imaginable to keep the dread secret from him until disintegration had been fully effected."

MacBeth probably came closer than anyone in diagnosing the latest Yankee bout of lousiness. To his mind, Wolverton had simply inherited a team that was "absolutely indifferent," and had no clue how to fix the disease. And like others, he had become wise to Chase and the growing suspicions that despite an $8,000 salary — in comparison, both Walter Johnson and Three Finger Brown were earning $7,000 — his indifferent play was not up to the standards of which he was capable. "Chase had somehow or other been a hoodoo to the Hilltop ever since he broke in," MacBeth wrote. "He has become unpopular with the masses, who believe he has not given Wolverton his best services."

For one reason, Chase sat out a lot of games in 1912, with real and not-so-real injuries. And it's a good bet that without managerial duties, he was throwing games more than ever. "My limit was $100 per game and I never bet against my own team," he told *The Sporting News* years later. "I wasn't satisfied with what the club owners paid me. Like others, I had to have a bet on the side and we used to bet with the other team and the gamblers who sat in the boxes. It was easy to get a bet. Sometimes, collections were hard to make. Players would pass out the IOUs and often be in debt for their

Looking spiffy in his Yankee duds, Harry Wolverton symbolized the no-nonsense look of the big league manager. Too bad he had so much trouble managing in the majors. (National Baseball Hall of Fame Library, Cooperstown, NY)

entire salaries. That wasn't a healthy condition. Once the evil started, there was no stopping it."

There was something else eating at Hal Chase in this summer of discontent. After more than four years of marriage, he and Nellie were getting divorced. It certainly didn't ease things that the divorce proceedings were daily fodder for many of the New York tabloids, which was contrary to the stereotype suggesting that journalists back then stayed clear of personal stories. They sure did a few a few years later when it came to Babe Ruth — remember the Babe's case of

gonorrhea, attributed in the newspapers to a bellyache from eating too many hot dogs? — who was generally liked. But with Chase's perplexing personality starting to grate, his personal antics weren't spared.

In courtroom proceedings, Nellie Chase accused her husband of an affair with "a blonde young woman." She might have thrown in Chase's lifestyle, in which he was spending less time at their home at 601 West 172nd St. and more with a pool cue and a fast crowd. It was the flash that went with it that had smitten Chase by 1912; "He loved to gamble, always had a $1,000 in his pocket," one old-timer told Lawrence Ritter in *The Glory of Their Times*. "A deck of cards or a pair of dice, he'd bet you on anything — anything."

When the divorce was finalized in September, Nellie, now living at the Amsterdam Inn, received custody of the couple's 3-year-old son, Hal Jr., and $100 a month in alimony, before moving to San Jose, of all things, to be near Chase's parents who loved her like a daughter. Years later, Chase described his life as "one great mistake after another" — the biggest of which was wrecking his marriage to Nellie. "Life would have smoother sailing all the way through had I appreciated (Nellie)," he told *The Sporting News* in 1941. "But I didn't appreciate her until it was too late. It was a fatal mistake and the kind that can never be corrected."

And the blonde? That would be Anna Cherurg, a Manhattan surgeon's daughter who Chase met through her brother, Rudy, a lawyer and a card player, whom the ballplayer was known to win large amounts from on more than one occasion. Chase and Anna were married in 1913 in Jersey City, but the lifestyle interfered again; they were divorced some years later after Anna accused him of a familiar pattern — spending money on other women and losing even more gambling.

On the field, the Yankee troubles continued. In a July 4 doubleheader in Washington, the Yankees "Cripples" as the newspapers had taken to calling them, were annihilated by the Nationals 12–5 in the opener. Then, they lost the nightcap 12–1, and Walter Johnson didn't even play. But he did the next day, pitching all 16 innings of a 6–5 Nationals win. With the Yankees at a woeful 19–49 — 30 games under .500 — things were in free-fall. Meanwhile, the Nationals were finally showing signs of life, settling into third behind only the Red Sox and the A's, with Johnson rounding into the superstar he'd be for the next two decades.

But even with 1912 hurtling toward the worst Yankee year in history, at least Farrell could be secure that plans for his new steel and concrete ballpark were progressing. After all, new ballparks had a way of invigorating its occupants; just ask the Pirates, who moved into Forbes Field midway through the 1909 season and won the World Series that year. Or the Red Sox, who had opened Fenway in April and seemed headed toward the A.L. flag.

By early August, Farrell appeared headed somewhere, or so it seemed. With the New York Institute for the Blind opting to knock the Hilltop down in favor of constructing a more lucrative series of residential apartment buildings, the Yankee owner had finally secured unrestricted building privileges for a ballpark to be built on a

pretty bluff at 225th Street and Broadway — about 50 blocks uptown, just north of the Harlem River — in the Kingsbridge section of the Bronx on the bed of the old Spuyten Duyvil Creek. With contractors set to begin filling in the marshy property, Farrell was anticipating a new home for the Yankees in 1913 or 1914.

Not that anyone was exactly dripping with nostalgia for the Hilltop. Jack Chesbro had once said that pitching there for two years was the limit for anybody, as the recent Yankee staff problems could testify. Anybody who has lived near the Hudson River, either in Manhattan or north in the Hudson Valley, would understand; the winds from the west are constant, which wreaked havoc for patrons and players alike. It was very often rainy too, and in the summer, unusually hot. MacBeth agreed, writing in *The Sporting News* that "even in the warmest weather, the playing benches are swept by treacherous breezes that penetrate the thickest sweaters." The effect extended to the field that in the summer was baked to near-asphalt hardness by the winds, making it hard on the players — particularly the Yankees who had to play half their games there.

The new ballpark probably wouldn't be ready for at least a year. So in the interim, Farrell was also at work lining up a ballpark to serve as a temporary respite. That would be the Polo Grounds, home of the Giants, headed as they were toward another National League pennant. Farrell could chalk up his fortune to a shrewd move he'd made back in the spring of 1911 in offering John Brush use of the Hilltop after the disastrous fire at the Polo Grounds. The Giants felt obligated to return the favor.

Meantime, the wreck of a season continued. On September 1, the New Yorkers were 45–78 — 33 games under .500. Exactly a month later, they were 49–100 — 51 games under .500 — and well behind even the Browns. September had indeed been the cruelest month, with the Yankees winning only four of 26 games.

Not that it had much effect on the A.L. pennant race. What race? At the other end of the standings were the Red Sox, which annihilated the rest of the circuit — going 105–47, 14 games better than Washington, which thanks to Walter Johnson's 33–17 record and league-leading 1.39 ERA, had their best season to date. But the Sox had Smokey Joe Wood who went 34–5, which included 13 straight wins and 10 shutouts. And they had the Chalmers Award winner Tris Speaker who put together a .383 batting average, which included a 30-game hitting streak.

For the World Series, the Red Sox drew … the Giants. A tough, veteran team, the N.L. New Yorkers were again paced by pitching — Mathewson, who went 23–12, and Marquard, who won 27 games, 19 of them consecutively in a streak that went from April 11 to July 3, which tied the 19th century record held by Tim Keefe of the 1888 Giants. At bat, the Giants reflected an overall boom in hitting — the N.L. hit .272 and the A.L. .265 the season — with Larry Doyle batting .330 and Fred Merkle banging out 11 home runs. But Boston took the tight seven-game Series — one game was called because of the darkness — with Wood winning three games.

It was the second of three consecutive N.L. pennants for the Giants and it underscored that they were still first in the hearts of New York baseball aficionados. For the Yankees, it was another contrast that however hard they tried, the seasons kept ending dismally. At least the end was fun — an October 5 game against the Senators at the Hilltop in which the tightly-wound Clark Griffith got silly. And as the *Times* sarcastically suggested in a headline — "Senators Force Yankees To Win" — it was about the only way that the New Yorkers could be assured of a good day at the ballpark.

It was 6–5 in favor of the Senators in the seventh when Griffith heard the final result of the Boston-A's game in Philadelphia that assured him of a second place finish. With the season all but finished, Griffith thought, "Why not?" So out of the lineup went the regulars — first baseman Chick Gandil; second baseman Frank LaPorte, the old Highlander; shortstop George McBride; third baseman Eddie Foster; and pitcher Jay Cashion, who had already replaced starter Long Tom Hughes. In went a gaggle of substitutes, including a couple of confirmed comedians, Germany Schaefer and Coach Nick Altrock.

The 35-year-old Schaefer was one of the funniest men to ever hit the bigs. A former mainstay with the Tigers and a veteran of two World Series, Schaefer was a utility infielder trying to hang on — by then, more known for his daffiness than his bat. There was the story about the argument he once had with former Detroit teammate Davy Jones, who was also his roommate. Schaefer was insisting that the Earth does not revolve and said he could prove it.

So they made a bet. That night in their hotel room, Schaefer filled up the bathtub with water and told him to look at it. That done, they went to sleep, woke up in the morning, whereupon Schaefer called Jones back into the bathroom and showed him the tub, still filled.

"Now," said the scholarly Schaefer, "it stands to reason that if the earth had revolved during the night, then the water would have spilled."

"I never thought of it that way," said Jones. "You win."

Altrock was a chip off the same block. He was 36 and had some good years pitching with the White Sox, where he had pitched in the '06 Series and won at least 20 games three years in a row. But by 1911, he hadn't pitched in more than a handful of games for years.

But there they were, entering the field at the Hilltop in the season's final game and the ballpark's last game ever. Altrock pitched, then moved to make way for Griffith, who moved to first.

"Nick Altrock, batting for Ty Cobb," he announced to no one in particular on stepping to the plate in the eighth.

"Get a hit Nick," yelled a bleacherite.

"If I do, I lead the league this year," Altrock countered. He didn't get a hit nor get a chance to lead the league. It was his only plate appearance of the year.

Then Griffith replaced Altrock and pitched to one batter — Hal Chase — who tagged him for a home run to right field. It was Griffith's only appearance of the year. For the record, it was the last home run ever hit at the rickety old ballpark, and was Chase's record 14th there, which was four more than the next highest Hilltop long ball batsman, Patsy Dougherty. A total of 262 home runs were hit in a decade at the ballpark, about one in every three games or so.

So out went Griffith, chased from the mound with mock anger by Altrock, replaced by the wise-cracking Schaefer in his first-ever big league pitching appearance. Schaefer went the rest of the way, with Griffith taking second and Altrock first. Oh yes, the Yankees won 8–6 for their 50th win of the year, against 102 losses. That put them an astounding 55 games behind, and perhaps most astounding of all, two games behind the Browns. So with that, "the most disastrous season that a New York American League team has had since the Johnson organization got a foothold here was concluded on the Hilltop," as the *Times* put it. Ninety years later, it is still the worst.

The final stats were dismal. Yankee pitching was a disaster — their 4.13 ERA was the team's worst ever and the highest in the American League since 1902. Everyone had losing records, including Ford at 13–21, Warhop at 11–19 and Caldwell at 7–16. Of the starters, the slender 5'9½" Warhop, listed at 176 lbs., had perhaps the best season with an ERA of 2.86. But the 28-year-old West Virginian had the unusual tendency of losing weight as the season wore on, which sapped his strength.

Yankee batters put up some respectable numbers. Chase hit .274 but made 27 errors, tops again for A.L. first basemen. At shortstop, Hartzell hit .272, in the outfield, Daniels hit .274 and catcher Sweeney had a career year, batting .268. Elsewhere, Wolverton no-names did okay and then quickly disappeared, never to be heard from again. One such player was Del Paddock, a third baseman acquired from the White Sox, who hit .288 in 45 games and never appeared again in the majors. Another was the imaginatively-named George Washington "Hack" Simmons, a Brooklyn-born shortstop bought from Detroit, who hit .239 and left the league. Remember the baseball term "cup of coffee," so named for a player's brief stay in the majors? It was the Yankees' year of coffee.

Attendance was atrocious. The Yanks drew only 242,194 in 1912 — a decline of more than 60,000 from '11 and the team's worst year except for its inaugural season back in '03. To put it in perspective, the Giants continued to draw, playing to 638,000 at the Polo Grounds. Even Brooklyn outdrew the Yanks; the Superbas, in their last season at old Washington Park, drew 243,000.

No way was Wolverton sticking around. This time, there was no question about it on Farrell's account, especially when somebody thought Wolverton may have, in fact, had a two-year contract. No doubt it was only for a year, Farrell replied, practically shoving Wolverton out the door. The official end came November 6 when a tight-lipped Farrell announced that in light of the dismal September, he'd be looking for a new Yankee skipper for 1913.

Farrell gave no inkling of who that might be. Speculation quickly settled on two National League veterans — former Giants mainstay and current Cardinals player-manager Roger Bresnahan, who also happened to invent the catcher's mask; and Cubs hero Frank Chance. Both were well-respected, level-headed baseball men who would wind up in the Baseball Hall of Fame. And both found themselves after the 1912 season very much willing to seek new opportunities — Chance, due to a money dispute and Bresnahan after a disappointing 63-win, sixth-place finish, a distant 41 games from first place.

So after a decade of disappointment, Frank Farrell was again looking for a new start.

21

A Bunion and an Onion

"If you want to get off this team, you have to take a number."

— *Dave Revering*

In the end, the announcement of the new Yankee manager came not in New York, but halfway across the country in Chicago, where Farrell had gone to confer with A.L. President Ban Johnson on the dire state of the franchise. For a decade now, it had been one of Johnson's primary goals to supply a contending team in Gotham; continued poor performance, he believed, could cause serious financial problems, and even imperil the whole league.

On January 6, 1913, Farrell and Johnson shook hands at American League headquarters and disappeared behind closed doors. When the door opened, Farrell strode the front of the conference room with big news. The choice as Yankee manager all along was Frank Chance, signed for an immense three-year contract at $25,000 per year — about $450,000 in 21st century dollars — and 5 percent of team profits.

It was a coup of some magnitude. "In securing Frank Chance to manage the Yankees, my ambition had been realized," Farrell said on returning January 10 to his New York office, where he found a stack of more than 100 letters and telegrams congratulating him. "I am confident that the completion of the deal is approved by the New York baseball fans, who deserve the best that our American League club can give."

Key to securing the managerial services of the 15-year veteran star was timing, for 1912 had been especially difficult for the man Chicago baseball writer Charlie Dryden coined "the Peerless Leader," or, when space was tight, simply "P.L." That was for the four National League pennants and two World Series his Cubs had won under his direction.

But by 1912, none of that had seemed to matter anymore. The season turned sour when Chance had quarreled bitterly that year with Cubs owner Charles Murphy over the amount the team would spend to obtain quality ballplayers. When Murphy refused to budge, Chance resigned in protest, despite winning 91 games and finishing third, behind only the Giants and Pirates.

The 36-year-old Chance who went by another nickname — "Husk" — was arguably the most respected player-manager in the game. He was tough as nails and willful. He hated to lose and was said to inspire his players like no other manager in the game. Chance was among the first baseball men to go against the grain and hire players who had been to college, which *Baseball Magazine* grandly surmised, "proves beyond doubt that educated men may possess true baseball instinct as well as the lad fresh from the sand pile."

A Fresno, California native, Chance had attracted attention in collegiate circles himself way back when—first with the University of California and then at Washington College in Irvington, California, where he studied dentistry. In between he played in sandlot leagues and, in 1898, caught the attention of Bill Lange, a former Chicago Colts outfielder. Although Chance's family wanted Frank to follow his father into banking, the young ballplayer was signed on Lange's recommendation and joined the Cubs, as they were known by then, as one of a handful of major leaguers to never spend so much of a day in the minors.

Chance spent the best part of the next three years riding the bench, and became so discouraged at times that he nearly quit. But he was smart and spent a good deal of his time on the bench, soaking up knowledge of the game, and finally after three years, got his shot. At first, Chance caught. But in 1903, his manager Frank Selee shifted him to first base and he became a star—hitting .327 and leading the league with 67 stolen bases. That was also the first year of a regular infield consisting of Chance, along with Joe Tinker at short and Johnny Evers at second that would become a legend.

In 1905 came the turning point of Chance's career. When Selee became too ill to continue as manager, the job was turned over to Chance, first because he was thought to be up to the job, and second, as was often done in the dead ball era, the team could save a few bucks with a manager who doubled as a player. Chance threw himself into the job, pulling off several deals that helped turn the Cubs into a N.L. power. He traded four players to the Superbas for veteran left fielder Jimmy Sheckard and acquired third baseman Harry Steinfeldt from the Reds; both players were integral to helping the Cubs become a power.

Chance's Cubs won N.L. flags in 1906, 1907, 1908 and 1910, including World Se-

ries in 1907 and 1908. Along the way, Chance earned a reputation as a tough, but fair taskmaster who could inspire his players. He was also a fighter, not in the nasty McGraw sense, but as a bad man to trifle with when provoked. There was the day at the Polo Grounds, when someone hit him on the back on the head with a soda bottle, whereupon Chance charged into the stands, his head bloody, and not only found the offender, but dished out a dose of pugilistic justice. Chance could be so serious and single-minded that once after a particularly hard defeat, he gazed on his wife, as though he had just suffered a death in the family.

"Cheer up, Frank," she said. "You still have me."

"Yes," said Chance, "and there were a couple of times this afternoon, I'd have traded you for a base hit."

But there was a dark side to Chance's baseball life. He was injury-prone—not in the pulled hamstring sense—but seriously, as someone often incapacitated by beanings. Getting hit in the head by a pitched ball has always been a serious occupational hazard of baseball, but it was particularly so in the dead ball era when batting helmets were decades from invention, the spitball was common and tight pitching, really tight, was more a part of the game than today.

Chance once estimated that he'd been beaned no fewer than 40 times. The most serious time was in 1911 when Cincinnati right-hander George Suggs clunked him on the temple with a fastball, and it was widely concluded that his playing days were finished. But Chance came back, but the first time at bat, collapsed at the plate. It was a sign that the end of a proud career was near; Chance played in only 31 games that year, hitting .241, more than 50 points below his career average. Other than a game here and there, he was done.

Later, it became clear just how intensely Chance had suffered after the 1911 beaning. In dispatches filed the following winter, syndicated baseball writer Hugh Fullerton called the suffering he had endured far more intense that was generally thought. For a month after the beaning, Chance couldn't sleep more than two hours at a stretch and spent most evenings pacing the floor to ease the pain, Fullerton wrote. The headaches lasted three months — and still he played, refusing to sit out. "They can't make me quit by hitting me on the head," Chance resolved.

The headaches eventually became so extreme that Chance could barely sleep at all — sometimes not falling asleep until noon and then going out that afternoon and playing ball. One day at St. Louis, he connected for a game-winning hit but is said to have not even seen the ball. Later, after Cubs second baseman Joe Tinker's throw went whizzing by Chance's head, Chance admitted that he had never even seen the ball and that the time had come to hang it up.

The end finally came just after the opening of the 1912 season when he collapsed in a game against the Reds. So Chance became bench manager, turning the duties at first base over to Heinie Zimmerman. "I owe Chicago a great deal, but I don't feel I owe baseball or the great Chicago public my life," he said. "They tell me that another blow on the head or another collapse like last year's would finish me."

Turning the team over to Joe Tinker, Chance quietly left the team in mid–September and journeyed to New York for treatment of his headaches. It came in the form of surgery to alleviate blood clots that were said to be causing the pain. Performing the surgery was Dr. W.G. Frolich of 33 East 60th St., who boldly pronounced Chance to be cured and in better health than he'd been in years. Breaking the story — more than three months later in December — was Joe Vila who declared Chance, by then back home in California, was in fine fettle and itching for a shot back at the big time.

Vila's December 28 dispatch was significant for another reason. It appears to be the first mention that Chance was in fact headed to New York to manage the Yankees, giving credence to the theory that it was Vila — he who had the ear of Farrell and Devery back in 1903 — who paved the way for Chance. Vila did so in a weird way, that is by quoting the good Dr. Frolich as waxing poetic on Chance's remarkable recovery while stating that the Peerless One would be able "to manage the Highlanders with all of his former skill." Suffice to say that it was in the foregone conclusion that Frank Chance was headed to the big city to run the Yankees in 1913.

But Chance himself made it all sound melodramatic, saying he was undecided right up the time he inked the contract's dotted line. "I honestly did not expect to sign," he said in Chicago after closing the deal, indicating he very nearly went home to his California orange grove instead. "When I arrived (in Chicago January 7), I had fully made up my mind that my interests lay in the West and that I could not afford to leave them at least for a year. Farrell, however, offered inducements much better than I had dreamed of, and even excluding my love for the game as a factor, I could not decline them."

Metropolitan baseball scribes could barely contain themselves. "New York has absolute confidence in Frank Chance," the normally sober MacBeth gushed in *The Sporting News*. "The former idol of the Cubs has put too many gray hairs in the head of John J. McGraw not to command the tenderest respect in this city."

Even McGraw himself was pleased. "Chance's coming to New York is the best thing that ever happened to the Giants," he said. "Put the Yankees up in the fight and it will help us as much as it will them. It's a curious thing, but this town has to have good baseball all the time to keep its fervor at high pitch."

Chance returned to California to settle affairs at home, but took the liberty to drop Farrell a few thoughts. First on his mind was changing the name of the team. His idea instead of Yankees, Highlanders, Hilltops, Hillmen, Kilties, Invaders, or any of the other monikers the team had gone by in its first decade? It was simple: the New Yorks. "McGraw's men have a copyright on the nickname Giants, and they deserve it, for they have accomplished big things in the National League," Chance wrote to Farrell. "They will always be Giants in the full sense of the word. Therefore, in calling our team the New Yorks we are appropriating something that doesn't belong to us.

"The nicknames Highlanders, Yankees and the others are meaningless," Chance added. "In cities outside of New York, they attract no attention.... We are going to try to bring New York to the top of the heap in the American League, and we will have 'New York' on our uniforms. I hope the newspapers and the baseball public will call us the New Yorks."

Sorry Frank, but they didn't, for 1913 was also the year the Yankees became, well, the Yankees. No more Highlanders or Kilties. And no "New Yorks" for that matter either. Credited with bestowing the famous nickname was newspaperman Jim Price — Fred Lieb's boss at *The Press* — and solely because it fit more snugly into the headlines than did "Highlanders." Price himself didn't stick around long enough afterwards to achieve fame as the originator of the nickname; when the *Press* merged with the *Morning Sun*, Price quit and became caretaker of the old Federal League park in Harrison, New Jersey, near Newark. For the Yankees, it was as good as time as any to nail down an official nickname, especially as the team prepared to shed the rickety old Hilltop for residence at the Polo Grounds.

When Chance arrived February 11 in New York, he had to quickly prepare for another new home, this one the team's spring training base. This year, the Yankees were set to become the first major league to travel beyond the U.S. for pre-season work. Their destination: Bermuda, where Farrell had secured the Hamilton Cricket Grounds. Joining them would be the Jersey City Skeeters, and the two teams would share the enormous grounds — about three times the size of most baseball fields — for workouts and a series of exhibition games.

For players used to spending their March in places like Macon and Atlanta, this was exotic. Leaving from Pier 42 on the Hudson River, Yankee players set sail in two groups — the last arriving March 3 after a two-day trip. Once in Bermuda, where there were few cars, players were given bicycles to get around. On the facilities, Farrell had spared no expense. They were first-rate, as was the cuisine at the training table, with provisions, like the drinking water, shipped in from New York twice a week. Even the weather behaved. "I feel sure that only Bermuda weather could have restored my old vim and put me in the excellent condition I am enjoying," said Chance. "Blame Bermuda if Frank Chance shows his oldtime ability around that first cushion."

Chance worked his team — and himself — hard. A disciplinarian who ruled by intimidation, Chance ran his ballplayers three times at each practice around the huge cricket pitch — a distance of more than a mile. He tolerated no carousing — not that there was much to do in Bermuda anyhow — and demanded they be in bed every night by 11:30 p.m. "I impressed upon them the early-to-bed rule," Chance said. "I told them that we might as well understand each other from the start."

Meantime, Chance worked to regain a piece of the old National League magic.

There was good reason: His plan was to take over first base himself and move Chase to second, a position the Prince had played in college and ever-so occasionally for the Yankees in past years.

Chase's purported move to second was the talk of camp. If anyone could do it, it was the smooth-fielding Chase. Sure, he was a lefty, and in playing second, would become the first lefthander on a major league level to play there since Billy Greenwood of Baltimore back in 1887. "The argument might be advanced that a nigh-sider is handicapped in playing second," MacBeth opined in *The Sporting News*. "But in Chase's case, it is different. Hal's remarkable speed will make up for any infinitesimal fraction of a second he may lose in making a turn to throw to a bag."

Farrell arrived in camp March 10 and announced himself highly pleased with his team, the training quarters and the weather — most likely in that order. What he and the others didn't realize at the time is that the coral base under the Bermuda turf was hard on the players' feet. And what Farrell wasn't sharing was how huge a pile of money that training in such an exotic locale was costing him. It wasn't yet an issue: With Chance at the helm, the team would be much improved — how could things get any worse than in 1912? — and make profits hand-over-foot.

That was the plan anyway. Lost in the hoopla was how disheveled the Yankees really were that spring. There were a host of new faces — most of them unproven or mediocre talent. Brought in to challenge shortstop Jack Martin after a .225 season were 25-year-old A's refugee Claud Derrick with 159 career at-bats and Malcolm Berry, a 33-year journeyman with 21 big league at-bats. At third for the moment was 21-year-old Johnnie Priest, who could have used one; he'd play two games and disappear, never again to don a major league roster.

You needed a scorecard to keep track of these Yankees. Eventually, Hartzell went back to short and Derrick to third. At least the outfield were known commodities, with Cree in left and Wolter, back from a broken leg, in center. Back in right was outfielder Bert Daniels, said to be in tip-top shape after spending much of the winter outdoors as a civil engineer with the New York Central Railroad.

The pitching, source of so many problems in 1912, had some consistency. Ford was back too, hoping to regain his rookie form, as was Warhop, 20 pounds heavier after off-season conditioning. After 50 wins in four big league seasons, big things were expected of Warhop, nicknamed "Crab." His mystifying underhand delivery, which the Bermudians found fascinating, was expected to yield big dividends. George McConnell, 8–12 in '12; Caldwell (7–16) and Ray Keating rounded out the probable rotation.

But the mainstays were having troubles. Chance quickly became a walking hospital ward, the victim of a spring cold and

A couple of dudes: Frank Farrell (left) and Frank Chance (right) take in Yankee 1913 spring training in Bermuda. (Brown Brothers)

a sore back, later to become lumbago, which trainer Charley Barrett did his best to treat with a large bottle of liniment. And although Chance's headaches were gone, the surgery had left him deaf in one ear. Less than a week later, Chase was injured all over again, when he twisted his right ankle while running the bases. The ankle swelled and three weeks later, was still in a cast. No, it wasn't smallpox this time, but for Chase, it was another lost spring.

The boat ride back to New York was a tough trip and every Yankee was said to be seasick. Maybe it was an omen. Back home in early April, the Yankees went to Brooklyn for a final spring tuneup against the Superbas and helped inaugurate spanking new Ebbets Field, baseball's latest steel and concrete, fan-friendly masterpiece. The Superbas, with a 22-year-old rookie centerfielder named Casey Stengel getting a base hit and scoring their second run, wasted a strong six-inning performance from Ray Caldwell, but won 3–2, much to the delight of the 30,000 Brooklynites who crammed every inch of the ballpark, including its marble rotunda. Could it be that the Superbas, whose last first-division finish had been in 1902, when Wee Willie Keeler played right field and hit .333, were finally showing signs of a pulse?

Seeing the pretty new park filled to its rafters with festive fans must have rubbed salt into Farrell's wounds. Never mind that Ebbets had somehow forgotten to build a flagpole or a press box — shades of future wackiness in Brooklyn. Farrell had moved his team into temporary quarters at the Polo Grounds with the understanding that the Yankees glorious new stadium would soon be going up. But already there were ominous reports of community opposition to the park, legal problems in filling in the creek that ran through the property and rising costs. Even then, it was beginning to look like the Yanks might never get their new ballpark.

If the ballpark was headed nowhere, neither were Chance's new charges as they prepared to open the Yankees' second decade with a makeshift lineup against Walter Johnson and the Nationals in Washington. It was a tall order, for the Nationals appeared even better than their second-place finish in '12, with their second-year manager Clark Griffith predicting a pennant. The main reason was that young Walter Johnson was rounding into a superstar and he drew the opening assignment on April 10, facing, not Caldwell as most had predicted, but 6'3" George McConnell, a Yankee rookie in 1912. That he had done it as a 35-year-old earned him the nickname, "Silver."

No wonder the overflow crowd of 15,841 was so festive. Another reason was the appearance at the game of President Woodrow Wilson, picking up on the custom that former President Taft had started the year in which the President tossed out the ceremonial first pitch, opening the season in Washington, D.C. Accompanied by his daughter Eleanor, Wilson arrived at the ballpark dressed in a fur-lined overcoat. Amid boisterous cheering, Wilson tossed his first pitch to Johnson who then handed the ball to Griffith for the President to autograph.

And with that, Johnson stalked to the mound to face the Yankees' Bert Daniels and opened the 1912 season by plucking him in the back with his second pitch. Daniels then stole second and took third when Nats first baseman Chick Gandil fumbled Harry Wolter's hit to the right side. Daniels then scored when George McBride threw home wildly. Barely into the Frank Chance era, the Yanks were ahead of the great Walter Johnson, 1–0.

But that would be all the offense for the afternoon. McConnell pitched well, but had one poor inning — the seventh — when he gave a two-out, two-run single to Danny

Moeller. It was enough for Johnson, who scattered eight hits, one of them from Yankee first baseman Dutch Sterrett, substituting for Chance and replacing Chase, who had moved to second to kick off the great infield experiment. As a Princeton undergraduate a few years back, Sterrett had been a student of the President's. The final was 2-1 Nationals. That Yankees run, by the way, would be the last one Johnson would allow until May 14. That was when the Browns scored against him in St. Louis to snap his streak of 55 consecutive scoreless innings, still the A.L. record.

Things didn't get immediately better. The Yankees lost the next day to Long Tom Hughes, and then went on to Boston, where Keating pitched the team's first win on April 15, 3–2. Returning to New York, the Yankees faced the Nationals on April 17 for their home opener and first game at the Polo Grounds.

The papers put it nicely, calling them the "reconstructed Yankees," but nobody was paying much attention, for the focus was again on Chance. The Peerless One got a hearty ovation from the 25,000 fans in attendance in addition to the obligatory barn full of floral tributes.

The first such tribute appeared shortly before game time; 10 feet high, it was carried to home plate by a squad of Big Tom Foley's Tammany Hall lackeys. More flowers came from the Friars, Frank Farrell and even new Giants President Harry Hempstead. Not to be outdone, a collection of New York area Californians then trudged to home plate and presented the new Yankee skipper with a dog — that's right, a white bull pup named Jimmy Britt — who had recently appeared at the Westminster Kennel Show. At least it stemmed the flow of flowers: The dog jumped up and licked Chance on the cheek, much to the delight of those assembled. Chance vowed to make him the team's mascot.

But the Yankees needed more than a mascot. For five innings, the game was close,

with the New Yorkers clinging to a 1–0 lead behind Silver McConnell. The floodgates opened in the sixth when the Nats scored three runs on errors by Hartzell and Chase, two singles and a stolen base. For the new second baseman Chase, it was one of two errors on that day — and don't think Chance wasn't watching. The final: 9–2 Washington.

The Yankees lost the next day to Long Tom Hughes, 7–5. They lost the day after that to Walter Johnson, 3–0, managing six hits with Chase committing another error. After a day off Sunday, they lost the series' final game on Monday, 8–4, managing only three hits against Hughes and making five more errors. The New Yorkers were barely hitting, fielding badly and not only losing, but doing so at home. Their 1–6 record was the worst start in the American League.

So Chance experimented. The next day in Philadelphia against the A's, he played first and moved Chase to center field. It didn't work and they lost 8–4. Ray Keating notched the Yanks' second victory after that, beating the A's 4–0. But the New Yorkers closed out the three-game series against the A's the next day — April 23 — losing 4–1 to Chief Bender, despite 11 hits. The Yanks had won only two of their first 10 games — matching the same miserable start of Wolverton's clueless 1912 team. And Wolverton had done it with considerably more style — remember how he'd been tossed after calling the umpire a leather-head mutt?

May was worse. The team lost all 12 home games and had yet to win at the Polo Grounds. Chance was desperate. He was injured again, this time with a bad leg, and had placed Chase back at first, Hartzel at second and Derrick at short. The team still wasn't hitting — principally Chase who was hovering just above .200 and not getting along much at all with his disciplinarian of a manager, especially when Chance barked his orders from the dugout.

So what else was new? Chase, who had

walked out on Elberfeld and engineered the dismissal of Stallings, didn't respond well to Chance's rages. Not only was the Peerless One, as the newspapers had taken to calling him—a play on words on Chance's well-earned nickname—steering clear of his manager, but he had taken to sitting on the bench to the side of his manager's deaf ear and mimicking him.

Chase would yell out the same order while scrunching his face to mock Chance. And he'd deliberately misinterpret his orders for the amusement of the other players. One who wasn't amused was Ed Sweeney, the catcher, who sympathized with Chance's health problems and told his manager what Chase was doing.

It no longer mattered that Chance had always enjoyed Chase's company. Any shred of friendship turned to quiet loathing. "I'm no stool pigeon," Chance said, glaring at his first baseman, "but you're not going to make fun of the big guy [himself] in front of me anymore." Combined with Chance's increasing doubts that his first baseman was playing every game hard, it meant that Prince Hal, as he had done so often in the past, was wearing out his welcome.

With little pitching and even less hitting, every win was like climbing a mountain. With the team headed nowhere, the criticism became a groundswell. The newspaper scribes took up the team's troubles. Most of their criticism was directed at Chance: "A hue and cry for the scalp of Frank Chance has been raised by some of the timorous fans of Manhattan, which reflects the old fickle affectations of fandom for the truly great," wrote MacBeth in *The Sporting News*. "It is rather painful to note that some baseball writers—who should know better—have been raffling at Chance just a trifle. Thy have been piqued that their predictions about the Peerless Leader getting off to an advantageous start have failed to date."

A mid–May road series in Chicago offered a respite for the beleaguered Yankee manager. On Saturday, May 16, nearly 36,000 people filed into Comiskey Park for Frank Chance Day, a tribute by his old mates to the former Cub hero. The crowd would have been more, but rain all morning and threatening skies through game-time kept it down. And never mind that the day was further marred when several spectators were injured when four sections of temporary seats collapsed: Chance received as big a tribute as anyone could remember. Festivities opened with a parade, featuring more than 700 cars. Then came enough flourishes to have impressed even Bill Veeck: circus and vaudeville acrobats, cabaret singers, trained dogs and tumblers. And then came that patented dead-ball tradition—floral tributes again—followed by speeches from just about every Illinois politician north of Cairo. With that, the Yankees went and lost 6–3; it was their 20th loss of the season against seven wins.

On May 27, the Yankees lost to the Red Sox—themselves in fifth place doldrums and unable to capture the magic of the year before, to remain deep in last with a 9–24 record. The day had started badly: During batting practice, third baseman Ezra Midkiff was struck in the stomach by a bat and had to sit out of the game, replaced by a journeyman infielder named Bill McKechnie, who'd played 44 games for the Yankees and hit .134, giving no hint of the managerial prowess that would land him in the Hall of Fame. Chance was forced to make another change in the third when Silk O'Loughlin tossed Harry Wolter for arguing at being called out stealing. The game itself was sloppy: The Yanks scratched out a run in the first but no more, with Hugh Bedient looking more like Christy Mathewson, going the distance in a 3–1 win, with the New Yorkers committing four errors.

It was afterwards that things got interesting — a blend of the old Yankee hoodoo, with genuine emotion and a bit of gossip thrown in for good measure. As usual, it involved Chase.

If Chase's mind wasn't fully on the game that day, he had good reason. That same day, he announced that he and 24-year-old Anna Cherung of 95 West 119th St. would soon be married, the second time the Yankee first sacker would tie the knot. That morning, he and Cherung had gone to City Hall in Jersey City, only to be told he did not have a certified copy of papers of his recent divorce, which had been finalized April 24.

But with Chase having to hurry to the Polo Grounds, Cherung returned to Jersey City, this time with the proper paperwork, and the marriage license was granted. She then went to the game and sent word to Chase, sitting on the bench, that things had been handled. As with most matters concerning Chase, the story was a major item in the next day's social columns of *The Tribune*.

Meanwhile, up in the Polo Grounds press box after the game, sportswriters Fred Lieb and Heywood Broun were wrapping up their game stories and about to board the 6th Avenue El for the ride back downtown, when Chance burst in, full of emotion and eager to talk about it.

"I want to tell you fellows what's going on," he said. "Did you notice some of the balls that got away from Chase today? They weren't wild throws; they were only made to look that way. He's been doing that right along. He's throwing games on me!"

The two writers were stunned. But they agreed to keep the substance of Chance's remarks to themselves. After discussing the conversation with Price, Lieb printed nothing about it in the *Press*. Neither did Broun, except for a short note in a *Morning Sun* column that Chance had told members of the press that Chase wasn't

playing to the best of the abilities and was letting some games get away with his inconstant play at first base.

After reading the Broun's comment, Farrell was mortified, at least on the surface. That afternoon, he stormed to the press box to discuss matters with the offending writer.

"That was a terrible thing you wrote about Chase," he thundered.

Broun countered. "I only said something that Chance told Fred Lieb and me," he said, "and he told us a lot more than I wrote in the paper."

After another rainout the following day, the Yankees went to Philadelphia for four games in three days against the A's. The results were much the same. On Thursday, May 29, Home Run Baker went deep in the seventh and scored the winning run in the ninth to beat Ray Keating 6–5. Baker was again the hero in a day-night doubleheader that Friday, going 3-for-8 and knocking another home run in 3–2 and 7–4 Philadelphia wins.

On the surface, the Saturday game wasn't much different: The A's chased 32-year rookie left-hander George Clark — what was about all the rookie oldsters? — with seven runs in the second and coasted 12–2. It would be Clark's only decision in a brief big league career that ended a few months later. Included in the Yankees' nine hits was a triple by the promising new shortstop Roger Peckinpaugh, just picked up from Cleveland, and a single from Chase. And with that, the Yanks descended deeper into last place, at 9–28.

It wasn't until the next day — Sunday, June 1 — that the true significance of the Saturday drubbing became apparent. Evidently, Chance had put the time presented by the two rainouts that week to good use. And "like a clap of thunder out of a clear sky," as the *Tribune* put it, came the news that the Yankee manager had been trying to put into place for weeks: Chase was gone, traded to the White Sox.

Apparently, Chance had been trying to unload him for weeks. Chicago responded after Chase was offered to every American League team, most of which refused Chase under any conditions or at any price. In return, the Yankees got an unproven no-name and a no-name with bad feet.

The unproven one — an "onion" in baseball lingo of the deadball era — was first baseman Babe Borton. Joining the White Sox in 1912, Borton had started well, hitting .371 in 31 games, and was hitting .275 in '13, when he was injured and relegated to the bench. The one with bad feet — bunions actually — was Rollie Zeider and was recognizable at least. A versatile infielder, he'd once hit as high as .253, but was unable to catch on to a starting position for the Sox. In the *Globe*, Mark Roth, later road secretary for the Yankees, wrote that the "Yankees traded Chase to Chicago for a bunion and an onion."

Everyone laughed at Roth's line. But the humor was apt because unloading Chase for two lesser players was a desperate move by a desperate team. Chance sanitized the move for the newspapers, saying Chase was the only New York player who could bring in two players the caliber of Borton and Zeider to the infield, where help was needed most. Uh-huh.

The reality was that Chase's anemic .212 batting average, spotty play and poor training habits didn't sit well with the hard-nosed Chance. Nor did the mimicry on the bench. Others argued that Chase was halfway out of the door when Chance thought he was dogging it during spring training, when, even with a bum ankle, he should have kept himself in better condition.

As usual, just about everyone had an opinion. "Handicapped with poor material, Chance began figuring on a trade involving Chase soon after the championship season opened," opined the *Sun*. "He played Chase regularly, however, to show other managers what he was worth. But oddly enough a majority of the American League teams refused to consider any kind of a proposition for Chase."

From Boston had came an offer of several benchwarmers for Chase. In Detroit, Hughie Jennings offered a catcher, but no one else. The irony is that almost every team had passed on Chase, but did nothing to encourage the end of his dubious ways. "What struck me then and has remained with me since," wrote Lieb in his memoirs, "was that the American League must have known the Chase record and the suspicions underlying what Chance told Broun and me. But instead of disciplining Chase or calling for an investigation, they let Farrell trade him to a club that was much higher in the standings (the White Sox were in fourth place at the time)."

Chance was said to have had his eyes on Zeider, whose play he had supposedly admired in the previous year's Cubs-White Sox post-season series. In Chicago, Charles Comiskey was giddy with excitement, saying that the acquisition of Chase practically guaranteed a White Sox pennant. For the Yankees, the trade brought to an end nearly 8½ of the rockiest, most erratic and occasionally stupendous years any one player could have for any one team.

Some write-ups of recent years have pointed to how shocked and disappointed people were at the trade. Surprised? Yes. But shocked and disappointed? No way, for a lot more people than Chance, Lieb and Broun were wise to the shenanigans of Prince Hal Chase by the middle of 1913. MacBeth summed it up best, when he wrote in *The Sporting News* that "Chase, as a winning factor for New York, was through some time ago."

"Ever since he jumped the club in 1908, Chase has been a disturbing element," MacBeth wrote. "He could not even take himself seriously when he managed the club in 1911.... It is to be hoped for the good of baseball that he reforms under (White Sox manager Jimmy) Callahan's command. Players like Chase come about once in a century. That he can play first as it never was and perhaps never again will be played is a well-known truth. That he will is a different matter."

So how did New Yorkers really feel about the trade? They expressed themselves Saturday, June 8, when who should arrive at the Polo Grounds for his first game as a member of the Chicago White Sox, but one Hal Chase?

Digging in to face Ray Keating in his first at-bat as a Chicagoan, Chase "did not cut an entrancing figure," the *Tribune* reported. Vigorous applause from the crowd of 15,000 quickly changed into hisses and boos, which grew louder and more sarcastic as the game wore on "until Hal became the target for a demonstration such as Johnny Evers and (Philadelphia second baseman) Otto Knabe have endured so exultingly for many years," the *Tribune* added in a reference to New Yorkers' particular venom for these two National League rivals of the Giants.

It didn't stop the Peerless One from getting two hits and scoring Chicago's first run. Such was the irony of a player who could turn it on when he felt like it. But it wasn't enough on a big day for the Yankees — two runs in the eighth and the winner in the ninth on two singles and a sacrifice to secure a 3–2 win. It was their first home win of 1913 after 17 straight defeats and a solitary tie at the Polo Grounds. "Yankees Win — Guns Boom and Rockets Flare," cooed *The Tribune*, with only slight sarcasm the next day.

It was a big day for Keating in more ways than one. For starters, he went seven snappy innings to beat 27-game winner Ed Walsh. And he did it on *his* day — the afternoon that a contingent of 1,100 people from his hometown of Bridgeport, Connecticut descended on the Polo Grounds to see their guy pitch. In doing so, they coughed up a bunch of gifts for their hero, including a loving cup, a silver bat, a diamond ring and — you guessed it — a horseshoe floral tribute. For good measure, Chance, Callahan and Walsh got floral tributes too. What exactly did these macho ballplayers do with all the flowers?

So New York was rid of Hal Chase. The reality however is that a Chase-less team was all part of Chance's larger mission to build a new team — quickly. Chance wasn't used to losing, hated it and took it on himself to wheel and deal and remake the Yankees his way. With Arthur Irwin sticking to business affairs, Chance watched the waiver lists, called his many friends in baseball to see who was available. And at least for now, Farrell was willing to go along.

Some moves worked. Others didn't. There was McKechnie, picked up from Boston in mid–April off the waiver list. He wouldn't stick with the Yanks, but would one day become a manager and wind up in Cooperstown. There was young Red Hoff, the left-hander from nearby Ossining and the slayer of Ty Cobb, who mopped up in two games and despite giving up not so much as a single run, was in early May sent packing to minor league Rochester of the International League. Hoff would resurface a year later and spend parts of two years with the St. Louis Browns before leaving the major leagues to enlist in the military during World War I.

Then came the pick-up of a man who one day would acquire his very own special moniker in the box scores. That would be "Peck," a smooth-fielding, moon-faced shortstop named Roger Peckinpaugh, picked up May 25 from Cleveland in exchange for Bill Stumpf and Jack Lelivelt. He joined the Yanks in the late–May disaster of a series against the A's in Philadelphia, and on May 29, went 3-for-3 in his first Yankee start. He continued to hit and fielded flawlessly — becoming the glue that held the unsteady infield together and one of the few bright spots in the Yankees' otherwise *annus horribilis.*

Chance had been trying to land the 22-year-old Peckinpaugh since the season's opening. To do so, he'd been pestering the Cleveland management, which already had a starting shortstop, Ray Chapman, who was exactly three weeks older than Peck and 100 points higher in batting average.

Peckinpaugh was still a catch. He was smart, knew and studied the game, and had the classic infielder's build — a big chest, broad shoulders and slightly bowed legs. Standing 5'10" and weighing 160 pounds, his hands were oversized and his throwing arm was a gun. He chewed Star Plug tobacco only when on the ball field, and said he'd spit into his glove and rub the ball in the goop for two reasons.

"Star plug was licorice flavored and it made my glove sticky," he'd tell the Cleveland *Plain-Dealer* years later. "It also darkened the ball and the pitchers liked that. The batters did not, but what the hell, there was [often] only one umpire."

Born in Wooster, Ohio, Peckinpaugh grew up in Cleveland, where he starred in football, basketball and baseball at East High School. His family was neighbors to Larry Lajoie, manager of the Naps, and when Lajoie, Peckinpaugh's idol growing up, offered him a $125 a month to play ball in 1909, the year after the young player graduated from high school, he wanted to accept.

But standing in his way was his father, John, a salesman and a former semi-pro player, who was opposed. The elder Peckinpaugh considered professional ballplayers a load of inebriated louts who lived in fear of real jobs, a hypothesis that wasn't so far off the mark.

So young Roger Peckinpaugh went to his former high school principal, Benjamin Ulysses Rannels, and asked his advice. Rannals urged him to sign the contract, but said to quit baseball if he couldn't make it to the majors in three years and go to college. He made it in two.

In 1910, Peckinpaugh was the sensation of spring training with the Naps, that is until Cleveland pitchers starting throwing curve balls. When that happened, Peckinpaugh's batting average promptly took a tumble from the .400 range, slithering right on down to the .200 level and the young shortstop was sent down to New Haven in the Eastern League.

When he emerged at the tail end of the 1912 season, it was to face Walter Johnson in his first official big league at-bat. Years later, Peckinpaugh would recall Johnson throwing the ball so fast that the batter could hear it. He got the Cleveland batsman on a foul pop-up.

"I thought I had achieved something just hitting the ball," Peckinpaugh said. "I fouled his fast ball twice."

Peckinpaugh had spent most of 1911 and 1912 with Portland of the Pacific Coast League, fielding well and begging pitchers in batting practice to throw him curves. "I knew if I got back up to Cleveland, five of every six pitches I would see would be curves," he would say, "so I knew I had to learn to hit them. It took me awhile."

So Peckinpaugh learned, hit in the .250 range, and, in time developed a distinctive batting style featuring a space as large as six inches between his hands. Some said he was copying Ty Cobb, but Peckinpaugh disagreed, saying he developed the style very much on his own, after hurting his left wrist sliding.

"I had worked too hard to become a regular so I told no one," he told the *Plain-Dealer* of the injury that led to his batting style. "In those days, you played hurt to keep your position. I kept experimenting until I found a style that would let me bat without hurting my wrist. I did most of the work with my right hand and got so I could punch the ball almost anywhere I wanted to."

As for Cobb, Peckinpaugh called him the greatest player he ever saw. "Cobb was a wild man on the bases and he came with his spikes high on a lot of infielders," he said. "But he never nicked me and I asked him why once. 'Because I respect your play,'" Cobb said.

As for the Yankees, they had found a shortstop but little else. With the team headed to oblivion, Chance took his license to wheel and deal to heart. He became Deal-A-Day Chance, who, with all the acumen of a used car salesman, discarded and found ballplayers, most of whom turned out to be one-shot wonders. On June 12, he waived catcher Dutch Sterrett, the Princetonian who'd shown promise, but was hitting a measly .171, had a bad leg and wasn't helping his cause by refusing to play Sundays for religious reasons.

Sterrett became expendable with the acquisition of another catcher, 21-year-old Dick Gossett, who also wasn't long in the big leagues when he hit .162 and was gone the next year — his career .159 career average preserved for posterity. Then, nine days after leading Sterrett to the door, a 22-year-old catcher, Jay Rogers, showed up from Richmond of the Virginia League. Five games later, he too was gone. His lifetime big league stats: eight at-bats, no hits.

Two days after Rogers, three more new Yankees turned up, each secured by Chance from a different place. From Mount St. Mary's College came outfielder Dan Costello; he'd hit .500 for the Yankees (okay … one-for-two) and play three years for the Pirates. From Galveston of the Texas League came first baseman Harry Williams, the brother of Browns outfielder Gus Williams,

who stuck for 27 games, hitting .256. And from New York City's very own Manhattan College came pitcher Jim Hanley, a Providence native whose career stats take up little room in *The Baseball Encyclopedia*: one game, four innings pitched, five hits, and a 6.75 ERA. You get the idea.

Nothing was working, all of which left the tightly-wound, increasingly-cranky Chance, well, even crankier. On July 2 at the Polo Grounds, he protested a 2–1 loss to the A's in which umpire Big Bill Dinneen actually ordered a replay of an at-bat that ended with the former pitcher-turned ump being popped in the head by the ball during an attempted 4–6–3 A's double play.

Big Bill's curious decision came in the fourth inning and essentially nullified a sharply-hit single by Borton that would have advanced Borton to second and Hartzell to third. Both runners had advanced when the ball, thrown by A's shortstop Jack Barry, found Dinneen's head, bounded high in the air, landed far beyond the first base line and rolled to the grandstand. "Big Bill had been standing in the hot sun for four innings, and Jack Barry's carom off the umpire's head had plenty of speed," the *Times* wrote, "so perhaps Bill's head was badly muddled."

Borton did his best on the replay. He reached first when Home Run Baker made a bad throw from third, sending Hartzell to second. Midkiff followed with a single that scored Hartzell, but instead of what could have been at least two runs came the day's lone Yankee tally. It was a tough loss.

But it was more than that. It was Borton's last hurrah. The "onion" wasn't hitting, so five days later, Chance shipped him to Jersey City and called up former Yankee Jack Knight, who had spent 1912 toiling with Washington.

That same day — July 7 — the catching situation went from tenuous to laughable. Actually, things had started deteriorating three days before when Sweeney went down with a broken finger in a doubleheader against Washington. Then, in another doubleheader against the Nationals, Gossett left the second game with a bad cut on his throwing hand. With no catchers, in went one Joe Smith, a local product signed at precisely noon the day before from Kingston of the New York and New Jersey League. Smith went 0-for-4 and played 12 more games, hitting .156. As Casey Stengel would say years later while managing the Mets, "Can't anyone here play this game?"

Apparently not. Two weeks later, Chance lodged another protest, this one with the Board of Directors of the American League claiming he'd been deliberately deceived by White Sox President Charles Comiskey in the Borton and Zeider deal. Borton was essentially useless, relegated to the minors. Zeider, meanwhile, was laid up in St. Louis, still suffering the effects of a nasty spike wound he'd received from Ty Cobb—*two weeks before the trade*. If his bunions weren't enough, poor Zeider had been in the care of a physician for the injury during his final weeks in Chicago.

"I never intimated," Chance said during a Yankee stop in Cleveland, "that I wished to have the deal rescinded in any way, but I do think that under the circumstances, Chicago should pay Zeider's salary and hospital expenses until such time that he is fit to report for duty."

But don't think for a moment that Chance ever regretted, even with a fraction of second, unloading Hal Chase. "I want no part of Chase's game," the Peerless Leader put forth in no uncertain terms. "Zeider in the hospital is worth more to the New York club than 10 Chases."

In time, the trade would have repercussions beyond Borton's ineffectiveness and Zeider's spike wound. Sensible as the trade appeared on the surface, Chase was still a

Farrell guy and the Yankee owners felt that Chance, in his angry haste to get rid of him, had been bilked. "The tension between manager and owners grew," wrote Frank Graham in his history of the Yankees, "with Chance accusing them of trying to run the club over his head."

That exact accusation wouldn't come for another year or so, but it's clear that the Chase deal combined with the general Yankee ineptitude was the trigger to what would become a steady deterioration of Chance's relationship with Farrell and Devery. What was it about Chase, now well out of New York, that caused complications?

For Farrell, Devery and their manager, it was the same old story: manager starts with toasts all round and a lot of optimism, but give it time and the situation deteriorates in a flurry of insults, innuendos and criticism. By early August, rumors were flying that Chance, fed up with the Yankee owners and fed up with his team's poor performance, was headed back to his orange groves in Glendora.

The rumors were met by a flood of denials. First, in the August 4 *Sporting News*, came MacBeth. "Frank Farrell has always been a very game sportsman—as game as Chance himself," he wrote. "The disappointing work of his players has in no manner shattered faith in the master of the great Cub machine of other days. Farrell realizes the obstacles that Frank Chance has to encounter. He realizes further that he needs a whole lot of baseball players."

Then it was Chance's turn. "I have not the slightest intention of resigning as manager," he said August 3. "Instead, I am working and planning to put a real pennant contender into the American League next season. It's slow work, to be sure, for I have to go into the bushes for new material, and then develop it for the big league."

He sure did. As August wore on, Chance continued to sign just about anyone who could walk in what became a kind of rolling audition for 1914. In came a fiery sparkplug of a rookie new third baseman, Fritz Maisel, "so small," the *Times* joked, "that the bleacherites can't see him until he gets down as far as second base." Maisel's heads-up play in his big-league debut on August 11 sparked Ray Caldwell's 6–2 win over the Browns. Maisel, who was 5'7½" and not *that* small, was a find, and would go on to play 51 games and hit .310.

That same day, three more new pitchers joined the Yankees. From Jersey City came Marty McHale. From Dayton of the Central League came Cy Pieh, and from Petersburg of the Virginia League came Georgia native Rebel Cooper. Of the three, McHale, a University of Maine product who'd thrown three straight no-hitters in college and had a cup of coffee with the Red Sox, would last the longest — two years-plus with the Yankees — for a 12–27 record. Chance's wheeling and dealing was certainly hit or miss — mostly miss.

As it turned out, games against St. Louis were about the only drama left in the Yankees' sorry season. Climbing out of last place and catching the almost-as-bad seventh-place Browns became the story line for most Yankee beat writers. On August 20, when the New Yorkers lost a doubleheader to the Browns, they fell eight games in back of St. Louis, and their chances of climbing out of the cellar seemed slim indeed.

But back at the Polo Grounds September 11, McHale shut out the Browns on a tidy four-hitter and Birdie Cree contributed three hits and scored a run in the 4–0 win, and the Yankees drew closer. And then eureka! Six days later, in a doubleheader split against the White Sox at the Polo Grounds — at the same time that the A's were beating the Browns — the Yankees caught St. Louis and sidled into seventh. It was the first time since September 23, 1912, and the glory days of Harry Wolverton that the Yankees were anywhere but last.

Not that whole hordes of people were hoisting cold ones in honor of the Yanks. The reality is that the 5,000 or so fans on hand to see them take on the White Sox couldn't see much of anything. Even so, the Yanks drew 357,551 in 1913, nowhere close to the Giants, but more than 115,000 above the dark days of 1912. After Russell Ford got clocked 9–3 in the opener, the Yankees and the White Sox played tit for tat in the nightcap, all in an increasing state of rainy, foggy autumn gloom.

It wasn't exactly the kind of high drama Ban Johnson had envisioned when he invented the American League. "The Yankees played a fine game in that tussle in the dark," opined the *Times* with a decided grain of salt. "Silk O'Loughlin says so and he was right up there behind the catcher and was the only one in the park who could see. The people in the grand stand looked into the darkness and followed the thrilling moments of the struggle with their ears. You could hear Silk shouting at the top of his lungs, 'Yourrr're Out!' or 'Yourrr're Safe!' or Tommy Connelly barking from the infield, 'Out' or 'Safe!'"

This much could be pieced together: the Yanks scored single runs in the first, second and sixth innings off Eddie Cicotte, the old Bostonian, and behind Ray Fisher, held off the Sox 3–2. Once again, Hal Chase, this time as a White Soxian, helped make it happen. In the first, Chase nailed Yankee center fielder Bill Holden at the plate on one play, but then uncorked a suspiciously poor throw to third in an attempt to get left fielder George Whiteman, who then scored. Chase, by the way, would compile vintage Chasian figures in 1913. Recovering from his ankle injury to bat .286 for Chicago and .266 overall, with a league-leading 27 errors at first base, 10 more than anyone else.

As for the game and the ever-increasing darkness, "The worst of it was nobody in the stands could tell whether the umpires were right or wrong, and so there was no chance to call the umpires names," the *Times* reported.

But by the eighth inning, with it an official game, even Silk admitted he had enough. Through the darkness came the foghorn voice of a spectator:

"For heaven's sake Silk, call the game. My wife don't know where I am and I've got to go home."

It was a reasonable request. With that, Silk called the game, the Yanks had won and they had crawled out from the basement of the American League. Chance vowed that they wouldn't return.

He was almost right. The Yankees did slide back, but then climbed out again for good on September 29 in a dramatic fashion—beating the Red Sox in a double-header at the Polo Grounds. Okay, so these weren't the World Champion Red Sox of the year before—battered by injuries, most notably to Smoky Joe Wood, who had come down with a bad arm—the Bostonians were fourth. But it was the first time the Yanks had beaten the Red Sox at the Hilltop since Hal Chase ran things back in June 1911—19 straight defeats ago.

The Yankees took a small measure of comfort in such trivia during that lost season of 1913. They had to, for it was dismal all the way around. At least they held on for seventh—finishing 57–94, 38 games behind the pennant-winning A's, and a game ahead of the Browns, last or next-to-last for the last four years.

The Yankees had poured through players like dishwater in 1913. There were 44 Yankees that year, including six catchers and a virtual parade of outfielders who came and went in a heartbeat. It didn't include a whole lot of hitting—the team's .237 average was tied with the Browns and ahead of only Chicago and its 3.27 ERA was ahead of only the Tigers. Only Cree, and Peckinpaugh, the team's leading batsmen at .272 and .268 respectively, compiled really solid seasons. Of the team's starting pitchers, only Cald-

well had a winning record at 9–8. Others didn't fare so well—Fisher went 11–16, Ford 13–18, Schulz 7–13, McConnell 5–15 and Keating 6–12. You get the idea.

Chance put the blame on something he recognized in hindsight had been a faulty decision, going to Bermuda. "The boys were completely knocked out by the climate, contracted all manner of ailments, including rheumatism, and suffered generally throughout the whole season," he said much later. "I do not say that my team would have been any better off had we trained elsewhere, but it is a cinch in opinion it could have been no worse. If next spring, I can bring my players to the barrier in proper condition, I feel that I will be able to make a far better showing than I did this season."

He also blamed Arthur Irwin for his lack of bringing in quality ballplayers. "How was it possible to collect so many mediocre ballplayers on one club?" Chance wondered aloud in comments not meant for attribution. Tensions were rising.

Not that Irwin's actions, or healthy players, or Hal Chase joining the temperance league, or much of anything else, for the matter, would have done much for the Yanks in '12. The A's, with big years from Eddie Collins, who led the A.L. with 125 runs and Home Run Baker, who batted .336 and drove in 126, cruised to their third A.L. flag in four years. And what a dreamy season for Walter Johnson and the Nationals, which finished in second, 6½ games back, thanks to the Big Train's 36–7 record and 1.09 ERA. With Johnson, the Nationals were an .837 team; without him, they were .486. No wonder Johnson became the first and only pitcher to earn the Chalmers Award.

Again, the A's opponent in the World Series would be the Giants, again paced by the game's top pitchers, including Mathewson and Marquard, both 23-game winners, and spitballer Jeff Tesreau, with 22. And just as in 1911, the A's again beat the injury-depleted New Yorkers in the Series, but this time needing only five games behind their mainstay pitchers, Eddie Plank, Chief Bender and "Bullet" Joe Bush. It was another bitter defeat for McGraw's Giants, well on their way to becoming the Atlanta Braves of the dead ball era — good enough to take the pennant, but seldom the Series.

But baseball officials had weightier things on their mind as they looked to 1914. Looming just ahead was another challenge — the Federal League, which was baseball's last serious attempt to establish a third major league. The "Flap Jack League," as writers soon took to calling it, had actually kicked off in 1912, but was only now giving the established National and American leagues a colorful run for their money, particularly after establishing itself at two spots in the critical New York market.

The New York strongholds were Harrison Park in Newark and the hastily rebuilt Washington Park in the Red Hook section of the borough, where the forgettable Brooklyn Tip-Tops stumbled to consecutive second division finishes in two seasons.

Outlaw baseball leagues are an American tradition. No exception when it came to the Federal League: It started with one John T. Powers of Chicago, who organized the Wisconsin-Illinois League in 1905, but had bigger things in mind — a professional league using players unaffiliated with other professional clubs that pooled their resources to make a profit.

Powers formed his next venture, the outlaw "Columbian League" in 1913, which became the Federal League. Convinced that baseball's bursting popularity could support eight primarily Midwestern teams, Powers kept peace with organized baseball by restricting league rosters to free agents and, in cases of teams in major league cities, sched-

uling league games when the major leaguers were on the road.

But the Flap Jack's low profile ended after 1913 when a faction of owners led by "Fighting" Jim Gilmore, a Spanish–American War veteran, self-made coal baron and owner of the league's Chicago franchise, forced Powers out of office with the intention of going big-time. From then on, the renamed Federal League added several ingredients to a beefed-up league — expansion into more lucrative Eastern cities, modern stadiums and the more aggressive pursuit of established major league stars.

As part of its master plan, Flap Jack magnates announced plans for the new Brooklyn franchise to resurrect old Washington Park, home of the N.L. Brooklyns before Ebbets Field. Those efforts paralleled successful efforts in Pittsburgh to use old Exposition Park, the former home of the Pirates, and in Chicago, where Charles Weeghman constructed an all-concrete and steel park called Weeghman Park, which became Wrigley Field.

At the time, the brothers Robert and George Ward, who owned the Tip-Tops — naming the team after their popular brand of bread — had tried to merely expand on Washington Park's existing wooden grandstand. But Brooklyn building codes forced them to totally raze the old structure and, as in Chicago, erect a new concrete and steel grandstand.

For Washington Park, it was the third leg of an odd life that had started in May 1883 and housed the Dodgers for five years, until it was destroyed by fire a week before another, more deadly tragedy — the Johnstown Flood. The park was named for General George Washington, whose headquarters in the Battle of Long Island during the Revolutionary War was in Gowanus House, which still stands on the same block. And the team's clubhouse: a stone building actually occupied for a time by Washington.

Rebuilt in less than a month, Washington Park housed the Dodgers again from 1898 to 1912. The new park, rebuilt in wood by the Dodgers, was actually catercorner to an earlier version of Washington Park. Total seating capacity for the renovated park was 18,000, including a covered grandstand, with the longest dimension a reasonable 400 feet in center-field, where the scoreboard rested on supporting legs so a fair ball could roll underneath.

Construction delays and cold spring weather kept the Tip-Tops from opening the 1914 season until May 11 against the gloriously-named Pittsburgh Stogies. As throughout the entire eight-team league, ticket pricing was identical to the major league clubs — $1 for box seats, 75 cents for reserved grandstand, 50 cents for pavilion seats and 25 cents for the bleachers. In keeping with the religious sentiment in "The City of Churches" and the laws of New York State, the Tip-Tops scheduled no home game for Sundays and played no road games on the Sabbath as well.

At the home opener, the Tip-Tops were already mired in fifth place, when Tom Seaton lost a tight 2–0 pitching duel to Pittsburgh's Howard Camnitz before more than 15,000. Both pitchers were among a number of former big leaguers who jumped to the new league. Among the others, many of whom were at the end of their playing careers: future Hall of Famers Edd Roush, Three Finger Brown, Eddie Plank and Chief Bender, along with one Hal Chase, gone in mid-season 1914 from the White Sox to the Buffalo Federals, where he'd pound the Flap Jack's blend of major- and (mostly) minor-league level pitching for a .347 batting average in 75 games.

A particular Federal League strength was its ability to exploit player disgruntlement. With many big leaguers growing increasingly resentful of the power that owners held over their lives, there was talk about the formation of a union. There were incidents aplenty: Back in '11 after Addie Joss

died and his Cleveland teammates voted to pass up the next day's game in Detroit in order to attend his funeral in Toledo, Ban Johnson wanted to order them back to work, but was talked out of it. Johnson was still miffed and later announced that the game had been postponed.

Sounding like a cross between Samuel Gompers and Allen Ginsburg, Walter Johnson summed up the situation in a 1911 *Baseball Magazine* article. "The employer tries to starve out the laborer, and the laborer tries to ruin the employer's business," he wrote. "They quarrel over a bone and rend each other like coyotes."

Player raids that continued into the Federal League's 1915 season brought on protracted lawsuits and legal skirmishes with the major leagues, particularly when it came to protecting legitimate stars like Christy Mathewson, who was said to be close to jumping (he didn't). It also created the need of strong franchises in the high-profile New York market. That got a considerable boost in the Tip-Tops' first home game in '15, when Benny Kauff, newly acquired from the defunct Indianapolis franchise, belted a three-run home run to help defeat Buffalo.

But upbeat beginnings couldn't save the Flap Jacks. Kauff won the batting title at .344, but the Tip-Tops fell to seventh place in the standings, beating out only the lowly Baltimore Terrapins. That did little to stop the declining attendance at Tip-Top games, even though the team, in desperation, slashed the 25-cent bleacher tickets to a dime and were actually planning to play night baseball — a full 20 years before its introduction in Cincinnati.

Things got worse when Federal League officials failed to persuade Judge Kenesaw Mountain Landis to dismiss the league's prolonged suit against organized baseball. The end came December 17, 1915, at the Waldorf–Astoria Hotel, where the N.L./ A.L. baseball establishment agreed to put up a sizable sum to compensate debt-ridden Federal League backers in exchange for disbanding the league. As part of the peace treaty, Chicago's Charles Weeghman was given controlling interest of the N.L. Cubs; and Phil Ball, the ice-making magnate, of the A.L. Browns.

For the Yankees in the winter of 1913 and 1914, the Federal League brought the same struggles to keep talent as other teams. Chance's focus that winter was a rangy, blond-haired 27-year right hander named "King" Cole, whose real name, Leonard, demonstrated why he'd stuck with his colorful nickname. Chance had managed Cole in Chicago where the Iowa native had strung together impressive records of 21–4 in '10 and 18–7 in '11, before suffering arm problems and waking up in the American Association. So after Cole went 23–11 and struck out 140 batters for Columbus in '13, Chance came calling and signed him in December to a Yankee contract.

But so did Joe Tinker, the new manager of the Flap Jack League's Chicago Whales. Cole signed with them too — in January — and the battle was on. In early February, the King cancelled a vaudeville performance to show up at Yankee offices, where he was welcomed by Frank Farrell and flamboyantly re-signed a Yankee contract for the original $3,300. But what about Tinker? The King, one of the few players of the era to have a personal attorney, settled things in the courts. The contract stuck.

Others didn't. All winter, Chance continued to clean house, ridding himself of Yankee mainstays like the 29-year-old Harry Wolter, displaced to Indianapolis of the American Association for the Yankees' new strategy: a youth movement. Wolter, who had made it back from his broken leg to bat .254 in '13, wouldn't reach the majors again until 1917, when he'd bat .249 for

the Cubs and close out a seven-year big league career with a lifetime .270 average.

Gone too was Russell Ford, he of the trick pitch and the winner of 73 Yankee games in four full seasons, the last two of which had been losing ones. Chance made it known that Ford wasn't wanted back, when he asked him to take a $2,000 pay cut. So Ford became another new Buffalo Federal and mowed down the inferior batters to post a 20–5 record in '14, the league's best.

The few veterans who did remain included Peckinpaugh, the Yankee shortstop of the present and future, and third baseman Roy Hartzell. The pitching staff remained relatively intact as well, with Ford's old mates Warhop, Fisher, Keating, Caldwell and Schulz headed south for spring training.

This year's destination was Houston. And it was with a sober, business-like air that 16 Yankee players, headed by Arthur Irwin, departed New York February 26 for the long, three-day train journey south. Unlike the previous season, when brass bands and flag-waving fans saw the ballplayers off, this year's version looked like a gang of young businessmen off to the annual meeting. The main reason was a whole new cast of characters; of the 16 on train, only two had been with the Yankees a year before. Another four had joined late in '13, leaving the majority untested and unknown.

Part of the new sobriety was that Chance had urged most of his pitchers to head for extra training in Hot Springs. And the Peerless Leader himself, said to be in splendid health with renewed spirits to match, was headed to Houston directly from California.

Headed that way, but from the opposite direction, was the other reason that nobody seemed to be paying much attention to the Yankees as they headed south. Call it a major case of bad timing, encouraged by one John McGraw, and it captivated the city.

Visit Pier 56 at the foot of West 14th Street at the Hudson River on the nippy morning of March 6 and you'd catch a festive throng of 300 baseball fans and officials — egged on by a stream of gushing newspaper headlines that had gone on for days.

It was New York's finest nautical baseball celebration — the homecoming of John McGraw and his all-star group of ballplayers, comprised mostly of Giants and White Sox, who sailed into New York Harbor. They were aboard the *Lusitania*, the infamous ship that a little more than a year later would be sunk by a German submarine, killing 128 American passengers.

But that tragedy was still to come. "The tooting of whistles and the shrill blasts of the sirens from every craft in the harbor (heralded) the welcome return of the baseball players," trumpeted the *Times*. For McGraw, it sounded "better than the thunder of 30,000 fans at the Polo Grounds."

The sirens of the harbor were only the start. Another crowd of 300, many of them Chicago friends of the White Sox, yelled a welcome from the boat *Niagara*. Back on land, ladies waved handkerchiefs and men vigorously pumped their hats in recognition of the 68-person delegation steaming up the Hudson toward home.

As the ship docked, "it could be seen that a change had come over the players," the *Times* said. In short, the Continent had turned them into dudes, using most of their time abroad by dressing for their homecoming in the latest fashions of Paris and London. "Mike Donlin was nifty in his new scenery, to say nothing of Germany Schaefer who looked as if he had just stepped out of a Bond Street toggery shop," the paper reported. Most dude-like of all may have been Umpire Bill Klem, who descended the

gangplank sporting a mustard-colored coat and walking stick.

They had done well on and off the field — having romped through 11 innings for King George in London, an audience with the Pope in Rome and playing before enthusiastic crowds in France, Egypt, Australia and Japan. It was an old-fashioned demonstration of American diplomacy through sports, the forerunner of ping pong diplomacy. Said the U.S. Ambassador to Great Britain, "This game has accomplished more toward getting the Americans and English together than any other thing."

The homecoming celebration continued on land. The next evening, another 600 admirers paid their respects in a gala banquet at the Biltmore that featured speech after long-winded speech, with guests paying $10 to squeeze their way into the mammoth banquet.

"You have performed a service to the game and your country will bear lasting results," thundered Governor John Tener of PA. "Wherever the game is implanted, there will indelibly be associated with it, the word, 'America'— the American game."

Yikes. How could the Yankees compete against that? Chance tried at least, appearing rested and upbeat while in Houston. "The impact of horsehide against second growth ash resounds through the air and the Peerless Leader is a kid again," wrote MacBeth in the March 12 *Sporting News*. "Yes, a real kid. The kind who led a celebrated bunch of Cubs to four National League pennants and two world's championships in the short span of seven fruitful years. He jokes; he laughs; at times he is tempted to sing."

Chance credited the r & r back home in California — and a glimmer of hope for what he said for a better team — as reasons for his optimism. "I have spent the winter out of doors," he told reporters, "and I feel fine." Chance was feeling so good that he was even entertaining thoughts of taking a crack at first base again. From New York, he ordered a specially-made head gear to protect him from his old nemesis — beanball injuries. That was short lived as Chance, who had batted all of 24 times in '13, took precisely one at-bat in 1914. It was the last of his nearly 4,300 major league at-bats in 17 big-league seasons.

For the most part, the untested Yankees did well that spring, feasting on minor league teams in Houston and Beaumont. On March 17, they even went to Texas City to take on the soldiers — the U.S. Army's 22nd Infantry, before 5,000 soldiers. It wasn't close, with the Yanks compiling 17 hits, four by Harry Williams, to coast 15–2. Those soldiers took a particular pleasure in watching the pitching of Rebel Cooper, a former Navy man, and King Cole, who wasn't pitching but umpiring — yes, umpiring. It was a good feeling all the way around — ticket money went to buy new uniforms for the Infantry team and to fix up the ballpark. Afterwards, Yankee players were guests for dinner and some inter-army boxing matches.

But Chance still ran a tough camp. Three days later, he fined Ray Caldwell $100 for breaking training rules. It was the second offense for Caldwell, whose offense was staying out way past the 11:30 p.m. curfew and not showing up for practice the next morning. Some figured he had jumped the team, not such a wild thought given the numbers of major leaguers leaving for the Federal League.

The Peerless One let go with a stern warning. "Caldwell has not far to go in big league baseball if he thinks he can train here like some people do on the Great White Way," he said. "I have stood for enough as far as Caldwell is concerned. He has been the only player who has not lived up to the training rules, and if he intends to play that kind of game with me, he is going to suffer for it." Caldwell didn't jump after all — paying the fine and getting down to business.

Heading north, Chance got tough again — banning poker-playing among his players in hotels in an effort to get their minds baseball-focused. "I do not think it does a ballplayer any good to sit for three and four hours in the morning at a hotel playing cards," he said as the team reached Richmond. "It makes them loggy, and they have not that pepper, which is required on the playing field in the afternoon." Chance, however, let up when traveling; players were allowed to play poker on trains.

So there was Caldwell, along with Cole, pitching well back at Ebbets Field in a late tune-up April 3 that the Dodgers won 1–0. Could these new-look Yankees be halfway decent after all? The veteran pitching staff appeared to give them some stability, as did a few strong position players, with Maisel at second, Peckinpaugh at third and the dependable Sweeney catching. And MacBeth in *The Sporting News* "refuses to predict a glowing future for the team that Chance has whipped together, but it certainly looks 100 percent stronger than that with which he set out last year."

Maybe not 100 percent stronger, but better. In their second season at the Polo Grounds, the Yankees broke well, humbling the World Champion A's in the opener 8–2 on a bone cold April 15 afternoon in Harlem. With Chance yelling the slogan "Be Alive" from the dugout — where, on earth, did that one come from? — the Yanks broke for four runs in the first, chasing Bullet Joe Bush and putting things away behind a string of hits by Hartzell, former Athletic Jimmy Walsh, Bill Holden, Doc Cook and Williams.

Who were these guys? With some exceptions, they were a bunch of players up for a cup of coffee — and who, in the early going, were playing over their heads. As for the few veterans, they had decent pitching and surprisingly good team speed on the base paths, but few dependable bats. It wasn't enough: After splitting a Memorial Day doubleheader against the A's, the Yankees were three games under .500 in sixth place, hardly the horrendous starts of the previous two years, but mediocre and still not fulfilling the promise for which Chance was hired.

At least Frank Farrell had his ballpark to think about. With seemingly everybody building glorious new parks more befitting of palaces, Farrell wanted nothing short of the best for his new ballpark in the Bronx. Finally, a place that the Yankees could call their own seemed to be in the cards — a situation made all the more critical by organized baseball's belief that a centrally-located park would discourage the Federal League from establishing a real foothold in Manhattan.

The previous July, Farrell had announced that the grandstand would be made of brick and terra cotta — essentially fireproof — at a cost of $250,000, with the field itself costing another $12,000.

Then, on March 29, Farrell grandly introduced further details, saying it would hold a Polo Grounds–like 40,000 — a steel and concrete double-deck grandstand, seating 20,000, open stands extending beyond both the right and left-field foul lines seating another 14,000, and another 6,000 or so who could stand. The field was to be among the largest in the major leagues — 325 feet to left, 330 feet to right and a deadball-like 550 feet to center.

With the announcement came an artist's rendering showing entrances to both decks of the grandstand that would connect with the platforms of the subway station. Construction on the field would start in April, it was said, with the foundation work to be completed by June and the whole thing to be done in time for the Yankees' 1915 home opener.

To support the new park, the New York Central Railroad agreed to build a six-track terminal between the main line station at Marble Hill and 225th Street, where 10-car trains would load and unload people who preferred to go by way of Grand Central Terminal. Express trains, it was said, would make it from Grand Central to the new park in all of 18 minutes.

More to the point were the unmentioned details. Legal problems in filling in the creek that ran past the park persisted, as did community opposition and the ever-rising construction costs. In the end, glorious plans of 40,000 fans cheering the Yankees in Kingsbridge remained nothing more than plans. Little more was heard of the projected ballpark until well after Farrell and Big Bill Devery had left baseball.

Only slightly more was heard of the Yankees that long 1914 season of discontent. Farrell and Devery, apt to leave Chance alone in the early going to buy and test his new players, were meddling again — hoping to push and prod the ever-anxious Peerless Leader into bringing home a winner.

Chance continued to wheel and deal. On May 27, he sold Rebel Cooper, by then a veteran of a single Yankees appearance, to the Red Sox, where he pitched 10 games over two years, compiling a lifetime big-league record of 1–1 before leaving baseball. Two days later, Chance responded to rumors that Ed Sweeney was about to jump to the Federal League and signed the dependable Yankees veteran catcher to a three-year deal.

On June 1, he signed Charlie Meara, a so-called "slugger," as the papers said, from Perth Amboy of the Atlantic League. Nothing against Meara, who was the team's leading slugger, but Perth Amboy to the majors in one jump? It showed: the 23-year-old Meara, nicknamed "Goggy," played four games for the Yankees, with two hits in seven at-bats. And that was that for Goggy's trip to the show.

On July 4, they split a doubleheader with the A's in Philadelphia, losing the afternoon contest to Joe Bush 6–2, to drop them 19 games below .500 and ahead in the A.L. standings of only Cleveland, its pitching decimated by the loss of its twin 20-game winners from '13 — three-time 20-game winner Vean Gregg, traded to the Red Sox, and Cy Falkenberg, off to the Flap Jack League's Indiana Hoosiers.

Three days later, the Yankees signed a 23-year-old catcher from the University of Pennsylvania named Pius Schwert, whose claim to fame was that his first name was actually Pius, the only man so named in big league history. The career of Pius Schwert, a Buffalo native, would mirror a lot of others that Yankees had signed the last few years — a few games here and there, and gone with the wind. Schwert's big league totals: a .217 batting average in 11 games over two seasons. Typical for another lost season of the deadball Yankees.

At least the Yankees had a partner in despondency that summer of 1914, the Austrian Empire. When Archduke Franz Ferdinand was assassinated June 28 by a Serbian student, Europe and shortly much of the world lurched into the terrible madness of world war. The patchwork of alliances made the conflict pan–European; Germany's invasion of Belgium to outflank France forced Britain and others into the pointless, protracted tragedy. In their arrogance, the kings who started it all thought the conflict would be over by Christmas, with their sides victorious, of course. But the war quickly became one of attrition, with each side trying to deprive the others of food and military supplies. Europe was soon a continent transected by trenches. Millions would die.

Declaring its neutrality, the U.S. and President Wilson tried gamely to carry on as usual. But when the British Navy successfully blockaded Germany, it helped bring the Americans into the conflict. Although that wouldn't happen until January 1917, U.S. newspapers quickly filled with ominous reports of troops on the march and eventually, the horrible trench warfare and mustard gas attacks of places like Verdun.

Back on the ballfield, June became a significant month for the Boston Braves as well. Dead last in the National League as late as July, the Braves, under former Yankee manager George Stallings, reeled off eight straight wins in early July, part of a 34–10 record that yanked them up to fourth place.

The Braves' improbable run continued. After climbing to fourth, they took nine straight to pull within seven games of the front-running Giants. By August 10, the Braves were in second, as they readied for a three-game showdown against McGraw's New Yorkers. They won all three and stormed into the lead by early September. Anchored by shortstop Rabbit Maranville and the former Cub Johnny Evers, the Braves won with timely, patient hitting, despite batting only .251; superb defense — career years from pitchers Dick Rudolph and "Seattle" Bill James and a touch of Stallings's passion. They became known as the "Miracle Braves," the talk and wonder of the baseball world.

Otherwise, the story of the 1914 season was all about the passing of the old guard and the entry of the new. On April Fool's Day came the sad news that Rube Waddell — he of fire engine, lion wrestler and whistling fastball fame — had died at 37 of tuberculosis in a San Antonio sanitarium. The eccentric, childlike Waddell, who had last pitched in the big leagues only four years before, had become weakened by a Herculean effort to help contain a winter flood in Kentucky. It was while he was living there in 1912 that a nearby dike broke and Waddell immediately volunteered to help stack sandbags to block the rushing stream.

Standing armpit-deep in freezing waters for 13 hours, Waddell contracted a nasty case of pneumonia from which he never fully recovered. Plagued by constant illness, which was exacerbated by his drinking, he pitched poorly for the Minneapolis Millers in 1913. Concerned by the drastic decline of Rube's health, friend and manager Joe Cantillon sent Waddell in early '14 to the San Antonio sanitarium, where he died. Penniless, Waddell was buried in an unmarked grave in a San Antonio potter's field, but within months, a number of Waddell's more well-to-do baseball friends passed the hat and provided him with a simple gravestone. Former A's teammate Ossee Schreckengost offered the best, most succinct insight into his old friend, "Rube Waddell had only one priority — to have a good time."

Later that month — April 22 — a 19-year-old pitcher named George Herman "Babe" Ruth threw a six-hit 6–0 win for Baltimore of the International League. His opponent: Buffalo, the second batter for which was Joe McCarthy, who would manage Ruth for 17 years as a Yankee. Less than three months later — July 11 — Ruth made his big league debut, pitching the Boston Red Sox to a 4–3 win over Cleveland. Although Ruth struck out in his first major league at-bat, his hitting would one day have huge consequences, both for the end of the dead ball era and the rise of the Yankees.

And what dead ball season could possibly sneak by without mention of Hal Chase? If anyone could be lured to the Federal League by the prospect of a few more dollars, it was the onetime Prince of New York. How Chaseian of him to do it by sticking a thumb in the eye of organized baseball — releasing himself after the '13 season from the White Sox and using the owners' 10-day notice clause to jump to the Flap

Jack's Buffalo Federals. When Chicago sued, the case wound up in federal court, where Judge Herbert Bissell hammered away at organized ball for setting up "a species of quasi peonage unlawfully controlling and interfering with the personal freedom of the men involved." Big words aside, the Judge made his point: Not a single big leaguer would ever be ordered by the court to return to his AL or NL club.

By early September, Chance had had enough. Irwin wasn't bringing in the level of talent he needed to make a go in the American League. When Ray Caldwell, who had become the Yankee ace, actually left the club after being heavily fined for breaking training rules yet again, Chance felt that the club had not backed him up in properly administering discipline. There was even a rumor that the front office was making overtures to the straying pitcher to come back, a move that Chance deplored given Caldwell's discipline problems. No wonder the comfortable life tending to orange groves back in Glendora was suddenly appealing to Chance.

What happened next had repercussions that went well beyond the ballfield. It not only unleashed a chain of events that wouldn't stop for years, but signaled the beginning of the end of the Frank Farrell-Big Bill Devery era. What happened was simple: Chance resigned, spelling out his demands in a letter to Farrell while on a road trip to Washington. First, he demanded his salary in full until the end of the season. Second, he held out the possibility that he'd consider staying if Irwin would go. Farrell agreed, sort of— saying he was willing to get a new scout, but refusing to fire his old comrade. And then Farrell did something else — proposing he and Chance meet back at the Polo Grounds on September 15 after that day's game against the A's.

Had the Yankees been able to play the rest of the year like they played that Saturday, they'd have been champions and not the A's. It was a barnburner of a game with big Ed Sweeney clubbing a dramatic ninth inning home run off Chief Bender into the lower-tier of the right field to take the Philadelphias, 2–1 and send many in the crowd of 9,000 into boisterous celebration. As the ball disappeared into the grandstand and Sweeney made triumphant tour around the bases, hundreds of fans surged onto the field and made the trip with him. "If everybody who ran down the line with Sweeney could have scored," the *Times* wrote, "the Yanks would have won by 500 runs."

Too bad that hadn't happened more often. It was directly after the game that reporters found Chance who announced his resignation, claiming that Farrell's "tight policy" and Irwin's wayward scouting would never bring a winner home to the New Yorks. "Anybody at all can manage a sixth or seventh place team," the Peerless One said. "But it is ridiculous to pay a man a high salary and then not give him the proper material to work with. Mr. Farrell will not spend the money that should be spent."

It was while delivering the news that Farrell and Big Bill surged into the room and started arguing with Chance. There were words. Then came accusations. Chance called Devery a "second guesser," the kind who would explain how things should have been done rather than how they should be done. Devery was more blunt and called his former manager a "quitter." So Chance lunged at the jowly, former copper, uncorking a punch that didn't land because the men were quickly separated. But it was enough to give the news hounds some good color to go with the day's big news.

In hindsight, the signs of Chance's growing dissatisfaction had been apparent for more than a year. There was the lingering feeling on the part of Farrell and Devery that the former Yankee skipper had unloaded their favorite son Chase a little too quickly and been bilked. There was the festering Irwin situation and the Caldwell mess. Things grew worse in late July when the Yankees, unbeknownst to Chance, announced that Clarence Kraft, a veteran of exactly three major league games with the Boston Braves, would be replacing steady, .260-hitting Charlie Mullen, recently picked up from Lincoln, Nebraska, at first.

"Nobody connected with the club has anything to do with the playing arrangements but me," an angry Chance said at the time. "I'm the boss on the field, and I intend to stay the boss." Kraft never suited up as a Yankee.

Then there was the relationship of Farrell and the blustery Devery. Long the Mutt 'n' Jeff of the baseball world, the two were showing the strain of all the losing by bickering among themselves on everything from ballfield doings to business transactions. So with the Yankees headed toward another poor showing — they were 60–73 and still ahead of only the Naps — the Frank Chance era was quite suddenly finished.

There was a catch: It was still only Saturday and Chance hadn't actually set his resignation until Tuesday. On Sunday the 13th, friends of the two held out a glimmer of hope that while Chance hadn't yet left town, he might be persuaded to patch up his differences with Farrell. But neither man was talking for the record and stuck to their stances — Chance saying that either he or Irwin would have to go, and Farrell refusing to fire his long-time scout.

Names of a new Yankee manager were thrown about; Roy Hartzell was rumored to be the new skipper, as was the old Highlander John Ganzel, now managing Rochester, and Hooks Wiltse of the Giants.

By Monday the 15th, there was still no change, and there was Chance on the coaching lines at the Polo Grounds as usual, greeted warmly by the fans and urging his men on with his deep baritone voice against the A's. There was his team, as usual, losing to the A's, this time 2–1, on a ninth inning Stuffy McInnis sacrifice that drove home Eddie Collins. Conspicuous in his absence at the game was Farrell, found by reporters anyway, but refusing comment on what must have been a downright confusing situation.

"In the event of Chance leaving today, who will manage the Yankees?"

"No comment."

"Will Chance stay to the end of the season?"

"No comment."

"What about the possibility of Ganzel taking over as manager?"

"I have nothing to say."

"Is it true that Arthur Irwin has left the team?"

In reply, Farrell said he was deeply interested in the European war.

On Tuesday, the A's beat the Yanks again, 3–1, in the New Yorkers' last home game of 1914. After the game, Chance quit for good, with Farrell agreeing to pay his full season salary of $20,000, which seemed like the most logical way out of the jam. The new manager for the rest of the season: Shortstop Roger Peckinpaugh, only 23 then, and still the youngest manager in big league history.

Chance hopped on a train and went home to California. Farrell, once again left with a team in shambles, was left to put his best spin control on the situation, as he'd done so many times in recent years. "Frank Chance and I parted friends," he said. "We are both sorry that the break came. I regard him as one of the best men in baseball, and keenly regret that luck broke so badly for him here."

In came the usual post-mortems, sparing neither man. "No doubt there is much to be said on both sides, but the charge that Frank Farrell holds his purse strings too tight is hard to believe," chimed in *The Tribune*. "He has spent a deal of money in trying to build up a winning team. The trouble is he has been badly advised in many a purchase and poorly served by one manager or another in passing along players who have proved highly valuable to other teams."

Not to be outdone, *The Sporting News* took the Peerless One to task. "Chance has not been a success as a team leader in New York," it wrote the September 17 edition. "He has had two years to show some of the leadership that was expected of him because of his success with the Chicago Cubs — and today, the Yankees are about as near tailenders as ever."

As the team's new manager, Peckinpaugh certainly tried. Heading a team that played its last 17 games on the road, he won nine and lost eight — the last one October 7 in a lopsided 10–0 loss to a makeshift lineup thrown together by the A's in Philadelphia. The game itself was memorable only because the Boston Braves, in town for the start of the World Series in two days against the A's, all went to the game. Yes, the Miracle Braves had done it, holding off the Giants to clinch the pennant on September 29.

So the first time in four years the Giants wouldn't be going to the World Series. Their post-season opponent: the Yankees, against whom they were set to play a best-of-seven series. On paper, the matchup looked lopsided, for the final Yankee statistics weren't very pretty: Finishing with a 70–84 record, tied for sixth with the White Sox, the team wiped out its credible 2.81 ERA with an abysmal, major-league low .229 batting average. So much for naughty Caldwell's splendid 18–9 record and 1.94 ERA — no wonder Farrell wanted him back — and Cole's decent 11–9 record; the team's highest average by a position player was .309, courtesy of the reliable Birdie Cree, with nobody else even remotely close. Rookie right fielder Doc Cook finished at .283, with Peckinpaugh at .223, and Maisel at .239. One bright spot: Team speed was apparent, with a league-leading 251 stolen bases.

It's a good job that Roger Peckinpaugh is warming up because he only got to manage the Yankees for 17 games in 1914. In later years, Peckinpaugh served as the longtime manager for the Indians. (National Baseball Hall of Fame Library, Cooperstown, NY)

Looking ahead to the Giants, excitement about the intracity series was oddly anti-climactic — and a sharp contrast to '08 when the city was salivating in anticipation at such a match-up. One reason was the expectations of Giant fans, spoiled by success and uninterested in attending any post-season series short of the Series. Another was lousy timing, for the Giants-Yankees best of seven series was due to take place almost day-to-day in conflict with the Braves-A's Series itself.

Besides, the Miracle Braves had become one of the great stories of the dead ball era and the nation was captivated. In New York, that was particularly apparent since they were owned by local sportsman James Gaffney and managed by Stallings, each with many friends in the area. Newspapers ran large ads for special trains running between West 23rd Street in New York and Huntingdon Street Station, the nearest station to Philadelphia's Shibe Park. And at Broadway & 42nd Street in Times Square, up went the dead ball era's version of a jumbotron — an oversized, 30-foot electrical scoreboard that used electric bulbs simulating the balls and strikes and movement of the base runners, and connected to the action at the ballpark through the telegraph wires.

There wasn't any need for electrical scoreboards in Times Square for the Yankees vs. Giants. There wasn't much interest. On October 8, the day before the

World Series started, only 7,640 showed up at the Polo Grounds to watch the Yankees nail Christy Mathewson for five runs, but lose 6–5 in the 10th when Larry Doyle drove home Bob Bescher, who had tripled off Ray Keating. For the 34-year-old Mathewson, it was uncharacteristic, but another revelation that his fabled fadeaway pitch was starting to desert him; Big Six had enjoyed a lackluster season in '14 for him, going 24–13, with a 3.00 ERA, the first time he'd ever been that high as a big league regular. It would be Mathewson's last winning season; two years later, he joined the Reds as manager.

Then, on October 9, the Yankees got even with Warhop's pitching and a nifty ninth inning two-run rally, thanks mostly to a streak of wildness by Big Jeff Tesreau, to edge the Giants, 2–1. But an even smaller crowd — 5,456 — showed up, which was only a few hundred more than went wild watching the World Series progress at the 71st Regiment Armory at 34th & Park, where life-like baseball players moved according to the news from the wires. The World Series couldn't have been more dramatic, with the Braves knocking out Chief Bender from a Series game for the first time ever; behind Rudolph, who finished 27–10, they coasted 7–1.

That became the pattern. On Saturday, October 10, the Yankees touched up Giant starter Rube Marquard in Game Three of their series, but lost 6-5 in the 10th on an improbable home run delivered by reliever "Steamboat" Al Demaree before 11,222. The series stood 2–1, Giants. In the other series — The Series —19-year-old Edward Behrndt of Philadelphia reported that interest was so high that he'd made $212 in

two days of scalping tickets outside Shibe Park. And the Braves won, taking Game Two on the road, 1–0 with Seattle Bill James edging Eddie Plank.

Back in New York, the Yankees and Giants soldiered on, drawing 14,040 for Game Four — another Giant victory, this one 6–1 behind the pitching of Art Fromme. Puncturing the game at the Polo Grounds were updates from the World Series Game Three at Huntington Grounds in Boston, where more than 35,000 giddy fans celebrated the Braves' dramatic 12-inning, 5–4 victory, with the winning run scoring on a wild throw by Joe Bush. The Braves were rolling.

So were the Giants, who clinched the New Yorkers' series the next day with a quiet 4–1 win behind a five-hitter thrown by Steamboat Al Demaree. A mediocre 10–17 during the regular season, Demaree was the post-season hero, who, the *Times* noted, "seems to be just rounding into form now that the season is over." It really was quiet, for more people could have fit into a Central Park softball field; a minuscule 1,508, the smallest crowd ever at a Yankees-Giants game, showed up for this fifth and final game of the series, taken by the Giants. The other series — uh, *the* Series — ended as well that day, in Boston where the Braves beat the A's 3–1 for an improbable four-game sweep.

How appropriate that the Yankee season of 1914 should end in such solitude: Although nobody thought of it at the time, the Frank Farrell-Big Bill Devery era was done, and with it the first phase in the history of a storied ball club. Sure, they would soon move things around. But getting there was going to take some work.

22

Money Talks

"There is no charity in baseball. I want to win the pennant every year."
— *Jacob Ruppert*

It is said that when Lyndon Johnson entered the room, the room was entered. A generation earlier, such a man was another Johnson — Ban — who came with requisite bearish looks and bluster, and never met a camera or a reporter's pad he didn't like.

But it was a different Johnson that stepped off the train in Grand Central in the first days of December 1914. No bluster this time — only minimal comments for the record. In this case, the A.L. President's trip from Chicago was one of quiet purpose, a secret mission intended to clean up a problem that had been festering for the past three years and showed no hope of improving. That mission: securing a new Yankee owner.

But when the *Sun* caught up with Johnson on December 9, he came clean. "Now that the news has leaked," Johnson admitted, "I will confess that my recent mysterious visit to this city was made in connection with the contemplated sale of the New York club. I will say further only a difference of opinion as to its value has kept the proposed deal in the air."

News that the Yankees were for sale had been in the air for a month by then. The prospective suitors were two men who presented polar opposites from the Frank Farrell-Big Bill Devery combination who had run and mismanaged the Yankees for 11 years. They were Jacob Ruppert, Jr. of Manhattan and the improbably-named Tillinghast L'Hommedieu Huston of Havana — and it would be their shrewd business acumen and deep pockets that would jumpstart the Yankees and lead them from the wilderness to the nation's most storied, professional sports franchise.

How different were they? For starters, Ruppert was a colonel and Huston a captain. Both men preferred both those monikers, which was particularly fortunate for Huston because it spared him from being called Tillinghast. Ruppert had earned his rank in the National Guard, and Huston from service as a captain of engineers in Cuba during the Spanish-American War. During World War I, Huston himself would become a colonel too, so honored for service in France building roads and railways under heavy German shell fire.

Both were rich and came prepared to shell out the kind of cash that would make the Yankees a winner. Otherwise, they presented an odd pair, Ruppert being the solid conservative and Huston the adventurer. As the aristocratic New York gentleman of leisure and business, the cerebral 47-year-old Ruppert would be out of fashion today.

The first baseball team he had managed was composed of neighborhood boys of his age on the Upper East Side, and although he later admitted that his enthusiasm for the game far exceeded his ability to play it, he was elected captain anyway. The reason: He bought the uniforms and equipment.

A future in baseball wasn't much in the cards anyway after Ruppert hurt his arm. He passed the entrance exams to the School of Mines at Columbia University, but decided that he didn't want to be a mining engineer, choosing instead to join the Ruppert Brewing Company, founded in 1851 by his father, Jacob.

The young Ruppert clearly had a knack for business. When he was 23, his father went away on an extended trip and young Jacob was placed in charge as general superintendent. He did so well that in 1890 the position was made permanent. By his late 20s, Ruppert had become general manager of the Ruppert Brewing Company (1693 3rd Avenue at 93rd Street) and within a few years, he had tripled production.

In some ways, Ruppert led the life of the young, wealthy late 19th century man about town. A lifelong bachelor, he directed a staff of servants that included a butler, maid, valet, cook and laundress in a 12-room mansion on the northwest side of 5th Avenue & 93rd Street. The mansion came with large grounds in the back that featured peach and apple orchards.

Ruppert was a man of diverse passions. At 32, he was elected to the first of four terms in Congress, where he served as a Tammany Democrat in the silk-stocking Republican Upper East Side. Ruppert attended the opera and the right parties. He collected first editions, race horses, jades and porcelains. And if that wasn't enough, he yachted, and, in 1933, sponsored the second Byrd Antarctic Expedition. At his country estate in the Dutchess County hamlet of Garrison along the Hudson River, Ruppert raised St. Bernards and

Boston terriers, kept a racing stable and even a score of monkeys.

Huston was different. A rumpled, earthy man with a jovial air, Huston did not collect jades or porcelains. Whereas Ruppert or a valet carefully selected his clothes each day, Huston often wore the same creased suit days on end. People and the need to connect were his passion and to his many friends, Huston was simply the "Cap," who liked nothing better than hanging with the writers at spring training and going on the road with his players. Huston's frequent companion, W.O. McGeehan of the *Tribune*, had another name for him. It was "The Man in the Iron Hat," a reference to the one distinctive detail of his attire, his derby.

A Cincinnati native and an engineer with restless ambition and a knack for making a buck, Huston fought for every dollar he ever made. He got rich by remaining in Havana after the Spanish–American War, and with little or no capital, setting himself up in business by building the docks and piers there.

Huston's special skill was in dealing with the politicians to ensure that the lucrative contracts came his way; from Havana, Huston would work on improvements to harbors in Santiago, Cienfuegos and Matanzas. "Never do anything you can hire someone to do for you," he once said. "It's the one who tells the other fellow what to do who reaps the profits."

Huston stayed in Cuba for more than 10 years, during which he moved easily into the sporting circles of wealthy Americans who enjoyed visiting Cuba to gamble and play. One such man was John McGraw, who met Huston during one of the frequent excursions there with the Giants. The two connected and became friends; when McGraw and his wife Blanche stayed several times at the Havana Country Club, the two men spent considerable time together.

After moving to New York, Huston

continued his friendship with the Giants skipper. And it was through McGraw that Huston met Ruppert, and the two became friends on their own, often meeting at the Polo Grounds to watch the Giants.

Ruppert was the first of the two to discover baseball. Actually, his efforts to secure a ballclub had started just after the turn of the century, when he had tried to buy the Giants, but gave up after Andrew Freedman rejected his offer and sold the team, in 1903, to John Brush. In 1912, the Colonel considered buying the Cubs, before changing his mind in the interests of sticking close to home. "I wasn't interested in anything so far from Broadway," he said.

What Ruppert wanted more than anything was to buy the Giants. He brought in Huston and approached McGraw who said there wasn't a prayer. Brush's widow and daughters were determined to keep the team in the family, with the team's new president and the late Brush's son-in-law Harry Hempstead heading things.

"But if you really want to buy a ball club, I think I can get one for you," McGraw said. "How about the Yankees?"

Neither man was interested. Own the Yankees, a pathetic stepchild next to its landlords, the lordly Giants, the toast of New York? No way, no how. But McGraw's vision was broader than theirs — and he set about showing them that a purchase could work. "The New York American League club would be a fine investment if a championship team could be assumed," he said. "I am sure that (you) are just the men to go ahead and get the necessary material."

McGraw, the lobbyist, was convincing. When at last, Ruppert and Huston relented, they found both Farrell and Devery receptive. The years of losing had taken their toll; Farrell and Devery, who had started out as friends, had become enemies and were barely speaking to one another by then. The last few years had been particularly hard on Farrell, who had spent a lot on players that

hadn't worked and gambled away even more at the track. Home crowds had grown noticeably thin as well, dropping to less than 360,000 in each of the previous four seasons. When Ruppert and Huston came calling, he had considered pledging his stock as security for a loan, forcing his hand.

And sounding like a man who was ready to pack it in, Farrell called his decision to consider to sell a mercenary one. "It is purely a question of paying me my price," he said December 10 when it appeared the sale was imminent. "Every man has his price and I have mine. If the prospective purchasers meet my terms, I shall be willing to step down."

The suggested selling price was $500,000. Ruppert and Huston countered with $400,000, leaving the two sides far apart. There were other problems — among them the catering contract of Harry Stevens, of all things. It turns out that Stevens had taken out a 10-year lease in the spring of 1914 at the Polo Grounds. Ruppert wanted the catering contract for himself, but he compromised and yielded. Stevens had his lease after all.

The negotiations dragged on; two days became three and turned into four and then five. Not wanting to inherit a completely hapless team, Ruppert and Huston were driving a hard bargain — asking that Ban Johnson guarantee them a name manager and five veteran players. And they demanded that the A.L. President put it into a legal document, which was considerably more than the good will toward that end, as Johnson had wanted.

Rumors ran rampant and made things more difficult. Without much to report, newspaper reporters acted as if the deal was all but sealed and wondered about the next Yankee manager. Miller Huggins's name came up, as did Hughie Jennings and even

Christy Mathewson. One report had Ruppert and Huston trading the surly Ray Caldwell to the Giants for Mathewson. Actually, the rumor wasn't all that far off; Big Six wouldn't play for the Yankees, but in two years, would leave the Giants to manage the Cincinnati Reds.

Dragging things out was Ruppert's insistence on sitting out many of the negotiations for some r-and-r in the Indiana resort town of French Lick. So when things still weren't settled by December 16, the magnates went to him. Off to French Lick went Huston, Johnson and White Sox owner and Johnson crony Charles Comiskey to continue the negotiations. Again, things stalled and there wasn't a whole lot to report, other than the fact that the meetings were closed and sandwiches were served. Translation: Nothing to report and little progress.

Ruppert's double-speak wasn't helping things. "I have already taken over the Yankees," he said from French Lick. "The price is the only thing that remains to be settled. This probably will be $450,000." And although he had yet to actually buy the team, it didn't stop him from announcing plans to put up a ballpark in the Bronx — this one near the same place in Kingsbridge that Farrell had wanted to build for years.

Then, on December 20, negotiations broke down, with the sticking point the prospective owners' insistence for a manager and the five veteran players. What was happening? As far as anyone could tell, Farrell and Devery were still the owners of the Yankees as a fog of mystery continued to surround the proceedings.

Proceedings? What proceedings, the *Times* wondered December 29. At least by then, Ruppert, Huston, Johnson, and Farrell had picked up again — this time back in New York at the Hotel Belmont, and again, behind closed doors for whole days, and aided by armies of secretaries and catered sandwiches — this time for lunch *and* dinner.

"The deepest part of the whole mystery is just this: What in the world could four men find in the Yankees to talk about all day long?" the *Times* asked. "Last season at the Polo Grounds, a great many of the fans could tell all about them in a few words."

They talked anyway and kept mum on specifics. "Details," said Ruppert, when asked about the subject of their discussion. "Details, details and more details."

Yes, but what details? "Oh just details," he said.

The fact is, however, that they were haggling over the same issues that had divided them for a month — Farrell's price and the Ruppert/Huston insistence that the A.L. cough up some good players. "They want a good club, a manager, a park and several other things which go to make up a successful baseball outfit," the *Times* wrote. "They also know that several owners of baseball clubs have been trying to get together a collection like this for years and have not succeeded yet."

But this was New York and it was imperative that Johnson make those concessions to keep the Federal League at bay and ensure that the Yankees be a stronger franchise than the sad sacks they had been for the last four years. On they talked and talked as 1914 headed toward closure. Finally, on December 31, it was done, with Ban Johnson announcing that the Yankees had been sold to Ruppert and Huston for a reported $500,000.

As part of the agreement, Ruppert was named Yankee President and Huston secretary-treasurer. Johnson's intervention was apparent, because the new owners got their players — a couple of outfielders, Hugh High from the Tigers and Walter Rehg from the Red Sox; first baseman Wally Pipp from Rochester; Elmer Miller from the St. Louis Cardinals and Joe Berger of the White Sox. If the intrusion of the A.L. president seems unduly autocratic today, consider another transaction he made that winter — ordering star infielder Eddie Collins from the A's to the White Sox, a move that became integral to making Comiskey's Chicagoans the class of the American League.

Ruppert and Huston even got a manager — Wild Bill Donovan, the old Tiger pitcher who had spent the previous two season managing Providence of the International League. "We will have to begin at the bottom with the process of reconstruction," Wild Bill said a couple of days later. "We will try to build up a harmonious club with all the men working together. That is an essential ingredient."

Then they did something really smart — hiring the shrewd Harry Sparrow as the team's business manager. A long-time crony of both McGraw and Huston, Sparrow had served in a similar position for the Giants and White Sox on their world tour. From the get-go, he gave the Yankees the kind of fiscal stability the team had lacked for years.

On January 30, 1915, the deed really was finished off, with the actual transfer of the team consummated. With Johnson back in town for the start of the A.L. winter meetings, in marched Ruppert, Huston, Farrell and Devery for one final go-round. The final price, as Ruppert had leaked some weeks before, was the $450,000 figure. True to a man of his elegance and prestige, Ruppert showed up with his lawyers and a certified check for $225,000, his half of the purchase price. Then it was the rumpled Huston's turn; reaching into his suit pocket, he pulled out 225 $1,000 bills, tossing them casually on the table.

And so it went that Jacob Ruppert and Cap Huston came into baseball, ending both the Farrell/Devery era and the first chapter of the Yankees' 100-year history. "For $450,000," the Colonel said years later, "we got an orphan ball club, without a home of its own, without players of outstanding ability, without prestige." Along the way, they got a franchise that for neither man had ever really been a long-term obsession and one Ruppert had seen in a few games — and then, "only because Walter Johnson pitched or Ty Cobb was a participant."

Good-bye American League doormats. Hello dynasty-in-the-making.

23

Endings

"I wish I'd known early what I had to learn late."

— *Richie Ashburn*

Some days later, Frank Farrell was said to have had pangs of regret about selling the Yankees. Nobody knows what Devery thought. The two former friends split the proceeds and headed in different directions, still arguing. Efforts by Joe Vila and others like Big Tom Foley and even Governor Al Smith to reconcile them didn't work. They died — Devery in 1919 and Farrell in 1926 — having never again spoken to one another.

For both men, the post-baseball years were hard. Farrell did well for awhile through the execution of subway contracts, but he continued to throw money around, particularly on gambling, and watched his savings dwindle away. He and his wife held on to their West End Avenue apartment, but at his death, Farrell left all of $1,072.

Devery didn't fare a whole lot better. Despite a lavish funeral and many headlines, he left only one asset — the sum of $2,500, representing his share of the original payment made by Harry Stevens for catering privileges at the Hilltop. For unknown reasons, the amount had lain untouched in Devery's strongbox. Throwing in his debts, it was reduced to $1,023.

Ruppert and Huston had secured a good deal for themselves, and wasted little time in making them winners. Cementing

their success was the arrival, in 1920, of a young slugger named Ruth; and the opening, in 1923, of baseball's grandest palace, Yankee Stadium.

By then, the Colonel was the Yankees' sole owner, having bought out Huston in 1922. And while Ruppert always had many interests, the Yankees became his consuming passion. That interest was personal and profound; at the same time, Ruppert expected big things from his "boys," as he called them. As he told Lefty Gomez when the star pitcher signed with the Yanks in 1937: "Now, go out and win 30 games."

Of the two, Huston was the first to go — in 1938 of heart failure while working at his desk at his Brunswick, Georgia, plantation. The Man in the Iron Hat, who late in life had tried to get unsuccessfully to get back in baseball by buying the Dodgers, was 71.

The Colonel's death, less than a year later in 1939 at the age of 71, prompted a heartfelt outpouring of affection. Some 15,000 people lined the streets around St. Patrick's Cathedral, where a Mass was held for the lifelong bachelor. Mourners ranged from celebrities to the rank and file — the kind of crowd who belonged at the ballpark, as the newspapers put it. As a man with a distinct love of life, Ruppert would have enjoyed it. He is buried near Lou Gehrig in Kensico Cemetery, Westchester County.

So what of some of the others? The most notable thing to be said for Ban Johnson is that he soldiered on, with his best days long behind him. Beginning in 1916 he antagonized owners in both leagues with several of his decisions concerning players. One person he angered was his old friend, Comiskey, and the two became bitter enemies. During World War I Johnson groveled before politicians to ensure the completion of the 1918 season, upsetting many patriotic fans. His atrocious handling of player unrest in the World Series that year almost resulted in Major League Baseball's suspension. In 1919 Johnson vetoed the sale of pitcher Carl Mays to the New York Yankees, but was overruled by the New York Supreme Court.

Johnson's influence was on the wane by the 1919 World Series. After the White Sox lost the first two games, Comiskey reportedly sent Johnson word in the middle of the night that a fix might be under way. Johnson allegedly responded, "That's the yelp of a beaten cur!" and went back to bed. To his credit, when he became convinced that the Series had not been played on the up-and-up, Johnson launched a full investigation, despite knowing that the exposure of a fix could destroy the National Commission and greatly reduce his own power.

When the details of the scandal came to light, the triumvirate was replaced by a single man, Judge Kenesaw Mountain Landis. Johnson clashed often with Landis but seldom received any support from the A.L. owners. At last, in July 1927, Johnson resigned as A.L. president, refusing to accept any compensation for the eight years remaining on his $40,000-a-year contract. Already ill, his health continued to decline

in retirement. Johnson died of diabetes in 1931 at age 67. In 1937 he was named to the Hall of Fame.

Most of Johnson's successes and failures can be traced to his own personality. Johnson was an utterly humorless autocrat devoted to his work. Unwilling to compromise, he lacked the political dexterity to influence those he couldn't bend to his will. At the same time he was completely fearless and an excellent organizer, and Major League Baseball would not be what it is today without Johnson. The A.L. was his creation, his life's work, and ultimately his monument.

It's not that Ban Johnson alienated everyone. One enduring friendship was with Clark Griffith, managing the Reds, when Johnson convinced him to return to the American League to take on the ailing franchise in Washington. He did so and the Old Fox had a home for life.

Griffith spent the next four decades with the Senators, becoming one of the grand old men of the game. One reason he never strayed far was that purchasing control of the woeful Senators put him in debt, from which he never recovered. Not only did his financial ills forever keep him at constant odds with his players, but it was the motivation for a change in his racial views. As early as 1911, with the Reds, Griffith began signing Cuban ballplayers, the first to seriously do so.

Griffith was often broke but combined sentimentality with a nose for box-office attractions. During the Depression, Griffith sold star outfielder Goose Goslin to Detroit, saying he could no longer afford him. But when the aging Goslin was released by the Tigers some years later, Griffith found a spot for him on the Senators' roster. And when war hero Bert Shepard had potential as a pitcher, but lost a leg in combat, Griffith signed him anyway.

Wartime blackout restrictions did not prevent Griffith from obtaining government approval to hold more night games than other franchises in order to provide more "r-and-r" for the federal workers in Washington, D.C. The ex-vaudevillian always knew what drew a crowd: In 1946 he installed the first device to record pitch speed — borrowed from the U.S. Army — so that Cleveland fast baller Bob Feller could record his speed and give the fans a pregame thrill.

Baseball historians credit Griffith with doing more than anyone to further the development of the relief pitcher. While in New York, he yielded to the pressures from his Tammany Hall owners and pitched his two premier starters, Jack Chesbro and Jack Powell, a colossal 845 innings in 1904. In 1905 both were markedly less effective, and completed many fewer games. The Old Fox finished many games for them himself, making a career-high 18 relief appearances that season.

By the time Griffith got to the Senators, he was a full throttle disciple of bullpen usage. He subsequently developed the first great relievers, Allan Russell and Fred Marberry, and in the 1924 World Series against McGraw's Giants, turned relief strategy into an art form. In Game Seven, Griffith sent in a succession of relief pitchers that led Mc-Graw, committed to the lefty-righty percentages, to remove star first baseman Bill Terry from the game. When Griffith finished up with the great Walter Johnson, the Senators went on to win the Series with a 12-inning triumph. Elected to the Hall of Fame in 1946, the Old Fox kept at it until 1955, when he died at the age of 85.

Remember the little girl whom hard-nosed Kid Elberfeld ran home to comfort back in 1908? Fast-forward two decades and here is the long-retired Kid, this time dressed in a natty suit and cap and back home at the farm in Signal Mountain, Tennessee — and being lauded all over again, this time as coach to his five daughters, all of whom were top athletes.

It started with the eldest, Nan, who became Arkansas single tennis champion and captained the family basketball team. It continued with Edith, Miriam, Dorothy and Ruth. All were outstanding athletes in everything from basketball to tennis, swimming and diving, and boxing — yes, boxing. The one somber note to the Elberfeld's second generation athletic prowess was Jack, the only brother of the five sisters, whose plans for a big league pitching career ended with a serious spinal injury from playing football.

It's fortunate that Elberfeld was one of the few dead ball players who invested his baseball earnings wisely — using it to put all five of his daughters through the University of Chattanooga, with one doing extra work at Columbia and another at Duke. "I had only four years of schooling myself," said Elberfeld, "but I was going to see to it my kids got the schooling that I missed."

"While I lived the life of a baseball star, the diamond was my schoolroom," the Kid said of his daughters in 1927. "I learned there some mighty valuable lessons which have been a lot of benefit to me in rearing my five girls. I have trained them all to proficiency in every American outdoor sport."

The irony is for all the attention Elberfeld received playing baseball, the athletic success of his daughters brought him a whole new round. The Ken Griffey Sr. of the '20s? Maybe not. But the Tabasco Kid clearly relished his role as the family patriarch of all those jocks, particularly at a time when women were starting to be recognized for athletics. "A mighty mite, that Elberfeld," wrote Will Wedge in the *Sun*. "His boys were mostly girls; The Kid was father of a team that swept the field in curls."

At the time, the Kid was long gone from the major leagues, but still active in his own right by managing a succession of minor league teams. Most notable were teams in the Southern Association, including Chattanooga, Little Rock and Mobile. His last job in organized baseball was in 1938, managing the team in Fulton, Kentucky. Afterwards, he returned to the farm in Tennessee, leaving periodically to coach at baseball schools. The end came in 1944; he was 69.

After leaving the Yankees, Frank Chance returned to California, where he operated an orange grove. For a time he was part owner and manager of a Pacific Coast League team in Los Angeles.

But the Peerless Leader grew restless in California, and in 1923 returned to the majors as manager of the Red Sox. Unfortunately, it was a familiar pattern, for Chance was again given little to work with, since most of the Red Sox talent had been sold off to pay owner Harry Frazee's debts. A hopeless team, Boston finished last.

Chance was slated to take over the White Sox when his health gave out, and he died in September 1924, six days after turning 47. His funeral in Los Angeles befitted a legend; surrounded by dozens of his friends, he was laid to rest with so many floral tributes that oversized trucks were required to carry them to the gravesite. At that day's San Francisco-Vernon Pacific Coast League game, fans and players bowed their heads for a two-minute silent salute.

In 1946, along with Joe Tinker and Johnny Evers, his partners in the Chicago infield, Chance was elected to the Hall of Fame.

No trucks were required for the floral tributes when the first of the old war horses, Willie Keeler, died on New Year's Day of 1923 in the front room of the flat at 1010 Gates Avenue in Brooklyn that he shared with his parents.

Unlike Chance, the death of the never-married Wee Willie at 50 was quiet and relatively serene; a few days before, he had told his brother, Tom, that if he was going to die, he at least wanted to see 1923 ushered in. On New Year's Eve, several family members and friends visited the old ballplayer — stepping outside just before midnight to listen to the church bells ring in the New Year. Going back in the house a few minutes later, they found Keeler sitting up in his bed and playfully ringing the little bell he had used to call his attendant. "He was playing the game of life as he played the game of baseball — until the last man was out in the ninth," opined the *Times*. A short time later, Keeler was dead of complications from heart disease and edema.

Keeler's last few years were a microcosm of how he had spent his life — quietly, among family and in the neighborhood where he played baseball as a youngster. In retirement, Keeler had earned income from his ownership in apartment buildings and auto dealerships, but when these investments went sour, it took a joint $5,500 gift in 1921 from the National and American leagues to keep him afloat. Few people had come calling those last few years, and those who did got few Keeleresque details of a long life spent in the game.

"Yes, I am back here at the scene of my early days," he had told a reporter a year or so before he died. "It was right here in this neighborhood that I first started to play ball. We were only sandlot kids, but what fun we did have."

His death unleashed a flood of old memories of a man who was arguably the greatest singles hitter ever. "I played six and a half years with Keeler, following him at bat," said Kid Elberfeld, "and he excelled more than Cobb or any other batter in history when it came to placing hits."

"He could place hits better than any other batter I ever saw," was John McGraw's assessment of his old Baltimore Oriole friend and teammate. "(Keeler) was a tremendous influence on the club — aggressive, smart, daunting. I am sorry to see him go."

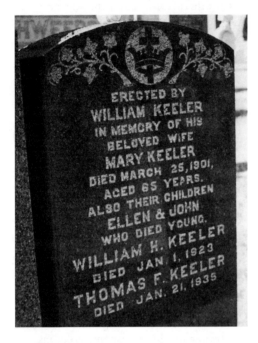

Willie Keeler's grave at Calvary Cemetery doesn't indicate it holds one of baseball's greatest — and most modest — players. While the gravesite is in Queens, at least it looks toward Keeler's native Brooklyn. (Photographs by Jim Reisler)

An old war horse himself, McGraw took Keeler's death harder than just about anyone. As hard-nosed and pugnacious as the Giant manager could be, he had a particular soft-spot in the heart for old ballplayers down on their luck. Bugs Raymond, the troublesome alcoholic pitcher of the teens, comes to mind. At 1010 Gates Street on the morning of the January 4 funeral, McGraw was visibly moved at seeing the body of his old teammate in the open casket. For more than five minutes, he knelt beside the coffin.

Later, McGraw and hundreds of others bowed their heads in tribute as the body was carried to the Church of Our Lady of Good Counsel in Brooklyn for a requiem mass. At Calvary Cemetery, just across the Queens border, where Keeler was laid to rest, McGraw, along with another former Oriole teammate, Hughie Jennings, and Willie's old Highlander roommate, Wid Conroy, each threw a spadeful of dirt on the casket as it was being lowered into the ground.

For New York baseball scribe Thomas Rice, Keeler was the game's best "place hitter," bar none. "Cobb and Lajoie were exceptional place hitters, and Wagner could knock a ball through a specified opening far more often than could most other brilliant batters," he wrote. "But Keeler was the most skillful place hitter in all of baseball history."

The Baseball Hall of Fame came calling in 1939. And today, Keeler may be best remembered of all things for his throwaway line of trying to "hitting them where they ain't."

So how best to end the story of the Yankees of the dead ball era? With none other than Hal Chase of course.

For the most part, it was more of the same for Prince Hal, and then some. Two months into the 1914 season while hitting a solid .267 for the White Sox, Chase did what so many big leaguers of the era did — he jumped to the Federal League. But unlike the others, Chase did it his way — actually giving 10 days written notice on June 23 to Charles Comiskey that he would be leaving the team. Chase's claim was ingenious: He claimed the 10-day clause that had previously been used only by owners to unload unwanted players had to work both ways to be fair.

And as with most things Chase, things quickly got complicated. Comiskey obtained a court order preventing Chase from playing in New York State. But State Supreme Court Justice Herbert Bissell sided with Chase and vacated the injunction. Bissell ruled that the traditional interpretation of the standard contract had produced what he called "a species of quasi-peonage unlawfully controlling and interfering with the personal freedom of the men employed." Quasi-peonage? Suffice to say it was a remarkable victory for Chase over organized baseball. But as time would tell, it earned Chase the enduring hatred of one Ban Johnson.

So Chase jumped. Joining the Buffalo Feds, he hit an impressive .347 in the remaining half-season to help them finish fourth. He did well in 1915 as well, batting .291 to lead his team and swat a league-leading 17 home runs — big numbers for a man who had never before hit more than four in a single season.

But when the Federal League folded in 1915, his name went into a common draft to absorb the ballplayers back into the established major leagues. It was Johnson's chance to exact revenge; as punishment for jumping Comiskey's Chicagoans, the American League ignored him en masse. But not the National League, where the Cincinnati Reds picked him up.

And as with most things Chase, it was a love fest at the start. "I intend to do the right thing in the future," Chase said on joining the Reds. "I want to square myself with the public."

He did for a time. In 1916, Chase batted .339 to lead the N.L. by 23 points and ranked among the leaders in virtually every offensive category. His debut was particularly dramatic; stepping in to bat for first baseman Fritz Mollwitz, who had been tossed from the game for arguing a third strike call, Chase drove the first pitch down the left field line for a ringing double. He was then sacrificed to third and stole home.

So much for those who said Chase's skills had eroded, even at the advanced baseball age of 33. In the midst of his best big league season, the Prince "played his head off" for new Reds manager Buck Herzog, according to newspaper accounts, and later in the season for replacement manager Christy Mathewson. Chase even behaved himself in the field, making a career-low 20 errors.

The Reds, however, were miserable in '16, finishing tied with the Cardinals for last at 33 games under .500 and 33½ games out. Things improved somewhat under Mathewson's management in 1917, when the Reds finished fourth with their first winning record in 12 years. But Chase's production dropped; he batted .277 and again led the league's first basemen in errors, this time with 28.

But the gig was nearly up. In the war-shortened 1918 season, the Reds continued to improve, sidling into third place and Chase once more hit well, batting .301. But on August 9, Mathewson suspended his first baseman for what was labeled "indifferent play." Press reports attributed the suspension to Chase's familiar tardiness. For a time, Mathewson played along, saying he'd soon be back in the lineup and "a layoff will do him good."

But as with most things involving Chase, there was a bigger story, said Jack Ryder in the *Cincinnati Enquirer*. "Hal Chase will never play another game for the

Reds so long as Mathewson is manager or at any other time," Ryder wrote August 10. "After Matty has a conference with (Reds') President (Garry) Herrmann, it is probable that Chase's baseball career will be ended. It's a tough finish for a player of pleasing personality and great natural brilliance, but it is inevitable."

Like Stallings and Chance before him, Mathewson was only the latest in a line of esteemed baseball men to harbor doubts about Chase's integrity. There were several incidents to choose from — among them, July 17, when Chase was said to have approached Giants pitcher William "Pol" Perritt with a proposal to join him on dumping that day's game. "I wish you would tip me off," he is supposed to have said, "because if I know which game you'll pitch then I can connect with a certain party before game time, you will have nothing to fear." Said Perritt, as quoted in *The Sporting News*, "I should have punched him in the eye."

Around the same time, Chase approached Reds pitcher Jimmy Ring with a similar offer. Coming in to relieve, in the ninth inning of a tight game with a runner on third against the Giants at the Polo Grounds, Chase paid a mound visit to Ring with a proposal for a payoff should the runner score.

Unnerved and confused, Ring reared back and unleashed his first pitch, a sinkerball that sailed far above home plate to walk in the runner. Hours later, after the Reds had lost the game, Ring, a New York native, was sitting with his fiancée in the lobby of the Ansonia Hotel when up walked Chase — a blonde woman on this arm, and outfitted in a dapper Brooks Brothers suit, spats and a derby, while puffing on a cigar. He plopped a $50 bill in Ring's lap.

"Take your girl to Gallagher's, Laddie," Chase said to Ring. "They've got the greatest steaks in New York."

Ring reported the conversation. So did Perritt, who added that Chase offered yet another Giants pitcher, Rube Benton, $800 to throw a game. Other allegations by Cincinnati teammates that Chase bet regularly against the Reds popped up too. "No use beating about the bush any longer or masking words," wrote William Phelon in *The Sporting News*, "(but) Chase is accused of throwing games after making bets that the Reds would lose."

Mathewson was said to harbor still another reason for reserving particular venom toward his onetime friend. According to a 1960 letter written by former *Cincinnati Post* sportswriter Tom Swope, it was common knowledge about the Reds of the dead ball era that Chase bet regularly on the club, sometimes to win and other times to lose. But the issue that got Mathewson seething, said Swope, was Chase's penchant for cheating at cards when playing the Reds' manager. Swope wrote that along with pitcher Mike Regan, Chase developed a series of signals involving the way he handled his ever-present cigar. "After a few sessions," wrote Swope, "Chase, always a crook, told Regan that they were up against a bad situation in bridge and should do something to even the competition."

The Prince seemed cooked. And yet, in a hearing after the season, he was quite miraculously cleared by National League President John Heydler. "It is nowhere established that the accused was interested in any pool or wager that caused any game to result otherwise than on its merits," he said. Heydler concluded with a plea for acceptance of the verdict and a second chance for Chase.

Come again? The only thing for certain was that Chase wasn't headed back to the Reds, particularly since Mathewson, by then serving in France as an officer in a chemical warfare unit of the American Expeditionary Force, firmly believed him to be guilty. Next stop then: the Giants, where Chase, having convinced his old friend John McGraw of his innocence, was slated for first base.

On the surface, Chase compiled a fine year for the Giants in 1919. At age 36, he hit .284 with five home runs, his second highest for a single season. He also stole 16 bases, a big jump from five the year before.

But even McGraw was finally growing wise to the shenanigans of Hal Chase. During an important series with the Reds in mid–August, Chase hurt his left wrist sliding into third base; it effectively kept him from batting or throwing the rest of the season. But McGraw claimed that team doctors could not substantiate the injury and said Chase was embellishing the problem. For good measure, he offered the evidence of a suspiciously-bad throw that Chase had made in the Reds series that had allowed three Cincinnati runs to score and cost the Giants the game.

"I became convinced that he purposely made dishonest plays that enabled the Reds to beat us in the four out of six games at the Polo Grounds," McGraw said. "In my opinion, Chase deliberately threw us down."

Chase's last game as the Giant first baseman was September 4 at the Polo Grounds against Brooklyn. Chase went 1-for-4 and helped turn a double play. His last game came September 25 as a pinch-hitter in the ninth inning against the Braves. He scorched a double although the Braves held on to win 8–4.

In February 1920, Chase and Giants third baseman Heinie Zimmerman were abruptly suspended. McGraw wasn't talking, nor was anyone else for that matter. "It appears almost as if a conspiracy was afoot among baseball officials and the press to let Chase quietly slip away from the game," wrote baseball historian Bob Lemke.

That was the plan anyway. But when Chase's teammate on the 1918 Reds, second baseman Lee Magee, was released from his new team, the Cubs, things got dicey. In retaliation, Magee threatened to go public with his revelations of big-time game fixing and gambling. Magee himself wasn't immune — and league officials subsequently obtained his confession at just about the time that Chase and Zimmerman were dropped from baseball.

Despite his confession, Magee sued the Cubs for back pay and his expected share of the 1920 World Series money. And unlike Chase's 1918 hearing, Magee's case went to open court, in Cincinnati in early June. Magee claimed that he had given Chase the money to bet on the Reds, but that Chase had doublecrossed him by using it to wager against their team instead.

The allegations wore on. Boston gambler James Costello testified that Chase and Magee had approached him on the morning of July 25, 1918, claiming that they had arranged for the Reds to lose the first game of that day's doubleheader by bribing Reds pitcher Pete Schneider. The fix didn't hold, however, when Schneider didn't pitch the first game, refusing to do so, he said, after being tipped off that something fishy was afoot.

It took the jury took only 45 minutes to dismiss Magee's claims against the Reds. And although Chase was never formally charged with anything, he was clearly and finally through with major league baseball after 15 years, a lifetime .291 batting average and some of the most spectacular plays ever seen in baseball history.

Even McGraw admitted he'd been had by Hal Chase. "I had absolute confidence in Chase when I signed him to play first base," the Giants' manager said. "When he was declared innocent of Matty's charges, I felt sure that he had done no wrong and was a victim of circumstantial evidence. I never was more deceived by a player than I was by Chase."

Unwelcome in organized baseball, Chase headed west, where he became a player and part-owner of the semi-pro Mission League's San Jose club. That ended after evidence of a bribery scandal and umpires refused to let him take the field.

Zimmerman and Magee didn't fare much better. It turns out that Zimmerman was dropped when McGraw learned that he had attempted to bribe Giant teammate Benny Kauff to throw games. His name surfaced again in 1921 when he turned the tables and publicly accused Kauff, pitcher Rube Benton and Fred Toney of throwing games. There was no evidence to support those claims, which appeared to stem more from vengeance. In later years, Zimmerman played semi-pro ball, and from 1929 to 1930, joined the infamous Dutch Schultz as a partner in a speakeasy. His later years were spent as a steamfitter; he died in 1969 in New York City. Magee soon faded to obscurity as well; he died in 1966 in Columbus, Ohio.

After the 1920 season came more hearings on baseball betting, in this case a Chicago grand jury that probed the granddaddy of vice — the fixing by eight Chicago White Sox players of the 1919 Chicago-Cincinnati World Series. It was baseball's blackest time; how fitting then that Chase's name came up prominently and often.

The tone was set early on when Rube Benton told a grand jury that Chase knew well in advance that the Black Sox would play to lose in key games and cleared $40,000 betting on the Reds. The White Sox players were eventually found guilty and banned for life from baseball. Chase himself was indicted and accused of being one of the principal parties in getting the bribe money and passing it on to the players. Facing extradition and prison sentence, Chase was arrested in San Jose but released on technicalities, and never forced to appear before the grand jury. His case was dropped from the court calendar, and Chase went to his grave fiercely denying he had been involved.

And just like that, Chase became a baseball footnote, dropped from the consciousness of the sporting public with a thud. Offered a job with the Sperry Flower Company, which would have given him a steady job and $300 a month, he turned it down in order to keep playing baseball. But Chase was getting older and drinking heavily, so playing baseball became increasingly problematic. He joined Madera in the outlaw San Joaquin Valley League, but was soon expelled as his past became more and more public.

Chase drifted to Arizona, where he played semi-pro ball for copper-mining league teams from a number of towns near New Mexico border. Joining him as members of one of those teams, the Douglas Blues, were Chick Gandil, Buck Weaver and Lefty Williams, three members of the disgraced White Sox. But he was seriously injured in a 1926 car accident and playing baseball became harder. The Copper League disbanded anyway in 1927.

Chase wasn't saying much for the record; what little he did say acknowledged some fault, but contained a tone of defensiveness. When in the mid–1920s, it was reported that he had been invited by the Mexican government to form a national baseball league, Chase considered it, saying "I would have an opportunity here in Mexico of playing baseball on a sound and honest foundation and demonstrate to baseball fans of the United States that I was the Dreyfuss, and not the Benedict Arnold, of organized baseball."

The truth is nobody much cared by then about a player well out of the mainstream. Chase's plans to be commissioner didn't work out. By then divorced for the second time, Chase resorted to old habits, hanging around pool halls and hustling for a few bucks. He took up odd jobs — operating a Tucson car wash and painting barns, chopping wood, doing just about anything in an attempt to keep body and soul together.

In 1931, Chase wrote to Commissioner Kenesaw Mountain Landis Jr. with the idea of restoring his name. In the letter, he wrote about his many mistakes and how much he'd learned from them. Landis responded that Chase was still a member in good standing of organized baseball, but asked that he expand on those mistakes. On his advice of his lawyer, Chase destroyed Landis' letter and never wrote back.

Hopping around the Southwest, Chase kept drinking and scraped by as best he could. He moved to Williams, Arizona where he worked at Dooley's Pool Hall. Back in Tuscon, he washed cars — 50 cents per car. By 1934, with the Great Depression in full swing, he did menial jobs for government relief programs.

For Hal Chase, the onetime Prince of New York, life had reached rock bottom. Recalling those days years later in an article in the *Arizona Daily Star*, Tucson resident Roy Drachman, by then in his early 80s, had particularly vivid memories of Chase. On the ballfield, Chase could still deliver, and when batting, the opposing first baseman would play so far back that he was in right field, Drachman recalled.

Otherwise, "Hal Chase was a bum when I knew him," Drachman remembered. At a pool hall in Nogales, a friend challenged Chase to demonstrate his batting technique with a pool cue. "He was swinging a pool cue at pieces of paper that were tossed to him," said Drachman. "Everyone was drunk."

In Nogales, Chase had taken to bumming money. Once, when visiting Drachman, he asked for a loan. But Drachman had only 15 cents. "We visited for a while," the Tucson resident recalled, "and when he got up to leave, he said, 'Roy, can I have that 15 cents? I can buy a loaf of bread.' I gave it to him and couldn't help thinking that a man in that position of needing such a pittance was really near the end of the line."

How true. Chase drifted back to Tucson, where he was living when, in December 1933, his old friend, newspaperman Joe Vila, was traveling west with the Columbia University football team, on its way to the 1934 New Year's Rose Bowl against Stanford. Traveling with the team was another friend from the past, onetime Highlander trainer Charley "Doc" Barrett.

It was there that a disheveled and broken figure stumbled into the city's swanky Hotel El Conquistador, where the team was staying, and asked to see Barrett. "And who should we ask is calling?" a member of the hotel staff asked.

"Chase," the man said. "Tell Doc it's Hal Chase."

Hearing that name for the first time in years, Barrett was stunned. Down to the lobby he went, anxious to rid himself of a man he was convinced was an imposter.

But it was hardly an imposter, but the onetime Prince of New York himself. Barrett stared at the disheveled old man, hesitant in both speech and step, and was astounded. The onetime friends embraced. Both men cried. It had been years since they had seen one another.

Hal Chase looked ancient, Barrett thought. "How old are you, Hal?" he asked. "Forty-six," the former ballplayer said. A local sportswriter disagreed, saying that Chase had told him recently that he was 48. But Barrett knew better and happened to know that in fact, Chase was 51.

Barrett introduced his old friend to New York writers traveling with the team, using the line, "Ever see him play first base?"

"Ever see him?" replied an incredulous Bill Corum of the *Evening Journal*, who knew all about Hal Chase. "How many times had I seen him," he wrote in the paper a few days later. "Hadn't I sat with my eyes glued on him in old Sportsman's Park (in St. Louis) until I could go back home to my own little country town and see him with my eyes shut. Hadn't I put my glove under my pillow at night and dreamed of the time when I would spear 'em out of the dirt with one hand like Chase."

Other writers, like Vila, soon gathered around Chase in an impromptu meandering down memory lane.

"His biggest thrill in baseball?" Corum asked. The long-ago day at Santa Clara College when Chase was discovered and knew he'd soon be going to the big leagues. The best first baseman? "George Sisler," Chase replied, "next ... to me," with no apparent sense of bravado. Sure, Sisler was good, "but I could go get that apple."

For Chase, it was all a wonderful, temporary way to forget his dire straits. "He was almost maudlin with joy over seeing Barrett," Corum wrote in his column a few days later. "Here was somebody who spoke his language ... and he couldn't talk. Even his once sharp, cunning mind was bobbing and weaving with his stumbling, shambling footsteps."

"What an object lesson in square shooting, because nothing made a bum out of Hal Chase but Hal Chase himself," Corum wrote. "He was one of those strange characters who are going to outsmart everybody and wind up outsmarting only themselves."

A year or so later, Chase was still in Tucson, where the 1935 City Directory listed his occupation as "ballplayer," despite the fact that he was 53 and hadn't played a big league game for 16 years. By 1937, he was back in California—living in Oakland and working part-time in a Works Progress Administration program, assisting plumbers and carpenters. By then, his health, wracked by years of drinking, was a mess; it was around then that he contracted beri-beri as well as kidney problems. Chase went sober in 1940, but it was too late for his health, which continued to falter.

In April 1947, while gravely ill at Colusa Memorial Hospital in Colusa, CA, the 64-year-old Chase sounded off in a long interview to *The Sporting News* about his many regrets, both in baseball and beyond. Foremost in his mind was a warning for all players not to make the kind of mistakes he had made. "If someone makes a proposition to you, play smart," he said. "Tell your manager or club owner. I was foolish and all the stuff I thought was so smart only robbed me of the kind of life I should be living today."

"I'd give anything if I could start in all over again. What a change there would be in the life of Hal Chase. I was all wrong, at least in most things, and my best proof is that I am flat on my back, without a dime."

Chase might have mentioned his philanderings that had destroyed two marriages and a relationship with his only son. Or his relationship with the rest of his family that was tenuous at best.

"You note that I am not in the Hall of Fame," he told *The Sporting News*. "Some of the old-timers said I was one of the greatest fielding first basemen of all time. When I die, movie magnates will make no picture like 'Pride of the Yankees,' which honored that great player, Lou Gehrig. I guess that's the answer, isn't it? Gehrig had a good name; one of the best a man could have. I am an outcast, and I haven't a good name. I'm the loser, just like all gamblers."

Hal Chase was still a patient at Colusa Memorial Hospital when he died May 18, 1947. It was the end of an era, the final act in the life and times of the New York Highlanders, once the kings of Washington Heights. "The most difficult thing in looking at Hal Chase's career and life is to put him in perspective," writes Daniel E. Ginsburg in *The Fix Is In*, a history of baseball gambling. "Chase is generally considered the most corrupt individual in the history of baseball.... At the same time, Chase was undoubtedly a great player."

With death came all the fond memo-

ries of plays made long ago, followed by obscurity. "He'll be remembered for a few days and then forgotten," Arthur Daley wrote May 20 in the *Times*, "recalled only occasionally as some old-timer, fumbling for a comparison, will hail a phenomenally clever rookie as 'the greatest fielding first baseman since Hal Chase.' It's the might-have-been which makes the career of Chase such an utter tragedy."

24

Postscript

"You get smart only when you begin getting old."

— Allie Reynolds

The lobby of Columbia-Presbyterian Medical Center gives a hint of the important work being done here this cold winter afternoon: doctors and medical staff rush about in their white jackets toward patients who need care. In from the parking lot come relatives of the sick; their expectant faces are tempered somewhat by a quick stop at the front desk to secure directions to the rooms and wards of loved ones.

It's a hurrying kind of place, one where everybody seems to rush about and give the place more the air of the Port Authority Bus Terminal at rush hour than a big city hospital. Pay enough attention to the bustle and you're likely to miss the small plaque that sits just across the way in the garden, near Broadway and 168th Street.

Yes, it's a little difficult to find in this sprawling complex of high rises and people rushing about in white lab coats. Best go the main lobby to ask a hospital security guard where to find the plaque.

"Plaque?" he asks.

"Yes, a plaque to commemorate a ballpark that was once here," the visitor says. "Ever heard about it? It was called the Hilltop and the original Yankees, the New York Highlanders, once played there."

"A plaque? Ballpark? Huh?"

"Yes, the plaque, from what I understand, is in the hospital garden," the visitor says. "It's bronze."

The guard thinks hard. Yes, maybe there is a plaque in the gated hospital garden across the street after all. Yes, indeed there is one, pipes in another security guard, on his break nearby. It was put in just a few years ago, he says.

"Well, if there is a plaque," says the first guard, "it's probably all green by now."

Directed to the garden, a visitor finds the plaque without too much trouble. In the shape of homeplate, it sits flush in the ground at about the midway point of the rectangular garden, next to a long hedge and near a wooden bench. And no, it's not green, as the security guard had suspected, but is actually rather spiffy and shiny in the sunlight, which filters in despite the buildings.

"Dedicated To Columbia-Presbyterian Medical Center and the community of Washington Heights by the New York Yankees," the plaque reads, "to mark the exact location of the home plate in Hilltop Park, home of the New York Highlanders from 1903 to 1912, later renamed the New York Yankees."

"Exact" location? Sort of. Dedicated in

September 1993, it commemorates the spot — more or less — where the Hilltop once stood. Diligent members of the Society for American Baseball Research determined the location — within 50 feet — of the old home plate with the aid of old photographs showing three existing apartment buildings on 168th Street.

* * *

Appearing at the 1993 ceremony to commemorate the plaque: one Chet "Red" Hoff of all people, the same man who on a May afternoon 81 years before at the Hilltop had reared back in the first major league

Hal Chase Slept Here: A plaque shaped as a homeplate on the grounds of Columbia-Presbyterian Medical Center in upper Manhattan is all that commemorates where the Hilltop once stood. (Photographs by Jim Reisler)

game and fanned Ty Cobb on three pitches — the last one a roundhouse curve that caught the great Detroit batsman looking.

Now with snow-white hair and bearing a still-firm, Marine-grip of a handshake, Hoff was a spry 102, basking in the recognition that of the 15,000 or so men who played major league baseball, he was the oldest. Recognition was late in coming to Hoff, who had left the game in 1918 for World War I and later returned to his hometown of Ossining, New York, where he worked for Rand McNally, before retiring to Florida in the 1950s.

But in 1991, when Hoff turned 100, he was interviewed by Joe Garagiola for the "Today Show" on NBC, prompting sudden fame and a slew of requests through the mail for autographs. From the Yankees came a uniform and a congratulatory letter. "I think I could still pitch nine innings," said Hoff at the time. "I might give it a try, considering the salaries they're making now."

Hoff never did suit up again. But his stories kept coming — particularly the one about striking out Ty Cobb, the first batter to face him as a big leaguer, which he enjoyed telling again at the ballpark commemoration. Finally, in 1998 — 86 years after his first game as a Yankee — Chet Hoff died in Daytona Beach, FL, at the age of 107.

Back in the rock garden, it's relatively quiet on this brisk day with the wind whipping in from the Hudson — so much so that you can shut your eyes for a moment, block out of the street noise and lose 90 years: Why here's Prince Hal Chase uncorking a bullet to nail a runner at the plate, but on the next hitter, arriving a split second late at the bag for the throw. Must be angling for an advance from the wise guys in the first base boxes.

Here's Willie Keeler sending a perfectly-placed single to advance the runner all the way from first to third. Here is Happy Jack Chesbro uncorking the wild pitch to hand the 1904 pennant to Boston. Uh oh, here comes Cobb with his Tiger teammates vaulting into the stands after a fan in 1912. Here's Clark Griffith and Frank Chance raging in the dugout, mostly with frustration — "If they could only have played the game like I did," you can hear them saying. Here is Kid Elberfeld ragging poor old Silk O'Loughlin; and here's Big Bill Devery tallying up the losses on the field and in his wallet, and wondering if his Highlanders would ever lick the voodoo they wore like a curse.

New York is like that — turn a street corner, take note of where you are and you're likely to be somewhere with a rich past. So it goes here in the hospital rock garden in the Washington Heights section of northern Manhattan, where the Hilltop once stood. Abandoned after the 1912 season when the Yankees moved to the Polo Grounds, the old ballpark was torn down in 1914 and the huge patch of grass turned into a tabernacle called the Fairgrounds where, three years later, Billy Sunday, the ballplayer-turned-evangelist, preached the gospel.

In 1925, the hospital went up and the Hilltop became a distant memory — that is, unless you want to shut your eyes for a moment and think back to a glorious time when giants of the baseball world once roamed....

Appendix: The First
Dozen Years — Statistics

1903:

American League Standings:

Team:	Won:	Lost:	Pct.	GB	BA	ERA
Boston	91	47	.659		.272	2.57
Philadelphia	75	60	.556	14.5	.264	2.97
Cleveland	77	63	.550	15	.265	2.66
New York	**72**	**62**	**.537**	**17**	**.249**	**3.08**
Detroit	65	71	.478	25	.268	2.75
St. Louis	65	74	.468	26.5	.244	2.77
Chicago	60	77	.438	30.5	.247	3.02
Washington	43	94	.314	47.5	.231	3.82

(World Series: Boston defeated the N.L. Champion Pittsburgh Pirates 5 games to 3)

League Leaders:
Batting Average:

N. Lajoie, Cleveland	.342
S. Crawford, Detroit	.335
P. Dougherty, Boston	.331
J. Barrett, Detroit	.315
B. Bradley, Cleveland	.313

Runs Batted In:

B. Freeman, Boston	104
P. Hickman, Cleveland	97
N. Lajoie, Cleveland	93
L. Cross, Philadelphia	90
S. Crawford, Detroit	89

Hits:

P. Dougherty, Boston	195
S. Crawford, Detroit	184
F. Parent, Boston	170

Pitching Leaders — Wins:

C. Young, Boston	28
E. Plank, Philadelphia	23
R. Waddell, Philadelphia	21
J. Chesbro, New York	21
B. Dinneen, Boston	21

Pitching — ERA

E. Moore, Cleveland	1.77
C. Young, Boston	2.08
W. Sudhoff, St. Louis	2.10
B. Bernhard, Cleveland	2.12
D. White, Chicago	2.13

New York:

(Manager: Clark Griffith)

Pos	Player	BA	HR	RBI
IB	J. Ganzel	.277	3	71
2B	J. Williams	.267	3	82
SS	K. Elberfeld	.287	0	45
3B	W. Conroy	.272	1	45
RF	W. Keeler	.313	0	32
CF	H. McFarland	.243	5	45
LF	L. Davis	.237	0	25
C	M. Beville	.194	0	29
OF	D. Fultz	.224	0	25
C	J. O'Connor	.203	0	12

Pitching:

Pitcher	G	IP	W-L	ERA
J. Chesbro	40	325	21-16	2.77
J. Tannehill	32	240	14-14	3.27
C. Griffith	25	213	14-11	2.70
H. Howell	25	156	9-6	3.53
B. Wolfe	20	148	6-9	2.97

1904:

American League Standings:

Team:	Won:	Lost:	Pct.	GB	BA	ERA
Boston	95	59	.617		.247	2.12
New York	**92**	**59**	**.609**	**1.5**	**.259**	**2.57**
Chicago	89	65	.578	6	.242	2.30
Cleveland	86	65	.570	7.5	.260	2.22
Philadelphia	81	70	.536	12.5	.249	2.35
St. Louis	65	87	.428	29	.239	2.83
Detroit	62	90	.408	32	.231	2.77
Washington	38	113	.252	55.5	.227	2.59

(No World Series that year: National League champions were the New York Giants)

League Leaders:
Batting Average:

N. Lajoie, Cleveland	.376
W. Keeler, New York	.343
H. Davis, Philadelphia	.309
E. Flick, Cleveland	.306
B. Bradley, Cleveland	.300

Runs Batted In:

N. Lajoie, Cleveland	102
B. Freeman, Boston	84
B. Bradley, Cleveland	83
J. Anderson, New York	82
D. Murphy, Philadelphia	77
F. Parent, Boston	77

Hits:

N. Lajoie, Cleveland	208
W. Keeler, New York	186
B. Bradley, Cleveland	183

Pitching Leaders — Wins:

J. Chesbro, New York	41
C. Young, Boston	27

E. Plank, Philadelphia	26
R. Waddell, Philadelphia	25

Pitching — ERA

A. Joss, Cleveland	1.59
R. Waddell, Philadelphia	1.62
O. Hess, Cleveland	1.67
D. White, Chicago	1.78
J. Chesbro, New York	1.82

New York:

(Manager: Clark Griffith)

Pos	Player	BA	HR	RBI
IB	J. Ganzel	.260	6	48
2B	J. Williams	.263	2	74
SS	K. Elberfeld	.263	2	46
3B	W. Conroy	.243	1	52
RF	W. Keeler	.343	2	40
CF	D. Fultz	.274	2	32
LF	P. Dougherty	.283	5	22
C	D. McGuire	.208	0	20
OF	J. Anderson	.278	3	82
C	R. Kleinow	.206	0	16
P	J. Chesbro	.236	1	17

Pitching:

Pitcher	G	IP	W-L	ERA
J. Chesbro	**55**	**455**	**41-13**	1.82
J. Powell	47	390	23-19	2.44
A. Orth	20	138	11-6	2.68
L. Hughes	19	136	7-11	3.70
C. Griffith	16	100	6-4	2.87

1905:

American League Standings:

Team:	Won:	Lost:	Pct.	GB	BA	ERA
Philadelphia	92	56	.622		.255	2.19
Chicago	92	60	.605	2	.237	1.99
Detroit	79	74	.516	15.5	.243	2.83
Boston	78	74	.513	16	.234	2.84
Cleveland	76	78	.494	19	.255	2.85
New York	**71**	**78**	**.477**	**21.5**	**.248**	**2.93**
Washington	64	87	.424	29.5	.223	2.87
St. Louis	54	99	.353	40.5	.232	2.74

(World Series: The N.L. Champion New York Giants defeated Philadelphia 4 games to 1)

League Leaders:

Batting Average:

E. Flick, Cleveland	.306
W. Keeler, New York	**.302**
H. Bay, Cleveland	.298
S. Crawford, Detroit	.297
F. Isbell, Chicago	.296

Runs Batted In:

H. Davis, Philadelphia	83
L. Cross, Philadelphia	77
J. Donahue, Chicago	76
S. Crawford, Detroit	75
T. Turner, Cleveland	72

Hits:

G. Stone, St. Louis	187
S. Crawford, Detroit	171
H. Davis, Philadelphia	171

Pitching Leaders — Wins:

E. Plank, Philadelphia	26
R. Waddell, Philadelphia	24
N. Altrock, Chicago	22
E. Killian, Detroit	22
G. Mullin, Detroit	22

Pitching — ERA

R. Waddell, Philadelphia	1.48
D. White, Chicago	1.76
C. Young, Boston	1.82
A. Coakley, Philadelphia	1.84
N. Altrock, Chicago	1.88

New York:

(Manager: Clark Griffith)

Pos	Player	BA	HR	RBI
1B	H. Chase	.249	3	49
2B	J. Williams	.228	4	60
SS	K. Elberfeld	.262	0	53
3B	J. Yeager	.267	0	42
RF	W. Keeler	.302	4	38
CF	D. Fultz	.232	0	42
LF	P. Dougherty	.263	3	29
C	R. Kleinow	.221	1	24
UT	W. Conroy	.273	2	25
C	D. McGuire	.219	0	33
OF	E. Hahn	.319	0	11

Pitching:

Pitcher	G	IP	W-L	ERA
A. Orth	40	305	17-16	2.86
J. Chesbro	41	303	20-15	2.20
B. Hogg	39	205	9-12	3.20
J. Powell	36	202	8-13	3.52
C. Griffith	25	103	7-6	1.67
A. Puttmann	17	86	2-7	4.27

1906:

American League Standings:

Team:	Won:	Lost:	Pct.	GB	BA	ERA
Chicago	93	58	.616		.230	2.13
New York	**90**	**61**	**.596**	**3**	**.266**	**2.78**
Cleveland	89	64	.582	5	.279	2.09
Philadelphia	78	67	.538	12	.247	2.60
St. Louis	76	73	.510	16	.247	2.23
Detroit	71	78	.477	21	.242	3.06
Washington	55	95	.367	37.5	.238	3.25
Boston	49	105	.318	45.5	.239	3.41

(World Series: Chicago White Sox defeated the N.L. Champion Chicago Cubs 4 games to 2)

League Leaders:

Batting Average:

G. Stone, St. Louis	.358
N. Lajoie, Cleveland	.355
H. Chase, New York	**.323**
B. Congalton, Cleveland	.320
S. Seybold, Philadelphia	.316

Runs Batted In:

H. Davis, Philadelphia	96
N. Lajoie, Cleveland	91
G. Davis, Chicago	80
J. Williams, New York	77
H. Chase, New York	76

Hits:

N. Lajoie, Cleveland	214
G. Stone, St. Louis	208
E. Flock, Cleveland	194

Pitching Leaders — Wins:

A. Orth, New York	**25**
J. Chesbro, New York	**22**
N. Altrock, Chicago	21
A. Joss, Cleveland	21
G. Mullin, Detroit	21
B. Rhoads, Cleveland	21

Pitching — ERA

D. White, Chicago	1.52
B. Pelty, St. Louis	1.59
A. Joss, Cleveland	1.72
J. Powell, St. Louis	1.77
B. Rhoads, Cleveland	1.80

New York:

(Manager: Clark Griffith)

Pos	Player	BA	HR	RBI
IB	H. Chase	.323	0	76
2B	J. Williams	.277	3	77
SS	K. Elberfeld	.306	2	31
3B	F. LaPorte	.264	2	54
RF	W. Keeler	.304	2	33
CF	D. Hoffman	.256	0	23
LF	F. Delahanty	.238	2	41
C	R. Kleinow	.220	0	31
UT	W. Conroy	.245	4	54
3B	G. Moriarty	.234	0	23

Pitching:

Pitcher	G	IP	W-L	ERA
A. Orth	45	**339**	**25**-17	2.34
J. Chesbro	**49**	325	22-16	2.96
B. Hogg	28	206	14-13	2.93
W. Clarkson	32	151	9-4	2.32
D. Newton	21	125	6-4	3.17

1907:

American League Standings:

Team:	Won:	Lost:	Pct.	GB	BA	ERA
Detroit	92	58	.613		.266	2.33
Philadelphia	88	57	.607	1.5	.255	2.35
Chicago	87	64	.576	5.5	.237	2.22
Cleveland	85	67	.559	8	.241	2.26
New York	**70**	**78**	**.473**	**21**	**.249**	**3.03**
St. Louis	69	83	.454	24	.253	2.61
Boston	59	90	.396	32.5	.234	2.45
Washington	49	102	.325	43.5	.243	3.11

(World Series: The N.L. Champion Chicago Cubs defeated Detroit 4 games to 0)

League Leaders:
Batting Average:

T. Cobb, Detroit	.350
S. Crawford, Detroit	.323
G. Stone, St. Louis	.320
E. Flick, Cleveland	.302
S. Nicholis, Philadelphia	.302

Runs Batted In:

T. Cobb, Detroit	119
S. Seybold, Philadelphia	92
H. Davis, Philadelphia	87
S. Crawford, Detroit	81
B. Wallace, St. Louis	70

Hits:

T. Cobb, Detroit	212
G. Stone, St. Louis	191
S. Crawford, Detroit	188

Pitching Leaders — Wins:

A. Joss, Cleveland	27
W. Donovan, Detroit	26
E. Walsh, Chicago	25
D. White, Chicago	25
E. Killian, Detroit	24
E. Plank, Philadelphia	24

Pitching — ERA

E. Walsh, Chicago	1.60
E. Killian, Detroit	1.78
A. Joss, Cleveland	1.83
W. Johnson, Washington	1.87
H. Howell, St. Louis	1.93

New York:

(Manager: Clark Griffith)

Pos	Player	BA	HR	RBI
IB	H. Chase	.287	2	68
2B	J. Williams	.270	2	63

Pos	Player	BA	HR	RBI
SS	K. Elberfeld	.271	0	51
3B	G. Moriarty	.277	0	43
RF	W. Keeler	.234	0	17
CF	D. Hoffman	.253	4	46
LF	W. Conroy	.234	3	51
C	R. Kleinow	.264	0	26
3B	F. LaPorte	.270	0	48
C	I. Thomas	.192	1	24

Pitching:

Pitcher	G	IP	W-L	ERA
A. Orth	36	249	13-21	2.61
J. Chesbro	30	206	10-9	2.53
S. Doyle	29	194	11-11	2.65
B. Hogg	25	167	9-8	3.08
D. Newton	19	133	7-11	3.18

1908:

American League Standings:

Team:	Won:	Lost:	Pct.	GB	BA	ERA
Detroit	90	63	.588		.264	2.40
Cleveland	90	64	.584	.5	.239	2.02
Chicago	88	64	.579	1.5	.224	2.22
St. Louis	83	69	.546	6.5	.245	2.15
Boston	75	79	.487	15.5	.246	2.28
Philadelphia	68	85	.444	22	.225	2.57
Washington	67	85	.441	22.5	.235	2.34
New York	**51**	**103**	**.331**	**39.5**	**.236**	**3.16**

(World Series: The N.L. Champion Chicago Cubs defeated Detroit 4 games to 1)

League Leaders:

Batting Average:

T. Cobb, Detroit	.324
S. Crawford, Detroit	.311
D. Gessler, Boston	.308
C. Hemphill, New York	.297
M. McIntyre, Detroit	.295

Runs Batted In:

T. Cobb, Detroit	108
S. Crawford, Detroit	80
H. Ferris, St. Louis	74
N. Lajoie, Cleveland	74
C. Rossman, Detroit	71

Hits:

T. Cobb, Detroit	188
S. Crawford, Detroit	184
N. Lajoie, Cleveland	168
M. McIntyre, Detroit	168

Pitching Leaders — Wins:

E. Walsh, Chicago	39
E. Summers, Detroit	24
A. Joss, Cleveland	24
C. Young, Boston	21

Pitching — ERA

A. Joss, Cleveland	1.16

| C. Young, Boston | 1.26 | W. Johnson, Washington | 1.64 |
| E. Walsh, Chicago | 1.42 | E. Summers, Detroit | 1.64 |

New York:

(Managers: Clark Griffith, 24 –32 and Kid Elberfeld, 27-71)

Pos	Player	BA	HR	RBI
IB	H. Chase	.257	1	36
2B	H. Niles	.249	4	24
SS	N. Ball	.247	0	38
3B	W. Conroy	.237	1	39
RF	W. Keeler	.263	1	14
CF	C. Hemphill	.297	0	44
LF	J. Stahl	.252	1	42
C	R. Kleinow	.168	1	13
UT	G. Moriarty	.236	0	27
C	W. Blair	.190	1	13
OF	I. McIlveen	.213	0	8

Pitching:

Pitcher	G	IP	W-L	ERA
J. Chesbro	45	289	12-20	2.93
J. Lake	38	269	9-**22**	3.17
R. Manning	41	245	14-16	2.94
B. Hogg	24	152	4-15	3.01
A. Orth	21	139	2-13	3.42
D. Newton	23	88	4-6	2.95

1909:

American League Standings:

Team:	Won:	Lost:	Pct.	GB	BA	ERA
Detroit	98	54	.645		.267	2.26
Philadelphia	95	58	.621	3.5	.257	1.92
Boston	88	63	.583	9.5	.263	2.60
Chicago	78	74	.513	20	.221	2.04
New York	**74**	**77**	**.490**	**23.5**	**.248**	**2.68**
Cleveland	71	82	.464	27.5	.242	2.39
St. Louis	61	89	.407	36	.232	2.88
Washington	42	110	.276	56	.223	3.04

(World Series: The N.L. Champion Pittsburgh Pirates defeated Detroit 4 games to 3)

League Leaders: N. Lajoie, Cleveland   .324
Batting Average: S. Crawford, Detroit   .314
   T. Cobb, Detroit   .377   H. Lord, Boston   .311
   E. Collins, Philadelphia   .346

Runs Batted In:

T. Cobb, Detroit	107
S. Crawford, Detroit	97
F. Baker, Philadelphia	85
T. Speaker, Boston	77
H. Davis, Philadelphia	75

Hits:

T. Cobb, Detroit	216
E. Collins, Philadelphia	198
S. Crawford, Detroit	185

Pitching Leaders — Wins:

G. Mullin, Detroit	29
F. Smith, Chicago	24
E. Willett, Detroit	21

Pitching — ERA

H. Krause, Philadelphia	1.39
E. Walsh, Chicago	1.41
C. Bender, Philadelphia	1.66
E. Plank, Philadelphia	1.70
A. Joss, Cleveland	1.71

New York:

(Manager: George Stallings)

Pos	Player	BA	HR	RBI
1B	H. Chase	.283	4	63
2B	F. LaPorte	.298	0	31
SS	J. Knight	.236	0	40
3B	J. Austin	.231	1	39
RF	W. Keeler	.264	1	32
CF	R. Demmitt	.246	4	30
LF	C. Engle	.278	3	71
C	R. Kleinow	.228	0	15
SS	K. Elberfeld	.237	0	26
OF	B. Cree	.262	2	27
OF	C. Hemphill	.243	0	10
C	E. Sweeney	.267	0	21

Pitching:

Pitcher	G	IP	W-L	ERA
J. Warhop	36	243	11-16	2.40
J. Lake	31	215	15-11	1.88
R. Manning	26	173	10-11	3.17
L. Brockett	26	152	9-8	3.01
S. Doyle	17	126	9-6	2.58
J. Quinn	23	119	8-5	1.97
T. Hughes	24	119	6-8	2.65
P. Wilson	14	94	6-5	3.17

1910:

American League Standings:

Team:	Won:	Lost:	Pct.	GB	BA	ERA
Philadelphia	102	48	.680		.266	1.79
New York	**88**	**63**	**.583**	**14.5**	**.248**	**2.59**
Detroit	86	68	.558	18	.261	3.00

Team:	Won:	Lost:	Pct.	GB	BA	ERA
Boston	81	72	.529	22.5	.259	2.46
Cleveland	71	81	.467	32	.244	2.89
Chicago	68	85	.444	35.5	.211	2.01
Washington	66	85	.437	36.5	.236	2.46
St. Louis	47	107	.305	57	.220	3.09

(World Series: Philadelphia defeated the N.L. Champion Chicago Cubs 4 games to 1)

League Leaders:

Batting Average:

T. Cobb, Detroit	.385
N. Lajoie, Cleveland	.384
T. Speaker, Boston	.340
E. Collins, Philadelphia	.322
J. Knight, New York	.312

Runs Batted In:

S. Crawford, Detroit	120
T. Cobb, Detroit	91
E. Collins, Philadelphia	81
J. Stahl, Boston	77
N. Lajoie, Cleveland	76

Hits:

N. Lajoie, Cleveland	227
T. Cobb, Detroit	196
E. Collins, Philadelphia	188

Pitching Leaders — Wins:

J. Coombs, Philadelphia	30
R. Ford, New York	26
W. Johnson, Washington	24
C. Bender, Philadelphia	22
G. Mullin, Detroit	21

Pitching — ERA

E. Walsh, Chicago	1.27
J. Coombs, Philadelphia	1.30
W. Johnson, Washington	1.35
C. Morgan, Philadelphia	1.55
C. Bender, Philadelphia	1.58

New York:

(Managers: George Stallings, 79-61, and Hal Chase, 9-2)

Pos	Player	BA	HR	RBI
IB	H. Chase	.290	3	73
2B	F. LaPorte	.264	2	67
SS	J. Knight	.312	3	45
3B	J. Austin	.218	2	36
RF	H. Wolter	.267	4	42
CF	C. Hemphill	.239	0	21
LF	B. Cree	.287	4	73
C	E. Sweeney	.200	0	13
OF	B. Daniels	.253	1	17
2B	E. Gardner	.244	1	24
SS	R. Roach	.214	0	20
C	F. Mitchell	.230	0	18

Pitching:

Pitcher	G	IP	W-L	ERA
R. Ford	36	300	26-6	1.65
J. Warhop	37	254	14-14	2.87

Pitcher	G	IP	W-L	ERA
J. Quinn	35	237	17-12	2.36
H. Vaughn	30	222	12-11	1.83
T. Hughes	23	152	7-9	3.50

1911:

American League Standings:

Team:	Won:	Lost:	Pct.	GB	BA	ERA
Philadelphia	101	50	.669		.296	3.01
Detroit	89	65	.578	13.5	.292	3.73
Cleveland	80	73	.523	22	.282	3.37
Chicago	77	74	.510	24	.269	3.01
Boston	78	75	.510	24	.274	2.73
New York	**76**	**76**	**.500**	**25.5**	**.272**	**3.54**
Washington	64	90	.416	38.5	.258	3.52
St. Louis	45	107	.296	56.5	.238	3.83

(World Series: Philadelphia defeated the N.L. Champion New York Giants 4 games to 2)

League Leaders:

Batting Average:

T. Cobb, Detroit	.420
J. Jackson, Cleveland	.408
S. Crawford, Detroit	.378
E. Collins, Philadelphia	.365
B. Cree, New York	.348

Runs Batted In:

T. Cobb, Detroit	127
F. Baker, Philadelphia	115
S. Crawford, Detroit	115
P. Bodie, Chicago	97
J. Delahanty, Detroit	94

Hits:

T. Cobb, Detroit	248
J. Jackson, Cleveland	233
S. Crawford, Detroit	217

Pitching Leaders — Wins:

J. Coombs, Philadelphia	29
E. Walsh, Chicago	26
W. Johnson, Washington	25
V. Gregg, Cleveland	23
E. Plank, Philadelphia	22

Pitching — ERA

V. Gregg, Cleveland	1.81
W. Johnson, Washington	1.89
J. Wood, Boston	2.02
E. Plank, Philadelphia	2.10
C. Bender, Philadelphia	2.16

New York:

(Manager: Hal Chase)

Pos	Player	BA	HR	RBI
IB	H. Chase	.315	3	62
2B	E. Gardner	.263	0	39
SS	J. Knight	.268	3	62
3B	R. Hartzell	.296	3	91
RF	H. Wolter	.304	4	36

Pos	Player	BA	HR	RBI
CF	B. Daniels	.286	2	31
LF	B. Cree	.348	4	88
C	W. Blair	.194	0	26
C	E. Sweeney	.231	0	18
SS	O. Johnson	.234	3	36
OF	C. Hemphill	.284	1	15

Pitching:

Pitcher	G	IP	W-L	ERA
R. Ford	37	281	21-11	2.27
R. Caldwell	41	255	16-14	3.35
J. Warhop	31	210	13-13	4.16
J. Quinn	40	175	6-10	3.76
R. Fisher	29	172	9-10	3.25
H. Vaughn	26	146	8-11	4.39

1912:

American League Standings:

Team:	Won:	Lost:	Pct.	GB	BA	ERA
Boston	105	47	.691		.277	2.76
Washington	91	61	.599	14	.256	2.69
Philadelphia	90	62	.592	15	.282	3.32
Chicago	78	76	.506	28	.255	3.06
Cleveland	75	78	.490	30.5	.273	3.30
Detroit	69	84	.451	36.5	.267	3.78
St. Louis	53	101	.344	53	.249	3.71
New York	**50**	**102**	**.329**	**55**	**.259**	**4.13**

(World Series: Boston defeated the N.L. Champion New York Giants 4 games to 3)

League Leaders:

Batting Average:

T. Cobb, Detroit	.410
J. Jackson, Cleveland	.395
T. Speaker, Boston	.383
N. Lajoie, Cleveland	.368
E. Collins, Philadelphia	.348

Runs Batted In:

F. Baker, Philadelphia	130
D. Lewis, Boston	109
S. Crawford, Detroit	109
S. McInnis, Philadelphia	101

Hits:

T. Cobb, Detroit	227
J. Jackson, Cleveland	226
T. Speaker, Boston	222

Pitching Leaders — Wins:

J. Wood, Boston	34
W. Johnson, Washington	32
E. Walsh, Chicago	27
E. Plank, Philadelphia	25
B. Groom, Washington	24

Pitching — ERA

W. Johnson, Washington	1.39

J. Wood, Boston	1.91	E. Plank, Philadelphia	2.22
E. Walsh, Chicago	2.15	R. Collins, Boston	2.53

New York:

(Manager: Harry Wolverton)

Pos	Player	BA	HR	RBI
IB	H. Chase	.274	4	58
2B	H. Simmons	.239	0	41
SS	J. Martin	.225	0	17
3B	D. Paddock	.288	1	14
RF	G. Zinn	.262	6	55
CF	R. Hartzell	.272	1	38
LF	B. Daniels	.274	2	41
C	E. Sweeney	.268	0	30
UT	D. Sterrett	.265	1	32
OF	B. Cree	.332	0	22
2B	E. Gardner	.281	0	26
OF	J. Lelivelt	.362	2	23

Pitching:

Pitcher	G	IP	W-L	ERA
R. Ford	36	292	13-21	3.55
J. Warhop	39	258	11-19	2.86
R. Caldwell	30	183	7-16	4.47
G. McConnell	23	177	8-12	2.75
J. Quinn	18	103	5-7	5.79
R. Fisher	17	90	2-8	5.88
H. Vaughn	15	63	2-8	5.14

1913:

American League Standings:

Team:	Won:	Lost:	Pct.	GB	BA	ERA
Philadelphia	96	57	.627		.277	2.76
Washington	90	64	.584	6.5	.256	2.69
Cleveland	86	66	.566	9.5	.282	3.32
Boston	79	71	.527	15.5	.255	3.06
Chicago	78	74	.513	17.5	.273	3.30
Detroit	66	87	.431	30	.267	3.78
New York	**57**	**94**	**.377**	**38**	**.249**	**3.71**
St. Louis	57	96	.373	39	.259	4.13

(World Series: Philadelphia defeated the N.L. Champion New York Giants 4 games to 1)

League Leaders:
Batting Average:

T. Cobb, Detroit	.390
J. Jackson, Cleveland	.373
T. Speaker, Boston	.363
E. Collins, Philadelphia	.345
F. Baker, Philadelphia	.337

Runs Batted In:

F. Baker, Philadelphia	117
D. Lewis, Boston	90
S. McInnis, Philadelphia	90
D. Pratt, St. Louis	87
J. Barry, Philadelphia	85

Hits:

J. Jackson, Cleveland	197

S. Crawford, Detroit	193
F. Baker, Philadelphia	190

Pitching Leaders — Wins:

W. Johnson, Washington	34
C. Falkenberg, Cleveland	21
C. Bender, Philadelphia	21
R. Russell, Chicago	21

Pitching — ERA

W. Johnson, Washington	1.09
E. Cicotte, Chicago	1.58
W. Mitchell, Cleveland	1.74
J. Scott, Chicago	1.90
R. Russell, Chicago	1.91

New York:

(Manager: Frank Chance)

Pos	Player	BA	HR	RBI
1B	J. Knight	.236	0	24
2B	R. Hartzell	.259	0	38
SS	R. Peckinpaugh	.268	1	32
3B	E. Midkiff	.197	0	14
RF	B. Daniels	.216	0	22
CF	H. Wolter	.254	2	43
LF	B. Cree	.272	1	63
C	E. Sweeney	.265	2	40
3B	F. Maisel	.257	0	12
UT	R. Zeider	.233	0	12

Pitching:

Pitcher	G	IP	W-L	ERA
R. Fisher	43	246	11-16	3.18
R. Ford	33	237	13-18	2.66
A. Schulz	38	193	7-13	3.73
G. McConnell	35	180	5-15	3.20
R. Caldwell	27	164	9-8	2.41
R. Keating	28	151	6-12	3.21

1914:

American League Standings:

Team:	Won:	Lost:	Pct.	GB	BA	ERA
Philadelphia	99	53	.651		.272	2.78

Team:	Won:	Lost:	Pct.	GB	BA	ERA
Boston	91	62	.595	8.5	.250	2.35
Washington	81	73	.526	19	.244	2.54
Detroit	80	73	.523	19.5	.258	2.86
St. Louis	71	82	.464	28.5	.243	2.85
Chicago	70	84	.455	30	.239	2.48
New York	**70**	**84**	**.455**	**30**	**.229**	**2.81**
Cleveland	51	102	.333	48.5	.245	3.21

(World Series: The N.L. Champion Boston Braves defeated Philadelphia 4 games to 0)

League Leaders:

Batting Average:

T. Cobb, Detroit	.368
E. Collins, Philadelphia	.344
T. Speaker, Boston	.338
J. Jackson, Cleveland	.338
F. Baker, Philadelphia	.319

Runs Batted In:

S. Crawford, Detroit	104
S. McInnis, Philadelphia	95
T. Speaker, Boston	90
F. Baker, Philadelphia	89
E. Collins, Philadelphia	85

Hits:

T. Speaker, Boston	193

S. Crawford, Detroit	183
F. Baker, Philadelphia	182

Pitching Leaders — Wins:

W. Johnson, Washington	28
H. Coveleski, Detroit	21
R. Collins, Boston	20
H. Dauss, Detroit	19
R. Caldwell, New York	18
D. Leonard, Boston	18

Pitching — ERA

D. Leonard, Boston	1.01
R. Foster, Boston	1.65
W. Johnson, Washington	1.72
E. Shore, Boston	1.89
R. Caldwell, New York	1.94

New York:

(Managers: Frank Chance, 61-76, and Roger Peckinpaugh, 9-8)

Pos	Player	BA	HR	RBI
IB	C. Mullen	.260	0	44
2B	L. Boone	.222	0	21
SS	R. Peckinpaugh	.223	3	51
3B	F. Maisel	.239	2	47
RF	D. Cook	.283	1	40
CF	B. Cree	.309	0	40
LF	R. Hartzell	.233	1	32
C	E. Sweeney	.213	1	22
C	L. Nunamaker	.265	2	29
2B	F. Truesdale	.212	0	13
OF	T. Daley	.251	0	9
IB	B. Williams	.163	1	17
OF	B. Holden	.182	0	12

Pitching:

Pitcher	G	IP	W-L	ERA
J. Warhop	37	217	8-15	2.37
R. Caldwell	31	213	18-9	1.94
R. Keating	34	210	6-11	2.96
R. Fisher	29	209	10-12	2.28
M. McHale	31	191	7-16	2.97
K. Cole	33	142	11-9	3.30
B. Brown	20	122	6-5	3.24

Source: *The Baseball Encyclopedia: The Complete and Official Record of Major League Baseball* (The Macmillan Company, 1969).

Home Attendance: (1903-1914)

1903:

New York (A.L.)	211,808
New York (N.L.)	579,530 (N.L. & major league high)
Brooklyn (N.L.)	224,870
Philadelphia (A.L.)	422,473 (A.L. high)

1904:

New York (A.L.)	438,919
New York (N.L.)	609,826 (N.L. & major league high)
Brooklyn (N.L.)	214,600
Boston (A.L.)	623,295 (A.L. high)

1905:

New York (A.L.)	309,100
New York (N.L.)	552,700 (N.L. high)
Brooklyn (N.L.)	227,924
Chicago (A.L.)	667,419 (A.L. & major league high)

1906:

New York (A.L.)	434,700
New York (N.L.)	402,850
Brooklyn (N.L.)	277,400
Boston (A.L.)	585,202 (A.L. high)
Chicago (N.L.)	654,300 (N.L. & major league high)

1907:

New York (A.L.)	350,020
New York (N.L.)	538,350 (N.L. high)
Brooklyn (N.L.)	312,500
Chicago (A.L.)	666,307 (A.L. & major league high)

1908:

New York (A.L.)	305,500
New York (N.L.)	910,000 (N.L. & major league high)
Brooklyn (N.L.)	275,600
Chicago (A.L.)	636,096 (A.L. high)

1909:

New York (A.L.)	501,700
New York (N.L.)	783,700 (N.L. & major league high)
Brooklyn (N.L.)	321,300
Boston (A.L.)	668,865 (A.L. high)

1910:

New York (A.L.)	355,857
New York (N.L.)	511,785
Brooklyn (N.L.)	279,321
Chicago (N.L.)	526,152 (N.L. high)
Philadelphia (A.L.)	588,905 (A.L. & major league high)

1911:

New York (A.L.)	302,444
New York (N.L.)	675,000 (N.L. & major league high)
Brooklyn (N.L.)	269,000
Philadelphia (A.L.)	605,749 (A.L. high)

1912:

New York (A.L.)	242,194
New York (N.L.)	638,000 (N.L. & major league high)
Brooklyn (N.L.)	243,000
Chicago (A.L)	602,241 (A.L. high)

1913:

New York (A.L.)	357,551
New York (N.L.)	830,000 (N.L. & major league high)
Brooklyn (N.L.)	347,000
Chicago (A.L.)	644,501 (A.L. high)

1914:

New York (A.L.)	359,477
New York (N.L.)	384,313 (N.L. high)
Brooklyn (N.L.)	122,671
Boston (A.L.)	481,359 (A.L. high)

Primary Source Notes

Chapter 1: The primary source was the Hal Chase file at the Baseball Hall of Fame Library and the paper, *The Life and Times of Price Hal Chase* by Gib Bodet.

Chapter 2: Primary sources were *The New York Times*, *The Sporting News* and the Ban Johnson file at the Baseball Hall of Fame Library.

Chapter 3: Primary sources were the books *Our Game* (Henry Holt and Company, 1991) by Charles C. Alexander and *The New York Yankees: An Informal History* (G.P. Putnam's Sons, 1951) by Frank Graham.

Chapter 4: Primary sources were the John Brush file at the National Baseball of Fame Library and the Leo Katcher book, *The Big Bankroll: The Life and Times of Arnold Rothstein* (Harper & Brothers, 1958, 1959).

Chapter 5: Primary sources were *The New York Times*, along with the following books: *Uptown, Downtown: A Trip Through Time on New York's Subways* (Hawthorn/Dutton, 1976) by Stan Fischler; *The Epic of New York City* (Old Town Books, 1966) by Edward Robb Ellis; and, *A Flame of Pure Fire: Jack Dempsey and the Roaring '20s* (Harcourt Brace & Company, 1999) by Roger Kahn.

Chapter 6: Primary sources were the Clark Griffith and Willie Keeler files at the National Baseball Hall of Fame Library, *The Sporting News* and *The New York Times*.

Chapter 7: Primary sources were *The New York Times* and the book, *Baseball: An Illustrated History* (Alfred A. Knopf, 1994) by Geoffrey C. Ward and Ken Burns.

Chapter 8: Primary sources were the Kid Elberfeld file at the National Baseball Hall of Fame Library and the following books: *The Big Bankroll: The Life and Times of Arnold Rothstein* (Harper & Brothers, 1958, 1959) by Leo Katcher; *Low Life* (Vintage Books, 1991) by Luc Sante; *July 2, 1903: The Mysterious Death of Hall-of-Famer Big Ed Delahanty* (Macmillan Publishing Company, 1992) by Mike Sowell; *Dead Ball: Major League Baseball Before Babe Ruth* (Franklin Watts, 1996) by Thomas Gilbert; and, *The Fix Is In: A History of Baseball Gambling and Game Fixing Scandals* (McFarland & Company, Inc., 1995) by Daniel E. Ginsburg.

Chapter 9: Primary sources were *The New York Times*, *The Sporting News*; and for a vivid description of the Philadelphia fire, *July 2, 1903: The Mysterious Death of Hall-of-Famer Big Ed Delahanty* (Macmillan Publishing Company, 1992) by Mike Sowell.

Chapter 10: Primary sources were the Jack Chesbro file at the National Baseball of Fame Library; *The New York Times*; and for a description of Iron Joe McGinnity's streak, the book, *More Strange But True Baseball Stories* (Random House, 1972) by Howard Liss.

Chapter 11: Primary sources were the John McGraw and Mike Donlan files at the National Baseball Hall of Fame Library and *The New York Times*.

Chapter 12: Primary sources were the Hal Chase file at the National Baseball Hall of Fame Library, particularly articles by Bob Hoie, "The Hal Chase Story" in *Grandstand Baseball America Annual 1991*; Greg Beston, "The Story of Hal Chase: How Baseball Officials Allowed Corruption to Exist in the Game from 1905-1919" (History thesis, Princeton University, 1997); and, Gib Bodet, *The Life and Times of Price Hal Chase.*

Chapter 13: Primary sources were *The New York Times*, *The New York Tribune* and various files at the National Baseball Hall of Fame Library.

Chapter 14: Primary sources were *The Sporting News*, the Hal Chase file at the National Baseball Hall of Fame Library and the books, *Where They Ain't: The Fabled Life and Untimely Death of the Original Baltimore Orioles, The Team that Gave Birth to Modern Baseball* (The Free Press, 1999) by

Burt Solomon, and *Our Game* (Henry Holt and Company, 1991) by Chales C. Alexander.

Chapter 15: Primary sources were *The New York Times*, *The Sporting News* and the book, *Low and Inside: A Book of Baseball Anecdotes, Oddities and Curiosities* (Breakaway Books, 2000) by Allen H. and Ira L. Smith.

Chapter 16: The primary source was *The New York Times*.

Chapter 17: Primary sources were the Henry Chadwick file at the National Baseball Hall of Fame Library, *The New York Times* and *The New York Tribune*.

Chapter 18: Primary sources were the George Stallings file at the National Baseball Hall of Fame Library; *The New York Times*; and the books, *The Baseball Astrologer and Other Weird Tales* (Total/Sports Illustrated, 2000) by John B. Holway; and, *The New York Yankees: An Informal History* (G.P. Putnam's Sons, 1951) by Frank Graham.

Chapter 19: Primary sources were *The New York Times*, *The Sporting News*, the Russell Ford and Roger Peckinpaugh files at the National Baseball Hall of Fame Library and the book, *The Glory of Their Times: The Story of the Early Days of Baseball Told by the Men Who Played It* (Macmillan, 1966) by Lawrence S. Ritter.

Chapter 20: Primary sources were *The New York Times*, *The Sporting News*, the Harry Wolverton file at the National Baseball Hall of Fame Library and the books, *The New York Times, The Century in Times Square* (*The New York Times*, 1999); *Everything Baseball* (Prentice Hall Press, 1989) by James Mote; *The Triangle Fire* (Carroll & Graf Publishers, 1962) by Leon Stein; and, *The Epic of New York City* (Old Town Books, 1966) by Edward Robb Ellis.

Chapter 21: Primary sources were *The New York Times*, *The New York Tribune*, *The Sporting News*, the Frank Chance file at the National Baseball Hall of Fame Library; and the book, *The Federal League of 1914-1915: Baseball's Third Major League* (Society for American Baseball Research, 1989) by Marc Okkonen.

Chapter 22: Primary sources were *The New York Times*, *The Sporting News*, and the Jacob Ruppert and Hal Chase files at the National Baseball Hall of Fame Library.

Chapter 23: Primary sources were *The New York Times*, and the book, *Lost Ballparks: A Celebration of Baseball's Legendary Fields* (Viking Studio Books, 1992) by Lawrence S. Ritter.

Bibliography

Books:

Alexander, Charles C. *John McGraw* (Viking Penguin Inc., 1988).

_____. *Our Game* (Henry Holt and Company, 1991).

_____. *Ty Cobb* (Oxford University Press, 1984).

The Baseball Encyclopedia: The Complete and Official Record of Major League Baseball (The Macmillan Company, 1969).

Cohen, Rich. *Tough Jews: Fathers, Sons, and Gangster Dreams* (Vintage Books, 1998, 1999).

Crichton, Judy. *America 1900: The Turning Point* (Henry Holt and Company, Inc., 1998).

Dickson, Paul. *Baseball's Greatest Quotations* (HarperCollins, 1991).

Ellis, Edward Robb. *The Epic of New York City* (Old Town Books, 1966).

Falkner, David. *The Short Season: The Hard Work and High Times of Baseball in the Spring* (Times Books, 1986).

Fischler, Stan. *Uptown, Downtown: A Trip Through Time on New York's Subways* (Hawthorn/Dutton, 1976).

Gilbert, Thomas. *Dead Ball: Major League Baseball Before Babe Ruth* (Franklin Watts, 1996).

Ginsburg, Daniel E. *The Fix Is In: A History of Baseball Gambling and Game Fixing Scandals* (McFarland & Company, Inc., 1995).

Graham, Frank. *The New York Yankees: An Informal History* (G.P. Putnam's Sons, 1951) … first published in 1943.

Gutman, Dan. *Baseball Babylon: From the Black Sox to Pete Rose, The Real Stories Behind the Scandals that Rocked the Game* (Penguin Books, 1992).

Holway, John B. *The Baseball Astrologer and Other Weird Tales* (Total, Sports Illustrated, 2000).

James, Bill. *Whatever Happened to the Hall of Fame?* (Simon & Schuster Inc., 1994, 1995).

Kahn, Roger. *A Flame of Pure Fire: Jack Dempsey and the Roaring '20s* (Harcourt Brace & Company, 1999).

Katcher, Leo. *The Big Bankroll: The Life and Times of Arnold Rothstein* (Harper & Brothers, 1958, 1959).

Lieb, Fred. *Baseball As I Have Known It* (Bison Books, The University of Nebraska Press, 1996).

Liss, Howard. *More Strange But True Baseball Stories* (Random House, 1972).

Longert, Scott. *Addie Joss: King of the Pitchers* (Society for American Baseball Research, 1998).

Lowry, Philip J. *Green Cathedrals* (Society for American Baseball Research, 1986).

Mathewson, Christy. *Pitching in a Pinch* (Bison Books, The University of Nebraska Press, 1994) … first published in 1912 by Putnam.

McCabe, Neil, and McCabe, Constance. *Baseball's Golden Age: The Photographs of Charles M. Conlin* (Harry M. Abrams, Inc., 1993).

McDonald, Brian. *My Father's Gun: One Family, Three Badges, One Hundred Years in the NYPD* (Dutton, 1999).

Mote, James. *Everything Baseball* (Prentice Hall Press, 1989).

Murdock, Eugene C. *Ban Johnson: Czar of Baseball* (Greenwood Press, 1982).

Mushabac, Jane, and Wigan, Angela. *A Short and Remarkable History of New York City* (Fordham University Press, 1999).

The New York Times: The Century in Times Square (*The New York Times*, 1999).

Okkonen, Marc. *The Federal League of 1914-1915: Baseball's Third Major League* (Society for American Baseball Research, 1989).

Okrent, Daniel, and Wulf, Steve. *Baseball Anecdotes* (Harper & Row, Publishers, Inc., 1989).

Ribowsky, Mark. *Don't Look Back: Satchel Paige in the Shadows of Baseball* (Da Capo Press, 1994).

Riess, Steven A. *Touching Base: Professional Baseball and American Culture in the Progressive Era* (University of Illinois Press, 1999).

Ritter, Lawrence S. *Lost Ballparks: A Celebration of Baseball's Legendary Fields* (Viking Studio Books, 1992).

_____. *The Glory of Their Times: The Story of the*

Early Days of Baseball Told by the Men Who Played It (The Macmillan Company, 1966).

Robinson, Ray. *Matty: An American Hero* (Oxford University Press, 1993).

Sante, Luc. *Low Life* (Vintage Books, 1991).

Scheinin, Richard. *Field of Screams: The Dark Underside of America's National Pastime* (W.W. Norton & Company, 1994).

Smith, H. Allen, and Smith, Ira L. *Low and Inside: A Book of Baseball Anecdotes, Oddities and Curiosities* (Breakaway Books, 2000).

Solomon, Burt. *Where They Ain't: The Fabled Life and Untimely Death of the Original Baltimore Orioles, The Team that Gave Birth to Modern Baseball* (The Free Press, 1999).

Sowell, Mike. *July 2, 1903: The Mysterious Death of Hall-of-Famer Big Ed Delahanty* (Macmillan Publishing Company, 1992).

Spatz, Lyle. *New York Yankee Openers: An Opening Day History of Baseball's Most Famous Team, 1903-1996* (McFarland & Company, Inc., 1997).

Stein, Leon. *The Triangle Fire* (Carroll & Graf Publishers, 1962).

Sullivan, Dean A. *Early Innings: A Documentary History of Baseball, 1825-1908* (Bison Books, The University of Nebraska Press, 1995).

Thorn, John; Palmer, Pete; Gershman, Michael; and Pietrusza, David. *Total Baseball, Fifth Edition: The Official Encyclopedia of Major League Baseball* (Viking, 1997).

Ward, Geoffrey C., and Burns, Ken. *Baseball: An Illustrated History* (Alfred A. Knopf, 1994).

Newspaper & Magazines:

Grandstand Baseball America Annual 1991, "The Hal Chase Story" by Bob Hoie.

The New York Times (1902-1915).

The New York Tribune (1903, 1911-1913).

Society for American Baseball Research: various publications.

Sporting Life.

The Sporting News (1903-1915).

Sports Collectors Digest, "Gambling Reds first baseman threw away career" (May 8, 1992) by Bob Lemke.

Papers:

Beston, Greg, *The Story of Hal Chase: How Baseball Officials Allowed Corruption to Exist in the Game from 1905-1919* (History thesis, Princeton University, 1997).

Bodet, Gib, *The Life and Times of Prince Hal Chase.*

Index